THE
EVOLUTION OF THE MONASTIC IDEAL

THE EVOLUTION OF THE MONASTIC IDEAL

FROM THE EARLIEST TIMES DOWN TO THE COMING OF THE FRIARS

A SECOND CHAPTER IN THE HISTORY OF CHRISTIAN RENUNCIATION

BY

HERBERT B. WORKMAN, M.A., D.Lit.

PRINCIPAL OF WESTMINSTER TRAINING COLLEGE

AUTHOR OF
'PERSECUTION IN THE EARLY CHURCH' 'CHRISTIAN THOUGHT TO THE REFORMATION' 'THE DAWN OF THE REFORMATION' 'THE LETTERS OF JOHN HUS' ETC.

WIPF & STOCK · Eugene, Oregon

Πολυμερῶς καὶ πολυτρόπως

πάλαι

ὁ Θεὸς λαλήσας

Wipf and Stock Publishers
199 W 8th Ave, Suite 3
Eugene, OR 97401

The Evolution of the Monastic Ideal
From the Earliest Times Down to the Coming of the Friars;
A Second Chapter in the History of Christian Renunciation
By Workman, Herbert B.
ISBN 13: 978-1-60608-293-5
Publication date 12/19/2008
Previously published by Charles Kelly, 1913

I DEDICATE

THIS SHORT STUDY OF A GREAT THEME

TO

MY BROTHER

𝔚𝔞𝔩𝔱𝔢𝔯 𝔓. 𝔚𝔬𝔯𝔨𝔪𝔞𝔫

SOMETIME FELLOW OF TRINITY COLLEGE, CAMBRIDGE,
HEAD MASTER OF KINGSWOOD SCHOOL, BATH

TOGETHER both, ere the high lawns appeared
  Under the opening eyelids of the morn,
We drove afield, and both together heard
  What time the gray fly winds her sultry horn.

PREFACE

I AM anxious that the reader, especially the critic—if such should deign to look at my pages—should understand clearly the intentions and limitations of this little book. I have not set out to write the history of Monasticism—a vast task, in some respects rendered needless by the great works that have been devoted to the subject, in other respects almost impossible because of the wide field of detail to be covered. Nor have I attempted a mere criticism of Monasticism, whether past or present. Every form by which human aspiration has attempted to realize the divine seems to me too sacred for destructive, negative criticism, however much we may differ from it. Nor will the reader find in these pages any account of the dress of the monks, the architecture of their churches, or the arrangements of the monasteries, themes that have been amply treated by competent writers. I have strictly confined myself to the history of the Monastic Ideal, tracing out the various stages in its evolution, and drawing attention both to the varying, concrete forms in which the Ideal has embodied itself, and to the effect of the Ideal upon the life and thought of the centuries. Works upon Monasticism abound, sometimes written by enthusiastic defenders, more often by those eager to expose its mistakes, both types, for the most part, based upon inadequate material or second-hand authorities.[1] I may at least claim that there is nothing in this book, in spite of imperfections of which no one is more conscious than the author, which is not the outcome of the honest study of the original sources, and of the best accessible modern literature. Throughout the work I have not made it my primary business to praise or blame, or to write as either advocate or judge—for, in such cases, judgement is too often, historically speaking, the result of an anachronistic outlook, of necessity unhistorical because it is anachronistic—but to give an impartial record of the development of a great ideal and of the lessons which it teaches. The Monastic Ideal, whether to-day it be true or false, has played a great part in the history of religion and life. We hold, therefore, that it is entitled to the reverent study of all those who recognize in the formative ideas of the past, whatever be their present value, the workings of one Master-mind, Who at sundry times and in divers manners hath spoken unto us by His Son. If some critics should accuse me of too indulgent treatment I must plead that sympathy seems to me the only key to understanding, and that the object of every historian must be to put himself into touch with the outlook of those whose spiritual experiences he is attempting to unfold.

[1] J. O. Hannay, *Spirit and Origin of Christian Monasticism* (1903), a work that I did not meet with until the following pages had passed through the press, is an exception. Mr. Hannay's work is, however, of limited range, and in some places suffers, as the author acknowledges in his preface, by his distance from a good library.

The reader will notice that I have called this study, "A Second Chapter in the History of Christian Renunciation." Some explanation is due for this sub-title. Some ten years ago, in the enthusiasm of youth and ignorance, I set out to write a short history of Christian Renunciation, intending, if I remember rightly, to compress it into one volume. But as I wrote the matter grew, and I was driven to alter my plans. In August 1906 I published a "First Chapter in the History of Renunciation,"[1] in a book entitled *Persecution in the Early Church*. The favour with which critics of all schools, in different countries, received this work led me to hope that a similar welcome might be given to a further instalment of the original scheme. After six years of work, sadly broken by the ever-increasing pressure of official duties, during the most part of which the manuscript has lain upon my desk, oftentimes, alas! reproaching me for my unavoidable neglect, I have ventured to publish "A Second Chapter in the History of Christian Renunciation." If it meets from the critic the favour which was bestowed upon my *Persecution in the Early Church* I shall feel that the delay has not been in vain. It has certainly enabled me to make use of some valuable works of but recent publication. "The Third Chapter" of my original design—the history of early missions—will shortly be published, in an abbreviated form, by the Student Volunteer Christian Union.

[1] This study of Renunciation was confined to Christian Renunciation, though not so stated. A similar restriction, admittedly unscientific, obtains in the following pages.

keep abreast of the most recent research in all its parts. To the critic who will forward the correction of any mistakes he may discern, or will indicate recent monographs that have been neglected, the author, in anticipation, now presents his thanks.

It is of importance that the reader further note that quotations from original sources are always enclosed in ' '; quotations from modern writers in " ".

WESTMINSTER,
    February 1913.

CONTENTS

	PAGES
ABBREVIATIONS AND EDITIONS	xv–xxi

CHAPTER   I.—HISTORIC SURVEY OF THE IDEAS OF
                MONASTICISM   1-74
              (For " Argument " of the Chapter see p. 2.)

   ,,   II.—THE HISTORY OF MONASTICISM AS AN
                INSTITUTION TO THE COMING OF
                BENEDICT   75–136
              (For " Argument " of the Chapter see p. 76.)

   ,,   III.—ST. BENEDICT AND HIS ORDER . .   137–180
              (For " Argument " of the Chapter see p. 138.)

   ,,   IV.—THE IDEALS OF MONASTICISM IN THE
                CELTIC CHURCH   181–216
              (For " Argument " of the Chapter see p. 182.)

   ,,   V.—THE DEVELOPMENT OF MONASTICISM
                FROM ST. BENEDICT TO ST.
                FRANCIS   217–268
              (For " Argument " of the Chapter see p. 218.)

   ,,   VI.—THE COMING OF THE FRIARS . .   269–316
              (For " Argument " of the Chapter see p. 270.)

   ,,   VII.—THE MESSAGE OF MONASTICISM .   317–352
              (For " Argument " of the Chapter see p. 318.)

APPENDIX A.—THE SOURCES OF OUR KNOWLEDGE OF
                EARLY MONASTICISM . . .   353–360

   ,,   B.—ADDITIONAL BIBLIOGRAPHY . .   361–363

INDEX   364–368

ABBREVIATIONS AND EDITIONS

N.B.—Works whose titles are fully quoted in the notes or to which only occasional reference is made are not given in this list. The abbreviations and editions of classical and patristic writers are not given. They are familiar to all students, or easily accessible. The student in doubt as to the best edition of the early Fathers should consult O. Bardenhewer, *Patrology* (Eng. trans. by T. G. Shahan, Freiburg in Breisgau, 1908). For patristics my references are, as a rule, to the edition of Migne, though in a few cases I have quoted the superior *CSEL*.

A. V. G. Allen *CI*	*Christian Institutions* (1898).
Anal. Boll.	*Analecta Bollandiana* (Brussels; in progress).
A.SS	*Acta Sanctorum*, the great, incomplete Bollandist collection. Quoted by the month and its volume, or occasionally by the month and its day.
E. Amélineau *HL*	*De Historia Lausiaca* (Paris, 1887). In Latin; with trans. of Coptic fragments.
,, *MG*	*Annales du Musée Guimet.*
E. C. Butler *HL*	*The Lausiac History of Palladius* (2 vols.; Camb. 1898, 190–; in *TS* vol. 6). See *infra*, p. 354 f.
B.M.	British Museum Library.
Cabrol *DACL*	*Dict. d'Archéologie Chrétienne et de Liturgie* (Paris; in progress). A vast work, mainly written by French Benedictine monks of Farnborough, a few volumes only of which have as yet (1912) appeared.
Cass. *Coll.*	Cassian, *Conferences.* See *infra*, p. 359.

ABBREVIATIONS AND EDITIONS

CSEL	*Corpus scriptorum ecclesiasticorum Latinorum* (Vienna; in progress). The volumes, unfortunately, are numbered in order of publication, and the works of the same author are often sadly separated. Supersedes Migne, *PL*, wherever issued.
DB	Hastings' *Dictionary of the Bible* (1898 f.; 5 vols.).
DACL	See Cabrol, *supra*.
DCA	Smith and Cheetham, *Dict. of Christian Antiquities* (1875; 2 vols.). Will be superseded by Cabrol, *DACL*.
DCB	Smith and Wace, *Dict. of Christian Biography* (1877; 4 vols.). Does not go beyond the 8th century.
DNB	*Dictionary of National Biography* (original edition).
S. Dill *RSWE*	*Roman Society in the last Century of the Western Empire* (2nd ed., 1899).
L. Duchesne *EHC*	*Early Hist. of the Christian Church* (Eng. trans. in 3 vols. from the 4th French ed.; London, 1910 f.).
,, *LP* or *Lib. Pont.*	*Le Liber Pontificalis* (Paris, 1886; 2 vols.).
W. Dugdale *Mon.*	R. Dodsworth and W. Dugdale, *Monasticon Anglicanum* (London, 1655; better eds. 1817, 1846).
ERE	Hastings' *Encyclopedia of Religion and Ethics* (in progress).
EHR	*English Historical Review.*
Greg. *Reg.* or Greg. Mag. *Reg.*	P. Ewald and L. M. Hartmann, *Registrum Epistolarum Greg. Mag.* in *MGH* (1891–9).
L. Gougaud *CC*	*Les Chrétientés Celtiques* (Paris, 1911); a good little compendium.
T. R. Glover *LLFC*	*Life and Letters in the Fourth Century* (Camb. 1901).

ABBREVIATIONS AND EDITIONS

G. Grützmacher *PAK*	*Pachomius u. das älteste Klosterleben* (Freiburg in Breisgau, 1896).
HE	*Historia Ecclesiastica* (of various writers: Socrates, Sozomen, Theodoret, Bede, &c.).
H. and S. *Conc.* or *Councils*	A. W. Haddan and W. Stubbs, *Council and Ecclesiastical Documents relating to Great Britain and Ireland* (Oxford, 3 vols., 1869–78).
E. Hatch *OEC*	*Organization of the Early Christian Churches* (3rd ed., London, 1888).
P. Helyot	*Hist. des ordres monastiques* (Paris, 1714–9; 8 vols.; new ed. by M. L. Badiche, Paris, 1858, in 4 vols.). See the remarks under Heimbucher, *OKK*.
HL	*Historia Lausiaca* (of various writers and editions. See especially *infra*, p. 354 f.).
HL (Gr.)	*Historia Lausiaca* in the Greek text. See *infra*, p. 355.
M. Heimbucher *OKK*	*Die Orden u. Kongregationen der kath. Kirche* (2nd ed., 3 vols.; Paderborn, 1907). An invaluable encyclopedia of literature and information that makes reference to the older works, *e.g.* Helyot, largely needless, save for the illustrations. For a complete bibliography of the more general works, see Heimbucher, i. 71–84.
C. J. Hefele *HC*	*Histoire des Conciles* (Paris; in progress; many volumes, each double). This translation by H. Leclercq of Hefele's great German work, *Conciliengeschichte*, with valuable additional notes and bibliography, is the one I have always quoted. It is much superior to the German, or to the Eng. trans. of the German.

PL	Migne, *Patrologiae cursus completus. Series Latina* (Paris, 1844 f.).
PG	Migne, *Patrologiae cursus completus. Series Graeca* (Paris, 1857 f.).
PRE	Herzog-Hauck, *Real-Encyclopädie f. protestant Theologie u. Kirche.* References, except where otherwise stated, are to the third edition. But the articles of Weingarten and others are in the second edition.
RS	The "Rolls Series" of English Historical Documents.
W. Reeves *AC*	Adamnan's *Vita Columbae* (Dublin, 1857). See *infra*, p. 202 n. 1.
H. Rosweyd *VP*	*Vitae Patrum* (Antwerp, 1615, 1628; also in *PL* 73, 74). This invaluable collection contains most of the Latin works mentioned in App. A, also certain translations of Greek works. Rosweyd's *VP* is very scarce, and Migne's reprint suffers from the fact that it is not complete, *e.g.* for the *Historia Monachorum* reference is made to *PL* 21.
Reg. Ben.	*Regula Benedicti.* See *infra*, p. 142 n.
S. Schiwietz *MM*	*Das morgenländische Mönchtum* (Mainz, 1904). (Vol. i. only has yet been published.)
E. G. Smith *CM*	*Christian Monasticism* (London, 1892). Chiefly essays contributed to *DCB*. Now out of print.
Sulp. Sev. *Dial.*	Sulpicius Severus. See *infra*, pp. 101 n., 104 n.
,, *VM*	Sulpicius Severus, *Vita Martini.* See *infra*, p. 104 n.
TS	*Texts and Studies.* Ed. Dean Robinson. Quoted by year of publication and author.

ABBREVIATIONS AND EDITIONS

TU	Texte und Untersuchungen zur Geschichte der altchristlichen Literatur. Ed. O. von Gebhardt and A. Harnack. Quoted by author and year of publication.
VM	Vita Martini. See Sulp. Sev., supra.
VP	See supra, Rosweyd, VP.
VCH	Victoria County Histories. Quoted by county and volume.
VS	Verba Seniorum. See infra, App. A, p. 360.
VA	Vita Antonii. See infra, App. A, p. 353.
H. Williams *CEB*	Christianity in Early Britain (1912). A learned and valuable collection of essays on the Celtic Church.
H. Weingarten *UM*	Ueber den Ursprung des Mönchtums in nachkonstantinischen Zeitalter (Gotha, 1877).
J. W. Willis-Bund *CCW*	Celtic Church of Wales (1897).
H. B. Workman *PEC*	Persecution in the Early Church (2nd ed., 1906).
H. Zimmer *CCB*	The Celtic Church in Britain and Ireland (trans. A. Meyer, 1902).
O. Zöckler *AM*	Askese u. Mönchtum (2 vols., paginated as one; Frankfort, 1897). This much augmented edition of his Kritischen Ges. der Askese (1863) covers the whole history of Asceticism from Buddhism to Methodism with select rather than full bibliography.

N.B.—In addition to the above list the student, anxious to obtain a limited bibliography of Monasticism, should also consult Appendix B, "Additional Bibliography," infra, p. 361 f.

CHAPTER I

HISTORIC SURVEY OF THE IDEAS OF MONASTICISM

Μὴ ἀγαπᾶτε τὸν κόσμον, μηδὲ τὰ ἐν τῷ κόσμῳ.
Καὶ ὁ κόσμος παράγεται, καὶ ἡ ἐπιθυμία αὐτοῦ, ὁ δὲ ποιῶν τὸ θέλημα τοῦ Θεοῦ μένει εἰς τὸν αἰῶνα.—JOHN, *1 Ep.* ii. 13, 15.

'Fecisti nos ad Te, et inquietum est cor nostrum, donec requiescat in Te.'—ST. AUGUSTINE, *Confess.* c. i.

'Otiosum non est vacare Deo, sed negotium negotiorum omnium.'—ST. BERNARD.

O happy in their souls' high solitude
Who commune thus with God and not with earth!
Lyra Apostolica, xxiv.

ARGUMENT

                                                                PAGE

§ I. The yearning for self-surrender — Renunciation and Monasticism—'Secular' and 'religious'—'Conversion'   3

§ II. The rise of Monasticism—Effect of Constantine's adoption of Christianity — Damasus and Ursinus — Ammianus Marcellinus — Protest of Monasticism against worldliness   6

§ III. Monasticism, at first, outside the Church—The failure to reform the Church—The protest of the lay spirit—Montanus — The opposition of the bishops — *Nolo Episcopari*—Monasticism and orthodoxy—The work of Athanasius—Of Augustine   11

§ IV. The individualism of Monasticism—Monasticism over against the State — The causes and results —'The despotism of the State—Its rottenness—Counsels of despair—Monasticism and Neoplatonism   .   . 22

§ V. Monasticism and isolation—Monasticism and the great cities—The yearning for the simple life—Illustrations: St. Guthlac; Hugh of Avalon—Absurd tales of beasts —Identification with nature   .   .   . 29

§ VI. Monasticism and Stoicism—Gnosticism—The defeat of Gnosticism—The Cathari—The victory of Gnosticism —Symeon Stylites—Anti-human ideals—Tales of self-denial—Divergence of East and West.   .   . 37

§ VII. Monasticism and Celibacy — Growth of Celibacy — Absence of social instinct — Exaggerated estimates and absurd relationships—Erotic novels of the times —Essential Dualism—Monasticism and the bath— *Militia Christi* 54

§ VIII. Monasticism and Poverty—Connotation of 'Poverty' —Monasticism and Obedience—Strange exaggeration —Theophilus and Mary—Mucius—Jesuitism .   . 66

                                                               pp. 1–74

CHAPTER I

HISTORIC SURVEY OF THE IDEAS OF MONASTICISM

I

IN every human heart, except, possibly, the utterly depraved, we find a yearning for self-surrender rising at times to a passion. Even in the worldling, buried deep beneath the deposits of self, there is an instinct he cannot explain, the power of which he may attempt to laugh away, that leads him, in spite of himself, in a moment of heroic decision to give his life a ransom for others. Few there are to whom there do not come at times visions of a nobler life. Like Bunyan's warrior, we tell the man with the inkhorn to write down our name in the roll of those who would join the immortals.

This imperial note of our higher natures can never wholly be silenced by the lower, and finds expression in every form of religion, however degraded or unreasoning. For the Christian, at least, self-surrender is the imperative call of the Master. 'If a man would come after Me, let him take up his cross and follow Me,' is still the absolute condition of discipleship. 'If a man love father or mother more than Me he is not worthy of Me' is one of those sentences so hard to interpret from the *a priori* standpoint, so easy to understand when we view its results in the life of the Church. The form this renunciation takes has varied with the changing years, nevertheless its essential feature is always the same; the print of the nails upon the hands and feet, the mark of the thorns upon the brow.

Throughout the universal Church, for almost a thousand years, there was one word which more than any other conveyed in itself the essential features of this renunciation. This was Monasticism. One word in its time plays many parts, and Monasticism, as we shall see later, came to stand for many different even opposing movements. Nevertheless in the main Monasticism and Renunciation for long ages were looked upon as almost interchangeable terms; in the sense, that is, that no real renunciation could be conceived of which did not end in some form of Monasticism. In the Middle Ages it is hardly too much to say that "the history of piety is the history of Monasticism."[1] So completely was the monk identified with the renunciant that a priest who was not a monk was regarded as still belonging to the world. He was a 'secular,' not one of the 'religious,' a term strictly confined to those who had adopted the monastic life.[2] In the same way 'conversion' had none of its modern evangelical significance, but connoted always the renunciation which expressed itself by reception into an order.[3]

[1] Harnack, *HD* v. 10.

[2] 'Religion' was used for the monastic life as early as the 2nd Conc. of Arles (443 or 452), c. 25 (Hefele, *HC* II. i. 472); 1st Conc. of Orleans (511), c. 11 ('Ascetics faithless to their vows who re-enter the world').

[3] 'Conversion' was used for the adoption of the *professio continentiae* as early as the Council of Orange (441), c. 22 (Hefele, *HC* II. i. 445);

Instead therefore of dismissing Monasticism with the sneer of Gibbon " at the unhappy exiles from social life, impelled by the dark and implacable genius of superstition,"[1] we shall do well to study, with the reverence which any ideal however faulty deserves, what were the causes which led men to the identification of 'religion' and Monasticism, and what have been the results of this ideal in the history of the Church.

At the outset it is well to point out that the writing of a formal history of Monasticism, much less of Asceticism, is far from our purpose. Even in the briefest outline this would form a task beyond our limits. But the evolution of Monasticism viewed from the standpoint of its inner meaning, that is as the expression in concrete life of the central principle of renunciation, is of more manageable proportions and ought not to be lightly dismissed. In the long story of renunciation in the Christian Church Monasticism forms a chapter even more striking in its variety, though perhaps less heroic in its appeal, than Martyrdom. Both alike sprang from the same root. By concentration upon this inner meaning of Monasticism, its development and varying forms, we obtain also a guiding thread which will save the reader from being lost amidst what, otherwise, might appear to be endless details. The various divisions and orders of Monasticism become correlated together, and the way is prepared, through the reduction to unity

---

the Conc. of Agde (506), c. 16; (see Leclercq's note in Hefele, *HC* II. ii. 988). Also at the 4th Conc. of Arles (524), c. 2.

In Benedict's *Regula* its meaning is already fixed (c. 58, 'noviter veniens quis ad conversionem'). By the time of Gregory the Great we have papal sanction for the identification of the 'religiosa vita' with Monasticism (Greg. Mag. *Reg.* iii. 17).

[1] Gibbon (ed. J. B. Bury), iv. 62.

of the whole, for the more detailed study, if so desired, of the several parts.

II

In the present chapter we propose, therefore, to enquire into the conditions which led to the adoption by the Church of Monasticism as the best expression in life of a perfect renunciation. Our enquiry, necessarily, will be many-sided. We may approach it from the standpoint of the times in which the idea was born, the environment of the idea; or from the inner contents of the idea itself. We purpose both.

The rise of Monasticism coincided, roughly speaking, with the loss of the Church in the world. Abandoning its early chiliastic conceptions, the Church had settled down into the acceptance of the 'world' as a definite part of economy, with which it must come to terms. Whatever the ultimate issue of the adoption by Constantine of Christianity as the official religion of this 'world' or State, its first effects were to lower the ideal of Christianity itself. Average morality had created the authority of the Church, and she in her turn legitimized average morality. In the striking phrase of Harnack, it seemed as if the net result of Constantine's action was to leave the 'world' "in possession of all except its gods."[1] The stalwart Christians whom Diocletian had killed had been replaced by a mixed multitude of time-servers and half-converted pagans.[2]

---

[1] Harnack, *Mon.* 28. Cf. *HD* iii. 131 n.

[2] We must beware of attributing the change wholly to Constantine. The amazing canons of the Council of Elvira (c. 300) show that rottenness had already crept into the Church. See Harnack, *EC* ii. 441, and for the canons of the Council, Hefele, *HC* I. i. 212 f.

The conviction of truth gave place to the acceptance of custom, the early chiliastic conceptions of the speedy reign of Jesus to an uninspired contentment with things as they were. "The Church," adds Montalembert, "has never known a period in which she was more tormented, more agitated, or more compromised"[1]— but the agitations were from within. She was garnished with all the resources that a world-empire and an age-long culture could offer her. But she seemed unconscious that she had purchased these things with a great price, a lowered standard of life, and a theology whose simplicity was spoiled by the systems of philosophy that she had tried to assimilate.[2] Once she had descended out of heaven as a bride adorned for her husband; but now the bridal dress was torn, the orange flower faded. She was rich and increased in goods, and knew not that she was poor and naked.

To outer seeming the victory of Christianity was complete. There was truth in the triumphant cry of Jerome:

'Even in Rome itself paganism is left in solitude. They who were once the gods of the nations remain under their lonely roofs with horned owls and birds of night. The standards of the military are emblazoned with the sign of the Cross. . . . The Armenian bowman has laid aside his quiver, the Huns learn the Psalter, the chilly Scythians are warmed with the glow of the faith' [*Ep.* 107 (2)].

But no one is more careful than Jerome to point out the superficiality of the success. If Jerome stood alone

[1] Mont. *MW* i. 188.
[2] "Occupied incessantly with questions as to the divine relationships and processions, the Church had lost sight of the message of Christ, of His history, and of His work of salvation" (Duchesne, *EHC* ii. 255).

we might discount or even disregard his invectives against the corruption of the Church, for his was the fatal gift of satire,[1] and the rhetorician's love of exaggeration. But, unfortunately, Jerome is not unsupported, and the picture that he draws of the Christian Rome of his time, in spite of its vivid colours, contains no small measure of truth.[2] Heresy mounted in triumph the throne of the world; Arians monopolized the sees of the Church, and even invaded, in the person of Liberius, the Chair of St. Peter.[3] The followers of Damasus in 366, in their struggle with the anti-pope Ursinus, won for him the papacy, but at the cost of one hundred and thirty-seven lives.[4] Once the Christians had laid down their lives for the truth; now they slaughtered each other to secure the prizes of the Church. Once Tertullian could record how the heathen remarked: 'See how these Christians love one another.'[5] Now Ammianus Marcellinus, the pagan historian, could write the bitter satire, as he speaks of Julian's recall of the Nicene exiles: 'He knew that there are no wild beasts so hostile to mankind as most of the Christians are to one another.'[6] The same writer, as he records for us the fight between Damasus and Ursinus, and the accompanying massacre of both sexes 'in the

[1] Cf. Sulp. Sev. *Dial.* i. 21, 'haec describenda mordacius beato viro Hieronymus relinquamus.' For Sulpicius, see *infra*, p. 101 n.

[2] See especially *Ep.* 22.

[3] The fall of pope Liberius († 24 Sept. 366) into Semi-Arianism, as the result of his banishment in 355 by Constantius to Beroea in Thrace, was, however, amply atoned for on his return to Rome (358). See Hilary, *Op.* p. 702 (*PL* 10, p. 714); Socrates, *HE* iv. 12; Mansi, iii. 210, 213, 377; Hefele, *HC* L ii. 918 f.

[4] Amm. Marcellinus, xxvii. c. 3. The *Gesta* speaks of 160 dead.

[5] Tert. *Apol.* 39.

[6] Amm. Marcell. xxii. 5 (4).

church of Sicininus,' adds a comment, more terrible than the invectives of Jerome :

'I do not deny that those who are ambitious for this thing (the See) ought to spare no effort to secure what they want. The successful candidate is sure of being enriched by the offerings of nations ; of riding about in carriages through the streets of Rome, as soon as his dress is composed with becoming care and elegance ; and of giving banquets so profuse and elegant that their entertainments shall surpass the sumptuousness of the imperial tables.'[1]

'Make me bishop of Rome,' said the prefect Praetextatus to Damasus, ' and I will forthwith become a Christian.' On all hands there is the same testimony. 'The doctrines of the Fathers,' writes Basil,

'are despised, the speculations of innovators hold sway in the Church. Men are rather contrivers of cunning systems than theologians. The wisdom of this world has the place of honour, having dispossessed the boasting of the Cross. The shepherds are driven out ; in their place grievous wolves are brought in which harry the flock. Houses of prayer have none to assemble in them ; the deserts ' (the reader will mark this conclusion) ' are full of mourners.'[2]

Or we turn to Gregory Nazianzen :

'At this time the most holy order is like to become the most contemptible of all. For the chief seat is gained by evil doing, not by virtue, and the sees belong, not to the more worthy, but to the more powerful.'

It was only the humblest priest who remained still so simple as to refuse with scorn the ten gold crowns which the Gallic traveller Postumian offered him : ' the Church,' he said, ' was not built up but rather destroyed by gold.'[3]

---

[1] Amm. Marcell. xxvii. 3 (2). But Marcellinus owns that many provincial bishops were distinguished for sobriety and temperance.
[2] Basil, *Ep.* 90 (to the bishops of the West). Cf. *Epp.* 70 and 92.
[3] Sulp. Sev. *Dial.* i. 5.

Against all this Monasticism was a protest. No true Christian could view without dismay the growing secularity of the Church. Rather a thousand-fold than these latter days of Ease in Zion a return to ancient simplicity and purity, even though accompanied by the poverty of Christ or the penalties of the martyrs. So, in spite of himself, the saint—whose long cry of despair echoes through all the writings of the times—was driven to construct a new form in which the old ideal of religion as the great renunciation might once again find expression. From the necessities of the case this new ideal was no longer as of old in the Church itself, nor even alongside the Church, nor did men seek for it in the apocalyptic visions of earlier days; [1] it lay above the Church, and, in a sense, even outside it. The saint preached once more the need of the narrow way and the strait gate, but the broad road with which he compared it was not only in the world. The hermit fled not so much from the world as from the world in the Church, from court bishops who fought for richer sees, from peoples who bore the name of Christ but who were still pagans at heart, from men who immediately they were made clerics 'enlarged the fringes of their garments, rode on foaming steeds,' and dwelt in houses of many rooms, with sculptured doors and painted wardrobes.[2] It was the snake in the grass that the monk dreaded; the open foe he could meet and crush.

[1] The last important theological representative of Chiliasm in the East was Apollinaris of Laodicea (*c.* 350). The old Chiliasm which had once been so important (see my *PEC* 153 ff.) died out as Monasticism began, or rather as the spirit which had inspired it took this new form.

[2] See the bitter description in Sulp. Sev. *Dial.* i. 21.

III

Monasticism was thus in its origin not merely an exodus of despair from the evils of the age, but even "a veritable stampede from the Catholic Church, as though that great creation of Christian energy were no better than the evil world from which escape was sought."[1] Even those who remained within the Church, men like Athanasius, the two Gregories, Augustine, cast longing eyes upon the purer ideal that lay outside. Thus from the first Monasticism lay over against the Catholic Church, with an ideal, life, and institutions of her own that claimed to be independent of, nay superior to, the institutions, life, and ideal of the Catholic Church.

We are so accustomed to think of Monasticism as one of the most formidable weapons that the Church has ever possessed, and of the monks as her most obedient and docile servants, that we find it difficult to realize how completely at one time the ideal of Monasticism lay outside, even opposed to, that of the Church. As an illustration we may mention the provision of Gregory the Great that no monk could obtain the cure of souls without thereby losing all his rights as a monk, nor could the secular obtain a position in the monastery unless he would first abandon his secular preferment.[2] But in nothing, perhaps, shall we see this better than by

---

[1] A. V. G. Allen, *Church Institutions* (1898), p. 139.

[2] Greg. Mag. *Reg.* vii. 40, viii. 17; cf. iv. 11, v. 1. But Gregory did not always carry out consistently this separation (Greg. Mag. *Reg.* iv. 18, ix. 7). The reader should note that quotations from the *Register* of Gregory the Great are always made from the edition of P. Ewald in *MGH*, the numbering in which differs considerably from that of St. Maur.

remembering that the Church has never yet directly founded one religious order. These have not sprung from the authoritative acts or provisions of councils or popes; in every case they have been the outcome of individual consecration and enthusiasm, seeking for itself some outlet that it could not find in the channels provided by the Church.

One result of the fact that Monasticism lay outside the Church may be seen in the curious circumstance that throughout its history Monasticism has rarely attempted to reform the Church, much less the State. The one exception is the great movement of the eleventh century associated with Clugny, the leader in which was Hildebrand. But, as recent research has shown, Hildebrand was not himself a monk but a spiritual Caesar who used the monastic ideal for his own purposes. Apart from this apparent exception—to which we shall return later—Monasticism has always been too individualistic, too conscious of itself, to attempt this larger ideal; its aim has been rather to reform itself. "The monk," according to Cardinal Newman, "proposed to himself no great or systematic work beyond that of saving his soul. What he did more than this was the accident of the hour." [1] "Historians have vied," writes Montalembert, "in praising Benedict's genius and clear-sightedness; they have supposed that he intended to regenerate Europe, to stop the dissolution of Society, to reconstruct public order, and so on. . . . I firmly believe that he never dreamed of regenerating anything but his own soul." [2] Provided we interpret this last sentence in a wide and altruistic sense, this will be true

[1] *Historical Sketches*, ii. 452–3.
[2] Mont. *MW* i. 436. Cf. Dom Butler in *Camb. Mod. Hist.* i. 540.

of all the great monastic leaders. Throughout its history Monasticism has been too intent upon the part to be conscious of the whole. Monks have sought to serve the Church, not by cleansing the inner courts, but by whitewashing the flying buttresses. In its first beginnings, and throughout its career, Monasticism has lost chance after chance of bringing in a real Reformation. If the energy with which men flung themselves into the formation and purification of an ideal that for the most part lay outside the Church had only been expended in the attempt to reform the Church itself, the history of Christianity would have been very different indeed.

Another consequence of Monasticism thus lying over against the Church is of the utmost importance. Monasticism in its origin was the protest of the lay spirit against any conception of religion which excluded the laity from the highest obligations or the supremest attainment. Until the end of the fifth century the monk was generally regarded as a layman, whose tonsure, in nowise an equivalent for orders, did not exempt him from the pains and penalties of the layman.[1] Now the rise of Monasticism as a lay movement coincided with the establishment of the Catholic Church upon a sacramental and sacerdotal foundation. Broadly speaking, by the fourth century the Church had committed herself to the proclamation of the coming of grace from without, through channels other than the man himself. Largely through the influence of Cyprian, the doctrines of Apostolic succession and a mediating priesthood had

[1] Conc. Chalcedon, c. 2; Hefele, *HC* II. ii. 772. By the time of Gregory of Tours, *de gloria Martyr.* 76 ('mulier filium ad monasterium adducens ut factus clericus'), monks began to be classed as *clerici*.

been made the foundation of Zion. Definite belief and external organization rather than holiness became the basis of union. The plea of Montanus [1] for the emancipation of the operation of the Holy Spirit from these rigid fetters, had been set aside. Against all this growing sacerdotalism the monk by his very existence was a silent, unconscious, but none the less potent protest. We see this clearly brought out in the *Life of Anthony*. Anthony is not only a mere layman; he neither goes to church, nor receives the Sacrament for years, and yet continues in the closest intercession with God.[2] In the Nitria eight presbyters sufficed for the spiritual administration of five thousand monks, whose lay character is shown by their not being allowed even to preach.[3] According to St. Basil: 'All the solitaries in the desert where there is no priest, take the communion themselves, keeping communion in their own home.'[4] In process of time the monk was often compelled, as a matter of fact, through the exigencies of providing for the ritual of the monastery, to join the priesthood,[5] but the special circumstance which brought this about

---

[1] For Montanism, see my *Christian Thought to the Reformation* (1911), 97 f. The best bibliography of the subject is a note by Leclercq, in Hefele, *HC* I. i. 129.

[2] "We cannot see how Anthony, during his twenty years of seclusion, can ever have been enabled to receive the Eucharist" (Duchesne, *EHC* ii. 390).

[3] 'Nullus praeter (primum presbyterum) alter aut sacra offert Deo, aut tractat, aut judicat' (Palladius, *HP* 2, in *PL* 74, p. 258).

[4] Basil, *Ep.* 93. But reservation of the Sacrament was possibly practised. Cf. Justin *1 Apol.* 65, last sentence.

[5] Instances are mentioned as early as by Cassian, *Conf.* iv. c. 1. Gregory the Great extended the custom (Greg. Mag. *Reg.* xii. 15), while Gelasius in a synod at Rome (11 March 494) shortened a monk's probation for the priesthood to one year (Jaffé, *RP* i. 85; Mansi, viii. 38).

never succeeded in making the priesthood the *esse* rather than the accident of his profession. We have a striking illustration of this in the fact that by the *Rule* of Benedict confessions were not made to a priest or monastic chaplain but to the abbot or to the whole brotherhood, even though they were laymen.[1] As a priest the monk had no place higher than his brethren, while throughout the annals of Monasticism we recognize that in the cloister the personal holiness of the monk— the underlying feature of which was his renunciation— is something higher than any succession can bestow. Except, possibly, in the Celtic Church [2] an abbot was never other than a presbyter, in spite of the papal sanctions which sometimes exalted him as to his position into the equal of a bishop.

But we are anticipating. Our immediate purpose is the demonstration that the monastic idea in its origin lay outside the Church. Monasticism, in fact, at first, in spite of its crude attempts at regulation, did not commend itself to the ecclesiastical authorities. Both in the East and West the new movement was bitterly opposed, especially by the bishops, sufficient proof in itself that Monasticism was not a primitive institution. In Egypt the monks and bishops were generally on opposite sides.[3] At Aquileia the ascetic community at the head of which were Jerome and Rufinus, was

---

[1] *Reg. Ben.* c. 46.
[2] See *infra*, p. 194.
[3] The opposition specially showed itself at the synod of Esneh (Ladeuze, *ECP* 188). The conflict comes out more clearly, as Grützmacher, *PAK* 52 f., shows, in the Coptic and Arabic recensions of the *Vita Pachom.* (see *infra*, p. 358) than in the Greek version. Grützmacher's deduction from this, however, is vitiated by his assuming the Greek to be the later, softened version.

broken up by the efforts of Lupicinus, the bishop of Stridon.¹ In Spain the synod of Saragossa (380) forbade clerics to become monks. Jovinian and Vigilantius even dared, the one to question the superior merit of celibacy over marriage, the other to protest against the whole monastic life as interfering with the duty of a Christian to his neighbour. Some bishops, *e.g.* Exsuperius of Toulouse, were bold enough to countenance their ideas, in spite of the violent invectives of Jerome, and of Jovinian's condemnation by pope Siricius.² In Rome at the funeral of the nun Blaesilla, the daughter of Paula, in 384, the people filled the streets, crying out: 'The young woman has been killed by fasts. . . . When shall this detestable race of monks be expelled the city? Stone them! Throw them into the river!'³ In the towns of Africa, especially in Carthage, when the people

---

¹ Jerome, *Ep.* 7 (5). For Stridon, see *infra*, p. 117 n.

² Of Jovinian, who died before 409, we know little save what we learn from Jerome's violent invective. For his "Protestant" theology, see Harnack, *HD* v. 57 n. His condemnation by Siricius took place in 390 in synods at Rome and Milan (Jaffé, *RP* i. 41). Vigilantius (b. about 370) was a Spaniard of Cazères who managed the estates of Sulpicius Severus, and at one time was the friend of Jerome. His denunciation of relics, alleged miracles, exaggerated estimate of virginity, &c., was published in Gaul about 406 and drew from Jerome a most abusive reply. The protest of Helvidius against the conception of the perpetual virginity of St. Mary must not be overlooked. For Jovinian, the student may refer to W. Haller, *Jovinianus; Die Fragmenta seines Schriften* (Leipzig, 1898). For Vigilantius, see A. Réville, *Vigilance de Calagurris* (Paris, 1902).

³ Jerome, *Ep.* 39 (5). For the heathen hostility, cf. Rutilius Namatianus, *de reditu suo*, i. 525—

non, rogo, deterior Circaeis secta venenis ?
tunc mutabantur corpora, nunc animi.

According to Rutilius, *l.c.* i. 489, they owed 'their Greek name of *monks*' to the fact that 'they wished to live without witnesses' of their crimes.

THE IDEAS OF MONASTICISM

saw a shaven crown they raised the hue and cry.[1] The illustrations of hostility in Gaul to the new order abound in the pages of Sulpicius Severus. Throughout his life, we are told, 'clerics and priests refused to recognize' the virtues of Martin, lest by so doing they should discover their own vices.[2] Even as late as the times of Gregory the Great we find numerous instances of persecution of the monasteries by a jealous episcopate that refused to punish monks who revolted from their abbot.[3] Nor was it bishops and priests alone that we find in opposition. Sulpicius tells a tale of how on one occasion he sat down with his Gallic servant to eat the scanty meal of a hermit, 'a bundle of herbs, and half a barley biscuit,' and quoted the words of Athanasius: 'Fasting is the food of angels.' 'We are not angels,' replied the sturdy rogue, 'we are only Gauls. It is foolish and inhuman to attempt to make us live like angels.'[4]

That the early monks with their profession of a higher life were generally laymen, may perhaps account for the hostility of many bishops in the fourth and fifth centuries to the new enthusiasm. We are inclined to forget this hostility owing to the fact that the holiest of the monks often became bishops; they were, in reality, consecrated by force to satisfy the admiration of the people. But of the reluctance of the monk to enter the

---

[1] Salvian, *de gubernat. Dei*, viii. 4 (in *PL* 53, p. 156).

[2] *Dial.* i. 26 (3); cf. i. 2 (3), ii. 24 (3), iii. 11, iii. 13 (6).

[3] For this opposition, see Greg. Mag. *Reg.* i. 12, ii. 29, v. 2, vi. 44, vii. 32, ix. 107, &c. About 473 we find similar opposition in Celtic Christianity (Williams, *CEB* 316).

[4] Sulp. Sev. *Dial.* 4. We may note that Lent as an institution obtained its hold about this time [Cabrol, *DACL*, ii. 2139 f.; G. Harford and M. Stevenson, *Prayer Book Dict.* (1912) 433].

episcopate, or even to become a presbyter,[1] we have too many instances to be lightly dismissed as a case of 'nolo episcopari.' Martin, for example, refused all the efforts of Hilary of Poictiers to make him a presbyter.[2] He was only captured and made bishop of Tours by a stratagem. A man pretended that his wife was sick, and so drew the saint from his lair. The bishops, among whom one called Defensor took a prominent part, were opposed to this invasion of their ranks by one whom they regarded, probably, as a Salvation Army fanatic. But the people would not be denied, and were wild with delight at an incident that attended Martin's consecration. The "reader" of the day could not obtain entrance into the church because of the crowd. So one of the officials in despair seized a Psalter and began to read. As chance had it this was his lesson: 'out of the mouths of babes and sucklings thou hast perfected praise, that thou mightest destroy the enemy and avenger (*et defensorem*).'[3] We are expressly told of the reluctance with which at the age of forty Macarius of Egypt received ordination.[4] Jerome, too, was only ordained in 379 against his will. According to some accounts "He never consecrated the sacrament or officiated as a presbyter";[5] while the monk's contempt

[1] *e.g.* the case of Abraham, *PL* 73, p. 285; the case mentioned in *HL* (Gr.) 68.

[2] Sulp. Sev. *VM* 5. He allowed Hilary to make him a deacon, however. For the date of this interview, see *infra*, p. 106 n. 3.

[3] Sulp. Sev. *VM* 9. Part of the amusement would be caused by the fact that *defensor* at this period was the title of an inferior civil magistrate who had much to do with taxes.

[4] *HL* (Gr.) 17 (2).

[5] *DCB* iii. 32. Cf. the letter of Epiphanius in Jerome, *Ep.* 51 (1), and Jerome's own account, *Contra Joan. Jerus.* 41, with its indifference if not contempt for ordination. Against this should be put

for apostolic succession is shown in his famous statement that in the early days bishops and presbyters were interchangeable terms, and that the hierarchy is an arrangement of human origin.[1] Aërius, the friend of the founder of Greek monasticism, Eustathius of Sebaste, went so far as to make this identity an *articulus stantis et cadentis ecclesiae*.[2] Other monks, whose repute for holiness exposed them to special danger, resorted to rude devices to avoid the episcopate, as in the case of the Coptic monk Ammon. When a certain town (Hermopolis Parva) desired to have him for its bishop, and dragged him from his solitude before the patriarch Timotheus of Alexandria,[3] he disqualified himself by cutting off his right ear, and threatened, if further pressed, to cut out his tongue.[4] When Theophilus of Alexandria tried to make Evagrius a bishop he escaped by flight.[5] To the end of his life Benedict of Nursia refused to be made a priest. Cassian, in fact, reckons 'the desire for the priesthood or diaconate' among the perils of the soul which the monk must avoid, and tells an amusing story of a monk who was so 'deluded by vainglory' as to 'give a striking sermon to the people' in the solitude

the remark of Postumian, who spent six months with Jerome and speaks of him as 'the presbyter who rules the church' at Bethlehem (Sulp. Sev. *Dial.* i. 8).

[1] Jerome, *Epp.* 69 (3); 146.

[2] Harnack, *HD* iii. 192 n.; Epiphanius, *Haeres.* 75, in *PG* 42.

[3] Bishop from 381-5.

[4] *HL* 12 (*PL* 73, p. 1104), or *HL* (Gr.) 11. For this Ammon, see also Soz. *HE* vi. 30, Soc. *HE* iv. 23. He could repeat by heart the *NT* and *OT*. When he visited Rome he refused to see any sights except the basilicas of St. Peter and St. Paul. If he was an Origenist (as Baronius and Rosweyd in *PL* 73, p. 1220, infer; but see *DCB* i. 102 and Butler, *HL* i. 174) he imitated his master in his mutilations.

[5] Soc. *HE* iv. 23. For this Evagrius († 398), who must be distinguished from the more celebrated Evagrius, see *DCB* ii. *s.v.* (12).

of his cell at Scete. He adds that the 'old maxim is still current: that a monk ought by all means to fly from women and bishops.'[1] Said the monk John of Lycopolis to Palladius when he visited him: 'If you desire to escape troubles don't leave the desert, for in the desert no one can ordain you a bishop.'[2]

This antagonism between the ideals of the cleric and the monk could not last. The new method corresponded too deeply with the yearning of the heart for the opposition to have any permanence. Few movements, in fact, secured their triumph more speedily. The rapid growth of Monasticism as the ideal of renunciation was due to other causes than its own value. By a strange accident a movement which in its early days had been, at times, identified with Marcionism and Origenism, became allied with orthodoxy; and the opposition to Monasticism with the doctrines of Arius and Apollinaris.

'The reason,' writes Sozomen, 'why these doctrines had not any extensive success in addition to the causes just mentioned, is that the monks of that day took part against them . . . for the populace (of Cilicia) had such reverence for the characters of the monks that they trusted their doctrine as orthodox, and shrank from those who held otherwise, just as the Egyptians were led by the monks of Egypt to oppose the Arians' (*HE* vi. 27).

Whatever the cause—whether the greater tenacity in orthodoxy of the unendowed monks over the endowed clergy, or the greater worldliness of the Arians, whether the influence of the story of Anthony and the assistance he gave to Athanasius[3]—the Arians set themselves to

---

[1] Cass. *Instit.* xi. 14, 16, 18. For Cassian and his works, see App. A, § V, *infra*, p. 359.

[2] *HL* (Gr.) 35 (11). For John, see *infra*, p. 72 n. [3] See *infra*, p. 94.

persecute Monasticism; and a belief in Monasticism became one of the marks of the orthodox party.[1] In Egypt the monks distinguished themselves by their fierce fanaticism for the most rigid and abstruse formulae of the faith. Fine shades of meaning in theological terms would bring them together in their thousands, chanting hymns and burning with desire to vanquish the enemies of the truth.[2] Some of the most disgraceful episodes in church history, e.g. the murder of Flavian at the "Robber Synod" of Ephesus, were the work of these fanatics.

More important than the alliance between orthodoxy and Monasticism—or rather perhaps one consequence of the alliance—was the support given to Monasticism by all the great leaders of the Church, both in the East and West. Basil, Chrysostom, Jerome, Augustine, never weary in singing its praises. But the reconciliation of the Church as a whole, East and West, to the new ideal was even more fully the work of Athanasius, who, more than all others, united in himself all that was most virile in the Christianity of the age. In 329 the great archbishop became acquainted with the institutions of Pachomius, in 333 he visited Tabennîsî during his pastoral journey through the Thebaid, and in 337, on his return from his banishment to Treves, he would hear of the visit of some of these Egyptian monks to Alexandria, in 'defence of the faith,' led by the

---

[1] Hatch, *OEC* 162 n. (In his references to Monasticism, Hatch as a rule is led astray by Weingarten, *UM*.) Cf. Basil, *Ep.* 257. For a striking illustration of this, see the story of Evagrius Ponticus in *HL* (Gr.) 38 (11), ' before whom one day three demons presented themselves in the guise of priests. One called himself an Arian, the second an Eunomian, the third an Apollinarian.'

[2] *Vita Pachom.* 27.

aged Anthony. The alliance between orthodoxy and Monasticism was completed by Athanasius writing the *Life of Anthony*,[1] a book that henceforth set the standard of conduct of the whole Church, and established the new ideal of Monasticism.

In the West the consciousness of opposition between cleric and monk, though never entirely absent, did not become so pronounced as in the East. This must be attributed in no small degree to the influence of St. Augustine. Augustine, in the working out of his Pauline reaction, had established his idea of the grace of God working for righteousness through the Church; and yet, by one of those contradictions in which he abounds, he had identified himself fully with the new Monasticism,[2] with its ideal virtually outside the Church. For Augustine had shown that Christianity possesses a double form; it is the authoritative visible kingdom, the City of God whose foundations are not in this present; it is also the inner kingdom of contemplation.[3] By this identification or conjunction he succeeded in bringing it to pass that Western Monasticism not only proved a handmaid to the Church, the most potent instrument in the realization of her aims, but yet was enabled at the same time to carry out her own ideal of a contemplative life, lying largely outside the Church.

IV

That the early monks were laymen is not the only consequence that we may trace of the fact that

---

[1] On this see App. A, § I, *infra*, p. 353.
[2] See *infra*, p. 254.
[3] Cf. Harnack, *HD* v. 77 f., 110 f., 137, 138, 152, 219.

in its origin Monasticism lay over against the Catholic Church, with an ideal other than, possibly higher than, that of the Church. "The dominating principle that pervaded Egyptian monachism in all its manifestations . . . was a spirit of strongly-marked individualism."[1] The very extravagancies and eccentricities which later writers have held up to scorn, were but the manifestations of this pronounced individualism in a rivalry of asceticism. Against the essential solidarity of the Catholic Church, as against the all-pervading tyranny of the organization of the Empire, the monk placed that individualism which must lie at the root of all conscious renunciation. His was the protest of the individual against the collectivism which tended, both in Church and State, by its institutions and functions, to lose sight of his value. The monk, whether in the East or West, was the voice in the wilderness crying the lost truth of the worth of one soul. He asked once more the old question, this time not as of old from the world but from the Church : 'what advantageth it a man if he shall gain the whole world and lose his own self ?' He recoiled from the growing conception of the kingdom of God as an organized society. Once more he heard the eternal words : 'the kingdom of God is within you.' Over against Cyprian's conception of a great imperial institution as the channel of grace, with its apostolically descended bishops, presbyters, and deacons, its elaborate system of sacraments, and its idea of solidarity in a common organization, the monk opposed the life of the soul, face to face with God, in direct not intermediate communion with Him, outside all institutions, cut off, possibly, by the physical facts of his renunciation

[1] Butler, *HL* i. 237. Cf. Cabrol, *DACL* ii. 3139.

from all sacraments, independent of all bishops and presbyters, and with a solidarity with his fellows limited to spiritual communion. Over every hermit's cell we might read the legend, "God and my soul"; an ideal altogether outside the ideal of the Catholic Church.

To this individualism we owe it also that Monasticism, as a system, in its origin lay not only over against the Church, but over against the State. In its first origins Christianity had lain over against the State because of its parousian conceptions. In the first enthusiasm of their chiliastic hopes the Christians had a tendency to forget the duties they owed to the State. The claims of the old 'world' that was 'passing away, with the fashion thereof,' and of the new world that men 'greeted from afar' were not easy to adjust. With the decay of parousian belief we have the rise of Monasticism, in which the adjustment was even less successful. In Monasticism, in fact, we find antagonism to the State one of the primal elements, an indifference or hostility at which we need not wonder, if we remember the then circumstances of the State against which it revolted. For the Empire was slowly sinking into ruin, as much from weakness within, bad methods of finance, a poverty-stricken middle class, the concentration of all wealth in the hands of the few, a hopeless bureaucracy, the stereotyping of all society into hereditary castes, an army of hireling barbarians—more terrible to its masters than to its enemies—as by attacks from without. The despotism of the Empire " as it grew old became at once feebler and more vexatious, exhausting a world which it could not even defend. It weighed upon all, and protected none." [1] "The ancient world," writes Harnack, "had arrived, by all the routes of its complicated development, at the bitterest criticism of and disgust at its own existence." [2] The fabric of Roman society and administration was honeycombed by moral and economic vices. Christianity had not as yet cured evils, so much as made the more thoughtful conscious of their presence, and of the tremendous organized πολιτεία or system which seemed bound up with them. Of the fourth and fifth centuries, equally with the first, is the description of Arnold true:

> " On that hard pagan world
> Disgust and secret loathing fell.
> Deep weariness and sated lust
> Made human life a hell."

A protest was bound to come and when it came to take the form of a reaction from the State to the individual. We see a similar revolt in the early days that followed the break-up of Greek civic independence and the substitution of imperialism. Philosophers despaired of the republic, and found a new subject for thought in the individual man. So once again. A protest is made, no longer by schools of Stoics and Epicureans, but by the noblest souls within the Church. Unfortunately the protest became a counsel of despair. When in a previous age the heathen had objected that

[1] Montalembert, *MW* i. 197. Cf. Jerome, *Ep.* 1 (3–8) for an instance of the oppression of the times.

[2] Harnack, *HD* iii. 127. On this matter see S. Dill, *Roman Society in the Last Century of the Western Empire*, bk. iv; Dill, *Rom. Soc. Nero to Aurelius*, 245–7; C. Bigg, *Church's Task in the Roman Empire* (1905), 119 n.; Boissier, *Fin du Paganisme* (1891), ii. 409–16.

the Christians were a useless people to the world at large, Tertullian had been able to reply :

> 'How can this be, since we mix with you as men. . . . We are not Brahmins or Indian devotees who live naked in the woods, or recluses in exile from other men. We avoid not your forum, your markets, your baths, your shops, your forges, your inns, your fairs. We are one people with you in all worldly commerce.'[1]

Two centuries later Tertullian—largely, we must own, as the result of his own writings—would have found some difficulty in writing this defence. An indifference which began by claiming that for the Christian to concern himself with politics is necessarily to defile himself with pitch, in course of time hardened into a fixed principle of withdrawal, or even of antagonism. Once more the old battle-cry rang out, though with a new meaning: 'Thy sons, O Zion, against thy sons, O Greece!'[2] From this antagonism to the State Monasticism throughout its long history was never delivered. To this antagonism, also, we owe the repeated attempts of emperors and kings, in the early days of Monasticism, to cut off from the monastic life their soldiers and civil servants.[3]

---

[1] Tert. *Apol.* 42. Cf. *Ep. ad Diognetum*, 5, 6.

[2] *Zech.* ix. 13. Cf. *PEC* 179 ff.; Tert. *Apol.* 38, 46; and the edict of Valens in 373 (*Cod. Theod.* xii. i. 63).

[3] In 593 the Emperor Maurice issued an edict to this effect, founded, to some extent, on an edict of Constantine ratified by pope Innocent I. (15 Feb. 404, Jaffé, *RP* i. 44). This edict led to an indignant protest by Gregory the Great (Aug. 593, Greg. *Reg.* iii. 61, 64). But at a later date he saw the justice of forbidding deserters from the army entering a monastery, and came to terms with Maurice. No *curialis* was to be received unless released from State obligations, and no soldier without careful enquiry and a three years' novitiate (Nov. 597, Greg. *Reg.* viii. 10). This prohibition Gregory strengthened in April 600 (Greg. *Reg.* x. 9).

To flee from difficulties rather than overcome them, to abandon a sinking ship rather than help to guide it into port, is not glorious; nevertheless the historian looking back can see justification for the action of the early monks. Reform from within seemed well-nigh impossible. There was no remedy that could heal the bad finance, weakened manhood, and lowered ideals that were bringing their inevitable punishment. Few writers, it is true, break the gloomy silence; but from the few we gather that not merely the Christian but the statesman looked upon the future as without hope;[1] nor were they, from their point of view, far wrong. The exhausted past to which they clung had within it no element of life. The old Pagan world was dying, slowly, it is true, but none the less inevitably. On every side the more thoughtful could see the gathering vultures. The world, in fact, could only be regenerated by a baptism of blood. When Attila, the scourge of God, and the other barbarians had done their work, and renewed by their rough surgery an exhausted Europe, then the monks who had abandoned a doomed Empire returned to conquer their victors. But in the meantime " men turned from the City of Destruction to realize a City of God in the desert and the cell." [2]

Nor must we overlook the element of life which underlay the conception. Monasticism was born in an age when the accepted idea—as we may see from the reorganization by Diocletian of the old Augustan Principate into the new absolutist Empire—was the existence of the individual for the sake of the State, and that outside the State he had no ground of being. That the Roman

[1] Cf. Dill, *Rom. Soc. Last Century W. Empire*, bk. iv. c. 2.
[2] Glover, *LLFC* 281.

Empire, or for that matter any other empire if such could have been conceived of as possible, existed for the sake of the individuals who composed it, was an idea that never entered the mind of either ancient or medieval thinkers. The State was viewed as an antecedent *a priori* principle.[1] East and West, pagan and Christian agreed in the belief that Rome's rule was from the nature of things eternal. But that rule was the rule of a machine in which the individual had ceased to have a place. To this idea Monasticism refused to bow the knee, and thus, by an indifference which at times seems almost criminal—especially if we overlook the causes which gave rise to it—prepared the way for the modern conception that the State exists for individuals, and has neither sanctions nor powers save such as they may confer.

We may trace, with Harnack, this essential individualism of Monasticism to the locale of its birth, Egypt and Alexandria. For the rise of Monasticism coincided with the renewed attention paid in Alexandria, both in the catechumen schools and by its Neoplatonist philosophers, to the Socratic maxim: 'Know thyself.' Origen was never weary of insisting that the soul nearest to God is not so much the soul that stands in need of nothing, as the soul for whom the highest good has become the knowledge of his own self. Here is the *diadema et regnum tutum*; this peaceful contemplation of the microcosm is itself the victory over the world.[2]

---

[1] This is not the place to enter into the modification of this idea introduced by Hildebrand's new conceptions of the primacy of the Church; for this, cf. in especial Hildebrand's epistle to Hermann of Metz (Jaffé, *Monumenta Gregoriana*, 453 ff., in Jaffé *BRG* ii.; Marten's *Gregor VII*, ii. 49 ff.).

[2] Harnack, *Mon.* 40.

So the monk fled into the desert that he might the more fully in the university of its solitudes pursue the knowledge of himself. But this self-knowledge, as the better school of the Neoplatonist claimed—for we may ignore the school which relied on magic—can only be won by a self-discipline the chief feature of which is its asceticism.[1] Only by a holy abstinence can a man rise clear of the entanglements of matter into a purer existence where he can contemplate and hold communion with the absolute. As Origen bluntly puts it: 'All evil which reigns in the body is due to the five senses.'[2] The gospel of Neoplatonism was the gospel of salvation by release from a world of sense. Thus in Monasticism as in Neoplatonism the individual finds himself by escaping from himself. This is, in fact, the only outcome of self-knowledge except despair. None the less it is a form of individualism. When we lose ourselves, as our Saviour has told us, we alone find ourselves.

V

The root principle of Monasticism lay in the intense desire for self-surrender. As we have seen, this could not find adequate expression in the Catholic Church as it then existed. This desire for self-surrender became at the same time a yearning for isolation. The modern reader is so accustomed to think of Monasticism as identical with Monachism, the lonely cell and the desert, that he scarcely realizes that these two spiritual

[1] Zöckler, *AM* 110–2; *ERE* i. 86. Cf. Harnack, *HD* ii. 336 f.; Workman, *Hist. of Christian Thought to Reformation*, c. 2 (6).

[2] How fully the doctrines of Origen commended themselves to the monks of Egypt we see from Sulp. Sev. *Dial.* i. 6, 7; cf. *HL* (Gr.) 11 (4).

forces, the desire for self-surrender and the yearning for isolation, are by no means necessarily one, and may even prove, as we shall see later, to be in opposition. The question, therefore, arises: how was it that in the Early Church they were looked upon, almost universally, as identical ? The answer is of some importance from more points than one.

The early monks, so far as we can discern, seem to have been chiefly recruited from the great cities. The reason is not far to seek. Early Christianity, following the lead of St. Paul, had found its chief opportunity in the towns. The bishop was from the first almost wholly a city officer; only slowly did the Church acquire influence over the country-side pagans,[1] and then chiefly by missions worked from the cities. In the fourth century Christianity was practically still a matter of the towns. But it was in the towns that life at this time was most hopelessly corrupt. The earnest Christian could see everywhere the trail of a heathenism nominally conquered, in reality still dominant. The theatres, the baths, the games of the arena, had been changed but little in their character by the introduction of a new religion. In the Coliseum gladiators still butchered each other to make a Roman holiday; in the theatres the greatest indecencies were still permitted; in most towns the baths were the centre of all that was effeminate and dissolute. Looking back we may see that there were ways of self-surrender more excellent, certainly more heroic, than the monk's flight

---

[1] But Zahn has shown that *paganus* does not mean 'villager,' as is so often stated, but 'civilian,' as opposed to the 'milites Christi' who have taken the oath of service to Christ. See my *PEC* 234 n. 3; Harnack, *Militia Christi* (1905), 68 f.

to the desert. But the Christian of the times, intent upon self-surrender, saw no alternative save total abnegation of the things of this world. The easiest way of obtaining this renunciation was expatriation to the desert place, anywhere, at any rate, away from the town. Theirs was the cry of Jeremiah, as of Cowper and of every wrestler with a hopeless world :

> "Oh for a lodge in some vast wilderness,
> Some boundless contiguity of shade,
> Where rumour of oppression and deceit,
> Of unsuccessful and successful war
> Should never reach me more. My ear is pained,
> My soul is sick, with every day's report
> Of wrong and outrage with which earth is filled."

The letters of Jerome give us many illustrations of this view. No one has painted more literally the corrupt life of the cities; no one panted more eagerly for the heaven of solitude. In his letter to Paulinus he owns that at present the duty of the Church lies in the towns :

'If you wish to take duty as a presbyter, live in the cities and walled towns. . . . But what has the monk to do with cities, which are the homes, not of solitaries, but of crowds ? . . . We have our masters in Elijah and Elisha, and our leaders in the sons of the prophets, who lived in fields and solitary places, and made themselves tents by the waters of Jordan. After the freedom of their lonely life they found confinement in a city as bad as imprisonment' [*Ep.* 58 (5). Cf. *Ep.* 2.].

Others, he continues, 'may think as they like, but to me the town is a prison, and solitude is paradise.' ' O desert,' he cries elsewhere,

'enamelled with the flowers of Christ. O solitude where those stones are born of which in the *Apocalypse* is built the city of the Great King ! . . . how long, brother, wilt thou remain in the shadow of roofs, and in smoky dungeon of cities ? Believe me, I see here more of the light ' [*Ep.* 14 (10)].

So in a letter to Rufinus he tells us of a hermit, his foster-brother Bonosus, who had settled on an island in the Adriatic, where he was alone ' with the sea that roared round its reefs.' There ' he beheld the glory of God, which even the apostles saw not save in the desert.'[1] Of Abba [2] John we read that he claimed: ' life in the peaceful retreats of the desert can only be compared to the bliss of angels.' So he mourned sadly that the effect of the large influx of monks into his solitude resulted in ' a cramping of freedom, and a quenching of the fire of divine contemplation.'[3]

We should err greatly if we classed this yearning for solitude with the spirit of Diogenes, or of Timon of Athens. Indiscreet utterances, it is true, may be quoted, and famous examples abound which tend in this direction. ' The greatest saints,' writes Thomas à Kempis, ' avoided the society of man, when they conveniently could, and did rather choose to live to God in secret.' He quotes with approval the saying of Seneca: ' As oft as I have been among men I have returned home less a man than I was before.'[4] But in reality both the practice and precepts of the better monks lay stress upon the need of spiritual communion. They claimed with Savage Landor that " solitude is the audience chamber of

---

[1] Jerome, *Ep.* 3 (4).
[2] The word ἀββᾶ does not connote superiority, and should not, therefore, be translated " abbot." It simply equals ' religious,' and is even given to a young girl of twenty-three years of age disguised as a monk (Lucot, *HL* p. 43). The corresponding title for nuns was ἀμμᾶς ; cf. *HL* (Gr.) 34 (6).
[3] Cass. *Coll.* xix. 5.
[4] Seneca, *Ep.* 7 ; Kempis, *Imit. Christi*, i. 20.

God." They maintained with the First Brother in Milton's *Comus* that it is in "sweet retirèd solitude" that

> "Wisdom's self
> Plumes her feathers, and lets grow her wings,
> That in the various bustle of resort
> Were all to-ruffled, and sometimes impaired."

The need of solitude was recognized; but it was solitude with an object. The anchorite of whom Postumian heard that he had lived alone for fifty years on the summit of Sinai, gave as his reason for refusing any interview with curious travellers: 'the man who is visited often by mortals could not often be visited by angels.'[1] The object of Paphnutius in penetrating inaccessible deserts was that 'with no human companions to disturb him he might be the more readily united to the Lord,' and 'enjoy the daily society of angels.'[2] 'The deeper insight into heavenly things,' writes Cassian, 'can only be gained in solitude.'[3] Elsewhere he contrasts life in the monastery and life in the desert, and claims that 'the higher life is that of the humble solitary,' for his is the blessing of the man 'who sitteth alone, and keepeth silence.'[4] But Cassian is careful to point out that solitude is not to be enterprised 'without a well-matured purpose.' For this higher life preparation must be made; as a rule, elsewhere. There is, in fact, nothing more fatal than 'to aspire to dwell in solitude before

---

[1] Sulp. Sev. *Dial.* i. 17. Cf. Thomas à Kempis: 'Whoso withdraweth himself from his acquaintance and friends will find God draw nigh to him with His holy angels' (*Imit. Christi,* i. 20).

[2] Cass. *Coll.* iii. 1.

[3] Ib. *Instit.* viii. 18.

[4] Ib. *Coll.* xix. 2, 5, 6, 8. Jeremiah, *Lam.* iii. 28.

we have got rid of our faults by the system of the coenobium.'[1]

This yearning for isolation was really, though unconsciously, on one of its sides a desire for return to a simple life. It was the cry in the soul of the countryman of old: 'to your tents, O Israel'; the free life of the fields over against the artificial life of the city. Probably at first the Christian who fled from his City of Destruction was conscious rather of that from which he fled than of the new life which he had found. Nevertheless, the new life of the country asserted itself in a new love of nature, hitherto all but unknown, so far as we can judge, in the old Roman world. Amid much that is insipid and absurd in the lives of the saints and hermits, there is much that fascinates by its breezy atmosphere, as by its larger sympathies with beasts and birds. Some of the earliest and most beautiful descriptions of the charms of the country will be found in the lives of the early hermits; they abound with evidences of a new sense of oneness with nature. 'How art thou content, Father,' said a philosopher to Anthony, 'since thou hast not the comfort of books?' 'My book,' he replied in words that distantly remind us of Shakespeare, 'is the nature of created things. In it when I choose I can read the words of God.'[2] We are told that after His temptation our Saviour found solace and repose among the wild beasts. So with the solitary ascetic who had fled the temptations of the town. The stories are endless of his companionship with bird and beast. Though at some risk of breaking in upon our argument we add a few, designedly taken from English life. Of St.

[1] Cass. *Coll.* xix. 11, 13. Cf. *ib.* ix. 7, 9, xix. 9, 10.
[2] *VS* iv. 16 in *PL* 73, p. 1018; quoted in Soc. *HE* iv. 23.

Guthlac, who had exchanged the life of a freebooter for prayer in the loneliest reaches of the Fens (Croyland), we read:

'Who hath led his life after God's will,' he said, 'the wild beasts and the birds become friendly with him. To the man who will live away from the world the angels draw nigh.'

But the angels were often the swallows which nestled in his arms.[1] Of Columban we are told that as he wandered through the woods " squirrels would run down from the trees and nestle in his cowl." [2] St. Godric, († 1170), who from a pirate became an anchorite at Finchale in Weardale, would not shoot even the stags who were destroying the young corn. When a hart fled to him in the chase, he sheltered it from the hunters, 'for he would not be a traitor,' he said, 'to his guest.'[3] It was at Bec that Anselm also, the archbishop of Canterbury, learned the same spirit.[4] Of Hugh of Avalon, the great bishop of Lincoln, we read that at his old home in the Chartreuse, before he came to this country,

'the little birds and wood mice who are commonly called squirrels, were domesticated and tamed by him to such an extent that they would leave their woods, and regularly at supper-time would come to share his meal with him, not only getting on his table, but eating out of his hand and his plate, and making themselves entirely his companions.' [5]

---

[1] Gray Birch, *Memorials of St. Guthlac* (1881), 37.

[2] *DNB* xi. 414.

[3] *DNB* v. 23, *s.v.* 'Godric.' Similar tales are told of Martin, Sulp. Sev. *Dial.* ii. 9; *Ep.* 3.

[4] Eadmer, *de vita Anselmi* (in *RS*, ed. Rule), ii. 18, 19. For similar tales of the Irish 'saints,' see Plummer, *VSH* i. Introd. cxli. f.

[5] Girald. Camb. *Vita Hugonis*, i. (1) [in Girald. Camb. *Opera* (*RS*, ed. Dimock), vii. 92]. St. Hugh's favourite bird was a wild swan which after he was bishop used to feed from his hand [*op. cit.* vii. 93; also in *Magna vita Hugonis* (in *RS*, ed. J. F. Dimock, 1864), iii. cc. 6, 7].

And so we might run on, multiplying tales, which oft-times bear a strong family likeness. Some, it is true, are ridiculous, without any of the charm that we find in Kipling's *Jungle Book*;[1] nevertheless even the most foolish bear witness to one result of Monasticism, especially in its eremite forms. The hermit who began with an almost Gnostic hatred of the created world, as the medium of temptation and the abode of sin, oft-times

[1] Of these absurd tales we may instance the lioness whom Postumian saw a monk feed with dates (Sulp. Sev. *Dial.* i. 13); the wolf who stole a loaf and for a whole week was racked with penitence (*ib.* i. 14);—Postumian's "traveller's tales" are usually of this order in spite of his 'calling Christ to witness that he invents nothing' (*ib.* i. 15);—the crocodile who used to carry Pachomius across the Nile on his back (*Vit. Pach.* 19 in *PL* 73, p. 241); the lion who performed strange gymnastics to get out of the road of hermit John (*PS* 181 in *PL* 74, p. 211); while another monk took lions to his bed habitually (*ib.* 18, *PL* 74, p. 128); and the two lions which dug the grave of the hermit Paul (Jerome, *Vit. Pauli*, 16). For other ridiculous beast-stories, see the story of Macarius of Alexandria and the hyæna's whelp. The hyæna in gratitude brought Macarius a sheepskin which the saint bequeathed to Athanasius, who in turn gave it to Melania. See *HP* c. 6 in *PL* 74, p. 276, where for Marcus we should read Macarius as in the Greek version *HL*, ed. Lucot, c. 18 (27). Variants of this last story will be found in Rufinus, *Hist. Mon.* c. 28; Rufinus, *HE* ii. 4; and Sulp. Sev. *Dial.* i. 15. The introduction into this story of Athanasius' name (on which Weingarten, *UM* 28–30, laid much stress as proof of fable, inasmuch as Melania did not come to Egypt until after Athanasius' death) is an interpolation. The Coptic version mentions merely 'Melania, the queen of the Romans.' See Amélineau, *MG* xxv. 235, 238; Butler, *HL* ii. 196.

We must remember that these beast-tales, in addition to serving as the novels of the times, had an underlying theological significance. The obedience lions, &c., give to the saints is the return to the state of the world before the Fall. Cf. *PS* 107 (in *PL* 74, p. 174). Possibly also " many of these tales go back to a time when no hard-and-fast line was drawn between men and animals " and are thus folk-lore survivals transferred to Monasticism (Plummer, *VSH* i. Introd. cxlv.). Cf. also *infra*, p. 306.

ended in an identification of himself with nature itself. But this made his Gnosticism an impossible belief.

VI

Hitherto we have treated Monasticism as arising from the unconscious opposition to the Catholic Church of an uncontaminated ideal of renunciation, and of an individualism bent upon its own salvation and opposed to the excessive tyranny of the State. But there were two other powerful factors at work, mainly philosophical, which must not be overlooked. We allude to the influence of Stoicism and of Gnosticism.

Stoicism as a philosophical system does not concern us, nor did it ever obtain any considerable footing in the Church. But the influence of the Stoic ideals was far-reaching, and in nothing more remarkable than in the presentation of Monasticism as the attainment of the Stoic ideal of $ἀπάθεια$, or the perfect domination over all the inclinations of nature. The monk is represented as having attained the supreme victory. Henceforth he is dead to self, dead to the senses, dead even to human respect[1] and to the desires for distinction; there is but one word that can describe his repose; he is $ἀπαθής$. In the quest of this $ἀπάθεια$ the first step is $ἀποταξία$ or the solemn renunciation of the world. The importance of this first step is generally emphasized in our monastic records by a detailed account of the circumstance which led to 'conversion.'[2]

[1] See the tale of Theophilus and Mary, *infra*, p. 71 f.
[2] The quest of $ἀπάθεια$ is well brought out in Palladius, *HL*. See Butler, *HL* i. 176, and the important passages collected in Cabrol, *DACL* ii. 3102 n., and the note in Lucot's edition of Palladius, *HL* p. 23 f.

From its earliest days Gnosticism had been the great foe with which Christianity, especially in the East, had been forced to fight for its very life. The investigation of Gnosticism forms no part of our purpose;[1] suffice that it was the emphasis of the old idea that has ever dominated under different forms and names the religions of the East, to wit, the essential dualism of God and the world, the absolute unconnectedness and opposition of soul and matter.

As a theological system, Gnosticism was defeated, not without dust and heat. No Demiurge of evil was allowed to place himself on the Throne, coeval and co-equal with God; no conception of an independent, unrelated *hylé* or matter, which lay at the root of all sin, could stand against the message of Advent: 'The Word became flesh and tabernacled among us, and we beheld his glory.' The 'resurrection of the flesh' (σαρκὸς ἀνάστασις) was made, even, a clause in the great Roman symbol.[2] A creed which began by breaking the bond between God and His creatures could not possibly justify itself as the religion of Redemption. Gnosticism as a system, with its endless series of emanations from God, and its opposing currents towards asceticism and licence, was thus defeated; but its defeat was in one sense only the beginning of its triumph. As an organized force, definitely bent upon the conquest of the Church, Gnosticism ceased to exist; it broke up into guerilla bands that effected more by their capture of individuals. The Church conquered, but

---

[1] For Gnosticism I may refer to my *History of Christian Thought*, c. 2 (3), or the fuller Harnack, *HD* i. c. 4. For Manichaeism, ib. *HD* iii. 316 f.

[2] A. C. McGiffert, *The Apostles' Creed* (1902), 164 f.

not without receiving scars of the conflict, some of which still remain. The Gnostics were defeated; they accomplished no small part of their purpose by crossing over into the ranks of the victors. The falsehood that was banished from the theological text-books of the schools found an impregnable refuge in the popular life and thought of the Church. In the East, especially, Gnosticism scarcely more than changed her name, and in the wilder forms of Monasticism won that victory which had been denied her as a philosophical system. In the West, she would, perhaps, have gained a still greater triumph had not St. Augustine succeeded in shaking off his early attraction for Manichaeism—in all essentials a re-statement of Gnosticism, if anything in more exaggerated forms—which constituted, as we learn from his *Confessions*,[1] his greatest difficulty in accepting Christianity.[2] In the West, largely through

[1] The saint doubts whether music can be right, simply because of the pleasure it afforded him. 'Sometimes,' he writes, 'I wish the whole melody of sweet music, to which the Psalms of David are generally set, to be banished from my ears, yea, and from those of the Church itself' (*Confessions*, x. c. 33). Elsewhere he tells us of his difficulty in sanctioning Church music at all: 'When it befalls me to be more moved with the singing than with the words sung I confess that I sin grievously, and then I would prefer not to hear the chanter.' He has the same difficulty with pleasant odours, in fact, with all things that have 'the enticing and dangerous beauty of sweetness' (*ib.* c. 35). Science he rejects as one of the 'lusts of the eye.' He is glad that he is as indifferent now to the transit of the stars as to the sights of the theatre; but eating, or rather the sense of satisfaction which it brings, is a continual difficulty for him (*ib.* x. c. 31). His famous epigram, 'Inter fæces et urinam nascimur,' could only have come from one who had developed an exaggerated doctrine of total depravity, which still, unfortunately, enslaves much theology.

[2] Zöckler, *AM* 169 ff.; Workman, *Christian Thought*, p. 115. For the Gnostic survivals in the theology of St. Augustine, see Harnack, *HD* v. 124 n., 211 n. Augustine's great opponent Julian strongly emphasizes and exaggerates these tendencies.

this conquest of St. Augustine's, Gnosticism never secured, with one exception, more than a transient footing. The very exception—the Gnostic heresy of the Cathari or Albigensians—was so late in its rise, so completely Eastern in its origin, so alien to the whole spirit of the West, that when it arose both theologians and people were slow to recognize its essentially Gnostic origin; in fact, to this day it deceives the sympathies of writers not a few.[1] Meanwhile it may suffice to note that in the West, Catharism or Gnosticism did not become formidable until Monasticism as a living expression of the need of self-surrender had virtually played itself out. We might even fairly argue that in the West Gnosticism was due rather to the failure of Monasticism to be true to its own ideal, whereas in the East a defeated Gnosticism early found refuge in a Monasticism modelled after its own heart. Justification for this argument would be found in the ease with which Francis of Assisi by his revival of primitive renunciation swept Europe from end to end altogether free of this long-continued heresy.

How complete was the influence of Gnosticism in the Monasticism of the East is evidenced by the tales that have come down to us, though the student would do well to remember that the very existence of these tales is proof that the deeds they chronicle were extraordinary, and not normal. But whether the saints whose virtues they extol were few or many, they bear witness to the Gnostic ideal that too often dominated Eastern Monasticism : that spiritual life can only find its highest perfection in the wildest asceticism. In the East the ideal monk of earlier days stood opposed

[1] On the Gnosticism of the Albigensians see my *Ch. of West in Middle Ages*, ii. 106–8, 182–9.

to a world which no Psalmist can claim as the Lord's, and over whose creation the morning stars should have wept rather than sung aloud. In the West, Monasticism grew more sane *pari passu* with its transition to an organized common life. But in the East, especially in Syria and Mesopotamia, where the eremite ideal was supreme, not only did Monachism end in monstrous austerities, but it developed a type of its own to which the mockery of later generations has given undue importance.

The typical saint of the East in whom we can best see these Gnostic elements at work, was Symeon Stylites[1]

---

[1] Born 390 at Sis near Nicopolis. There are two other canonized saints who bore his name. The more famous of these, born at Antioch in 521, died at Theopolis in 596. (Evagrius, *HE* vi. 23.) For the life of Symeon we have two accounts in the *VP* (Rosweyd). The one by Antonius his disciple, who was with him in his last moments (c. 16). A Latin translation of this is in *PL* 73, pp. 325-34, The other is in Theodoret's *Philotheus* (or *Theophiles*), c. 26, a Latin translation in *PL* 74, pp. 98-108. The best edition of both Antonius and Theodoret is by H. Lietzmann, *Das Leben des Sym. Stylites*, in *TU* v. 32 (Leipzig, 1908), with good life of Symeon (p. 238 f.). A contemporary of the saint, incorrectly called Cosmas, and a Syrian bishop, James of Sarug in Mesopotamia († 521) (*DCB* iii. 327), also wrote accounts, the latter in verse, portions of which are preserved in Asseman *A.MM* (Rome, 1748) ii. 227-346. The so-called 'Cosmas' was used by Evagrius in his account of Stylites in his *HE* i. 13-14 (in *PG* 86, p. 2454 f.); several MSS. still exist. There is a monograph on these Syrian lives by H. Hilgenfeld, in Lietzmann, *op. cit.* 79-195. For the whole subject of Pillar-saints, see the monograph of H. Delahaye, *Les Stylites* [in *Compte rendu du troisième Congrès des Caths. à Bruxelles*, Sept. 1894 (Scient. hist.), 1895, 191 ff.; also published separately (1895)]; also T. Nöldeke, *Studies from Eastern History* (trs. J. S. Black, 1892), c. 7. "Some Syrian Saints." According to Lucian, *de dea Syria*, c. 28, at the shrine of the Syrian goddess Atargatis at Hierapolis-Bambyce twice a year a man (φαλλοβατεῖς) ascended a colossal pillar for seven days' intercourse with the god. But according to Theodoret, who calls this form of asceticism new, Symeon knew nothing of this.

—'that great miracle of the world,' as Theodoret calls him; 'that angel upon earth, that citizen in the flesh of the Heavenly Jerusalem,' as Evagrius claims. For thirty-seven years this strange being, the 'glory of Antioch and Syria,' worked out the rudest penitence that the world has ever known, on the top of a column which the devotion of his admirers, or his own desire to escape their attentions, gradually raised from four cubits to forty in height,[1] and which seemed to an eye-witness but three cubits in breadth. Even before he mounted the pillar to which he was chained (A.D. 423)—no doubt there was a cage on the top to prevent his fall—the rigour of his asceticism was such that, in the words of his admiring disciple Antonius, 'when he walks vermin drops from his body.'[2] He began his monastic life as an enclosed anchorite (413–23) by dwelling for forty days in a cave with his right leg fastened by an iron chain to a stone, 'though the iron chain did not hinder the flight of his soul.' When the bit of leather which protected his skin from the iron was removed, admirers counted in it twenty fat bugs which Symeon had refused to disturb. At another time he dug a trench in a garden and daily buried himself in it up to his head through a whole summer. His fame as a saint was unequalled throughout the East. Arabs, Persians, Armenians, strangers even from Spain and Britain journeyed to gaze on this prodigy of austerity. The letters which he dictated from his pillar to his disciples on the dogmas of the Councils of Ephesus and Chalcedon were looked upon as authoritative pronouncements. Kings and emperors crouched at the

---

[1] *i.e.* equal to 20 metres.
[2] No uncommon thing: cf. Sozomen, *HE* vi. 34.

foot of his pillar, cherishing, as if they were precious pearls, 'the worms that dropped from his body,' gazing with awe as Symeon touched his feet with his forehead 1244 times in succession—at this figure his admirers lost count—or stood all night motionless with his hands stretched out to heaven. He was called 'the most holy martyr in the air'; men spoke of him as

'standing midway between heaven and earth, holding communion with God; from the earth offering supplications as an ambassador of God' (Evagrius, *HE* i. 13).

For two months before his death crowds gathered round his pillar to receive his last words. On his decease (2nd Sept. 459)[1] his corpse was carried to Antioch with more than imperial pomp, 'to be a wall and bulwark' to that defenceless city, while his pillar was enclosed on the heights of Telnishé in a splendid church which no woman was ever allowed to enter.[2]

Symeon had been regarded by the monks of the Nitria as a radical innovator. They sent to know why, 'abandoning the beaten path which the saints had trodden, he was pursuing another, altogether unknown.'[3] But, nevertheless, the greatness of Stylites did not lack the tribute of imitation.[4] A succession of pillar-saints enclosed in boxes or palings, at heights varying from ten to sixty feet, witness to his repute; their boast was to bear his name. One saint, Thalelaeus, passed ten years

[1] For date, see Lietzmann, *op. cit.* 234–5.
[2] Pillar and church still exist in ruins. See C. J. M. de Vogüé, *Syrie Centrale* (Paris, 1865–77), i. 141–54.
[3] Evagrius, *HE* i. 13.
[4] For imitators, see Moschus, *PS* 27–8, 36, 129 (*PL* 74, p. 132 f.), and cf. *infra*, p. 53 n. One of the Stylites, called Symeon Fulminatus († 1180), because he was struck by lightning, wrote considerable treatises (ed. by J. Gretscher, Ingolstadt, 1603).

in a tub suspended in mid-air from poles. 'As he had a big body he was bound to sit bent up, with his head on his knees.'[1] Jerome speaks with admiration of another who lived in an old cistern on five figs a day.[2] Henceforth in the East, in all places where the spirit of Anthony rather than of Pachomius triumphed,[3] the ideal life of renunciation was too often either the dreary and barren quietude—if indeed the word quietude may rightly be applied to the desolation of a life out of which all human instincts have been forcibly uptorn—or else the wildest rigours of asceticism. Especially is this true of the monks of Syria and Mesopotamia. Feebler successors of Symeon penetrated deserts hitherto inaccessible, for instance Paphnutius, who because of his solitude was surnamed 'the buffalo.'[4] There they were exposed to attacks and destruction by 'Blemmyan robbers.'[5] Some buried themselves in the darkest caves, or established themselves 'in islands near the Nile habitable by none but monks, since the saltness of the soil made them unfit for cultivation,' and where every drop of water had to be carried over three miles 'with sandy mountains in between.'[6] Some, acting on a mistaken interpretation of Psalm xlix. 20 [7] that by living like cattle they might recover the lost likeness to God, aspired to reduce themselves to the level of beasts; of others the naked body was only covered by their long hair, or by the coarsest

---

[1] Theodoret, *Phil.* 28 (*PL* 74, p. 110).
[2] Jerome, *Vita Pauli*, 5.   [3] See *infra*, p. 125.
[4] Cass. *Coll.* iii. 1, xviii. 15; *HL* (Gr.) 47 (3, 5).
[5] Cass. *Coll.* vi. 1. In 373 the monks of Raïthu, in Sinaï, were massacred by them (Duchesne, *EHC* ii. 407 n.).
[6] Cass. *Instit.* v. 36.
[7] LXX version (*Ps.* xlviii. 21), ἄνθρωπος ἐντιμῇ ὢν οὐ συνῆκε, παρασυνεβλήθη τοῖς κτήνεσι τοῖς ἀνοήτοις καὶ ὡμοιώθη αὐτοῖς.

THE IDEAS OF MONASTICISM 45

goat-skins.¹ One set, who dwelt round Nisibis, were called *Boskoi* or ' Grazing Monks ' from their imitation of the madness of Nebuchadnezzar. ' When meal time came,' writes Sozomen, ' they took sickles and sallied forth to cut grass, and on this they made their repast as if they were cattle.' ² Some hung large weights on their necks and loins ; ³ others confined themselves like beasts, in a cage so small that they could neither stand up nor lie down.⁴ Acepsimas ' lived sixty years shut up in his cell, neither seeing nor speaking, but with gaze turned in upon himself and God.' He became so bent that one day a shepherd shot him, thinking that he was a wolf.⁵ Another, Marcianus, divided a pound of bread into four parts to last for four days.⁶ Cyriacus of Bêth ' Âbhê in Mesopotamia stood for hours on one leg like a crane, until he fainted with exhaustion.⁷

Innumerable tales bear witness to the charm of an impossible, even anti-human ideal. By the monks their lives were regarded, in the phrase of Theodoret,⁸ as ' pietatis palaestrae,' wrestling rings in which they were ' the athletes of God.' Of Macarius of Alexandria ⁹ we

¹ Sulp. Sev. *Dial.* i. 17.
² Sozomen, *HE* vi. 33. A more modern case was Euthymius of Thessalonica, b. 823. See K. Lake, *Early Days of Monasticism on Mount Athos* (1909), p. 44.
³ Theodoret, *Philotheus*, 10, and especially c. 29 (in Migne, *PL* 74, pp. 61, 112).
⁴ Theodoret, *op. cit.* cc. 2, 3, 27.
⁵ *Ib.* c. 15.   ⁶ *Ib.* c. 3.
⁷ Thomas of Margâ, *Book of Governors*, ed. E. A. W. Budge (1893), i. p. 112.
⁸ Theod. *Phil.* 30 (*PL* 74, p. 114). But the phrase and thought are common.
⁹ See *HL* in *PL* 73, p. 1116, 74, pp. 272–5, 362 or *PG* 34, p. 1057, or ed. Butler, *HL* ii. 53 or Lucot, *HL* cc. 17, 18. The student must distinguish clearly between Macarius of Egypt and Macarius of

read that 'if ever he heard of any one having performed a work of asceticism' he was all on fire to do the same[1] —an attempt " to break the record " in subduing the flesh.[2] One day Macarius of Alexandria was stung by a gnat. In his impatience he killed it. Conscious of a lost opportunity of bearing mortification with resignation, he deliberately lived for six months in the marshes of the Nile near Scete, maddened by gnats 'whose sting can pierce the hides of boars.'[3] When the same Macarius —whose usual abode was a windowless cell of sun-dried mud in the Nitria, but who during Lent lived in an underground lair in the "Cells,"[4] so narrow that he could not stretch his feet—visited the monks of Tabennîsî in order to see for himself 'their great method of life,'

Alexandria. Palladius [*HL* (Gr.) cc. 17, 18 or in *PL* 74, p. 267] tells us (p. 270) that on his journey to 'the Cells' in 390–1 he did not meet Macarius of Egypt ' for he rested in the year before I entered these solitudes' (*i.e.* in 389, Butler, *HL* ii. App. 7), but 'I saw Macarius the presbyter of Alexandria in the place called Cellae where I lived for nine years, during three years of which he was still alive.' For the different men that bore the name Macarius among the early Egyptian monks, see Butler, *HL* ii. 193–4 n.; *DCB* s.v. 16 and 17; Heimbucher, *OKK* i. 98 f.; Schiwietz, *das morgenländische Mönchtum* (1904), i. 97–106. Macarius of Egypt began life as a fruit seller in Alexandria, and at the age of 30 became a disciple of Anthony. A *Vita* by a contemporary monk Serapion in Coptic has been recently published by Amélineau (*MG* xxv. 1894 with Fr. trs.). Amélineau (*op. cit.* Introd. 29) calls him, not without justice, the St. Francis of Egyptian Monasticism. Such was the impression produced by his austerities that we find an Arabic writer in the 15th cent. (Al-Makrizi; see Butler, *HL* ii. 193 n.) mentioning the tradition that 'he never ate fresh bread, but took old shoes softened in a mess of palm leaves.' The body of Macarius of Alexandria († 393 or 394) is still preserved in the monastery that bears his name, Deir Mar Makar (A. J. Butler, *Ancient Coptic Churches of Egypt*, i. 287).

[1] *HL* (Gr.) 18 (1).   [2] Butler, *HL* i. 238.
[3] Butler, *HL* ii. 48; *PL* 74, p. 270; Lucot, *HL* p. 121.
[4] For the 'Cells,' see *infra*, p. 127 n.

the monks murmured with astonishment and anger at the sight of a saint whose 'fleshlessness' (ἄσαρκος ἄνθρωπος —they called him) put their lesser austerities to shame.[1] And well they might. 'Old man,'[2] said Pachomius to him, in his ignorance who he was, 'you are not able to be a monk or to endure their habits of toil and life.' His reply to this challenge had been a fast performed in silence, and standing, for forty days, broken only by nibbling at the leaves of palms. 'For seven years,' as Palladius tells us, 'he ate nothing cooked by fire,' so that the bones of his face 'stood out naked beyond the wont of men.' Arsenius, who had at one time (383) filled the post of tutor to the emperor Arcadius, the son of the great Theodosius, won in his later life more enduring fame. When forty years of age he abandoned the court with 'its slaves in silken garments,' set sail for Egypt and established himself as an hermit in Scete. There he occupied himself with weaving baskets of palm leaves, of set purpose only changing the water in which the leaves were moistened once a year. The fetid smell was his punishment for the perfumes of his early life.[3] It is characteristic of early Monasticism that when Arsenius, whose speech and manner betrayed that he was no poor stranger, first applied to be made a monk, he was kept standing while the rest sat at their food. After a while a biscuit was flung to him, which

[1] *HL* c. 20 in *PL* 73, p. 1109; or c. 18 (12) in *HL* (Gr.); also *HP* c. 6 in *PL* 74, p. 270.

[2] This shows the effects of the austerities. Macarius cannot possibly have been more than forty-five at this time, for the mention of Pachomius fixes the date as before his death in 346.

[3] For Arsenius (b. 354, d. 449), see *Verb. Sen.* in *VP* (*PL* 73, p. 762 ff.). His life by Theodore of the Studium is in *A.SS* July 19. To balance this tale of the palm leaves (*l.c.* 764) the student should note the beautiful vision of the world (*l.c.* 763).

he ate kneeling. 'He will do,' cried the brethren, and welcomed him to their number.

The mortifications recorded of some of the Egyptian monks were appalling. Some passed days without food —the trial fast of Paul the Simple, when applying to Anthony that he might join his hermits, lasted four days [1]—while others never partook of food until sunset.[2] In the week before Easter some kept an almost unbroken fast, as we learn from Dionysius of Alexandria.[3] Some never drank except on rare occasions.[4] Adolius, a Syrian monk of Jerusalem, only broke his fast during Lent one day in five. A Cilician hermit named Conon for thirty years only had one meal a week.[5] Others trained themselves to do without sleep; 'Until he slept the eternal sleep,' writes the admiring Palladius, 'Adolius never slept except during the three hours before dawn,' so that 'the demons feared to approach him.'[6] 'First persuade the angels to sleep,' replied Dorotheus to those who urged him to rest or at any rate to lie down when attempting to sleep. In his case tired nature asserted itself. 'Frequently when eating,' writes Palladius, 'he was so sleepy that the bread fell from his lips.'[7] Sisoes, a Syrian, to overcome the

---

[1] *HL* (Gr.) c. 22. For the slow development of Christian Fasting, see *ERE* v. 765 f.

[2] The monks of Pachomius, when eating, covered their heads with their hoods, as if ashamed of the act [*HL* (Gr.) 32 (6)].

[3] Dion. Alex. *Ep. ad Basilid*, (*PG* 10). Cf. Jerome, *Ep.* 130 (17).

[4] The most astonishing case was that of Ptolemaeus, who for five years lived on the dew that he gathered with a sponge off the stones; *HL* (Gr.) 27 (1).

[5] *PS* 22 in *PL* 74, p. 130.

[6] *HL* c. 104 in *PL* 73, p. 1192; *HL* (Gr.) c. 43; *HP* c. 30 (*PL* 74, p. 346). Cf. *HL* (Gr.) 18 (3).

[7] *HP* c. 1; *HL* (Gr.) c. 2.

temptation to sleep, placed himself at night against a dangerous jutting crag of rock; for fifteen years Pachomius slept upright in the midst of his cell. Arsenius slept in a standing position every night except Saturday; on this night he prayed from sunset to sunrise.[1] About the year 400 a monk named Alexander († 430), once an officer of the imperial court at Constantinople, actually founded an order of the *Aksemetae* or 'Sleepless Ones,' first on the Euphrates, then afterwards at St. Memnas in Constantinople. Day and night the work of prayer and praise never ceased. Their most celebrated monastery, that of the Studium near Constantinople, bears the name of the noble Roman, Studius, who founded it (c. 460). A branch of the order was established in the sixth century at St. Maurice in the Valais (Switzerland).[2]

There was the same abstinence as regards dress. One monk, Sarapion, a contemporary of Anthony, never wore anything save a muslin vest,[3] and his example found many imitators. More lasting in their repute were the *inclusi*, who spent their lives shut up in a cave or cell, some of them for more than eighty years. One of the earliest of these was the harlot Thais (c. 350) who was fed through a window by the nuns of a neighbouring convent. Day and night she sobbed aloud,

---

[1] Margâ, *Book of Governors*, i. p. cli–ii. Thomas of Margâ, himself at one time an inmate of Bêth 'Âbhê, wrote his *Book of Governors* about 850. It gives us a full account of that famous Nestorian monastery and its rulers. Thomas was well acquainted with the *Hist. Laus.* of Palladius, and the incidents Palladius gives us of asceticism in Scete are all reproduced by Thomas at Bêth 'Âbhê (Budge, *op. cit.* Introd. i, p. xxxiv).

[2] *DCA* i. 13; Zöckler, *AM* 263–4; *A.SS* Jan. i. 1018 ff. (Life of Alexander).

[3] *HL* 83 (*PL* 73, p. 1178 f.) or *HL* (Gr.) 37.

'O my Creator, have mercy upon me.' Another, Alexandra of Alexandria, who was immured in a tomb, was visited by the elder Melania. For ten years she had never seen the face of man nor woman.[1] At an early date the custom spread to the West. Palladius tells us of an *inclusa* at Rome who spent twenty-five years in silence.[2] When asked whether she were alive: 'I believe,' she answered, 'that I am dead to the world.' She was at any rate alive enough to resist the suggestion of Sarapion—he of the muslin vest—that she should show that she was 'dead' by throwing off her clothes, and then cross the city, carrying them on her shoulders. So Sarapion left her in scorn for 'her arrogance of mind.'[3] Very soon councils found it necessary to lay down rules for the *inclusi*. They were ordered to obtain the licence of the bishop,[4] and to prove their fitness for their task by a probationary discipline in a monastery.[5] In later years the *inclusus* was walled or nailed up in his cell, and sealed in with the bishop's ring. Only a little aperture was left for the passing in of provisions, nor were other clothes given him than those he was wearing. Thus was he left in his living death to end his days alone, and blessed was the monastery that possessed attached to it, or in its precincts, so illustrious a saint.[6]

[1] Palladius, *HL* (Gr.) 5, or *PL* 73, p. 1095.
[2] Ib. *HL* 85 (*PL* 73, p. 1182); *HL* (Gr.) c. 37 (12).
[3] Cf. H. Joly, *Psychol. des Saints*, 63. The early date of this *inclusa* (see *infra*, p. 116, n. 4) leads to some suspicion.
[4] Synod Frankfort (794) c. 12 (Hefele, *HC* III. ii. 1057).
[5] Synod of Vannes (465) c. 7 (Hefele, *HC* II. ii. 905); Agde (506) c. 38 (Hefele, *HC* II. ii. 997); 1st Orleans (511) c. 22 (*ib.* 1013); 7th Conc. Toledo (646) c. 5 (*ib.* III. i. 287); Conc. in Trullo (692) cc. 41, 42; three years' probation (*ib.* III. i. 568).
[6] For the *inclusi*, see L. C. Pavy, *Les recluseries* (Lyons, 1875). From the tale in Palladius of the *inclusa* of Jerusalem who fell into sin

And yet, as if in rebuke of our strictures, and as a warning against hasty generalization, it is of these very Eastern monks that we find related some of the sweetest tales of self-denial. As if to prevent us from judging by externals, whose value differs for different ages, it is of the extremist Sarapion that there is told the charming story of his conversion of the harlot Thais, near whom he now lies buried.[1] We have seen the excesses of Macarius of Alexandria. The same Macarius when offered by a traveller a bunch of grapes, despite his longing to taste them, handed them to the first hermit he could find who was hard at work, and so, as he deemed, needed them more than himself. He, too, would have liked the refreshing fruit, but determined to give them to another. And so they were handed round from one to another, until at last they were brought back to Macarius.[2] Nor were the lives of all spent in useless asceticism. Many of them wrote valuable contributions to the polemics or theology of the times.[3] At Arsinoe (Suez) swarms of monks in harvest-time helped to cut

we see that the attendant on such *inclusae* was sometimes a man; *HL* (Gr.) 28.

We have two sets of rules made for *inclusi*, the one by Grimilach of Metz in the 9th cent. in 69 chapters (in *PL* 103, p. 575 f.), the other by Ethelred, the Cistercian prior of Rievaulx († 1166) in 78 chapters (Holsten-Brockie, *CR* i. 291 ff.; i. 418 ff.).

[1] *PL* 74, p. 661, where the tale is put down to Paphnutius. But as Rosweyd surmised, the tale should be attributed to 'Sidonius,' *i.e.* Sarapion or Serapion Sindonius or 'Sarapion with the muslin vest.' Abbé Nau has shown this in his *Histoire de Thais* (*MG* xxx. 51). The story of Thais in its present form was worked up into a morality in the 4th century. It has recently been popularized by Anatole France. The tombs of Thais and Serapion were discovered at Antinoë by A. Gayet in 1901 (Cabrol, *DACL* i. 2338-40).

[2] *VS* in *PL* 73, p. 765.

[3] Complete list in Heimbucher, *OKK* i. 152-5.

the corn of the fellaheen.[1] Others introduced into the world new conceptions of benevolence, and were hard only upon themselves. We hear of one monk, Macarius by name,[2] a jeweller in his youth, who erected a hospital, in the upper floor of which he lodged women, in the lower men. When visited by a miserly woman of Alexandria, he offered to give her of ' his gems.' ' Which do you wish to see first,' he asked, ' my jacinths or my emeralds ? ' Then he led her to his lepers : ' Behold my jacinths.' After that he showed her his cripples : ' See my emeralds.'[3] Nor must we forget, according to a beautiful legend which deserves to be true, that it was another Eastern monk, Telemachus, who put a stop by his death to the crime of centuries, and closed for ever the slaughter of gladiators in the Coliseum.[4]

But the Gnosticism that so completely entrenched itself in Eastern ideals had but little influence in the West, at any rate when once Augustine had won his victory over his Manichaean temptations. Between the Monasticism of East and West there soon ceased, in fact, to be any links of connection save their common origin. Even before the rise of Benedict, the saner spirits of the West shrank back from the excesses of Eastern fanaticism. Sulpicius Severus, with all his

[1] Sozomen, *HE* vi. 28.

[2] This Macarius is mentioned by Cassian, *Conf.* xiv. 4. He must not be confounded with the two better known Macarii.

[3] *HL* c. 6; *HP* c. 2 in *PL* 74, pp. 256–7. In the story of the monk who acted as midwife, *HL* (Gr.) 68, we have a semi-erotic element introduced. For hospitals founded by monks, see Heimbucher, *OKK* i. 157.

[4] Theodoret, *HE* v. 26. Unfortunately the games continued after this date, and, as Gibbon pointed out (iii. 258, ed. Bury), the absence of all chapel, memorial, &c., to Telemachus is against the story; cf. Gregorovius, *Rome in Middle Ages*, i. 118.

reverence for St. Martin, refused to allow that it was necessary 'to be covered with your own hair instead of a garment, if you would be visited by angels.' The divergence, in fact, between East and West was inevitable, and is one of the many illustrations of the varieties of religious experience produced by a changed environment.

> "The victorious West
> In crown and sword arrayed"

could give up many things at the call of the Church:

> " She broke her flutes, she stopp'd her sports,
>   Her artists could not please.
> She tore her books, she shut her courts,
>   She fled her palaces."

But even in the wilderness she could not renounce her genius for activity and organization. For the West the " patient deep disdain " of a " brooding East " for the actual facts of life in the long run was an impossibility. Divergence of ideals was inevitable, and, in spite of the fact that Monasticism in the West was really an Eastern importation, this divergence was not slow in making itself apparent.[1]

---

[1] Instances of excess were, however, not altogether wanting in the West, especially before Benedict of Nursia. Thus Gregory of Tours († 594) tells us of one 'athlete of Christ,' a hermit called Lupicinus, who kept a huge stone 'which two men could scarcely lift' on his back 'for a whole day while he sang to God' [Greg. Tur. *Vit. Patrum* 13 in *MGH* (*Script. Rer. Merov.* ed. Arndt and Krusch, i. 715)]. We hear also of a Wulflaich of Treves, a Western imitator of Stylites, whose renunciation drew great crowds until his bishop demolished his pillar (Greg. Tur. *Hist. Franc.* viii. 15, ed. cit. pp. 333–5). Julian of Randan in Auvergne stood upright on his feet until they were diseased (Greg. Tur. *Hist. Franc.* iv. 32); Senoch of Tours loaded himself with chains (ib. *Vit. Pat.* 15); Portian tortured himself by chewing salt without water even in the heat of summer (ib. *Vit. Pat.* 5).

Of this early divergence of ideal we may select a famous illustration. Nothing, in fact, throws greater light upon the contrast between East and West than to remember that the age in which Symeon Stylites died, mourned by the whole East as the greatest of the human race, witnessed also the death of the typical hero of the West, pope Leo the Great (10 Nov. 461). The glory of the one was that he lived for nearly half a century on a lofty column, and died without the sin of descending; the other forced Attila to have mercy on the prostrate Romans.[1] In the East the dervish still remains the ideal of the renunciant, whether in the Christian, Muslim, or Buddhist world; in the West the colossal figures of such monks as St. Gregory or St. Bernard are both the interpreters and symbols of a different ideal. The chasm that divides the two is the age-long gulf between East and West. But to this divergence we shall return again.[2]

VII

In our studies of the causes which led to the rise of Monasticism, we have dwelt, as yet, rather on the environment than on the content of the idea itself. But this last is of no less importance than the first.

Monasticism, as we have seen, in its origin was the effort of the nobler spirits in a dissolute age to recover more completely the lost ideal of renunciation. But such renunciation was not left vague and indeterminate. On the contrary, it was sharply defined in every detail.

---

[1] For this incident, see W. E. Beet, *Rise of the Papacy*, 262 f.; *Lib. Pontificalis*, ed. L. Duchesne, i. 239; *DCB* iii. 654. Even if the importance of Leo in this embassy be exaggerated it does not alter the current tradition.

[2] *Infra*, p. 152 f.

THE IDEAS OF MONASTICISM

Complete renunciation centred itself round three points: poverty, chastity, and obedience; or the renunciation of the world, the renunciation of the flesh, and the renunciation of self-will.[1] All of these in process of time came to be definitely guarded by solemn vows. These three vows correspond to the three greatest needs of the age in which Monasticism was born. The old world was dying, as a result of its unbridled luxury, sensuality, and disorder. The one hope of the world lay in the reconstruction of a society upon some nobler basis. Nor must we forget that the exaggerated forms that these remedies assumed were the result, to no small extent, of the monstrous forms of the disease. In times of plague and pestilence only the wisest are able to avoid the exaggerations of fear.

From the first Monachism rested upon celibacy, in whose preservation Cassian detects six degrees of excellence, the sixth degree being proof against all attacks of the imagination.[2] Chastity was the chiefest virtue; to this abstinence and poverty were but ancillaries. Said Jerome in his letter to the lady Eustochium: 'God is not pleased by the rumblings of our bowels and the emptiness of our bellies in themselves. But without their aids our chastity cannot be guarded.'[3] So completely, in fact, was chastity taken for granted by the monk that in the *Rule of Benedict* there is no mention of any vow thereof, only of obedience.[4]

---

[1] For the growth of these ideas, see Zöckler, *AM* 151-65.
[2] Cassian, *Coll.* xii., an analysis that won't bear translation.
[3] *Ep.* 22 (11).
[4] Married monks, living in 'outer cells' with their wives and children, are, however, found at Bêth 'Âbhê in 594, and were driven out. Cf. *infra*, p. 193. Possibly they had taken the vow of chastity after their reception as married men (Budge, *Book of Governors*, i. p. cxliv, ii. 58).

The modern reader is so accustomed to identify Monasticism with the vow of chastity, and to think of the Roman priesthood as under the same obligation, that he scarcely remembers that in this matter, as in much else, Monasticism at first lay rather over against the practice of the Catholic Church than formed part of it. For in spite of the development of the idea of celibacy as a duty [1] Monasticism arose at a time when we see in the Church a marked reaction against extreme views. "The *Canons of Hippolytus* and the *Egyptian Church Order* protest against the idea that marriage hinders from prayer." [2] Not merely were many of the clergy married, as, for that matter, the majority are still married in the Eastern Church, but even married bishops were not infrequent; for instance, the father of Gregory Nazianzen, Synesius of Ptolemais,[3] and others. At the Council of Nicea the motion to impose conjugal abstinence on bishops was vetoed through the influence of the aged confessor Paphnutius.[4] The Council of Gangra anathematized those who refused to attend the ministrations of a married priest.[5] The practice of the Catholic Church—as distinct from its ideals—up to the time of Hildebrand [6] is undoubted, or rather, would be, but for the interested polemics of Roman writers. Were it not that there can be no greater mistake than to estimate the practice of the rank and file by the ideals of its saints and leaders, it is remarkable that every

---

[1] For this, see *infra*, p. 79 f.   [2] *ERE* iii. 493.

[3] Synesius is very outspoken on the subject. See his *Ep.* 105 in *PG* 66, p. 1485. Other instances are given by Leclercq in Hefele, *HC* II. ii. 1335-6.

[4] Soc. *HE* i. 11; Hefele, *HC* I. i. 620.

[5] Canon 4. For date, &c., see *infra*, p. 128, n. 2.

[6] See also *infra*, p. 152, n. 1; 234.

Father after the first three centuries, Basil, the two Gregories, Ambrose, Augustine, Jerome, Chrysostom exhaust language in the effort to exalt virginity; that, too, at a time when Monasticism itself was but inchoate. Nothing is more common in the literature of the early Church from Tertullian onwards than discussions on the relative merits of marriage and celibacy; but we are never left in any doubt as to the side on which the verdict will be given. Marriage is only a secondary good for those unable to preserve their continence. The unclean beasts, said Jerome, went into the ark in pairs; the clean by sevens—a symbol of the relative ease of entering Paradise.[1] 'Marriage,' said Martin, 'belongs to those things which are excused (*ad veniam*), but virginity points to glory.'[2] Jerome goes so far as to tempt Paula to consecrate her daughter to virginity by giving to her the proud but profane title of 'mother-in-law of God.' For marriage he has but one reason for which he can give it even limited praise: 'because it bears me virgins';[3] though he owns that 'married women, as such, are not outside the pale.'[4] He compares virginity to wheat, wedlock to barley, and fornication to cow-dung, and adds that 'to prevent a person pressed by hunger from eating cow-dung, I may allow him to eat barley.'[5] Almost the sole distinction in this matter between the Manichaeans and the orthodox lay in the contemptuous admission of the Church that 'in a great house there are also vessels of wood and earthen-

[1] Jerome, *Cont. Jovin.* ii. 15; *Ep.* 22 (19).
[2] Sulp. Sev. *Dial.* ii. 10 (6).
[3] Jerome, *Ep.* 22 (20).
[4] Jerome, *Ep.* 22 (2). The student should read the whole of this famous letter with its vivid picture of Roman society.
[5] Jerome, *Cont. Jovin.* i. 7; *Ep.* 48 (15).

ware, as well as vessels of silver and gold.'[1] The natural result followed. In some Christian writers woman is treated with scorn as the source of all evil, the deadly temptress without whose baleful influence man would never have lost his Eden.[2]

The reader who may dip into these survivals of another age and thought will be conscious at once of something that chills, apart altogether from his aversion to the theological attitude. The cause, he will find, is the social selfishness with which the whole matter is considered, so complete that at times it becomes sublime. The social instinct, social claims, that larger altruism which forms to-day the hope of the age, seem altogether wanting. The question is argued from the standpoint of spiritual Robinson Crusoes; no conception even of a possible Man Friday, to whom the Christian may owe a love that is something more than charity, ever seems to cross the mind. Life is viewed from an individualistic standpoint complete enough to satisfy the crudest disciple of Hume or Rousseau. The utmost concession that some of the extremer men will grant to the argument that their principles if carried out would destroy the race, is to fall back upon the ability of God, if needful, to provide other means of propagation.[3] Such a view differs from anarchism merely by the absence of every ray of hope. To some extent this was the reflection of the anarchism of the times. 'Dearest daughter in Christ,' writes Jerome, as he

---

[1] Jerome, *Cont. Jovin.* i. 40.

[2] Cf. the Syrian Aphraates (Burkitt, *Early East. Christianity*, 134 f.). Eng. trans. in *NPN* xiii. 365.

[3] Cassian, *Instit.* vii. 3, is more judicious in this matter than Jerome, *Cont. Jovin.* i. 36.

narrates the doings of Alaric, 'will you marry amid such scenes as these?'[1]

We need, therefore, feel no surprise at the absurd relations between men and women to which Monasticism gave rise in its carrying out of these ideals into practice. We are told of one virgin who refused to see even Martin himself, bishop and miracle-worker though he was, and Martin praises her for her refusal.[2] He himself never allowed a woman to touch him save once, and then he could scarcely escape the contagion, for it was a queen who flung herself at his feet, and insisted on waiting upon him.[3] Even St. Augustine would not see any woman save in the presence of a third party. Pior, an Egyptian monk, for fifty years refused to see any member of his family, even when they came to visit him. When, on her appeal, his bishop at length bade him visit his sister, he obeyed, but took care, writes his admiring biographer, to keep his eyes closed all the time.[4] The abba Apollos refused to go to his father's funeral, pleading that he himself had 'been dead to this world for twenty years.'[5] The remembrance of one's relatives, in fact, is represented by Anthony as a temptation of the devil, and Sulpicius relates how Satan once tempted a monk to return and convert his wife and son, 'a plausible appearance of spurious righteousness' for which he suffered by being 'possessed by a demon.'[6] We hear of a nun who, when she was dying,

[1] *Ep.* 123 (12).   [2] Sulp. Sev. *Dial.* ii. 12.
[3] *Ib.* ii. 6. 7. Palladius, relating that an old nun once sat with himself, speaks of it as a case of marvellous ἀπαθεία.
[4] *VS* in *PL* 73, p. 759; *HL* (Gr.) 39.
[5] Cassian, *Coll.* xxiv. 9. For the same reason Apollos refused to help his brother to save his ox when in the swamp.
[6] *Vit. Ant.* 36; Sulp. Sev. *Dial.* i. 22.

refused, for the sake of his soul, to let her brother see her.[1] Cassian tells us of a monk who after fifteen years had a 'huge packet of letters' brought to him from his 'father and mother and many friends in Pontus.'

'"What thoughts," said he, "will the reading of these suggest to me? They will incite me to senseless joy or useless sadness." ... So he threw the whole packet into the fire, all tied up just as he had received it, crying: "Away, ye thoughts of my home; try no further to recall me to those things from which I have fled"' (*Instit.* v. 32).

When Melania lost her husband and two out of her three sons within the same week,

'not a tear fell; she stood immovable, and falling at Christ's feet, as if she were laying hold on Him herself, she smiled: "More easily can I serve Thee, O Lord, in that Thou hast relieved me of so great a burden."'

When another of Jerome's friends—'of all the ladies in Rome the only one who had power to subdue him'—Paula, a descendant of the Gracchi and of Scipio, was urged by her children not to leave them for the desert, 'she raised dry eyes to heaven, and overcame her love of her children by her love of God. She knew herself no longer a mother.' So Paula, indifferent to the scandal which, as Jerome acknowledges, was caused, 'uplifted the cross of the Lord' and set off for Palestine, leaving her little son behind to grow up a heathen, a renunciation that led to results different from the outcome of the tears and prayers of Monnica the mother of St. Augustine.[2]

Remembering these things we are prepared for the exaggerated estimate of the value of celibacy which characterized the Eastern monk. One of the leaders

---

[1] *VS* in *PL* 73, p. 872.
[2] Jerome, *Epp.* 39 (4); 45 (4); 108 (6).

of the Mesopotamian Church, the Persian sage, bishop, and monk Aphraates (fl. 345) went so far even as to make baptism a privilege reserved for celibates—a fact which may perhaps account for the common reservation of that sacrament until late in life.[1] We hear of one man, the hermit Abraham, who fled from his marriage feast to a cell two miles off. When his friends found him he blocked up the entrance.[2] When Theonas, with whom Cassian held several conferences, found that his wife would not consent to live apart from him : ' it is safer,' he said, ' to be divorced from a human being than from God.' So he stripped himself of his goods and fled to a monastery.[3] After this for fifty years he never changed his shirt, nor washed his face and feet. ' In his face,' we read, ' one could discern the purity of his soul.' A girl of Alexandria, on discovering that it was her bright eyes that led a youth to pester her with his base offers of love, took up a weaver's shuttle and dug them out.[4] A certain Abba Paulus

' had made such progress in purity of heart in the stillness of the desert, that he would not suffer, I will not say a woman's face, but even the clothes of one of that sex to appear in his sight' (Cassian, *Coll.* vii. 26).

Apparently contradictory to this, yet one in its root, is the answer of an abbess to a monk who, when he met her, turned out of his way : ' If you were a true monk,' she replied, ' you would not know whether we were women or not.' Of another monk we read that when he found it needful on a journey to carry his aged mother over a

[1] F. Burkitt, *op. cit.* 125 ff.   See also *infra*, p. 81.
[2] *PL* 73, pp. 283, 292.
[3] Cassian, *Coll.* xxi. 9, 10.   Cassian only half approves.
[4] *PS* 60 in *PL* 74, p. 148.

stream, he carefully wrapped her up in his cloak, lest by touching this 'fire' 'the remembrance of other women should return.'[1] Exactly opposite to this in their outer manifestations, though springing from the same root, were the dangerous practices of the *Agapetae*, female Christian ascetics who lived together with men, though both parties had taken the vow of continence. These spiritual marriages, possibly in origin an attempt to substitute brotherly love for marriage, were very common with the Valentinians, Montanists, and the Encratites, and in the third and fourth centuries were held in favour also in the Catholic Church,[2] as also with the early 'saints' of the Celtic Church. From such spiritual marriages, designed as an aid in subduing the flesh, the step to concubinage was but slight. By the sixth century the worst construction was put by both populace and Church upon all such connections,[3] and every effort was made to stamp them out.[4]

When we turn from real life to the novels and hagiographic literature of the period we find this sexual aversion oftentimes taking a dangerous, erotic form. The writers of these tracts for edification love to play with fire, though, possibly, remembering Jerome's famous letter to Eustochium, we impute to them a sensitiveness that in reality they did not possess. In the romance of *Nereus and Achilleus* there is a voluptuousness of treatment which is not atoned for by its exaltation at all costs of chastity at the expense of marriage—it is,

[1] *VS* in *PL* 73, p. 872-3.

[2] See *ERE* ("Agapetae") i. 177 f. On the whole subject see H. Achelis, *Virgines subintroductae* (Leipzig, 1902).

[3] Conc. Toledo (589) c. 5; Hefele, *HC* III. i. 225.

[4] Achelis, *op. cit.* 33 f.

writes Dom Leclercq, "la dissertation d'un carabin en presence d'une vierge." [1] Other instances of an over-strained chastity degenerating into erotics could be adduced, e.g. the story of Drusiana in the *Acts of John*,[2] or the myth of Polyxena in the *Acts of Xanthippe and Polyxena* [3] with its disparagement of marriage.

If from these illustrations—a few only out of many that we have noted in Rosweyd's *Vitae Patrum* and elsewhere—we turn to the question: what was it exactly that gave to celibacy this extraordinary hold as an ideal? it will not suffice to answer that the renunciation of the best and deepest human instincts is necessarily the best and deepest renunciation. This would overlook the fact that the monastic writers seem to look upon the sexual instinct as altogether devilish. Even the possession of a body becomes a sin, the *fons et origo* of all evil. As a result of this half-veiled Gnosticism, throughout the vast literature of Monasticism, with rare exceptions, there runs one constant refrain, the apostrophe of the dying Pachomius to his body: 'Alas, why was I ever attached to thee, and why should I suffer because of thee an eternal condemnation!' [4]

[1] Cabrol, *DACL* iii. 1163. For the romance see *A.SS*, May. iii. 11 f.

[2] Pseudo-Abdias, v. 4 in Fabricius, *Cod. Apoc.* ii. 542.

[3] Ed. Dr. M. James in *TS* (2) no. 3. Cf. the story of Theophilus and Mary, *infra*, p. 71. Even when the tales are without eroticism, e.g. *HL* (Gr.) 70, they show a tendency to dwell round the sexual passion. The tale of Moses [*HL* (Gr.) 19] is of a different order, and would delight the heart of every schoolboy. Moses was an Ethiopian slave who became a brigand-chief. Becoming penitent, he fled to the desert, and was there attacked by four robbers. They had mistaken their man. Moses tied the four up and carried them off to the nearest church. Explanations followed, and on hearing that the monk was the once famous bandit Moses, the four robbers 'glorified God' and became 'converted.'

[4] *Vit. Pach.* 46 in *PL* 73, p. 265.

From this attitude Monasticism rarely found escape, except indeed when it lost its original earnestness. Even brother Giles, the joyous companion of St. Francis, falls into the same strain:

> 'Our wretched and weak human flesh is like the pig that ever delighteth to wallow and befoul itself in the mud, deeming mud its great delight. Our flesh is the devil's knight; for it resists and fights against all those things that are of God and for our salvation.' [1]

To the monk man is ever a duality rather than a unity, the soul chained to the flesh as a prisoner to a corpse. We have echoes of the same idea, unless indeed it be a pure mistranslation, in the funeral service of the Anglican Church, with its committal of 'this vile body' to the worms. To the same idea we owe many of the absurdities and repulsive practices of early Monasticism. Some monks deemed it a sin, or at least a snare, to bathe, because of the dangers of seeing themselves undressed. 'Why should Paula,' asked Jerome, in a strangely mixed metaphor, 'add fuel to a sleeping fire by taking baths?'[2] Paula responded to his appeal by maintaining, 'with knitted eyebrows,' that 'a clean body and a clean dress mean an unclean soul.'[3] Hence it was but a step to the general neglect of cleanliness characteristic of the whole movement. "The Church," writes Havelock Ellis, "killed the bath."[4] Athanasius boasts that his Anthony 'never changed his vest, nor washed his feet,' and the example of Anthony, as we have already noted, was widely followed.[5] The *Rule* of Pachomius

---

[1] *Little Flowers of St. Francis*, trs. Arnold, c. 8.
[2] Jerome, *Ep.* 107 (11).   [3] Jerome, *Ep.* 108 (20).
[4] See the proofs in Cabrol; *DACL* ii. 97 f.
[5] *VA* 47, 60. Cf. Isidore in *HL* (Gr.) 1 (2); *ib.* 38 (12).

THE IDEAS OF MONASTICISM

strictly forbade all washing save in case of sickness. The great Roman lady, Melania, boasted that 'except for the tips of the fingers' she never allowed water to touch her, in spite of her doctors.[1]

There were other considerations which powerfully contributed to the formation of the ideal of celibacy. Celibacy, as we have seen, was not merely the struggle of the soul to escape the bars of the flesh; it was, in part, the reaction of individualism against the tyranny of a society which seemed to be altogether evil. As is commonly the result in reactions against society, individualism became anarchic. Similes also played their part in the formation of the idea. As is usually the case in an unscientific age, they exercised an influence out of all proportion to their value in logic. The Church was regarded as the *Militia Christi*, the army of Christ's soldiers in a holy war which should bring in the kingdom of heaven.[2] But no victorious army can ever live in ease and indulgence; soldiers are called upon rather to deny themselves many delights that theirs may be the greater triumph.

'No soldier,' pleads Tertullian, 'takes luxuries with him. He marches to battle not from his sitting-room, but from the camp, where all kinds of hardship and inconvenience are to be met with' (*ad Mart.* 3).

Hence it was felt that the soldiers of Christ—and the monk is but the soldier on campaign, with scanty food as befits 'the rations of service'[3]—must bind themselves, in their warfare with the forces of the world, by the same

[1] *HL* (Gr.) 55 (2).
[2] See Harnack's monograph *Militia Christi* (1905) the appendix of which contains a full list of the passages in early Christian literature on this idea and on its importance. Cf. also my *PEC* 184 ff.
[3] Cassian, *Instit.* iv. 5.

restrictions as the soldiers of the emperor at Constantinople or Rome. We see this idea in the answer of Martin to the request of a certain monk that his wife, 'who had taken the oath of allegiance in the same service as himself,' should be allowed to live with him. '"Tell me," said Martin, "have you ever stood in the line of battle?" "Frequently," he replied. "Well then, did you ever in the line of battle see any woman standing there or fighting?"' By 'this true and rational analogy,' Martin convinced the monk that he must abandon his wife.[1]

VIII

The second fundamental virtue of the monks was the renunciation of wealth, or 'property.' This was regarded from the earliest times as one of the marks of the perfect. 'Blessed are ye poor,' sneered Julian when he confiscated Church property, 'for yours is the kingdom of heaven.' The priests might resent the Apostate's logic, the more so because they could scarcely deny that, in the opinion of the times, he was arguing the matter from the standpoint of the Apostles. For the early Church was saturated, through and through, with Ebionite ideas. In some writers 'poverty' is as much the essential mark of the Christian as it afterwards became of the Spiritual Franciscans. Wealth was one of the things which it was the Christian's business to renounce, though alas! complete renunciation was achieved but by the few. For the higher orders of the ministry 'poverty,' at first, was considered an in-

[1] Sulp. Sev. *Dial.* ii. 11.

dispensable qualification.[1] Only with the decay of early enthusiasm did the clergy begin to amass wealth.[2] But whatever might be the neglect in this matter of the seculars, for the regulars, from the earliest days onwards, poverty was regarded as absolutely essential. Nevertheless the reader should note that even for the monk 'poverty' became in time a mere technical term, the meaning of which it was certainly not easy to discover from outer appearances. In the beginning 'poverty' was real, the absolute renunciation by the individual of all share in the world's wealth, 'the naked following of a naked Christ.' But in the expansion of Monasticism, circumstances, which proved stronger than the ideals of the monks, filled the monasteries with wealth. When Caesarius of Arles[3] insisted on the postulant making a legal act of alienation of his wealth, the final step, possession by the monastery, was inevitable. Then 'poverty' became little more than a name for the individual's renunciation of all private ownership of this wealth, except his use and rights as a member of a corporation to whom alone it was deemed to belong. But as a member of this corporation the most insignificant unit was certainly far from poor.

To the causes which produced this change in the connotation of 'poverty' we shall return later. But meanwhile we should note that appropriation by the individual was always strictly forbidden. 'If any man calleth aught his own,' said Basil, 'he maketh himself a stranger to the elect of God.'[4] In Egypt,

---

[1] On this see Hermas, *Shep.* Sim. i., ix. 20; Lucian, *Prot. Peregrinus*, 13; *Didaché*, xi. 4–6 (cf. *Matt.* x. 9–10, xix. 21); Euseb. *HE* iii. 37 (2).

[2] See my *PEC* 153.   [3] See *infra*, p. 123.

[4] Basil, *Regulae brev. tract.* Interrog. 85 in Basil, *Op.* (ed. Garnier, Paris, 1839) ii. 629.

however remunerative the toil of individual monks, all must go into the common treasury, 'except two biscuits with three pence.'[1] The monk who, 'through inadvertence or ignorance,' boasted of 'my book, my tablet, my pen, my cloak, my shoes,' or who attempted 'to seal anything with his own seal,' was guilty of a sin execrated in all *Rules* and which Columban punished with six lashes.[2] No tale of the Middle Ages is more familiar, or more often quoted with approval, than the story of the monk Justus whom Gregory the Great, shortly before his election as pope, when he was still abbot of his own foundation of St. Andrew's, discovered in possession of three gold pieces, and whose dead body he ordered to be cast out on the dunghill with the three gold coins he had left behind.[3] To the same horror of individual appropriation we must trace the rise in later ages of the Spiritual Franciscans with their emphasis on the absolute necessity of evangelical poverty.

The third fundamental idea of Monasticism, first specifically introduced by Pachomius, was the renunciation of the will. This is sometimes called obedience, sometimes humility; in reality, from the Monastic standpoint the two tend to become one. The two are related as cause and effect; they are different aspects of that com-

---

[1] Cassian, *Instit.* iv. 14.

[2] Cf. Cassian, *Instit.* iv. 13, and Benedict Aniane, *Conc. Regularum*, c. 42 (in *PL* 103, p. 1058).

[3] See Greg. *Dial.* iv. 55. There is another account in the *Vita Greg. Mag.* by John the Deacon, i. 15, 16 (*PL* 75, p. 68). Hus (to cite one of the many medievals) quotes this story with approval [F. Palacky, *Documenta Mag. J. Hus.* (1869), 14–15; or *Monumenta Hus.* (1558), ii. 51 *b*.; Eng. trans. in Workman and Pope, *Letters of Hus* (1904), pp. 42–4]. There is another version of what is evidently the same tale in John Diac. *Vita Greg.* ii. 45, quoted from a Greek book Λειμών, *i.e.* Moschus, *PS* c. 192 (*PL* 74, p. 220).

plete self-renunciation which is higher than any mere outer surrender. The man who has nailed his inner self to the cross cannot be otherwise than humble; while the humble man will show his humility by a perfect obedience. 'The first degree of humility,' said St. Benedict, 'is ready obedience.' 'Our life in this world,' he adds, 'is like Jacob's ladder, which has been erected towards heaven with its lowest rungs in a humble heart.'[1] 'Monasteries,' wrote Cassian at an earlier date,

'are not founded on the whim of any man who pleads his own renunciation of the world. . . . No one is allowed to preside over the assembly of his brethren, or over himself, until he has learned that he is in nowise the lord or arbiter of himself' [*Instit.* ii. 3 (1)].

'It is a great matter,' writes Thomas à Kempis, 'to live in obedience, to be under a superior and not to be at our own disposing. It is much safer to obey than to govern.'[2]

This insistence upon obedience and humility was naturally one of the marks of the increasing emphasis of the cenobite as distinct from the hermit life, and grew, therefore, with the growth of the corporate form of Monasticism. Without humility and obedience life in a brotherhood becomes impossible. This is the foundation principle upon which the order and welfare of a monastery must depend. Its corollary was government by one head. True, the attempt was made, at the close of the fourth century, in the Priscillianist monasteries of Spain, to regulate monastic life on democratic models and to reduce the abbot to little more than a counsellor; but the attempt was necessarily

[1] *Reg. Bened.* 5, 7.   [2] *de Imit. Christi*, i. 9.

doomed to failure.[1] Monasticism could never be content with a measure of obedience sufficient for utilitarian ends. The system demanded humility and obedience so complete as to destroy that very individuality of which Monasticism, in its rise, had been an expression. The records abound with illustrations of humility and obedience, not only incomprehensible to the modern mind, but which make manhood itself a contemptible thing. Humility must be perfect; so the hero of God will strip himself even of his reputation if only by this means he may reach complete self-abasement; nay he will even glory in shame, using the words in a literal and not figurative sense. As Hus put it in one of the last letters that he wrote: 'Some argue that a man who submits himself to the Church wins merit by his humility when he confesses to guilt, though it be granted that he is innocent.'[2] The monk who attempts to retain his reputation becomes guilty of that incomplete renunciation which was the sin of Ananias and Sapphira. So we read of one saint under whose bed a stolen book was placed by his enemies. When the book was found he was not careful to maintain his innocence.[3] Again, Cassian tells the story of a certain abbot, Pinuphius, whose humility was so blessed that when he saw that all men reverenced him 'either for his life, or for his age, or for his priesthood'—for he was a presbyter—he withdrew from the convent he ruled and fled into the far recesses of the Thebaid, and entered as a lay novice a monastery where he

---

[1] For this remarkable Priscillianist *Regula consensoria* see Holsten, *CR* i. 136-7; Cabrol, *DACL* ii. 3221.

[2] Workman and Pope, *op. cit.* 260; Palacky, *op. cit.* 136.

[3] Cassian, *Coll.* xviii. 15.

was unknown. There he was set to dung the garden. When discovered and brought back, 'for like a city set upon a hill his saintliness could no longer be hid,' he once more fled to the monastery where Cassian was staying, 'which was at no great distance from the cave in which our Lord was born.'[1]

The strange contempt for reputation, to which the cultivation of this species of humility led, cannot be better illustrated than by the tale of Theophilus and Mary. About the year 530 there appeared in the streets of Amida, a city on the Tigris, the modern Diarbekir, a mime and his female companion, who seemed to be a prostitute, though as they regularly disappeared at nightfall this last was but a surmise. The suspicion was sufficient, however, for the governor to issue an order that she should be handed over to a brothel. She was rescued by a Christian lady named Cosneo, who exhorted her to a better life. She listened with downcast look, but forthwith returned to her comrade. At a later date it was discovered that the strange pair were the children of noble citizens of Antioch. They had completed the renunciation of all their wealth by silently enduring the reproach of living in shameful immorality—for a virtuous maiden an unnatural self-abnegation, to this age inconceivable, but which won for Mary in Syria an extraordinary reputation.[2] A similar story is told of Marina, a virgin who dressed as a man and who was taxed with being the father of a foundling. She did not deny the charge, nor was

---

[1] Cass. *Instit.* iv. 30–1; *Coll.* xx. 1 (also in *PL* 73, p. 833).

[2] T. Nöldeke, *Sketches from East. Hist.* (1892), pp. 233–5. For a similar tale in the case of a priest, see *HL* (Gr.) 70.

her innocence discovered until they laid her out for burial.[1]

A humility which could thus become abject—no other word can describe it—naturally resulted in an obedience not merely contemptible but even criminal in its disregard of all sense of personal responsibility. The early writers relate with pride illustrations which need no commentary. We hear of a certain John the Short, who, when bidden by his superior to water a log of firewood, spent a whole year on this task, carrying water a distance of two miles 'as though it had been a divine command.'[2] At another time the said John, on hearing the command: 'Run, John, and roll hither that huge rock,' essayed the hopeless task.[3] A similar tale is told of Paul the Simple who, when sixty years of age, fled into the desert because of the wreck of his home by his guilty wife. When Anthony saw him he told him that the condition of salvation lay in implicit obedience.

---

[1] *PL* 73, p. 693. The tale was told to Hus (see my *Letters*, 260) with the object of getting him to recant even though he felt he were innocent of any heresy that needed recantation. The reader will note the erotic element in these tales or novelettes. We have a good illustration of this in the romance of the virgin of Corinth and her rescue from the brothel to which she had been condemned for being a Christian. *HL* (Gr.) 65; Cf. *PEC* 302 n., 371.

[2] Cassian, *Instit.* iv. 24. Cf. *Coll.* i. 21, xxiv. 26. In Sulp. Sev. *Dial.* i. 19 the wonder grows; the watering is for three years, at the end of which the log sprouts; while Postumian saw it 'standing with green branches'! And in the Coptic Life of John the Short (Amélineau, *MG* xxv. 347) old men eat of its fruit! John the Short must not be confused, as is so often done with John of Lycopolis († 395), who was noted for his powers of clairvoyance, and in whom the emperor Theodosius (379-95) had such confidence that he sent to consult him with reference to the conduct of a military expedition [*HP* 22 in *PL* 74, p. 301; *HL* (Gr.) 35 (2); a statement accepted by Gibbon (ed. Bury, iii. 181)].

[3] Cassian, *Instit.* iv. 26.

He promised. Whereupon Anthony bade him stand in prayer until he should return. 'Throughout the heat of the day and the dew of the night' the novice stood until, on the next day, Anthony returned fully satisfied with his test.[1] We are told of another monk who, when ordered to cross a river that swarmed with crocodiles, obeyed at once. As a reward the reptiles 'licked his body, but did not hurt him.'[2]

But the classic illustration of criminal obedience is the story given us by Cassian of the Abba Mucius.[3] Mucius had entered a convent, together with his little lad of eight. Lest the sight of the lad should win back the father to the world, the two were placed in separate cells. The better to wean the father from the vanity of his affections his child was dressed in rags and systematically neglected. To test Mucius' progress in grace the child was beaten with rods. 'But the love of Christ conquered,' and the heart of the father remained unmoved, 'nor did he grieve over the lad's injuries.' As a last proof of his piety, 'one day when he saw the lad in tears,' Mucius was ordered to throw him into the river. This 'work of faith and obedience would have been accomplished' had not the brethren hindered 'this second Abraham'; 'when the child was thrown in they, somehow, snatched him from the bed of the river.' If this illustration were isolated we might pass it by as a freak; but, unfortunately, similar stories abound, related with a relish which shows us the opinion of the early monks that of such was the kingdom of heaven. The

---

[1] *HL* in *PL* 73, p. 1126. For this Paul, see *HL* (Gr.) 22.

[2] *VS* in *PL* 73, p. 789.

[3] Cassian, *Instit.* iv. 28-9. Petschenig (ed. *CSEL*), however, reads Patermucius.

more absurd the obedience, the more it was regarded 'as the trampling under foot of all shame and confusion out of love for Christ.'[1]

Even the Rule of Benedict, with all its sanity, cannot allow the individual judgement much discretion as to the limits of obedience. 'If a brother is commanded to do anything that is impossible . . . let him represent the matter to his superior, calmly and respectfully. . . . If the superior still insists . . . let the junior be persuaded that it is for his spiritual good.'[2] If there come a knock at the door, the monk, even if engaged in writing, must spring up at once, 'without waiting to finish the stroke he had begun.'[3]

Of all this there could be but one result. The exaggeration in Monasticism of obedience, after passing through the military phases of the Templars and other similar orders, was bound to end in Jesuitism. The Society of Jesus was founded upon the perfect exploitation of the renunciation of the will. But between the earliest monks and the followers of Loyola there is the continuity and development of twelve hundred years of monastic life.

[1] Cassian, *Instit.* iv. 29. The Jesuit Rosweyd has indexed these illustrations with admiration in his ed. of the *VP*. They perfectly illustrate the Jesuit position: 'Obedentia ad perfectionem compendiosa.' Cf. also Sulp. Sev. *Dial.* i. 18; Cassian, *Instit.* iv. 10.

[2] *Reg. Bened.* 68.

[3] Cassian, *Instit.* iv. 12.

CHAPTER II

THE HISTORY OF MONASTICISM AS AN INSTITUTION TO THE COMING OF BENEDICT

> The vast frame
> Of social nature changes evermore
> Her organs and her members with decay
> Restless, and restless generation, powers
> And functions dying and produced at need,—
> And by this law the mighty whole subsists:
> With an ascent and progress in the main;
> Yet oh! how disproportioned to the hopes
> And expectations of self-flattering minds.
>
> WORDSWORTH, *Excursion*, bk. vii.

It is no small matter to dwell in a religious community, or monastery, to hold thy place there without giving offence, and to continue faithful even unto death.

THOMAS À KEMPIS, *Imitatio Christi*, i. 17.

ARGUMENT

§ I. Monasticism not primitive — The Early Church and Ascetism—Hermas and his *Shepherd*—The Second Century—Gnostic Gospels—*Acts of Paul and Thekla*—Hierakas—The Marcionites—Monasticism and Asceticism—'The resurrection of the body'—Serapis and Mithra — Sacrifice passes into self-sacrifice — Sexual abstinence and the Sacraments. . . . 77

§ II. Monasticism in Egypt—Serapis—Pachomius—His importance—Philo and the Therapeutae—The Essenes . 85

§ III. *The Life of Anthony*—Its influence—Anthony—*Life of Paul*—The power of demons—The note of triumph—Anthony and the clergy—Anthony and Orthodoxy—Anthony and Augustine—The reality of the spiritual . 92

§ IV. *Life of Martin*—Secret of its success—Story of Martin — His death — His popularity—Origin of the word "chapel" 101

§ V. Monasticism in Syria—In Mesopotamia—Basil and the Greek Church—Monasticism in the West—Jerome—Monasticism in Gaul—Lérins—John Cassian—Caesarius of Arles 110

§ VI. Monasticism and the need of *Rules* — Pachomius — Schenoudi—St. Basil—Accounts of early travellers—Palladius — John Cassian — Postumian — Amorphous condition in the West—Gyrovagi and Sarabaites . 124

pp. 77-135

CHAPTER II

HISTORY OF MONASTICISM AS AN INSTITUTION TO THE COMING OF BENEDICT

I

FROM the study of the content of the Monastic ideal we pass to the story of Monasticism as a concrete institution. At the outset the student will need some explanation of the fact that it took Monasticism three centuries to establish itself within the Church. With but slight authority in the precepts,[1] certainly none in the practice of the Author of her faith (whatever may be said of Elijah or John the Baptist), the Church had hesitated long in endorsing this conception of the more excellent way. This is indeed only what we might expect. Christianity was the daughter of Judaism; and in Judaism, with the exception of the Essenes and Therapeutae, "chastity and marriage were considered to go hand in hand." Until its later periods Judaism was not ascetic.[2] To assert with Montalembert that "the first Christians lived as the monks have lived since,"[3] is, in one sense, correct. For all Christians,

[1] *Mark* x. 21, 29, 30; *Matthew* xix. 12, 21. Cf. *1 Cor.* vii. 25 f.; *Luke* xviii. 22. Cf. F. W. Farrar, "Fasting in Holy Scripture" (*Expositor*, 1893, 339 f.).

[2] *ERE* i. 66; *ERE* ("Chastity") iii. 492.

[3] Mont. *MW* i. 219. The arguments for a primitive Monasticism are given in L. Bulteau, *Essai de l'Histoire Monastique d'Orient*

in every age, the law of their life is the same : *via crucis, via lucis*. But this does not mean that we draw Montalembert's inference that the early Christians were monks in all but name and dress. Jesus, it is true, lived in community with His disciples, but the community life was far removed from that of the monastery. In the earliest age, though asceticism might be practised and commended, hermits were few, monks there were none.[1] Self-abnegation was essential; but the joy of the Resurrection was still too near for men to strain after the unnatural. "Christianity," writes Zöckler, "was a religion, not of asceticism, but of faith and love."[2] The birth of the Church was as the birth of the year, 'with gladness and singleness of heart.'[3] The statement is correct provided we make due allowance for the eschatological hopes. Buoyed up with the belief in the immediate return of Christ—'Maran Atha'[4]—such asceticism as the Christians practised was rather the preparation for coming victory, than that counsel of despair to which, as we have seen already, Monasticism in part owed its origin. The brotherhood

(Paris, 1680), and S. Schiwietz, *Das morgenländische Mönchtum* (Mainz, 1904), i. 1–45. Cf. Heimbucher, *OKK* i. 86 f. H. Leclercq (in Cabrol, *DACL* ii. 3081) owns that "until the commencement of the fourth century there was not even a commencement of codification" of ascetic principles.

[1] The argument of Cassian, *Coll.* xviii. 5, that Monasticism was founded by the Apostles, died down, and then was revived by Anthony and Paul, is, of course, without any justification.

[2] Zöckler, *AM* 136. Cf. F. Burkitt, *Early East. Christianity* (1904), 118 f.; Harnack, *HD* i. 67, 205.

[3] *Acts* ii. 46, RV. Black, *Culture and Restraint*, c. 11, contains some good remarks on the teaching of Jesus and the Apostles as to Asceticism. But the best account is in Zöckler, *ERE* i. 73 f., or more fully, *AM* 136–48, 151–60. Cf. also *ERE* iii. 272, 492.

[4] *1 Cor.* xvi. 22. Cf. Workman, *PEC* 154, 232–3.

of disciples had not yet yielded to those dissolvent forces of worldliness and Gnosticism which, at a later date, drove the purer-minded to seek the lost Christianity in the wilderness. In one of the earliest documents of the post-apostolic age, the *Shepherd* of Hermas, Hermas, in the opening vision seeing the beauty of Rhoda, reasoned in his heart, ' Happy were I if I had such an one to wife, both in beauty and character.' In one of his 'Similitudes' Hermas, with a charming simplicity that to a later age would have seemed impossible, tells us how the virgins pressed him to stay with them till eventide, and how he lay down in the midst of them, 'they doing nothing else but pray.'[1] Even if these utterances of Hermas be interpreted as referring to spiritual marriages,[2] the attitude of mind is very different from that afterwards developed in Monasticism. Tertullian, with all his severity of outlook, could still plead at the commencement of the third century that the Christians were in no sense ' dwellers in woods,' or 'exiles from life.'[3] In the *Clementine Homilies* the picture drawn of married life is perfect and unexaggerated.[4]

In the second and third centuries asceticism, especially in the matter of chastity, became more pronounced. At first it was the protest of the heretic against the catholic. The Marcionites, for instance, admitted no married person to baptism unless he con-

---

[1] Hermas, *Shepherd*, Vis. i.; Sim. ix. 11. The *Shepherd* was probably written during the episcopate at Rome of Hermas' brother Pius, *i.e.* probably between 140–55. For the date, see the discussion in my *PEC* 220 n.

[2] See *supra*, p. 62.

[3] Tert. *Apol.* 42 (quoted *supra*, p. 26). Cf. his remarks on the happiness of marriage in *ad uxor.* 8.

[4] *Clem. Homil.* 13.

sented to a separation.[1] At Sinope in Paphlagonia, where Marcion's father was bishop, there were recognized virgins.[2] In the Gnostic Gospels the apostles are represented as zealous ascetics and vegetarians. The *Gospel according to the Egyptians* makes general virginity a condition of the coming of the kingdom of God. 'I am come,' said the Saviour, 'to suppress the acts of woman.'[3] In the *Acts of Thomas* the separation of husband and wife is made the price of eternal life.[4] Thomas arrives in India at the moment of the marriage of the king's son. So powerful is his sermon on the evils of marriage that the young couple, after passing the night in deliberation, announce that they have devoted themselves to celibacy. In the *Acts of Paul and Thekla* St. Paul pronounces a blessing on those 'who have a wife, and are as if they had not.'[5] The inherent pollution of all matter was a cardinal tenet with the followers of Saturninus, Basilides, and Tatian, as well as with the Encratites and other Gnostic sects.[6] Tatian pronounced

---

[1] Tertul. *adv. Marc.* i. 29; iv. 11; v. 5. Aphraates pushed this still further: see *supra*, p. 61.

[2] Epiphan. *Haer.* 42 (1) in *PG* 41, p. 696.

[3] A. Hilgenfeld, *N.T. extra can. receptum* (Leipzig, 1866), iv. 45.

[4] R. A. Lipsius and M. Bonnet, *Acta Apost. Apocrypha* (Leipzig, 1903), ii. (2) 114 f.

[5] In Gregory of Tours, *Hist. Franc.* i. 42, *de gloria confessorum*, 32 (best ed. see *supra*, p. 53 n.), we have an historical instance of this in the case of Injuriosus of Auvergne. Gregory tells the tale of the young wife's effective pleadings with great relish, and it certainly is a contrast to the terribly low level of animal life that he depicts. In Cabrol, *DACL* iii. 1165 f., there is a valuable collection of inscriptions in which married people bear witness to life-long chastity, &c., one of which dates back to the year 378. Cf. also the illustrations in Palladius, *HL* (Gr.), cc. 8 (Amon), 67 (Magna).

[6] On these see Irenæus, *adv. Haer.* i. 24, 28; Harnack, *HD* i. c. 4; *DCB* ii. 118. One set of fanatics who gave much trouble in the 4th cent. were the Messalians, Euchites, or 'Enthusiasts,' who renounced

marriage to be 'corruption and fornication.'[1] The followers of Hierakas in Egypt, repudiating, as did the Marcionites, 'the resurrection of the flesh,'[2] dreamed of a paradise where none entered save the celibate.[3] With the Montanists marriage is practically proscribed. Though the Church gained the victory over the heretics, and in her official creed gave an exaggerated value to the σάρξ strangely at variance with St. Paul's explicit denial that the flesh rises again, yet in the process of the fight she absorbed some of the heretics' ideas. Catholic Christians could not be outdone by heretics and heathen in self-renunciation. The renunciation upon which all Christian life must be founded tended to become more specific. The 'flesh,' the resurrection of which was made an article of faith, was looked upon as the one enemy in actual life that must be trampled under foot. Celibacy and the preservation of virginity were increasingly regarded, if not as the expiation of sin, yet as the greatest gift that could be laid at the crucified feet of Christ,[4] the one specifically Christian

all property, lived on alms, and did nothing but pray (Εὐχή; hence their name). On these see *ERE* v. 570.

[1] Euseb. *HE* iv. 29 (3). Encratites = Ἐγκρατεῖς, *i.e.* "continent."

[2] The student should remember that the clause in the early Roman symbol known as the Apostles' Creed, σαρκὸς ἀνάστασιν, must not be translated as "resurrection of the body." It is impossible that the clause would have assumed this form if the ideas of Anthony had assumed prominence at the date of its composition.

[3] Epiphan. *Haeres.* 67 (2, 46) in *PG* 42. On Hierakas see Harnack, *HD* iii. 98 f. He did not believe that children could be saved.

[4] "Tertullian was the first who definitely regarded ascetic performances as propitiatory offerings and ascribed to them the 'potestas reconciliandi iratum deum.'" See Harnack's valuable note in *HD* ii. 132. Methodius echoed his view in the Eastern-Church, *ib.* iii. 110 f.

virtue,[1] though as yet there was no separate estate of such as lived this higher life. By the time of Cyprian the vow of virginity was regarded as binding, its breach a matter for the penances of the Church.[2] In the Spanish Council of Elvira (c. 306) this view received definite sanction in a canon.[3] From this it was but a step to a definite liturgy for the consecration of virgins,[4] and to the definite association together of such as adopted this manner of life.[5]

Those who claim for Monasticism an early origin in Christianity, in reality pay her no homage. For Monasticism was not the flight of cowards to the wilderness from the persecution of Marcus Aurelius or Decius. When the penalty for confessing Christ was the cross or the stake, there was no need to find an artificial cross. The ideal of self-surrender was then to be found in the martyr, the highest celibacy in those immortal virgins who, like Blandina or Felicitas, submitted themselves to all the tortures which paganism could devise rather than surrender the proud title of 'slave of Christ.'[6] It was not persecution but rather its cessation that made the hermits; they were the later growth of a primitive idea due to the triumph of the Church, or rather of the world, in the peace of Constantine. All

---

[1] See Harnack's note, *HD* iii. 128, on Ambrose, *de virgin.* i. 3; and cf. *HD* v. 28. [2] Cyprian, *Ep.* 61 (to Pomponius).

[3] Conc. Illiberit. can. 13. Hefele, *HC* I. i. 229. This canon passed into Gratian's *Decretum* as Causa xxvii. q. i. c. 25.

[4] For an excellent study of the growth of this sentiment, see H. Koch, *Virgines Christi* in *TU* (1906) xxxi. (2).

[5] We see these associations first in the Pseudo-Clement *Epp. de virgin.* i. 6; ii. written at the commencement of the 3rd cent. Of these Epps. there only remain Greek fragments and a Syriac version, the latter trans. into Latin in F. X. Funk, *Op. Pat. Apost.* (1901) ii.

[6] See my *PEC* 313, 349.

that persecution had done had been to familiarize some who had fled from the Decian tyranny with the solitary life among the deserts and mountains.[1]

But when the age of persecution was past Monasticism rapidly, and not unnaturally, became the recognized, perfect form of the self-surrender essential to the Christian. All those ascetic yearnings and instincts which had hitherto found full scope in the battle for the faith, must now find their exercise in another field. The bloody struggle of the martyr gave place to the self-immolation of the eremite. Moreover, the attempt of Christianity to obtain the mastery of the world coincided, it would appear, with an upward spiritual movement among mankind at large. The old heathen conceptions were striving to adapt themselves to the enlarged spiritual and human outlook of a world which was no longer local in its instincts but imperial. The search of the philosophers for the universal principle in knowledge and thought, resolved itself among the more thoughtful into the desire to find some universal object of faith. We are not concerned, in this connection, with the directions in which men sought to satisfy this larger vision; nor with the growing spirituality which students have discovered in the three great rivals of the Christian faith: the worship of the Great Mother, the worship of Isis and Serapis, and the religion of Mithra.[2] These three religions, with the stress that they laid upon atonement, vicarious sacrifice, immortality, and mystic rapture, prepared the old world in more ways than one for the

---

[1] Euseb. *HE* vi. 42. Cf. *Vit. Constant.* ii. 2 (persecution of Licinian). See *infra*, p. 95.

[2] See further on this in my *PEC* 87-8; or the full discussion in Dill, *Rom. Soc. Nero to Aurelius*, iii. c. 3, and book iv.

religion which was to satisfy, at last, the hunger and thirst of humanity by a more perfect vision of the Divine.

But in all these religions the doctrine of renunciation, especially in the form of asceticism, holds a prominent place,[1] as in fact it had done and still does in the religions and customs of the primitive races. Penitential abstinence, especially chastity, formed part of the preparation without which the worshipper could not approach the gods or be initiated into the holy mysteries.[2] The priesthood of Vesta was not the only religion in which we find the tabu of chastity. For all the priests of Isis asceticism and chastity formed a lifelong obligation. The use of woollen garments, of wine, pork, fish, and certain vegetables, was absolutely forbidden to them. Monasteries, as we shall see later, form a definitely recognized part, at any rate in Egypt, of her sacerdotal caste. According to some writers—though the matter is not certain—in all the forty-two temples of Serapis, especially in the great temples of Memphis and Heliopolis, there were ascetics whose cloistered life was of the strictest.[3] In the worship of Mithra there were grades of ascetics, and companies of virgins. Asceticism, in forms not far removed from those familiar to us in the Christian Church, was "in the air"; it was part of the evolution of the higher spiritual forms from the lower. The conquest of Christianity over its rivals was not the

[1] Cf. *ERE* i. 107.

[2] Cicero, *de Legibus*, ii. 19–24. The student should consult the article on "Chastity" (Introductory) in *ERE* iii. 474 f. for a full exposition of this.

[3] *Inclusi* or κάτοχοι. See *supra*, p. 49; Zöckler, *AM* 96; Weingarten, *UM* 30–6. The κάτοχοι were of both sexes (Amélineau, *HL* 2). It is possible, however, to interpret κάτοχος as ="possessed" by the god, a common classical usage (see Cabrol, *DACL* ii. 3056 n.). But this does not seem to me likely.

crushing out but the absorbing in of tendencies which we find in evidence in all the religions of the age. In all the religions of the ancient world, in the early centuries of our era, the idea of sacrifice that had at one time been predominant was tending to pass away into the loftier conception of self-sacrifice. Hence the rise of Monasticism, which was, in fact, by a natural transition, "the inheritance of the Church, not its invention; not the offspring, but the adopted child."[1] Just as the religions of India, Egypt, and Greece demanded from the worshipper a period of sexual abstinence, so in Christianity continence was required as a preparation for both Baptism and the Eucharist.[2] But in the process of transfer we find development. Just as the sacrifices of Mosaism gave place to the idea of the Atonement on Calvary, so, if we may compare the reflection with the reality, the slaughter of the martyr gave place to the self-devotion of the eremite.

II

The emphasis we have laid upon the enthusiasm with which Christianity, both in the East and the West, adopted the Monastic life as the highest ideal and expression of Renunciation, would have a mischievous result if it led the reader to overlook the growth and evolution of the idea itself in the experience of the Church. For the history of Monasticism is not the study of a fixed idea the content of which was changeless, its expression undetermined by environment. On the contrary, Monasticism shows its life by its adaptation to different local needs, and by the method in which it

[1] E. G. Smith, *CM* 3.
[2] *ERE* iii. 483; Westermarck, *Hist. of Marriage* (1901), 151 f.

changed itself so as to suit the changing centuries. The essential elements of the idea, it is true, remain the same whether in the fourth or the fourteenth century; in the same way that chemical analysis reveals to us that the essential elements of water are the same whether it takes the form of cloud, rain, snow, or ice; and that diamonds, coal, blacklead, and soot are different forms of one basic principle. But, after all, the forms that the elements take cannot be neglected because, in the last result, science shows that they can be reduced to one. Similarly in the history of the doctrine of renunciation, nothing is more instructive than to note the institutional changes through which Monasticism passed in the course of its long development.

In the Church Monasticism first appeared in Egypt, a land by climate and circumstance well adapted for its rise and growth.

> "To Egypt first she came; where they did prove
> Wonders of anger once, but now of love.
> The Ten Commandments there did flourish, more
> Than the ten bitter plagues had done before." [1]

The precise nature of the influence upon Monasticism of heathen examples and ideas is a matter of much dispute. Some have argued that the Egyptian hermit was the last man to owe aught except hatred to the dying cults around him. His illiberal zeal would lead him to eschew rather than to imitate any institution with a pagan prototype. Others, on the contrary, have maintained that "asceticism in Egypt was indigenous," [2] that the

---

[1] G. Herbert, *Church Militant*.

[2] Amélineau, *MG* xx. Introd. 17. But according to F. Petrie, *Religion and Conscience in Early Egypt* (1898), 122–3, asceticism did not exist in the Egypt of the Pharaohs. Cf. *ERE* iii. 497.

rise of Monasticism coincided with the conversion to Christianity of the monks of the great heathen Serapeum of Memphis, who transferred to their new faith their old institutions, including the tonsure.¹ In support of this theory they have appealed to the case of the Copt ² Pachomius, the real founder of Egyptian Cenobitism.³ They maintain that before he became a Christian he had lived as a recluse (κάτοχος) in the temple of Serapis at Schénésit,⁴ in the southern Thebaid. The illustration would appear, however, to rest upon an error.⁵ The temple was in ruins, and Pachomius,

¹ For a survey of pre-Christian Asceticism, see Zöckler, *AM* 33-135, or *ERE* i. 65-71, 80-109. For Egyptian Monasticism, E. Preuschen, *Mönchtum u. Serapiskult* (2nd ed., Giessen, 1903), or the very full S. Schwietz, *MM*. Both writers totally reject the theories of Weingarten.

² It may perhaps be advisable to explain, for the sake of the young student, that Copt is the Arabic transcription of Αἰγύπτιος with the first syllable lost. The Coptic language is really the old Egyptian written in Greek letters. Curious to say, no Coptic writing that is not about Christianity and written by Christians has yet been found (Amélineau, *HL* 18; Budge, *Coptic Biblical Texts*, lxxii. f.).

³ For sources of his life, see Appendix A, § IV, p. 357. The best accounts of Pachomius, from very different standpoints, are given us by Amélineau, *MG* xvii.; Grützmacher, *PAK*; and Ladeuze, *ECP*, whose narrative is specially to be trusted. There is a good summary of the organization of Pachomian monasteries in Cabrol, *DACL* ii. 3114-23.

⁴ Gr. Χηνοβόσκιον. Modern Quasr-es-Saïad; see Ladeuze, *ECP* 173 n. 2.

⁵ I have followed Ladeuze, *ECP* 158 f., who seems to me on this matter to be the best guide. Weingarten, *UM* 36, started the theory and was followed by Zöckler, *AM* 194, though cf. *ERE* i. 75; Grützmacher, *PAK* 39. But Butler, *HL* i. 235 n.; Cabrol, *DACL* ii. 3054, 3091; J. Mayer, *Die Christliche Askese* (Freiburg, 1894), 37; Heimbucher, *OKK* i. 106 reject. The Memphitic and Arabic versions of the *Vita Pachomii* (see *infra*, p. 358) know nothing of the story. For the Serapeum reference may be made to Brunet de Presle, *Mémoires sur le Sérapeum de Memphis* (in *Mém. de l'Acad. des Incript.* 1852).

who had recently received his discharge as a soldier, had sought it out that there he might live the hermit life. He was already praying for the light. As he grew his vegetables and ministered to poor travellers or to the sick in the neighbouring villages,[1] the light broke, and he received baptism as a Christian. Soon after his conversion he sought out an anchorite named Palaemon, with whom he dwelt for some years, learning both the weakness and strength of the solitary life. Then he took the great step which has given him immortality. Beginning with three disciples, he gathered the hermits of the Thebaid into his first monastery, destined rapidly to grow into a congregation of nine monasteries, at Tabennîsî—" the palm garden of Isis "—near Denderah.[2]

On the importance of Pachomius we shall have occasion to dwell later. He marks the second stage in the development of Monasticism; the hermit passes into the cenobite.[3] For Pachomius had grasped the truth which had eluded the hermits, that " to save souls you must bring them together." The inspiration which under-

[1] Ladeuze, *ECP* 161, points out that this was totally alien to the recluses of Serapis.

[2] The Gr. form Ταβέννησις became wrongly divided, as early as Sozomen, *HE* iii. 14, into Ταβέννη νῆσος, giving rise to the misconception still current that the monastery was on the island of Elephantine in the Nile. Tabennîsî (the modern Dechna) was near Pabau, another Pachomian house, whose modern Coptic name is Faou or Phbôou. See Butler, *HL* ii. 205–6; Zöckler, *AM* 196 n.; Grützmacher, *PAK* 97 n.; Amélineau, *Géog. de l'Égypte à l'époque copte*, 331 f.; Cabrol, *DACL* ii. 3112.

The dates of Pachomius are very doubtful. I give those of Ladeuze, *ECP* 222 f.: b. 292; in 313 or 314 enrolled as a soldier; 314 or 315 retreated to the ruined temple; 9 May 346, death of Pachomius. With these we may compare Grützmacher, *PAK* 23 f. For the numbers in his monasteries, see *infra*, p. 111.

[3] A certain Aotas had made the attempt before, but without success (*Vit. Pach.* 77).

lies this conception entitles Pachomius to a foremost place among religious leaders, and, whatever may have been his debt to the cult of Serapis, it was from Christ alone that he had learned this deeper truth. Nor was his work restricted to men. Under the influence of his sister Mary he organized two monasteries for women, the first near Tabennîsî, a second soon following at Tesminé,[1] a number which soon increased to a dozen.[2] To the monasteries of Pachomius there came in 333 a traveller, the great Athanasius, whose sympathies were shown in later visits that he paid to these new institutions. If, instead of devoting his pen to the praise of the hermit life, Athanasius had written an account of the community life inaugurated by Pachomius and established by him under a *Rule*, the two centuries that were to elapse before its principles were developed by St. Benedict might have been considerably shortened. As it was, Pachomius suffered the neglect which too often attends those who are before their age, nor were his monasteries free from the defects of first attempts. False visions, suicides, and a few carnal falls witness to the imperfect accommodation of means and ideal.[3]

There are other pre-Christian sources of the Monastic ideal to which we may turn with more confidence than to the Serapeum of Memphis. Among the Jews of Alexandria and Egypt—in numbers, as we shall do well to remember, about one-sixth of the whole population of the country [4]—the principles of Monasticism

[1] On the name and site of this place see Ladeuze, *ECP* 175 f.
[2] *HL* (Gr.) 59 (1).
[3] Cabrol, *DACL* ii. 3104. The failures, exaggerated by Amélineau, are exhaustively discussed by Ladeuze, *ECP* 327 ff.
[4] See *PEC* 113.

seem to have been fully developed at the dawn of the Christian era. In the *de Vita Contemplativa*, the authorship of which may be assigned, with some certainty, to Philo,[1] as well as in other works of the same writer, we see how a sect of the Jews near Alexandria, called "Therapeutae," or "devotees,"[2] were accustomed to leave all, and retire into the country, especially to the hills on the south side of Lake Mareotis. There they led an austere life of poverty, chastity, meditation, and labour.[3] This life they called 'the philosophical,' and as proof of their claim, 'when feasting luxuriously on doctrines, did not remember their food for three days.'[4] That Eusebius considered these Jewish Therapeutae to be Christians may well be regarded as one indication of the influence of Jewish ascetic ideals upon the new faith, as

[1] See F. Conybeare, *The Contemplative Life* (Oxford, 1895), who in this agrees with Eusebius, *HE* ii. 17. Reference may also be made to the conclusive work of P. Wendland, *Die Therapeuten u. die philonische Schrift vom beschaul. Leben* (Leipzig, 1896). The attack of Grätz (iii. 463 f.) on its genuineness may thus be dismissed. Conybeare reverts to the opinion held by scholars since the Reformation that the Therapeutae were Jews and not Christians. Lucius, *Die Therapeuten* (Strasburg, 1879); (cf. Harnack, *PRE*² art. "Therapeuten"), follows the Jewish historian Grätz and all the Fathers in identifying the Therapeutae with Christian (Gnostic or Montanist) monks, as Eusebius, *HE* ii. 17 (17), had done. In this he was followed by Schürer, *Jewish People in Time of Christ* (Eng. trs. 1886), div. ii. vol. iii. p. 357. The matter is still under discussion (see the vast literature in Cabrol, *DACL* ii. 3063 n.–3068 n.), but on the whole, Conybeare may fairly claim to have established matters as they were before the publication of Lucius' volume (see espec. Conybeare, *op. cit.* 337–48; and cf. Cabrol, *DACL* ii. 3071 f.). For Jewish asceticism, cf. Zöckler, *AM* 120 f., who also (*l.c.* p. 128 f.) endorses Conybeare.

[2] Philo [*op. cit.* in Euseb. *HE* ii. 17 (4)] interprets as "physicians," but without justification. See Lightfoot, *Ep. Col.* 352.

[3] Conybeare, *op. cit.* 261–75; Euseb. *l.c.*

[4] Euseb. *HE* ii. 17 (18). They held solemn spiritual banquets once every seven months.

indeed we see also in the case of the Colossian heresy. At a later date St. Ambrose tried to discover in Jewish usages a precedent also for Christian nuns; but the passages that he quoted or allegorized from the *Song of Songs* are but a slight foundation upon which to build.[1]

But little change was needed to develop the principles of the Therapeutae into those of Anthony or Pachomius. The same is true of another sect of Jewish ascetics, the Essenes, though the frequent bathings for the remission of sins which formed a strong feature of one Essene sect called "Hemerobaptists" or "morning bathers,"[2] certainly formed no part of early Christian Monasticism. Of the Essenes, whose centre was on the shores of the Dead Sea, the foundation principle was the old Gnostic or Persian idea of the malignity of matter. As part of their struggle to avoid pollution they rejected animal food, avoided wine and warm baths, and wore linen rather than wool because of its higher ceremonial purity. Their ideal was a semi-nomad corporate life with entire community of goods, and unconditional obedience to the head. They accepted marriage, otherwise regarded as an abomination, as needful for the preservation of the race. But, at best, woman was a

[1] Ambrose, *de Virg.* The whole book is full of remarkable exegesis. According to E. G. Smith, *CM* 214, Ambrose quotes in defence of the existence of Jewish nuns 2 *Macc.* iii. 19, "the virgins that were kept in ward," but I cannot find the reference.

[2] Lightfoot, *Ep. Col.* 402. The translation "daily bathers" would appear to be wrong. The emphasis is on bathing at dawn. Another similar sect was the Sampsaean, on whom see *ERE* v. 267; Lightfoot, *l.c.* 374; Hippolytus, *Haer.* ix. 13, 15 ff. For the Essenes the student should master Moffatt's article in *ERE* v. 396 f. In this article Moffatt shows (as against Lightfoot, *l.c.*) that the non-Jewish elements are of Neopythagorean not of Persian origin.

mere instrument of temptation,[1] and marriage, when possible, should be neglected. One part of their discipline consisted, as with St. Benedict, in manual labour. But it is not easy to decide to what extent their customs were ascetic in aim, or the survivals of primitive habits.[2]

III

Among the factors in the rapid growth of Monasticism we must not overlook the extraordinary influence exerted in the fourth and fifth centuries by two remarkable biographies, the *Life of St. Anthony*, and the *Life of St. Martin*. Of the first work the author is somewhat uncertain. After the manner of the times, it was attributed to the great Athanasius,[3] in whose lifetime it was undoubtedly published, thus securing for it future respect, while testifying to the high regard in which it was already held. The basis of fact which underlies the biography of St. Anthony, supplies the smallest part of its influence. This is due rather to its theme—the narrative of the triumph of a simple, unlettered Copt, by the grace of God and by the help of his hermit life, over every form of temptation.

Anthony, who was born about the year 251 in the village of Coma in Middle Egypt not far from the Thebaid,[4] was brought up in a godly home. At the age of twenty, Anthony, who, by the death of his parents in infancy, had been left in possession of a large farm,

[1] Lightfoot, *Ep. Col.* 85-6.
[2] See F. Conybeare, "Essenes" in Hastings' *DB*, and cf. *ERE* i. 63, *ib.* i. 99 (the sect is there regarded as of exotic origin).
[3] For an investigation of the authenticity and historical value of the *Vita Antonii*, see *infrâ*, Appendix A, § I, p. 353.
[4] Sozomen, *HE* i. 13.

heard the divine call. Chancing to enter a church as the Gospel for the day was being read—If thou wouldst be perfect, go sell all that thou hast and give to the poor—he took the words, as did St. Francis at a later date, as addressed to himself.[1] He sold all, gave his wealth to the poor, reserving only a small portion for his sister.[2] Shortly after, hearing the words, 'Take no thought for the morrow,' he sold even his reserve. Then 'freed from all the chains of this world he entered upon his rough and arduous task.' He sought out a venerable old man who was living an ascetic life near his village.[3] To him he joined himself, supporting himself by the labour of his hands, and giving all that he did not need to the poor. But his toil and renunciation brought him no peace, only perpetual conflict with Satan, and the Valley of the Shadow of Death with its hideous noises and unhallowed thoughts.[4] After passing thirty-five years of incessant temptation—his home for part of the period in one of the village tombs,[5] for twenty years in a disused castle abandoned by the snakes as he entered[6] —the battle was at last gained. One night, after the usual struggle with evil thoughts, he saw the Devil cowering at his feet like a black child. 'I have deceived many,' wailed the Spirit of Impurity, 'I have cast down many, but, as in the case of many, so in thine, I have been worsted in the battle.'[7] From all parts men

[1] Recent discoveries show that it was probable that the version used was Coptic (see E. A. W. Budge, *Coptic Biblical Texts*, 1912). Otherwise the matter might have thrown light on Anthony's alleged ignorance of Greek (*infra*, p. 353).

[2] VA 2, 3.

[3] Such ascetics were called ἀποτακτικοί. They are often mentioned in the *Acta* of martyrs.

[4] Cf. especially VA 4, 8.   [5] *Ib*. 7.
[6] *Ib*. 11.   [7] *Ib*. 4.

now flocked to the triumphant saint, bringing to him their diseases of body and soul.

To escape this pressure Anthony crossed the Nile, as the third century drew to its close, and journeyed for three days until he came to a mountain—the Inner Mountain of Anthony, as it was afterwards called to distinguish it from his former abode—not far from the Red Sea.[1] There, beside a spring of water, clear and cold, in the midst of wild beasts that he had tamed, he tilled his little garden, wove his baskets, and taught the hermits who gathered round him. About the same time (c. 305), all unknown to Anthony, far down the Nile the monk Pachomius was founding his great monasteries at Tabennîsî. Twice Anthony left his mountain and journeyed to Alexandria, once in 310 or 311, when the emperor Maximin renewed the persecution in Egypt. 'Let us go,' he said, 'to the glorious triumphs of our brethren.' But no one dared to touch him as he stood in the public place girt with white, or followed the confessors to the place of death.[2]

His second appearance in Alexandria was more memorable still. In extreme old age Anthony came to the help of Athanasius against the Arians.

'No age, no sex remained at home. I say nothing about the Christians, for the Pagans even and their priests rushed to the church crying out: Let us see the man of God. They were

---

[1] The modern Deir Anba Antonios (*VA* c. 24; *HP* c. 9 in *PL* 74, p. 280; Cabrol, *DACL* ii. 3130). His first 'mountain' was at Pispir (Gebel-el-Ter) near the Egyptian Babylon [*HL* (Gr.) 21 (1)], thirty miles east of the Nile (Cabrol, *DACL* ii. 3134).

[2] *VA* 23 and for the persecution *PEC* 278–9. Anthony did not leave until after the martyrdom of bishop Peter, which took place in 311 [Euseb. *HE* vii. 31 (32)] on either Nov. 24 or 26 (the dates of his festival).

anxious to touch were it but the hem of his garment, believing that the touch would benefit them much.'[1]

His purpose accomplished, Anthony returned to his beloved solitudes. 'Fish die,' said he, 'when they are drawn to land, and monks lose their strength in towns, so let us hasten back to our mountain.'[2] And now 'he saw that it was time for him to set sail, for he was an hundred and five years old.' 'I perceive,' he said to his monks, 'that I am called by the Lord.' So he summoned two of his children to him, related to them the story of his conflicts, then gently and humbly passed away : 'As he looked death in the face, his countenance was so glad that you might know that he saw already the multitude of angels descending to carry away his soul.' In obedience to his last words his disciples secretly buried his body, 'and nobody knows to this day where it is hidden.'[3]

Anthony, if we judge strictly by time, was not the first Christian hermit. In the height of the Decian persecution (*c.* 250) many of the Christians had escaped to the deserts.[4] Among them, if we may accept the story of Jerome, in its bare outline probably true,

[1] *VA* 41–2; Theodoret, *HE* iv. 24; Jerome, *Ep.* 68 (3). The date was probably between 335–8, possibly 27 July 337 (Larsow, *Die Festalbriefe des heil. Athanasius*, 28 n., 29 n.; Grützmacher, *PAK* 56 n.). Athanasius re-entered Alexandria on his return from Treves on 23 Nov. 337. See Duchesne, *EHC* ii. 156 n.; Hefele, *HC* I. ii. 682 n.

[2] *VA* 53.

[3] *VA* 58–9. Date probably 17 Jan. 356 (Jerome, *Chron.* s.v. Robertson, *op. cit.* 218 n.). But the chronology of Anthony's life is very difficult. See Zöckler, *AM* 187. The two disciples who buried him are called Macarius and Amatas [Jerome, *Vit. Paul.* 1. Palladius, *HL* (Gr.) 21 (1)]. This Macarius must be distinguished from the Macarius of Egypt and Macarius of Alexandria. See *supra*, p. 45 n.

[4] Eusebius, *HE* vi. 42. Cf. Soz. *HE* i. 12.

was one, Paul, at that time a youth of sixteen, who withdrew to a cave in a far-off mountain. But when the storm was passed he did not return, but lived and died in extreme old age in his cave near the Red Sea [1] under the shadow of the palm-tree from whose leaves he had woven the tunic which at his death he bequeathed to Anthony, the 'illustrator' as Jerome puts it of the life of which Paul was 'the author.' [2] With this tunic, runs the legend, Anthony, who had visited him before his passing,[3] was wont to invest himself at Easter and Pente-

[1] The modern Deir Anba Boulos, *i.e.* Paul.

[2] Jerome, *Ep.* 22 (36).

[3] Butler, *HL* i. 231, sees nothing unreasonable in this visit. But it is not in the *VA* and should be rejected. Jerome's *Vita Pauli* (in *PL* 23, p. 17 f.; Greek versions in *Anal. Boll.* ii. 561 ff., also published by Bidez at Ghent in 1900) was written in 376 before his visit to Egypt. It cannot therefore claim any first-hand knowledge, and, as Jerome himself states (*l.c.* c. 1), is chiefly derived from stories set afloat by Amatas and Macarius. It seems to me a valueless imitation of the *VA*, evidently written for purposes of edification (cf. cc. 17 and 18). To its wild fictions Jerome seems to refer in his dedication: 'I have taken great pains to bring my language down to the level of the simpler sort' [*Ep.* 10 (3)]. The existence of Paul has been doubted *e.g.* by Weingarten, *PRE*² x. 759, who only echoes doubts that Jerome frankly owns were current in his day (cf. Jerome, *Vita Hilarion*, c. 1). To this we must add the complete absence of all early references even in the *Vit. Antonii*. On the other hand, Dom Butler properly argues (*HL* i. 231-2; cf. Zöckler, *AM* 183-4) for Paul's existence from the monastery Deir Anba Boulos, visited by Postumian probably about 402 (*DCB* iv. 447. Sulp. Sev. *Dial.* i. 17. 'I also went to the place where also lived the blessed Paul, first of hermits'). We have also references in Jerome, *Chronicle*, sub. ann. 359 and in his *Ep.* 22 (36) (*PL* 22, p. 421). Cf. Cassian, *Coll.* xviii. 6, which, however, is probably only taken from Jerome. In any case we know nothing of Paul except his existence (cf. Jerome's confession, *Vit. Pauli*, c. 1 *fin.*).

For the Coptic *Vita Pauli* with Fr. translation see Amélineau, *MG* xxv. (Paris, 1894). Amélineau argues that it is the original which Jerome translated (*op. cit.* Introd. iv-xiv). But Jerome did not know Coptic, and the existence of a Syriac version the

cost ' as with the armour of a dead hero.' [1] Nor was Paul alone. Palaemon, the teacher of Pachomius, Psenosiris, and others, all witness to the charm of the solitary life.

This simple statement of the story of Anthony's life will not give the reader any due insight into the reasons for its extraordinary influence. How great it is as a work of art may be seen by contrasting it with the short but soulless imitation, the *Life of Paul* by Jerome. In this romance, the chief figure of which is not Paul but Anthony, hippocentaurs and satyrs meet with Anthony and hold converse with him; while at the end, two lions dig Paul's grave.[2] In reality the *Life of Anthony* was produced at the psychological moment. With consummate art it presented Monasticism as the one adequate solution of the difficulties of life. We must not forget that everywhere men lived in dread of the powers of evil; superstition was triumphant. In the *Historia Lausiaca* of Palladius nearly all the ills of life are attributed to the agency of demons. The Devil and his angels were regarded as foes almost omnipotent, certainly omnipresent. The powers of darkness 'filled the atmosphere which extends between earth and heaven,' thus 'fortunately, by Divine Providence, withdrawn from human sight.'[3] But the author claimed that for the monk:

"The ancient Prince of ill,
Look grim as e'er he will,"

---

same as the Coptic, which states that Jerome is the author, disproves this theory (Butler, *HL* i. 285; Zöckler, *AM* 184; Schiwietz, *MM* 50 n.; *Anal. Boll.* xx. 121 ff.; Grützmacher, *Hieronymus*, 161 n.).

[1] Jerome, *Vita Pauli*, 16. [2] Jerome, *Vit. Pauli*, 7, 16.

[3] Cass. *Coll.* viii. 12. On the current ideas concerning devils see *ib.* vii. 9–25, 27, viii. c. 8; Palladius, *HL passim*; Amélineau, *HL* 111–21; and my *PEC* 130–2.

is absolutely the most futile of beings.[1] 'Thou art utterly despicable,' said Anthony to the Spirit of Impurity cowering at his feet, 'thou art black of soul, yet weak as a child, nor shall I henceforth cast one thought on thee, for the Lord is my helper.' Once as he lay on the ground in exhaustion the Devil came: 'Here am I,' cried Anthony, 'and I shun not the fight.'[2]

We have the same consciousness of victory elsewhere. One night Anthony was thinking of the destiny of the soul when a voice came from without:

'"Anthony, arise! come forth and see." And when he lifted up his eyes he beheld a vast and hideous shape, reaching to the clouds, and other winged beings which strove to rise. And as they rose the monster stretched forth his hands to catch them, and if he could not then they soared aloft, untroubled for the future. And Anthony knew that he looked upon the passage of souls to heaven' (*VA* c. 38).

No blows or torments of the Evil One can separate Anthony from the love of Christ. For him monastic renunciation is absolute triumph, and that too from its essential principles; Monasticism brings peace. 'By his experience,' says Cassian, 'the blessed Anthony established that demons cannot possibly overwhelm the soul unless they have first deprived it of all holy thoughts.'[3] From all this world of devils Neoplatonism had offered release; man could rise from plane to plane, ever growing more free from matter, until at last he reached the sphere of not-being. But this escape was only for the philosopher; the people did not count. The *Vita*

[1] Cf. *VA* 5, 16, 43 in *PG* 26, pp. 835 ff.
[2] *VA* 8. For the powerlessness of the Devil against the monk cf. *Vit. Pach.* 49 (*PL* 73, p. 267); *HL* (Gr.) 19 (9), 22 (10), 38 (8) *et passim*.
[3] Cass. *Coll.* viii. 19.

Antonii, with that democratic instinct which is inseparable from all true Christianity, pointed out a road that all might tread. 'Trouble not at the loss of thy bodily eyes,' said Anthony to a blind friend, Didymus by name, 'for thou hast the eyes with which the angels see, and with which thou mayest behold God.'[1] 'Christianity,' sneered Celsus, 'is a faith fit only for fullers and bakers.' But the *Vita Antonii*, centred as it is round low-caste monks and a Copt who knew no letters, claims that of such is the kingdom of heaven.

Many are the tales told of Anthony which enable us to discern in him no mere fanatical ascetic, but a great soul that had learned the lessons of renunciation. But the common sense of the monk, or, as some would have it, the skill of the writer, is best seen in the way in which he is careful not to stir up against the Monasticism that he advocates the ill-will of the Church. He rather seeks to allay the troubles and doubts so prominent in the case of Pachomius, if we may trust the Coptic versions,[2] by making Anthony most dutiful to all clerics, even to the humblest presbyter.[3] The writer claims that

---

[1] This incident is quoted by Jerome in writing to comfort his blind friend Castrutius (*Ep.* 68; date 397). The incident took place on Anthony's second visit to Alexandria (*supra*, p. 95 n.). From Jerome it found its way into *VS* 218 (*PL* 73, p. 809).

[2] On this see *infra*, App. A, § V, p. 358.

[3] See *supra*, p. 15 f. This passage, which seems to me certainly not to be part of the genuine *Anthony*, is so important that I quote it at length (in Evagrius' version): 'Nam omnes clericos usque ad ultimum gradum ante se orare compellens, episcopis quoque atque presbyteris, quasi humilitatis discipulus, ad benedicendum se caput submittebat. Diacone vero . . . ad orandum Dominum sibi praeponebat, non erubescens, et ipse discere' (*VA* 39; *PL* 73, p. 456. In the Greek version, c. 67). Curious to say Athanasius makes no reference to this deference of Anthony to priests even when writing to Dracontius, who had refused the episcopate.

there is an alliance between orthodoxy and the new religious life. He illustrates this by the story, true no doubt in its bare outlines but improbable in its details, of how Anthony, though an illiterate Copt with no knowledge of Greek, had yet come to Alexandria to the help of Athanasius, and by his logic and eloquence discomfited the Arians. The Arians, as we read their history, were not thus easily routed, unless indeed we have here another illustration of the age-long influence in Egypt of the dervish or solitary fanatic.

But these factors would not of themselves explain the extraordinary influence of the work. For this we must fall back upon a higher cause. The secret of its success, as Bishop Westcott has pointed out, lies in the fact that the *Vita Antonii* presents the "spiritual world as one intense reality." Everywhere the writer represents Anthony as face to face with the eternal. "What are to us figures, were to him sensible truths, and he was strong because he felt the awful grandeur of the conflict in which we, no less than he, are engaged."

The influence of this work was extraordinary, more especially after its speedy translation into Latin by Evagrius, the friend of Jerome, about the year 373. Augustine tells us a story of the conversion at Treves, through casually reading the book, of one of the officials of the Ministry of the Interior, on his way back one afternoon from the games of the Circus. 'If I choose,' he cried, as he finished the story, 'I can be the friend of God from this moment.' But the book was one of the agents under God in the conversion of a greater soul than this unknown official. It was from reading in this work the story of Anthony's own conversion, and from hearing of its influence upon others, that Augustine

MONASTICISM AS AN INSTITUTION 101

himself first realized, as he tells us, the gulf that lay between his own low level of ideal, in spite of all his opportunities and learning, and the holiness attained by the ignorant Copt, 'whose name, though held in high honour by thy servants, I had never heard of till that hour.'[1] To this work we must also attribute St. Augustine's own pronounced leanings to Monasticism.

IV

Another work, second only in importance to the *Life of St. Anthony* in the spread of Monasticism, especially in the West, was the remarkable biography of St. Martin of Tours, written by Sulpicius Severus,[2] his disciple

[1] August. *Confess.* viii. 6–12. Augustine quotes the work as anonymous, and this has been considered a strong argument against its Athanasian authorship; but Augustine would use the Latin version, the preface of which ascribes the work to Athanasius.

[2] The reader will find a most interesting study of Sulpicius in Glover, *LLFC* 278–302. Sulpicius Severus was born in 363 near Bordeaux. About 393 he gathered other ascetics round himself at Primuliac near Béziers (for the details of this establishment see Cabrol, *DACL* ii. 3194). According to Reinkens, *Martin v. Tours* (Breslau, 1866), he died about 406. The tale that in his last years he fell into Pelagianism, and on repentance abjured speech for ever 'to expatiate by silence the sin he had contracted by speech,' is very doubtful, and seems to be due to a blunder of Gennadius (*Vir. Ill.* 19) misunderstanding a phrase in a letter of Paulinus of Nola to Sulpicius ('confugisti ad pietatis silentium,' *Ep.* v. 6 in *CSEL* xxix. 29). For other references of Paulinus to Sulpicius, see *Epp.* 1 (10, 11); 5 (6, 13); 11 (6); 24 (1). The *Vita Martini* (*VM*) was written during Martin's life, for Martin's death is narrated by Sulpicius in his *Ep.* 3, which may be regarded as a postscript. The *Chronicles* of Sulpicius (written about 400) became the standard history text-book of the sixteenth century and was ignorantly placed on the *Index Expurgatorius* (Symonds, *Renaissance in Italy*, vi. 222). They are of considerable value inasmuch as, according to Bernays, they incorporate matter from the lost books of Tacitus.

The best edition of the *Opera* of Sulpicius is by Halm (*CSEL*,

and literary exponent. The influence of this work was extraordinary. In the book-shops of Rome 'nothing commanded a readier sale or fetched a higher price.' At Carthage and Alexandria everybody was reading it, while Egypt sent a request for a continuation. Even Athens, the home of a culture altogether alien to Monasticism, in the triumphant words of Sulpicius 'now knew that Socrates in his prison was not braver than Martin.' Such indeed was the interest excited by the book that the mere rumour of a discourse on Martin, in which fresh details would be given of his life, drew together, unexpectedly, a large congregation of all classes of society.[1]

The reader who shall take up this work, and ask the secret of its influence, will not have far to go. No one can read it without falling in love with its rough, tender-hearted hero. The book lifts life into a higher level; it brings before us—and that too in the age of Julian the Apostate—the heights of Christian power and peace accessible, through the new method of renunciation, not to the wise and wealthy, not to priests and bishops, but to the poorest and meanest of the laity. The book is filled with that peace of God which passeth all understanding. For Martin, as for Anthony, the Devil is not merely impotent, he is beneath his feet. 'Martin held the Devil ever under the power of his eyes.'[2] We see this peace in the story of how Martin, on his journey over the Alps to Pannonia, undertaken with the object of converting his parents, 'fell into the hands of robbers,

Vienna, 1866), to which all my references are given. There is also an edition in Migne, *PL* 20, p. 159 f., and a translation by A. Roberts in *NPN* vol. 11. Of Paulinus the best ed. is *CSEL* vol. 29.

[1] Sulp. Sev. *Dial.* i. 23, iii. 17; cf. i. 26, iii. 1.
[2] Sulp. Sev. *VM* 21.

one of whom lifted up his axe and poised it above Martin's head.' 'Are you not afraid?' they asked of their captive, who lay stripped at their feet:

'Then indeed did Martin most stoutly reply that never before had he felt so safe, for he knew that the mercy of the Lord would be specially with him in temptation. He was only in trouble over the robber, inasmuch as he was showing himself unworthy of the mercy of God. Thereupon he preached to the robber the Word of God' (*VM* 5).

The result was the robber's conversion.

Another secret of the success of the *Life of Martin* is the emphasis that it lays upon the power of grace to save to the uttermost. In an age when the Church was becoming sacerdotal and worldly, the book, in spite of its over-emphasis of the miraculous, thrills us with its intense passion for souls. Once, when entering Paris, attended by the usual crowd, at the city gate that in spite of all revolutions is still named after him, he met a leper of hideous appearance. Amid the shudders of the crowd Martin stepped up to him, kissed and blessed him.[1] Such a man despaired of none, neither the rude robbers, nor even the Devil himself. When the Devil tried to persuade Martin that certain men had so fallen away from grace that they were no longer within the scope of pardon, Martin cried:

' "If thou thyself, wretched being, wouldst but desist from thy pursuit of men, and repent thee of thy deeds, I have such a confidence in our Lord Jesus Christ that I would promise thee mercy." '[2]

In the same spirit he could never be persuaded to remove one of his persistent slanderers, the priest Brictio, from his sacred office, in spite of the many

[1] Sulp. Sev. *VM* 18.   [2] *Ib.* 22. Cf. Burns' familiar lines.

accusations brought against him. 'If Christ,' he replied, 'bore with Judas, why should not I bear with Brictio?'[1] This combination of bravery, tenderness, and peace, is the characteristic of the man, and runs through the whole book. But we are never allowed to forget that, in the opinion of the writer, the virtues of Martin are the virtues of monastic renunciation.

Renunciation is, in fact, the keynote of the whole, the charm of its tales, the secret of its influence. Martin[2] was born about 336[3] at Sabaria (Sarwar), a town of Pannonia, now part of Hungary. His father was a Pagan, who had risen from the ranks to the command of a cohort. A soldier has no home, and little Martin was brought up at Pavia in North Italy with but scanty education. At the age of ten, in spite of the remonstrance of his parents, he became a catechumen. His father retaliated by procuring his impressment in the army when a youth of fifteen.[4] So for five years Martin was a soldier in Northern Gaul, probably serving in the cavalry.[5] But even the temptations of the army could not seduce him from following the precepts of Christ. There is no tale more beautiful

[1] Sulp. Sev. *Dial.* iii. 15.

[2] The only primary authority for Martin is Sulpicius Severus; the *Vit. Martini* (= *VM*); *Sacred Historia*, ii. 45 f.; *Dial.* ii. and iii.; and certain of his *Epp.* Gregory of Tours has given us three books on the miracles wrought by Martin's relics. From these two all later writers work up their narratives, bishop Venantius Fortunatus of Poictiers († 600) and Paulinus of Perigueux (c. 470) turning the *VM* into hexameters. The references in Sozomen, *HE* iii. 14, are valueless.

[3] See *infra*, p. 105 n., for this date.

[4] For military service and Christianity, see *PEC* 181 f. Military service at this time was in low repute, and recruits were branded as if they were slaves (Dill, *RSWE* 235 ff.).

[5] See Lecoy de la Marche, *S. Martin* (Tours, 1881), 85 f.

than that of how Martin, when the troops were stationed at Amiens, encountered at the gate of the city a poor naked beggar. It was mid-winter; the snow lay deep, but the youth of eighteen at once took off his cloak— for his purse was empty—cut it in two and gave half to the beggar, amid the jeers of his barrack companions. But that same night

'Martin had a vision of the Christ clothed in the same half cloak with which he had clad the beggar. Ere long he heard Jesus proclaim in a clear voice to the hosts of angels that stood around: "Martin, though but a catechumen,[1] hath clothed me with this robe"' (*VM* 3).

Sulpicius adds that 'in no wise puffed up with human glory Martin hastened to receive baptism.'

For two years after his baptism, which took place when he was twenty,[2] Martin continued to serve in the army. About this time also he paid a visit to Hilary of Poictiers, who was anxious to ordain him a priest. In December 358 [3] he won his discharge. In consequence of his brilliant victory at Strassburg (357) and subse-

[1] As was so commonly the case, Martin had deferred his baptism. Cf. the remarkable case of Constantine the Great.

[2] See *VM* 2.

[3] The chronology of Martin is difficult. Assuming that Sulpicius (*VM* 4) is right in his mention of Julian as 'Caesar,' the incident must be the campaign of Julian in 358 (on which see Gibbon, ii. 280 f.), and in any case could not have taken place before Dec. 355. Deducting 22 we get the date of birth as 336, or at earliest 334, instead of the usual date 316. This latter date is, however, clearly wrong in any case; for as Hilary did not become a Christian until 350 or bishop until 353, this would throw Martin's visit to him out of gear with Sulpicius' *VM* 5, unless we assumed a 15 years' interval between his leaving the army and his visit to Hilary, of which Sulpicius gives no hint. To date the incident of the discharge in 355-6, though giving an opportunity for the first visit to Hilary (see *infra*), seems to me difficult, as Julian took no part in any campaign that year.

quent successful campaigns against the Franks, Julian the Apostate, who on 6 Nov. 355 had been appointed 'Caesar' by the emperor Constantius, granted a donation to the soldiers. Martin, who was at Worms, boldly claimed that as his share he should be allowed ' to become a soldier of God.' For this he was imprisoned, but speedily released. His immediate movements are uncertain; but about this time he undertook a journey to Pannonia [1] with the object of converting his parents. Thence he retired to Milan. His stout opposition to Arianism had already led to his public scourging, and Auxentius the Arian bishop drove him from the city to the island of Gallinaria [2] in the Gulf of Genoa (359). In 361, on the return of Hilary from exile, Martin, who had failed to intercept Hilary in Rome, followed him to Poictiers,[3] and shortly afterwards adopted the monastic life,[4] a step that led to large consequences.

On the after life of Martin, on the miracles that he wrought or was thought to have wrought—many of

[1] See *supra*, p. 102. The visit to Pannonia is usually placed (as Sulp. Sev. *VM* 5) after his visit to Hilary. I have attempted to rectify the chronology by placing it before. Sulpicius tells us that the Milan incident occurred while Hilary was in exile (*VM* 6).

[2] Urgo or Gorgona, near the modern Allenga.

[3] Hilary was in exile 'in Asia' from June 356-9. He then received permission to return, but took nearly a year over it. Martin's visit cannot therefore be dated before 360-1. To date the visit in 355 (*DCB* iii. 56) after the discharge is to disregard Sulpicius' statement *re* Julian (*supra*), and to date earlier is to overlook in addition that Hilary was already a bishop at that time (*VM* 5), who tried to ordain Martin a presbyter. The date of this first visit to Hilary is therefore a great difficulty. The easiest way out seems to me to take it as paid while Martin was still a soldier. [The chronology of Martin that I have given was worked out before I had seen Reinkens' *Martin v. Tours*, 245–57, which practically gives the same conclusions.]

[4] *VM* 6. See *infra*, p. 120.

them undoubtedly cures of neurotic cases[1]—on the respect that he inspired even in such rough characters as the usurping emperor Maximus[2] or in the ferocious freebooter Avitianus,[3] on his humility—as a bishop Martin would never sit on the usual throne, but always on a 'rude little stool such as those in use by the lowest servants'[4]—on his boundless generosity and unfailing tenderness, and on his noble efforts to save the Priscillianists from persecution[5]—it is no light honour to have been the first to protest against capital punishment for heresy—our scanty limits forbid that we should dwell. His name will ever be surrounded with the pure glory of goodness.

'O man thrice blessed,' writes his biographer, 'in whom there was no guile, who judged none and condemned none, and never returned evil for evil. No one ever saw him angry or disturbed or in sorrow or laughter. He was always one and the same,

---

[1] The question of medieval miracles lies outside my limits. But no one can study the records of Monasticism and airily dismiss the whole as instances of the untruth of the biographers, as was done until recently by some unscientific historians (e.g. Milner, *Ch. History*, ii. 193). The questions of what did happen and how did it happen can only be approached on the lines of strict investigation, not of *a priori* generalizations, either on one side or the other. The psychological question of the bearing on veracity or trustworthiness of the state of mind that expects miracles needs investigation. I may state that I have not allowed it to weigh against an author's veracity, if otherwise probable, however evident his leaning to the credulous. To the modern mind the two things are connected in a way that does not appear to be true of the medieval (cf. my remarks in *PEC* 129–30).

[2] *VM* 20. *Dial.* ii. 6.   [3] *Dial.* iii. 4, 8.

[4] *Dial.* ii. 1.

[5] *Dial.* iii. 11 f. Cf. Sulp. Sev. *Sac. Hist.* 50–1, whose remarks are worth reading. Martin's effort to save the persecution of the Priscillianists (on whom see Hefele, *HC* II. i. 66, 108, 481; *DCB* iv. 470 f.; Duchesne, *EHC* ii. 419 f.)—a dark chapter in the rise of intolerance—is one of the noblest incidents in his life. With Priscillian as a preacher of asceticism Martin would have much sympathy.

and seemed something other than mortal, wearing on his countenance a sort of celestial joy. Never was anything on his lips but Christ, never a feeling in his heart but piety, peace, and pity' (*VM* cc. 26, 27).

The death of Martin was in keeping with his life. Hearing that the clerics of Condate [1] 'were at variance among themselves, Martin, wishing to restore peace, although he well knew that the end of his own days was at hand, did not shrink from undertaking the journey.' His object accomplished, he purposed to return to his monastery. But the sudden failure of his strength showed that his work was finished. 'Lord,' murmured the dying man, his thoughts going back to his early life,

'"I will serve under Thy standard as long as Thou shalt prescribe. But if now Thou art merciful to my many years, good, O Lord, is Thy will to me, for Thou Thyself wilt guard over those for whose safety I fear."'

When the hour of his passing came he ordered his friends to lay him upon the ground : 'How else,' he asked, 'should a Christian die except among ashes?' In his last moments he thought he saw the Devil, whom he had so often met and overthrown, standing close to him:

'"Why do you stand here, bloody monster?" he cried. "Thou shalt find nothing in me. Abraham's bosom is ready to receive me." As he uttered these words his spirit fled, and those who were present testified to us that they saw his face as if it had been the face of an angel.' [2]

---

[1] There were several towns of this name in Gaul. As the one in question must have been in the diocese of Tours it was probably the modern Candes on the Loire (Lecoy, *op. cit.* 359).

[2] The year of his death is not quite certain, though the day, 11 Nov. (Martinmas), is beyond dispute. The year is usually stated as 397, but more probably it should be 401. Cf. Reinkens, *op. cit.* 253 f. (See *Dial.* iii. 13, where the reading *sedecim*, 'he lived sixteen years

MONASTICISM AS AN INSTITUTION

The popularity of St. Martin both during his lifetime and after his death was unbounded. Few saints have so stamped their name on later generations. Every would-be renunciant of the world began his vocation, if possible, by visiting the saint's tomb. Every monastery had an oratory that bore his name. Within a few years of his death churches were dedicated to his memory in Italy, Spain, and Gaul.[1] When Ninian, the first preacher of the gospel to the Northern Picts, built his rude stone church at Whithern or Candida Casa in Galloway, it was with the name of Martin that it was dedicated,[2] whilst the church of St. Martin at Canterbury, the oldest church in England, was in existence long before the mission of St. Augustine.[3] There are few old towns in which his name is not still perpetuated in the name of church or road, nearly four thousand dedications in France alone witnessing to his hold upon the people. Nor was his fame limited to Christian lands. Even before his death a heathen Egyptian 'sailing on the Tuscan sea' was heard to cry

after this,' gives us the date of death; for the date of execution of Priscillian (to which reference is made) is 385. For the reading *undecim* there seems no authority, and it is this reading that has given us 397.)

[1] For an example of the method whereby dedications of ancient churches to St. Martin have been used to determine the date of the introduction of Christianity into certain parts of Brittany (*infra*, p. 197), see de la Borderie, *Hist. de Bretagne*, i. 201-2. According to Lecoy de la Marche, *op. cit.* 500, there are 3675 churches dedicated to him in France and 425 'bourgs, hameaux ou villages' that bear his name. Germany is similar: 64 churches in the diocese of Cologne, 68 in Treves, 23 in Mainz, &c. (Heimbucher, *OKK* i. 172).

[2] Bede, *HE* iii. 4. There seems no authority for the later legend that Ninian heard of Martin's death while the church was building.

[3] Bede, *HE* i. 26; H and S, *Councils*, i. 15, 37; and for Martin's connection with Britain, *ib.* i. 13.

out in the agony of a great storm, 'O God of Martin, save us';[1] while the writings of Sulpicius Severus carried the story of this Greatheart of Gaul through the Roman Empire 'from the Fortunate Islands to the northern ice.' By a curious irony of etymology his memory is preserved in every Nonconformist place of worship throughout the English-speaking world. For among the relics of the Merovingian kings there was none that was so venerated as the little cloak (*capella*) of St. Martin,[2] the tunic that he had cut at Amiens. This cloak accompanied the kings everywhere; it was the surety of victory in their struggle with their foes; on it all solemn oaths were sealed. The oratory where it was guarded by numerous priests called *capellani* became known from its priceless treasure as the *capella* or chapel of St. Martin. From this royal oratory the name has passed not only to all the other oratories of the Roman Church, but to the places of worship of those the majority of whom may never have heard of the tunic of St. Martin, but who yet bear their unconscious testimony to the far-reaching influence of this glorious saint.

V

We shall have occasions elsewhere to note other factors in the *Life of St. Martin* which conduced to this extraordinary popularity; though the student who reads the book for himself—if he put on one side modern difficulties with reference to the miraculous—will

---

[1] Sulp. Sev. *Dial.* iii. 14.

[2] For the history of this relic, see Cabrol, *DACL* iii. 381 f.; and for the derivation of *capella*, *ib.* iii. 409 f.

need no arguments to convince him of its merits. Suffice for the moment that we remember that these virtues and graces are definitely linked, both in the *Life of Anthony* and in the *Life of Martin*, with renunciation, or rather with Monasticism as the perfect expression of renunciation. The influence of these works and of the lives that they portrayed was seen in the rapid spread, both in the East and West, of the new movement. In every land, in spite of the hostility of the Church, never more pronounced than in its opposition to Martin, the new institution came to stay. In Egypt, so rapid was the spread of the new cult under the lead of Pachomius that Rufinus could utter the exaggerated boast: ' the multitude of monks in the deserts equals the population of the cities.'[1] According to Palladius, in his sixteen monasteries Pachomius ruled over three thousand monks, while in the Nitria there were five thousand, dwelling in fifty lauras.[2] Schenoudi, also, is said to have had under his care nearly four thousand monks and nuns.[3]

From Egypt Monasticism was introduced into Syria by Charito of Iconium, whose life, as it has come down to us, is mostly legendary,[4] and by Hilarion of Gaza.[5]

---

[1] Rufinus, *Hist. Mon.* 5.

[2] *HL* 7 (2), 32 (8); Ladeuze, *ECP* 204–5. In his preface to the *Reg. Pach.* Jerome exaggerates the number into 50,000, and in *VP* (in *PL* 73, p. 433) we have the absurd statement that the monastery of Macarius at Pernoudj contained 15,000.

[3] Leipoldt, *Schenute v. Atripé* 93.   [4] In *PG* 115, pp. 899 ff.

[5] For Hilarion we have Jerome's semi-historical *Vita Hilarionis* (in *PL* 23, p. 29 f.), written at Bethlehem about 390; sundry notices in Sozomen, *HE* iii. 14, vi. 32; and in the *VP* (*PL* 73). A hitherto unknown *Vita* has recently been published at Constantinople (1898) in the 'Ανάλεκτα 'Ιεροσολ. Σταχυολογίας. The student should consult Zöckler, *Hilarion v. Gaza* in *NJDT* (1894) iii. 146–78; or, for opposite view, W. Israel, *Die Vita S. Hilarion* in *ZWT* (1880) 129–65.

Hilarion was born at Tabatha near Gaza about the year 291. Owing to his abilities he was sent for further education to Alexandria, but there became a Christian and a follower of Anthony. At the age of fifteen he returned to Gaza and established himself as a hermit, dwelling for twelve years in his little cabin of 'chips and broken tiles.' In this eremitism Hilarion was not alone, for there already existed in Syria an indigenous growth of pre-monastic asceticism, whose members were known as *B'nai Q'yāmâ* or "Sons of the Covenant."[1] The ground was therefore already prepared for further developments. Such were the crowds that flocked to Hilarion that in his sixty-third year he once more set off on his wanderings, in spite of the pleadings of his agonized followers. But neither Mesopotamia nor Sicily could protect this wonder-working saint from the people that were drawn to him. At length he found a cave in Cyprus sufficiently inaccessible to visitors, and there he passed away (21 Oct. 371). 'Go forth, my soul,' murmured the dying saint, 'why do you hesitate? You have served Christ nearly eighty years; do you still fear death?' Within a few years of Hilarion's death monasteries and lauras had arisen in all parts of Palestine; the lead in organization being taken by Epiphanius of Eleutheropolis.[2]

---

[1] According to F. Burkitt (*Early East. Christianity*, 128 f.) these were the baptized laity of the Syrian Church, and therefore celibates (see *supra*, p. 61). For further on this matter, see the criticism of Burkitt by R. H. Connolly in the *JTS* vi. 522–39.

[2] For the later developments in Palestine, see Heimbucher, *OKK* i. 116 f; Cabrol, *DACL* ii. 3161 f. S. Vailhé, *Répertoire alphabétique des monastères de Palestine* in the *Rev. de l'Orient Chrét.* (Paris, 1900), gives historical notices of 137 Palestinian cloisters. For a description of their condition in the 8th cent. see Tobler and Molinier, *Itinera et Descriptiones* (Geneva, 1879), i. 302.

The founder of Monasticism in Mesopotamia was Mar Awgîn (Eugenius)[1] the Egyptian. Mar Awgîn († 363) was originally a pearl-fisher near Suez, who forsook all and betook himself to the monastery of Pachomius. Thence he departed for Mesopotamia and built a monastery in the mountains near Nisibis. The details of his life are legendary and uncertain; but with Aphraates, who lived in a monastery near Mosul between the years 336 and 345, we come upon certain ground. So rapid was the spread of the monastic life throughout the East that by the end of the fourth century we find it firmly established in Mount Sinai, Armenia, and Persia.[2]

Of greater, more lasting importance was the introduction of Monasticism into the Greek Church. The first Greek to countenance the monastic system seems to have been Eustathius of Sebaste,[3] an episcopal vicar of Bray in the Arian controversies of the times; but the real founder was the famous St. Basil († 379),[4] who in the year 357 set out on his travels with the sole

---

[1] For Mar Awgîn (whom Sozomen, *HE* vi. 33, calls Aones, though cf. Zöckler, *AM* 233 n.), see E. W. Budge, *Book of the Governors*, i. Introd. pp. xliv, cxxv–xxxi. E. Butler (*Camb. Mod. Hist.* i. 526) rejects him as unhistorical, and the date is certainly suspicious. His chronology is uncertain. Assemann puts his foundation at Nisibis before the Council of Nicea (325); others in 333.

[2] Heimbucher, *OKK* i. 119–21; Cabrol, *DACL* ii. 3142–3.

[3] Siwas in Armenia Minor. For Eustathius († c. 380), see Soc. *HE* ii. 43; Soz. *HE* iii. 14; and for his life *DCB* s.v. (4); Loofs, *Eustathius v. Sebaste*, Halle (1898).

[4] The contention of E. Marin, *Les Moines de Constantinople* (Paris, 1897), 4–6, for monasteries in Constantinople founded by Constantine is rejected by the best scholars, as also his belief in a pre-Constantine monastery founded in 240 by bishop Castinus (*op. cit.* 3). According to Callinicus, *Vita Hypatii* (Leipzig, 1895), p. 8, Constantinople only possessed one monastery (St. Isaac's) in the year 384.

object of studying Monasticism. Few bishops of the Eastern Church, not even Chrysostom himself, have left behind them a greater name for saintliness and indefatigable energy than Basil. As Athanasius was the great champion of Catholic faith against Arian error when at the flood, so Basil in the East, Ambrose in the West, were the chief instruments in the hand of God in repairing the breaches when the first fury of the storm was over. From 370–79 from his see at Caesarea Basil practically ruled the Eastern Church by the fervour of his piety, the strength of his intellect, and the width of his outlook; this, too, in spite of a sickly constitution which made it difficult for him to travel without pain, and which rendered even his abstemious meals of 'vegetables and salt a weariness to him.'[1] 'Thanks very much,' Basil once answered with a smile, when the sub-prefect of Pontus threatened that if he did not yield to his demands he should be torn with combs, 'Thanks; by such laceration you will cure my liver, which, as you see is wearing me away.'[2]

As indicative of Basil's attitude to Monasticism, this letter, written about 375 to Eustathius, will be read with interest. Human documents of this sort are of perennial value:

'Long time had I spent in vanity and had wasted almost the whole of my youth in the idle toil of studying that wisdom which God has made folly. Then at length, raised as from a deep sleep, I gazed upon the marvellous light of Gospel truth, and discerned the unprofitableness of the wisdom taught by the rulers of this world, which are coming to nought. Much did I bewail my wretched life, and pray that guidance would be vouchsafed to

---

[1] Basil, *Ep.* 41 § 1.
[2] Greg. Naz. *Orat.* 43 § 57. This Oration is a panegyric on St. Basil of great power and beauty.

MONASTICISM AS AN INSTITUTION

me for an entrance into the doctrines of godliness. And, above all, was it a care to me to reform my heart, which the long society of the corrupt had perverted. So I read the Gospel and perceived that the best start toward perfection was to sell my goods and share them with my poor brethren, to be altogether reckless of this life, and to rid my soul of all sympathy with things on earth. I earnestly desired to find some brother who had made the same choice, that with him I might make passage over the troublesome waves of this life. Many did I find in Egypt, in Palestine, in Syria, and Mesopotamia, whose abstinence and endurance I admired, and at whose constancy in prayer I was amazed : how they overcame sleep, being subdued by no natural necessity ; having ever a high and free spirit in hunger and thirst, in cold and nakedness ; not regarding the body, nor willing to spend any thought upon it, but living as if in flesh not their own ; how they showed in deed what it is to sojourn in this world, and what it is to have one's conversation in heaven.' [1]

As the result of his travels Basil withdrew, about the year 358, to his solitude on the Iris near Neocaesarea in Pontus, and there lived in a roofless hut on bread that wrenched the teeth from the jaws. From these extravagances, into which he seems to have been led by Eustathius, Basil afterwards escaped. Greek and Russian Monasticism has remained much in the form which the *Rule* attributed to him first impressed upon it.[2]

The introduction of Monasticism into the West, though really the development of tendencies already at work, may be said to have been due to the great

---

[1] Basil, *Ep.* 223 (2). Other letters of Basil on the same subject are numerous: cf. 22, 23, 44, 45, 46. See also Greg. Naz. *Epp.* 5–7 ; *Orat.* 20 ; Greg. Nyss. *de Basil* (funeral oration) ; Sozomen, *HE* vi. 17.

[2] *Infra*, p. 153. For the later history and numbers of the Basilian monasteries, see Heimbucher, *OKK* i. 125–41. The chief reforms were by Theodore of the Studium († 826). Many of the Basilian monasteries, especially among the Ruthenians, are R.C. (Heimbucher, *OKK* i. 136 f.).

Athanasius.[1] To the remarkable influence of his *Life of Anthony* we have already alluded. But Athanasius did more than assist the new movement with his pen. On the 16th April 339, some years before this work was written, Athanasius once more set out from Alexandria [2] as a fugitive and journeyed to Rome, in which city he abode three years. There, in the house of the Christian widow with whom he lodged, he met the lady Marcella. From his lips she learned the story of 'Anthony, who was still alive, of Pachomius and of his virgins and widows.'[3] In consequence of the impulse thus received towards the ascetic life Marcella was the first in Rome to make the monastic profession,[4] though continuing to live with her mother in her palace on the Aventine.[5] Either into this monastery or into an offshoot from it we find Marcellina, the sister of Ambrose, seeking admission on Christmas Eve, 352.[6] The naturalization of the new institution in Italy, thus begun by Athanasius and

---

[1] For the origins of Monasticism in Italy reference should be made to the monograph of E. Spreitzenhofer, *Die Entwicklung des alt. Mönchtums in Italien* (Vienna, 1894).

[2] For the date, see A. Robertson, *Select Writings of Athanasius* (*NPN Lib.*), Introd. p. lxxxii (Hefele, *HC* I. ii. 695, dates in 340). Athanasius was accompanied by two monks: Isidore, ' who never touched a bath ' (*HL* 1), and Ammon (Soc. *HE* iv. 23), who never stirred out to see a single sight in the city.

[3] Jerome, *Ep.* 127 (5); really a memoir of Marcella.

[4] The total silence of the catacombs shows that Monasticism in Rome was of late origin, at any rate was unrecognized. But the story of Sarapion Sindon's visit to Rome (*supra*, p. 50) shows that monastic tendencies were there before Marcella.

[5] Jerome, *Ep.* 47 (3). Marcella died a few days after the sack of Rome by Alaric as a result of injuries then received [*Ep.* 127 (13)], leaving all her wealth to the poor. Her sister Asella was made a church-virgin at the age of ten (*Ep.* 24). She lived on bread and salt, often fasting two or three days at a time.

[6] Ambrose, *de Virg.* iii. 1.

Marcella, was continued by Eusebius of Vercellae,[1] by Rufinus, by Ambrose, above all by Jerome, who in this as in much else formed the connecting link between East and West. In 404 Jerome translated into Latin the *Rule of Pachomius*, thus introducing to Italy the more organized form of the Egyptian ascetic movement. But of greater importance than any single writing was the constant emphasis of Monasticism which we find in his *Letters*, of which a volume, addressed to Marcella had been published in 392 for the benefit of the nuns in her Aventine palace.

The views of Jerome on Monasticism are well known, and their importance cannot be exaggerated. Born in 346 at Stridon in Dalmatia [2] he had at an early date come under ascetic influences, possibly through intercourse with Eusebius of Vercellae. These were strengthened by a visit to Antioch and Syria (374–79), where for four years he lived in a cell in the desert of Chalcis, weaving baskets and copying books. He found that 'through fear of hell he had condemned himself to prison,' and in a later letter he describes his spiritual struggles and esctasies. Driven away by the ill-will of his fellow-monks—for Jerome was never happy unless he were hewing some Agag in pieces before the Lord—he returned to Rome (382), and there met Paula and her three daughters, Blaesilla, Eustochium, and Paulina, who, with the older Marcella and Asella, formed a band of patrician ladies devoted to the ascetic life. To these he poured out his soul in praises of virginity; his letter to Eustochium, by the grossness of its allusions, forming the most

[1] *Infra*, p. 253.
[2] Stridon was destroyed by the Goths in 378. Its situation is uncertain; see Grützmacher, *Hieronymus*, 105–6.

remarkable document that a saint ever wrote to a pure-minded girl. In 385 he was compelled to leave Rome, having failed, fortunately for the Church, to secure the papal chair. So he set off with Paula and Eustochium to Palestine and Egypt, all finally establishing themselves at Bethlehem in a monastery and nunnery built for them with Paula's wealth. There Jerome lived for the remaining thirty-four years of his stormy career, engaged in those literary works which have given him deathless renown, and which he dedicated to these great ladies.[1] One by one he saw his friends slip away—Paula in 403, Marcella in Rome in 410, and Eustochium in 418. He died (20 Sept. 420) as he had lived, amidst troubles and controversies; his monasteries attacked by swarms of angry Pelagian monks (418), himself nursed through a long illness (419) by the younger Paula and Melania. He was buried by the side of Paula and Eustochium, near to the grotto of the Saviour's birth.

With Jerome Monasticism is the one perfect form of renunciation; he never wearies in dwelling on its merits. He is not unconscious of the difficulties in the way of the would-be renunciant:

'I have passed through troubles like yours myself. Now it is a widowed sister who throws her arms around you. Now it is the slaves who cry: "To what master are you leaving us"? Now it is a nurse bowed with age, and a body servant loved only less than a Father, who exclaim : " Only wait till we die, and follow us to our graves." Perhaps, too, an aged mother, recalling the lullaby with which she once soothed you, adds her entreaties.'

But he mentions these difficulties only to add that 'the

[1] The friendship of Jerome for these ladies led to scandal in later years. In the dedications of his writings it was common for scribes to scratch out their names and substitute 'venerable brothers'! (Cabrol, *DACL* ii. 3178 n.).

love of God and the fear of hell will easily break such bonds,' for the 'battering-ram of natural affections will recoil powerless from the wall of the Gospel.'[1] But his experiences in early life made him see the valuelessness of the hermit, with 'his chains and his dirt,' and his claim to 'judge the world from the depths of his caves,' in comparison with the more organized monastic forms.

By the end of the fourth century monasteries of both sexes abounded in Italy,[2] and in the isles of the Mediterranean. "There was much in the monastic life thoroughly in keeping with what remained among Romans of their pristine sternness; it was a congenial reaction from the luxury and effeminacy of the day."[3] In the next century we find the new movement receiving not only the support of St. Augustine but of the papacy. Sextus III (432-40) founded a monastery on the Appian Way, and Leo the Great established one in connection with St. Peter's.[4] But the Monasticism thus introduced, though not without the elements of a Rule,[5] was too often of the Eastern type, attended with the usual Eastern

---

[1] Jerome, *Ep.* (14) 3, a very rhetorical passage on the monastic life written to Heliodorus, who had turned back to more clerical duties (373). Jerome's views on Monasticism can be best gathered from a study of the following Epistles: *Epp.* 14; 17 (his life at Chalcis); 22 (the remarkable letter to Eustochium); 23 (*re* Lea); 24 (*re* Asella); 38, 39 (*re* Blesilla); 46; 66 (*re* Paulina); 107; 108 (*re* Paula); 125; 127 (*re* Marcella).

For the chronology of Jerome's early life and writings the best account is in G. Grützmacher, *Hieronymus* (Leipzig, 1901).

[2] See Zöckler, *AM* 329-31. Spreitzenhofer, *op. cit.* 17-35, gives the full list, compressed in Heimbucher, *OKK* i. 157 f., 164, 198-9.

[3] *DCA* ii. 1221.

[4] Duchesne, *Lib. Pont.* i. 213, 216, 222, 234, 239. Cf. Spreitzenhofer, *op. cit.* 11.

[5] Cf. Jerome, *Ep.* 130 (15), written in 414.

disorders. Rules, where they existed, were local, and often depended on the will of the abbot.[1] The transformation of this Monasticism into a form more akin to the genius of the West was not the work of a day. But, as we might expect from the Roman genius, between Jerome and Benedict we see the monastic profession taking more and more a definite, solemn form, with suitable restrictions and commensurate obligations.[2]

In South Gaul Monasticism seems at first to have appeared at Marseilles, though not, we gather, under the happiest auspices. The indiscretions, if no worse, of the 'Sarabaitae' and 'Gyrovagi'—two classes of monkish vagabonds that drew down the wrath of Benedict [3]—justified the opposition of the bishops. The new ideal would have had but scanty hopes of survival had it not been for the influence of the famous Martin. He gathered around him, first at Ligugé [4] then at Marmoutier [5] near Tours, eighty disciples who dwelt in holes hollowed out of the rocks that there overlook the Loire. They were clothed with 'garments of camels' hair,' [6] and spent their time in transcribing books, in prayer, and in deeds of love.[7] Their greatest delight was to accompany Martin on his episcopal visitations. So great was the influence of Martin that

[1] Cf. *Reg. Benedict.* c. 1, ' Primum (genus) coenobitarum, hoc est monasteriale militans sub regula *vel abbate.*'

[2] The steps are clearly detailed in Cabrol, *DACL* ii. 3187 f.

[3] See *infra,* p. 134 n.

[4] *i.e.* Locociagense (Sulp. Sev. *VM* 7), founded about 361. See *supra,* p. 106 n.

[5] *i.e.* majus monasterium. This derivation is better than to regard it as a corruption of ' Martini monasterium.'

[6] Sulp. Sev. evidently had in his mind *Matt.* iii. 4. He can hardly be taken literally in Gaul.

[7] Sulp. Sev. *VM* 10.

when he died two thousand monks followed him to the grave.¹ Though he left no *Rule*, and had allowed his disciples considerable latitude, his *Life* spread his ideals far and wide. In the south of Gaul, where the islands along the Riviera were already a favourite monastic refuge, Honoratus († 429), shortly before 410, landed at Lérins with a band of monks, drove out the serpents with which it swarmed, and established the famous monastery which, within a few years, became a seminary of Gallic bishops and supplied the Church with a rule of faith ² whereby to distinguish Catholic truth from heresy. The alliance between Orthodoxy and Monasticism was complete, nor did an uncritical generation notice that one of the first effects of Vincent's formula, if strictly applied in past days, would have been to rule out Monasticism itself as a Catholic form of life.

From Lérins and Marmoutier monks spread over the face of Gaul. About 410 John Cassian returned from his journey to the East and settled at Marseilles.³ There, over the burying-place of a martyred Roman soldier, " in the midst of those great forests which had supplied the Phoenician navy, and which in the time of Caesar reached as far as the coast, whose mysterious obscurity, also, had so terrified the Roman soldiers that the conqueror to embolden them had himself taken an axe and struck down an old oak," ⁴ Cassian gathered (413–416) into his two monasteries of St. Victor and St. Mary over 5000 monks and nuns. For their

¹ Sulp. Sev. *Ep.* 3. See for date, *supra*, p. 108 n.
² For the famous rule of Vincent of Lérins († c. 450), ' Quod semper, quod ubique, quod ab omnibus creditum est,' see his *Commonitorium*, c. 2, published in 434.
³ For Cassian's life and works, see App. A, § V, *infra*, p. 359.
⁴ Montalembert, *MW* i. 464.

benefit he published the codes of monastic life that he entitled *Institutes* and *Conferences*. Nor was success limited to Marseilles and Lérins. About this time we hear as far north as Rouen of monks 'emaciated by fasting,' who kept up a perpetual chant in the cathedral, as well as of a 'choir of virgins.'[1] 'Not only,' cries Cassian in triumph, 'the countries of the West, but even the isles now flourish with great crowds of brethren.'[2] Cassian probably was referring to the islands off the Riviera; possibly, however, he was thinking of Ireland, in which Christianity was already organizing itself on a monastic basis.[3] Within a few years of Cassian's death we see the commencement also of Monasticism in Germany, through the missionary labours of Severin († 482) the apostle of Noricum, whose benevolent rule saved his flock in times of famine and flood, and protected them from the exactions of the Rugian barbarians.[4] In Africa and Spain, on the contrary, we see loss and decline. The vigorous Monasticism which had established itself before the close of the fourth century was largely overwhelmed by the Wisigoth and Vandal invasions. But the conversion of Spain under Reccared in 587 from Arianism to Catholicism gave Monasticism a new opportunity, soon to be blighted by the Muslim conquests.

Nevertheless, in spite of these advances, monasteries were still few in number in the West as compared with

---

[1] S. Victricius, *de laude sanctorum*, c. 3 in *PL* 20, p. 445.

[2] Cassian, *Coll.* iii. Pref. Cf. Paulinus of Nola, *Ep.* 18 (5), to Victricius (in *CSEL*, 1894, xxix. 132).

[3] *Infra*, c. 4.

[4] The *Vita Severini* was written by his friend Eugippius in 511. Best ed. is by P. Knöll in *CSEL* ix. (2), 1886. For other founders of German monasteries (*e.g.* Fridolin), see *infra*, p. 201 f.

the East, a fact attributed by Cassian to the laziness of Western monks as compared with their brethren in Egypt.[1] Though in the sixth century their numbers increased, the life of the monks themselves inclined to grow stagnant. Each monastery, in spite of the tendency to uniformity given by the writings of Cassian, was a little world in itself, governed by different rules—some by the *Rule* of Cassian,[2] others by that of Caesarius of Arles († 542), who has given us the first known *Rule* for nuns;[3] some, as for instance the monasteries of Spain,[4] adopted that of Basil, or patched up a *rule* to suit their own needs from the *Rules* of Anthony,[5] Pachomius, or Macarius.[6] Some were a Rule unto themselves, as in fact Martin himself had been; a state of things which, when without the enthusiasm and saintliness of St. Martin, often issued in a Monasticism without *Rule* at all. In some cases a divided allegiance was given under the roof of the same monastery to several *Rules* at once.[7]

[1] Cassian, *Instit.* x. 23.

[2] Zöckler, *AM* 341; Smith, *CM* 56, deny that Cassian published a *Rule*. Until recently it could only be inferred from the *Concordia Regularum* of Benedict of Aniane (see Holsten, *CR*). But the text of the *Rule* of Cassian has recently been found in Munich, and some fragments in the Escurial. See H. Plenkers, *Untersuchungen zur überlieferungsgeschichte der ältesten lateinischen Mönchsregeln* (Munich, 1906), pp. 70-84.

[3] In *PL* 67, p. 1105 ff.; briefly in Heimbucher, *OKK* i. 200, *DCA* ii. 1236. There is an analysis of it in Cabrol, *DACL* ii. 3201 f. For Caesarius the best biography is by A. Malnory, *St. Césaire* (Paris, 1894).   [4] Heimbucher, *OKK* i. 203.

[5] Anthony never wrote a *Rule*. That which went by his name was the compilation of the Syrian abbot Isaiah (in Holsten, *CR* i. 6 f. or *PL* 103, p. 425).

[6] *DCA* ii. 1222; *PL* 103, p. 435.

[7] For these various *Rules*, see Heimbucher, *OKK* i. 176-9; *DCA* ii. 1229-38 (a very full account); and for mixed *Rules* in the same monastery, Greg. Tur. *Hist. Franc.* x. 29 (*MGH rer. Merov.* 441).

VI

Nothing is more instructive than to note that from the very first Monasticism seems to have been conscious of its need of regulation. Undoubtedly, as the meaning of the word ' monk ' shows, Monasticism started with the individual hermit, seeking by himself to save himself; the monk was strictly the anchorite. In the background of monastic history we see the lofty figure of the protagonist in Egyptian Monasticism, the hermit Anthony, while Pachomius himself began his religious life under the hermit Palaemon. But so quickly did Monasticism pass through its merely individualistic stage, that we find, almost as soon as it emerges out of the mists of romance into the light of history, the solitary hermit—the μοναχός strictly so called— joining himself unto others, seeking to adapt his life to a common rule. Hermits and anchorites, it is true, still survived, especially in Lower Egypt, and in the desert that went by the name of the ' Cells,' but only as the exceptions for whom new names had to be found, inasmuch as their own name had been appropriated by the conforming majority. Monasticism, in fact, almost as soon as it was born, passed through its first transition; monachism gave place to cenobitism, at first the loose organization of the laura or cluster of cells around some common centre, later the stricter rule of a monastery. Thus, by three stages of development,[1] the ' monk ' becomes the brother of the common life, the mark of whose life is not so much his isolation as

---

[1] Cf. K. Lake, *The Early Days of Monasticism on Mount Athos* (1909), p. 5–7, 100–1, on the developments of Monasticism in Mount Athos.

his socialism. But at this development we need feel no surprise; it falls in perfectly with the laws of all true renunciation. For renunciation, though it starts with the individualistic standpoint, cannot long content itself with this. By a law of being the renunciant cannot remain a law unto himself, or condition his salvation by himself.

Of the historical truth of this position there can be no doubt. The study of Monasticism has been obscured and hindered by the way in which for many centuries romance has been mistaken for fact. In popular writings the idea of a religious Robinson Crusoe has had a hold out of all proportion to its actual accomplishment. So long as men regarded the *Life of Anthony* or that of *Paul* as the chief documents on the subject, so long as Pachomius was but a name and Schenoudi unknown, it was natural for historians to exaggerate the more individualistic side, the origin of Monasticism in monachism. The student who realizes the great importance of Pachōmius as the real founder of Egyptian monachism can have no justification for this error. Pachomius rapidly passes from the hermit, a law unto himself, into the head of a well-organized, self-supporting community of nine monasteries. In the accounts which have come down to us we see him laying down rules and regulations, the outlines of organization, a congregation, a chapter, and a system of visitation for the separate monasteries from the head monastery at Pabau (to which Pachomius had transferred his residence from Tabennîsi), that reminds the student of later developments at Citeaux.[1]

After Pachomius the greatest figure in the history of

[1] See *infra*, p. 243. For the system of visitation from Pabau, see Cabrol, *DACL* ii. 3118; Ladeuze, *ECP* 173, 286.

Egyptian Monasticism is that of Schenoudi of Atripé, whose fortress-monastery is still existing to-day under the name of the "white monastery" (*Deir-el-Abiad*).[1] Schenoudi, whose name, even, until recent times was lost to the world of letters,[2] would appear to have been responsible for one development of the Pachomian principles. Pachomius had aimed at doing away with the life of the hermit; Schenoudi looked upon the community life of the monastery as a possible preparation for the few who stood the test to take up the more rigorous life of the solitary. That the tests were too severe even for the lesser austerities of the monastery is evidenced by the constant insubordination against which Schenoudi thunders in vain, and which he tried to repress by corporal punishment. We still possess a letter written to the 'mother' of a convent of nuns, in which he orders the exact number of blows of the rod that must be given to the sisters for various faults in which they had been detected. One of his monks actually died from the castigation inflicted by the abbot.[3] Like Benedict of Aniane at a later date,[4] he seems to have mistaken minuteness of regulation and harshness of discipline for the mainsprings of true renunciation.

---

[1] For its situation, see Cabrol, *DACL* ii. 3113; A. J. Butler, *Ancient Coptic Churches of Egypt* (Oxford, 1884), ii. 351–61, plan on p. 352.

[2] Schenoudi [b. about 334, d. 451; see Leipoldt, *op. cit.* 44–7; but Bethune-Baker in *JTS* (1908) 601–5 contends for 7 July 466] has been made known to us by the researches of Ladeuze, *ECP* 116 f.; Amélineau, *Vie de Schenoudi* (Paris, 1889); and J. Leipoldt, *Schenute von Atripé* (in *TU*, xxv, 1903). As he spoke and wrote in Sahidic Coptic he is never mentioned by any Greek or Roman writer, not even by Palladius, who must have seen his monastery on his visit to Panopolis. In consequence he disappeared from view until recent Coptic discoveries.

[3] Leipoldt, *op. cit.* 141–3.   [4] See *infra*, p. 227.

The introduction by Schenoudi of vows, or rather of an approximation to vows, a matter unknown to Pachomius, was one natural result of this tendency.[1]

The influence of Pachomius and Schenoudi must not be exaggerated. Egyptian Monasticism remained divided between two tendencies corresponding roughly with the immemorial geographical divisions of the country. In Upper Egypt, where the influence of Pachomius was supreme, his example was almost universally followed. Monasticism south of Lycopolis to the districts of Ethiopia became a system of cenobitism. Even in Lower Egypt, where the influence of Anthony predominated, the pure eremitical type tended to die out in favour of a loose but effective community life.[2] The monks who claimed the mountains of the Nitria,[3] a desert some sixty miles south of Alexandria, for their own, or who, under the lead of Macarius the Egyptian, dwelt in the nitrous wastes of Scete, soon became a republic five thousand strong, dwelling in fifty 'lauras' or congregations, capable of striking terror into the heart of Roman governors by the unity of their orthodoxy.

We see the same tendency elsewhere. When St. Basil the Great introduced Monasticism into the Greek Church, at first, as we have seen,[4] he was led astray by the extreme austerities of his then friend but later foe, Eustathius

---

[1] The matter is not certain. See Amélineau, *op. cit.* 44; Leipoldt, *op. cit.* 109, 195–6. We see the same tendency to formal vows in Basil, *Reg. fus. tractat.* 14 (*PG* 31, p. 950).

[2] There was a Pachomian monastery as far north as Canope near Alexandria.

[3] For the situation of the Nitria—the Wady Natron—of Scete, and of the "Cells" (Τὰ Κελλία) see Butler, *HL* ii. 187–90; Cabrol, *DACL* ii. 3126–7; or the investigations of Amélineau in *Géog. de l'Égypte à l'époque copte* (Paris, 1893), 433–52.

[4] *Supra*, p. 113.

of Sebaste. Won over, as he owns, by the 'coarse cloke, the girdle, and the shoes of untanned leather,'[1] for a while he adopted the hermit life. But his common sense, assisted, possibly, by the condemnation of Eustathius and of the excesses of Monasticism at the synod of Gangra,[2] soon cleared away extravagances. 'God,' he wrote, 'has made us, like the members of our body, to need one another's help.'[3] So Basil organized his monks into communities to which he gave a *Rule* more full, minute, and organic than that of Pachomius.[4] Even the intensely individualistic and now schismatical settlements on Mount Athos, soon after their first establishment, recognized a common chief called the 'Protos,' and a common centre at Caryes, where three times a year they all assembled for worship.[5]

This early striving after order, this determination on the part of the monastic renunciant to bring himself under that discipline which is only possible in a common life, is evidenced for us not merely in the *Rule* of Pachomius and in the regulations of Schenoudi, but appears plainly in the accounts of early travellers. The monastic

---

[1] Basil, *Ep.* 223.

[2] The date of this council is very doubtful, but would appear to be about the year 340. See Hefele, *HC* I. ii. 1029 f., and cf. *DCA* i. 709. There can be little doubt that the Eustathius condemned (Canons 12–19, with the Synodical Letter and the Epilogue) for false asceticism was the bishop of Sebaste.

[3] Basil, *Reg. fus. tract.* 7. Cf. *Ep.* 295.

[4] *Supra*, p. 126. For the *Rule* of Basil in its two forms (*fusius tractatae* and *brevius tractatae*), the first draft of which was probably by Eustathius of Sebaste (Soz. *HE* iii. 14), see Zöckler, *AM* 287 f.; Cabrol, *DACL* ii. 3147; *Opera Basil* (ed. Garnier), ii. 199 f. There is a good analysis in *DCA* ii. 1233.

[5] K. Lake, *op. cit.* 92; Heimbucher, *OKK* i. 133–5. Date about 950. Heimbucher gives the present number of monks on Mt. Athos as 7522, of whom 3615 are Russians.

institutions of Egypt, and in part also of Syria, as they existed at the opening of the fifth century, have been described for us by four eyewitnesses of repute and intelligence. These early travellers—Rufinus, or whoever was the author of the book which perhaps Rufinus merely translated;[1] Palladius, the author of the *Historia Lausiaca*, whose account of the Pachomian monastery of Panopolis (Akhmīm) is the most complete that we possess;[2] the Gallic monk Postumian, the narrative of whose second journey to the East is related for us in the lively *Dialogues* of Sulpicius Severus;[3] and Cassian, another Gaul, whose first journey to Egypt was made about the year 385,[4] and whose description is as complete as it is shrewd in tone and wise in sentiment—all show us a Monasticism in which extremes of asceticism, though no doubt admired, are related as exceptions rather than as the rule.

Palladius,[5] who spent two years in the Nitria, has given us an account of the manner of life of the hermits,

[1] See *infra*, App. A, p. 357.   [2] *HL* (Gr.) 32 (9).
[3] Date about 403. See *DCB* iv. 447.
[4] *Infra*, App. A, p. 359. One of the most interesting narratives of Egyptian Monasticism is lost. Between 380–88 a virgin of Bordeaux usually called Silvia but whose name seems to have been Eucheria, visited the monasteries of Jerusalem, Edessa, Sinai and the Thebaid. The last part (Thebaid) is lost; the previous parts have been published as *S. Silviae Aquitaniae Peregrinatio* [ed. Gamurrini, Rome (1887); also ed. P. Geyer in *CSEL* xxxix. (1898), p. 37 f. under the above title]. The general reader may content himself with Glover's interesting account of her pilgrimage in *LLFC* c. 6. Eucheria was, possibly, a daughter of the consul Eucherius (381), the uncle of Theodosius. (See Duchesne, *EHC* ii. 403 n.) But Lucot, *HL* 344 n. gives the name as Etheria and dates between 533–40. Cf. W. Heraeus, *Silviae Peregrinatio* (Heidelberg, 1908). Another famous lady traveller was the elder Melania. The difficulties and dangers of these pilgrimages were very great.
[5] For Palladius, see App. A, p. 355.

from which we see clearly that they were by no means without organization, though the whole system was still voluntary, and each was allowed to discipline himself as he liked.[1] They lived apart or together, as they pleased, in their 'lauras' or clusters of windowless cells, oftentimes deserted tombs. We are told that they were allowed the use of wine, and that they wore rough linen clothes. There were churches in the desert in which on Saturdays and Sundays—for the keeping sacred of both days was common throughout Egypt [2]— the monks assembled for Communion. In Scete alone, according to Cassian, there were four, each with its presbyter; in the Nitria, however, there was but one large church, for evensong was sung by the brethren each in his own cell. Here and there we see a monk counting his beads; one, Paulus, reckoning three hundred prayers a day by little pebbles.[3] The stranger, says Palladius, who suddenly came on the scene, ' would think that he was transplanted into Paradise.' But the ' Paradise ' at times became uncommonly like an American backwood-camp. Summary justice prevailed; great whips hung on palms near the church for beating erring monks, robbers, and others. Strangers—'whom,' says Rufinus, ' the monks ran out from their cells to meet, like a swarm of bees '—were granted a limited hospitality; they were then set to work at the grindstone or in the kitchen, or, in the case of those of better

[1] This description of the Nitria is taken from *HL* 7 (*PL* 73, p. 1098, or Butler, *HL* ii. 24); Rufinus, *Hist. Mon.* 21, 22 (ed. Preuschen, p. 83 f.). For the present state of the Nitrian monasteries, see A. J. Butler, *Ancient Coptic Churches of Egypt*, i. c. 7.

[2] See Butler's excellent note, *HL* ii. 198–9.

[3] *HL* (Gr.) 20 (1). This seems the earliest mention of a rosary (*PL* 74, p. 279, and cf. *DACL* i. 2338 *s.v.* Antinoé).

birth, at the copying out a text.[1] With another matter, also, the observant stranger would be struck: the emphasis laid upon the learning by heart of the Psalter and New Testament. One monk, as he walked with Palladius the forty miles to Scete, recited a portion 'of the Psalter, the *Hebrews, Isaiah*, a part of *Jeremiah*, then *Luke*, and then *Proverbs*.' In the monasteries of Pachomius such memorization was obligatory.[2]

In the *Institutes* of Cassian we see this tendency to organization even more clearly brought out; nor is the value of the evidence lessened when we remember that Cassian only came in contact with eremitical monachism. Unlike Palladius, he never visited the Pachomian foundations. Cassian gives us the results of his own personal investigation; and the ideal that from his travels he deemed best to be introduced into his new convent at Marseilles is founded, in almost every detail, upon the Egyptian precedents. It is impossible to read these works without realizing that Eastern Monasticism was not so completely amorphous as some writers would have us believe. Regulations abound; some dealing with details of dress,[3] in others care is taken as regards the repetition of the Psalter:

'It is not,' says Cassian, 'the number of the verses but the intelligence with which they are repeated that must be our aim: Better to sing two verses with understanding, than a whole Psalm with wandering thoughts' [*Instit.* ii. 11 (1)].

---

[1] Writing was recognized as an eremitical exercise. See Butler, *HL* ii. 36 (the meaning is obscured in the Latin, *PL* 74, p. 263); also *HL* ii. 120, 133 for the monks of Tabennîsî. It is highly probable that the fine *MS* called H of the *Epp.* of St. Paul was the work of Evagrius of Nitria [see Butler, *HL* i. 103-60, and *HL* (Gr.) 38 (10)].

[2] *HL* (Gr.) 26 (3); Butler, *HL* ii. 96. According to *PL* 73, p. 326, Symeon Stylites learned the whole Bible in four months.

[3] *Institut.* Bk. 1.

So the round of prayers is to be judiciously interwoven with the chanting of the Psalms, 'in order that no weariness may creep in among us.'[1] Emphasis is placed upon punctuality,[2] the prevention of waste and breakages —a heavy punishment for the brother who carelessly lost three lentils in preparing the soup—and other virtues of the common life.[3] But this common life was not as yet the common life of the family—for this we must wait until Benedict—but that of an aggregate of individuals, each living in his own cell,[4] or in the house of his trade.[5] Everything was still individualistic and voluntary in this spiritual democracy.

The account given by Postumian, in spite of his love of the incredible, his crude science, and his tendency to exaggerate the value of the life of the recluses upon Mount Sinai, bears out the same conclusion. He tells us that 'for the most part the monks resided together in companies of one hundred.' Even his tales of 'incredible obedience,' exaggerated and repulsive as they may seem to a later generation, witness to an ideal that lies at the root of all community life. So great was the influence of this regulated cenobitism in diminishing extravagance and madness, that Cassian gravely discusses how it is

'that the devils have not now the same power as they had during the early days of the anchorite, when their fierceness was such that but a very few stedfast men, and those advanced in years, were able to endure a life of solitude.'

---

[1] *Instit.* ii. 11 (2).   [2] *Ib.* iii. c. 7.
[3] *Ib.* ii. 3. Cf. the *Rule* of Pachomius, cc. 8, 9, 125.
[4] The continued cell-life even of monks in a *coenobium* is clearly brought out in Cassian, *Instit.* ii. 12, 14, 15. This is the second stage in monastic development; see *supra*, p. 124.
[5] See *infra*, p. 155.

So great is the change from the times when in the colonies of the hermits 'they did not dare to go to bed all at once, by night, but took turns. While some snatched a little sleep, others kept watch and devoted themselves to prayer and the Psalms.'[1]

We have dwelt upon this matter at length because of its importance. Writers not a few have considered Eastern Monasticism as if it were wholly made up of fanatics or irregulars with a sprinkling of more ordered communities. In doing this they have, we think, fallen into the usual mistake of mistaking extremists for representative men. There is always a danger, in the twentieth as well as in the fourth century, lest the extremist-colour too powerfully the presentation which we may form of any subject. In all ages there is a tendency to judge a movement by its most prominent exponents, in forgetfulness that the main body always lags behind its leaders, and that the tales that have survived of special devotion or fanaticism have survived just because they were the exception and not the rule. Eastern Monasticism, it is true, contained within its borders fanatics and madmen not a few, and in the East the madman is always regarded as but one remove from the saint. But Eastern Monasticism contained a larger average of well-regulated, if at times indiscreet, adherents. Schenoudi and his *Rule* does not bulk so largely in popular imagination as Symeon Stylites; his real importance is vastly greater. Of the two lines upon which Monasticism developed, the eremitical and cenobite, the latter from the first was supreme. Historically considered, the figure of St. Anthony, though a favourite with poets and

[1] Cass. *Coll.* vii. 23.

painters, is of secondary influence to that of St. Pachomius.

Nevertheless, in spite of all the efforts of Pachomius, Martin, Cassian and others, to regulate Monasticism, it still remained, even in the West, somewhat amorphous, prone to many of the diseases of hysterical subjectivism. Especially noticeable, in spite of the emphasis placed upon it by Caesarius of Arles, was the lack of 'stability' —the technical name for the permanent attachment to one monastery. Jerome, Cassian, and Benedict alike mention, as one of the pests of Monasticism, the Sarabaites[1] who

'want to imitate rather than truly aim at evangelical perfection, who are anxious to be reckoned by the name of monks, without emulating their pursuits or practising their discipline,'

'whose shaven heads,' as Benedict puts it, 'lied to God'; and the Gyrovagi—'worse in every way than the Sarabaites'—'who wander where they will, and do what they like.' 'Of their life,' adds the saint, 'it were better to keep silence than to speak.' In Africa Augustine

[1] For the Sarabaites (? Hebrew סרב to be rebellious) see Cassian, *Coll.* xviii. 7; Jerome, *Ep.* 22 (7) (called there 'Remoboth'). Benedict begins his *Rule* by reprobating the Sarabaites ('tertium monachorum teterrimum genus') and 'gyrovagi' (*Reg. Ben.* c. 1). The pest was not soon destroyed. 'The gyrovagi' lingered on into the 11th cent. See Baltherus of St. Gallen, *Vita Fridolini* (see *infra*, p. 201 n. 3) in *MGH rer. Merov.* iii. who in the first chapter speaks of himself as 'gyrovagus.' A capitular of Charles the Great in 802 is directed against the 'Sarabaitae' [*MGH Leg.* II. i. 91]. The wandering of monks was forbidden at an early date. Cf. Conc. Chalcedon (451) c. 4 (Leclercq's note in Hefele, *HC* II. ii. 780); in Trullo (692) cc. 42, 46.

Since printing the above note I notice that Schiwietz, *MM* 238-9, derives 'Remoboth' from the Coptic *rem* = men, *i.e.*, "men of the cloister," and agrees with Revillout that Sarabaitae is the Coptic scheere-abêt, *i.e.*, "sons of the cloister." This seems more probable than a Hebrew derivation.

tells us of monks who refused to work, preferring rather to wander about selling amulets and false relics.[1] Even poverty was often disregarded by so-called renunciants, 'who wore openly upon their fingers rings with which to seal up what they have stored.'[2] The profession was, in fact, as yet too generally uncontrolled, a liberty which in this case tended to become licence. Sulpicius was right in his anticipation of disaster when he wrote that 'there is in Gaul no more destructive evil than spurious righteousness.'[3] In the sixth century, in fact, Monasticism in Gaul, in spite of the renown given to it by St. Martin,[4] as elsewhere, presented symptoms which must inevitably have issued in decay, had it not been for the new life given to it by Benedict of Nursia.[5]

[1] August. *de opere monachorum*, c. 28, written about 400 to induce monks to work. (Best ed. in *CSEL* vol. 41.) Cf. also the Messalians, *supra*, p. 80 n. On Monachism in Africa see H. Leclercq, *L'Afrique chrétienne* (Paris, 1904), ii. 73-7.

[2] Cassian, *Instit.* iv. 15.

[3] Sulp. Sev. *Dial.* i. 21, and for the looseness of monks, ii. 8 (3).

[4] Since this chapter has been paginated there have come under my notice four critical, not to say sceptical, articles by E. C. Babut on *St. Martin* in the *Rev. d'hist. et de litt. relig.*, vols. 1 and 2 (Paris, 1910, 1911). As regards the incident at Worms (*supra*, pp. 105-6), which M. Babut dates in Aug. 356 (*op. cit.* ii. 56 cf. *supra* 105 n.), M. Babut is of the same opinion as I have expressed on p. 106 n. that the common chronology is impossible. For the date of Martin's death Babut (ii. 46) inclines, without sufficient reason as it seems to me, to the old date of 397 (see *supra*, 108 n.). Babut's views as to imitation by Sulpicius of the *Vita Antonii* seem to me to be exaggerated. Plagiarism in medieval times was "in the air," and did not mean what it means to the modern, as I have shown in my *Letters of Hus*, exposing the wholesale plagiarism, if that is the right word to use, of both Wyclif and Hus from Gratian's *Decretum*.

[5] Of the general life and condition of Western monasteries before Benedict, there is a good study in E. Spreitzenhofer, *Die Entwicklung des alt. Mönchthums*, 37-107.

CHAPTER III

ST. BENEDICT AND HIS ORDER

Quisquis ergo ad patriam caelestem festinas, hanc minimam inchoationis regulam descriptam adjuvante Christo perfice; et tunc demum ad majora quae supra commemoravimus doctrinae virtutumque culmina Deo protegente pervenies. Amen.

Explicit *regula Benedicti*.

Some unadvised persons, by reason of their over-earnest desire of the grace of a devoted life, have overthrown themselves because they attempted more than they were able to perform, not weighing the measure of their own weakness, but following the desire of their heart rather than the judgement of their reason.

THOMAS À KEMPIS, *Imit. Christi*, iii. 7.

ARGUMENT

§ I. Benedict of Nursia—His importance—Literary history of his *Rule*—His life—Foundation of Monte Cassino—His character—'*Inspexit et despexit*'—Success of his Order ... 139

§ II. Causes of Benedict's success—His *Rule*—Characteristics—The reign of Law—Inner principle—Self-surrender rather than self-conquest—Contrast of Monasticism in East and West—Benedict and labour—Pachomius and labour—Effect on Europe—Benedict's Socialism—The work of Cassiodorus—His life—His literary activities—Monastic schools and libraries ... 145

§ III. Benedict's opportunity—Gregory the Great—Alliance of Monasticism and the Papacy—Causes of this alliance—The False Decretals—Monastic Privileges—Their danger ... 162

§ IV. Gregory the Great and Missions—Their importance for Benedictinism—England—The coming of Augustine——Winfrith and Germany—Double monasteries—Their history—Archbishop Theodore—Private monasteries . 172

pp. 139–180

CHAPTER III

ST. BENEDICT AND HIS ORDER

I

THE life of St. Benedict of Nursia forms the turning-point in the history of Monasticism. Before Benedict's time Monasticism, though showing itself to be no exotic incapable of transplantation to other climes, had been essentially a plant of Eastern growth. After his life the Monasticism of East and West became so diverse in character, that henceforth they may be regarded as two different systems. Some change in a system transplanted from East to West was of course inevitable, if only as the outcome of a changed climate. Habits of life that might suit the Thebaid could not possibly be adopted in the colder regions of Western Europe, as, in fact, Cassian had owned in his preface to his *Institutes*. Nor could the Roman world have much patience with any movement that led to no practical issue, and which did not seek to establish itself on the recognized lines of a guild or society.[1] In the Latin Empire, especially in Italy, individualism, pure and simple, had but slight chance of survival. The old ideas of duty to the State still retained some hold on the minds of the best citizens. In the West also, chiefly through the influence of Augustine, the conception of

[1] On this matter see my *PEC* 67-72.

the Church as the Kingdom of God was far stronger than in the East. Any ideal of life and renunciation that men might figure to themselves was bound, therefore, in the West to come into much closer contact with the Church than in the East, where to this day, as we have already noted, Monasticism lies rather alongside the Church than within it. Change was inevitable; the direction of that change was determined by the life and influence of Benedict of Nursia.

Benedict was born at Norcia—'frigida Nursia' as Vergil calls it—a little town with crumbling walls that nestles under the Apennines in Umbria, at a time when the old Roman world was crumbling into ruin, dragging down with it, as it might seem, the Church itself.[1] A Roman of the Romans, a scion of one of its most illustrious patrician houses,[2] he was destined to give another illustration of the Roman genius for organization, and of its power to produce an ordered cosmos out of chaos. 'From his infancy,' we are told,

[1] The usual date for Benedict's birth is 480. See Grützmacher, *op. cit.* 4–7. What we know of Benedict comes to us, mixed with legend, from Gregory the Great (*Dial.* ii. also iii. 16, written in 593 or 594, in *PL* 66, pp. 126–204), who relates it as in the main he received it from four of his disciples, one of them Constantine his successor at Monte Cassino. The short *Vita* in verse by Marcus Poeta (6th cent.) contains a few details, but is of little value (in Tosti, *op. cit. infra*, App. A; also Mabillon, i. 28 ff.). Works on Benedict are numerous. We may single out the critical work of G. Grützmacher, *Die Bedeutung Ben. v. Nursia u. sr. Regel in der Gesch. des Mönchtums* (Berlin, 1892); and F. Dudden, *Gregory the Great* (2 vols., 1895), ii. 160 ff. (a capital sketch). Abbot Tosti's *St. Benedict* (Eng. trs. by W. R. Woods, 1896; full of printers' blunders) is uncritical and sentimental.

[2] Possibly the Anician, to which also Gregory is said to have belonged (Dudden, *op. cit.* i. 4, ii. 162). The Church of S. Benedict *in Piscinula* is on the site of the family palace of Benedict in Rome (Tosti, *op. cit.* 20–4).

'he carried the heart of an old man'—words that will seem pathetic to a generation more sympathetic with childhood than was that of Gregory. Disgusted by the pollutions that he saw around him as a youth in Rome, he began his religious life at the age of twenty [1] by retiring to a cave in the gorge of the Anio, where at one time Nero had built himself a palace, with artificial lakes above it.[2] This Nero had abandoned in terror after a narrow escape from being struck by lightning, and solitude had long since claimed for her own the scene of the emperor's orgies. So for three years Benedict lived alone, inflicting upon himself dire austerities, and waging war incessantly with Apollyon. Probably he would have perished of hunger had not a friendly monk, Romanus, fed him with bread saved from his own allowance. This he lowered down the cliff to Benedict by a long cord. So far there was nothing to distinguish Benedict from the other Western imitators of Egyptian Monachism. Like the anchorites of the Thebaid we see him dwelling in a cave,[3] clothed in the skins of beasts, mistaken by the shepherds for a wild animal, overcoming his temptations by rolling naked in the thorn thickets. The fame of so ardent a young saint soon drew to the gorge would-be disciples, or high-born personages bringing their little sons to entrust to his care. His disciples he formed into twelve communities of twelve,[4] with a prior at the head of each.

[1] Gregory states that he was a 'puer,' and the usual age is given as 14. But Tosti, *op. cit.* 27, 44, shows reason for believing that he was older. Cf. Butler, *HL* i. 252 n.

[2] 'Sublaqueum,' whence Subiaco. For Nero's connection, see Tac. *Annals*, xiv. 22.

[3] *Il sagro speco* of Italian legend and of the modern monastery.

[4] The usual apostolic number in all monastic migrations.

Driven from Subiaco by an irruption of shameless women, sent for the purpose by a dissolute priest named Florentius, Benedict with a few companions journeyed to Monte Cassino on the border of the still wild Abruzzi.[1] There he desecrated the temple of Apollo which crowned the summit of the mountain, once a Roman and Pelasgic citadel,[2] cut down the sacred grove in which rude peasants still sacrificed to demons, and built in its place what was destined to become the most illustrious monastery of Christendom, the oratory of which he dedicated to St. Martin. Tradition yet points out the place where Benedict knelt before he laid the first stone. To this monastery he gave in 529—the year in which the Schools of the philosophers at Athens were closed after a continuous existence of over a thousand years, and the Code of Justinian was promulgated [3]—his famous *Rule*.[4] His object he tells

[1] According to Tosti, *op. cit.* 87–8, he arrived on 27 Feb. 529.

[2] The earlier names of Casinum were Casca and Eraclea.

[3] The reader will make his own reflections over the coincidence of these three most remarkable movements, than which no other three have done more to mould Western civilisation.

[4] The original autograph of the *Regula*, on the destruction of the monastery in 589 by the Lombards, was carried to Rome, but was restored to Monte Cassino in 717 by pope Zachary. When in 883 the monastery was again destroyed by the Saracens it was carried to Teano and lost when that monastery was burnt in 896. Two copies, however, had been made, one in 560 by Simplicius, another in 787 for Charles the Great (Jaffé, *BRG* iv. 359); this last was seen by Paul the Deacon, *Ep.* 1. To the diffusion of this Caroline text we owe the general purity of the *Rule*. No doubt in process of time (before 680) there have been several interpolations (especially in c. 29), none of which, however, are fundamental [Zöckler, *AM* 358; see fully L. Traube, *Eine Textgesch. der Regula hl. Ben.* (Munich, 1898, in *Abh. d. k. b. Akad. der Wiss.* t. 21 (3) pp. 601–731), and cf. C. Butler, *The Text of St. Benedict's Rule* (1899; in the *Downside Review*, 223–33) and in *JTS* (1902) iii. 458–68]. The Rule has been often published (*e.g.* Holsten, *CR* i. 113 f.). The most important

us was 'to form a school of divine servitude, in which, we trust, nothing too heavy or rigorous will be established.'[1] Men of every type and condition flocked to the new 'school,' whether as inmates, or, as Totila the fierce Goth, to visit its revered head whose "quiet influence for good was felt like the sunshine."[2] For fifteen years Benedict watched over the welfare of his monks; then the end came. He survived by but a few days his twin sister Scholastica, who had adapted to her sex the work of her brother, and whom once a year he allowed himself to meet at the foot of the mountain.[3] He died (21 March 543) standing beside her grave, with his arms extended to heaven in prayer, and was buried by her side,[4] where once had stood the altar of Apollo. His whole character is summed up

sections are printed in C. Mirbt, *Quellen zur Gesch. des Papsttums* (3rd ed., Tübingen, 1911), 71 f. Good modern eds. with commentaries or critical notes, are C. Brandes (Einsiedeln, 1856); better still, E. Schmidt (3rd ed., Regensburg, 1902); E. Woelfflin (Leipzig, 1895); D. O. H. Blair, *The Rule of St. Benedict* (with Eng. trs., 2nd ed., London, 1906; uncritical); A. L'Huillier, *Explication ascétique et historique de la règle de S. Benoit* (2 vols., Paris, 1901), and Dom Butler (1912); and cf. P. E. Spreitzenhofer, *Die hist. Voraussetzungen der Regel des hl. Ben.* (in *JB des Schotten-Gym.*, Vienna, 1896). The oldest commentaries upon the Rule are those of Paul the Deacon († 799; *In sanctam regulam commentarius*, published at Monte Cassino, 1880); Smaragdus († 824; in *PL* 102, p. 689 ff.); and Benedict of Aniane (*infra*, p. 226). For complete list, see Heimbucher, *OKK* i. 215, who also (i. 218 f.) gives a good analysis; cf. Grützmacher, *op. cit.* § 5.

[1] *Reg. Ben.* Prologue.
[2] Dudden, *op. cit.* ii. 167. Totila's visit was in 542 (Greg. Mag. *Dial.* ii. 14, 15), a date which helps to fix the death of Benedict.
[3] Greg. Mag. *Dial.* ii. 33 (*PL* 66 p. 194.)
[4] The question whether his whole body is still there, or whether a portion was stolen in 653 and transferred to Fleury on the Loire, has been for centuries a matter of hot dispute between Italy and France.

in the inscription which the traveller may still read on the old Roman tower at Monte Cassino in which he dwelt: *Inspexit et despexit*—'He saw the world and scorned it.' For one night shortly before vespers, as he was gazing from the windows of his cell, a mystic light shone round him and he saw the whole world gathered as it were into one ray of sunlight. But, as his Master of old, *inspexit et despexit*.[1]

Within two centuries of his death the Order Benedict had founded had swarmed like bees into every land of the West. The very use of the word "Order" points to the revolution that he effected. Before his day, strictly speaking, outside the Pachomian system there were no 'Orders'—there was only the Monastic method of life in which every monastery was more or less autonomous and a rule to itself. For this disunion Benedict, while preserving self-government, substituted the ideas of solidarity, without, however, the machinery that in later days was needed to secure it. The result showed the wisdom of this new conception, and how perfectly it met the desires of the age. Even the older foundations embraced Benedict's *Rule*, whether voluntarily or under pressure from the papacy, in preference to their own, as a more perfect expression of monastic life; while its quickening impulse on the age was felt in the establishment of an enormous number of new houses. From these there passed out a stream of missionaries, who not only carried Christianity into the heart of heathendom, but at the same time took their own ideal with them. The conquest of the heathen was marked by the rise in all directions of Benedictine abbeys, the frontier posts, as it were, of the new kingdom. "Scarcely

[1] Greg. Mag. *Dial.* ii. 35.

had the Empire fallen asunder when Roman monks, barefooted, the cord around their loins, fearlessly traversed as conquerors those districts of the Ultima Thule and the wildest regions of the West which the consuls of old had vanquished with difficulty at the head of their legions."[1] At one time the total number of Benedictine foundations in Western Europe is said to have been not less than fifteen thousand,[2] a vast number that is, probably, an exaggeration.

II

The reader, remembering the long list of failures in Monasticism, who would seek the cause for the success of Benedict in the saint's character, as given us in the traditional picture, will find himself face to face with a psychological puzzle, from which the only escape is to fall back upon the manifest exaggerations in the *Vita* of Benedict's austerities and ill-balanced discipline. Nor will he find the solution in any startling novelty in the *Rule* itself. Its virtues were the familiar monastic virtues of abstinence, long periods of silence, humility, and obedience. All immoderate asceticism, it is true, is eliminated through the saving regulation that 'the abbot so dispose all things that the brethren may do what they have to do without just cause for

---

[1] Gregorovius, *Rome in the Middle Ages* (Eng. trans.), ii. 11.

[2] For a bibliography of the literature of Benedictinism, see Heimbucher, *OKK* i. 205-211. The following may be singled out: J. Mabillon, *Annales ordinis S. Benedicti* (6 folios. Paris, 1703-39; Lucca, 1739-45: a vast storehouse down to 1157). Two English works are the classical R. Dodsworth and W. Dugdale, *Monasticon Anglicanum* (best eds., London, 1817, 1846), and E. L. Taunton, *The Eng. Black Monks of St. Benedict* (2 vols., London, 1898).

murmuring.'[1] Chastity, as we have already noticed, was taken for granted, and is not even mentioned. Its duties were worship, reading, and manual labour, all of them familiar to us in the precepts and lives of Benedict's predecessors. A fundamental law, of course, was the absolute community of all property. He who reserved for himself but one gold piece was to be regarded as a new Simon Magus. Obedience, prompt—' sine mora '—cheerful, zealous to God, and to the abbot as God's representative, was essential.[2] In everything the decision of the abbot, or of his officers, was final, the entire government of the monastery depending upon his will.[3] From the decisions of the abbot, however impossible, there could be no appeal,[4] though this autocracy was modified in practice by the democratic freedom of the chapter-meeting which the abbot was bound first to consult.[5] In its details, in fact, Benedict's *Rule* was by no means new, and shows a familiarity not merely with that of Cassian,[6] but with the *Rules* of Pachomius, of Serapion, of Macarius, of Basil, the reading of which he commands,[7] and, as modern research has shown, with the *Rule* of Schenoudi.[8] But a closer acquaintance reveals that the resemblances, after all, are but superficial.

The *Rule*, in fact, was founded upon the past in much the same way as is one of Shakespeare's masterpieces

[1] *Reg. Bened.* 41.
[2] *Ib.* 5.
[3] *Ib.* 65.
[4] *Ib.* 68. Cf. *supra*, p. 74.
[5] *Ib.* 3.
[6] For his great indebtedness to Cassian, see Cabrol, *DACL* ii. 3185, n. 5; to Cassian and Basil, see Grützmacher, *op. cit.* 40 f.
[7] *Reg. Ben.* 73.
[8] See *supra*, p. 126. How did he get over the Sahidic Coptic text? Cf. Ladeuze, *ECP* 305 n. 2.

upon the *Chronicles* of Holinshed, or on the *Plutarch* of Thomas North. Its genius lies in the way in which it presents its materials, incorporating into one organic whole the successes and failures that had preceded it, accommodating Monasticism, hitherto alien in outlook and character, to European conditions and environment. Above all, " that which gives the chief value to this *Rule* is that it is manifestly the work of an impetuous temperament to whom the years have taught self-restraint." [1] The *Rule* is instinct with the Roman genius for organization and solidarity. Attachment to the order is to be the one earthly passion, an attachment rendered the stronger by the vow of 'stability' which bound the monk to his first monastery. For the vagrancy and lawless individualism which in the Sarabaites and Gyrovagi [2] had brought discredit upon the movement, Benedict substituted the settled, ordered community. Henceforth the monk was tied down to his domicile, but that domicile is a Christian home of which the abbot is the father. In estimating the astonishing success of the *Rule* it is not sufficient to point out, with Gregory the Great, that the *Rule* is a masterpiece of 'clearness and discretion.' [3] We should rather do well to claim with Dr. Gasquet that the success of the *Rule* lay in its being " the transition from the uncertain and vague to the reign of law." [4] This supreme emphasis of law, as distinct from arbitrary regulation, completed the revolution begun by Pachomius, and which had been furthered by a long succession of abbots, Cassian,

[1] H. Leclercq in Cabrol, *DACL* ii. 3238.
[2] *Supra*, p. 134.
[3] Greg. Mag. *Dial.* ii. 36 (in *PL* 66, p. 200), 'discretione praecipuam, sermone luculentam.'
[4] Gasquet, Pref. to Montalembert, *MW* i. p. xxi.

Caesarius of Arles, Fructuosus of Braga, and others. The old individualism, with its private ventures in asceticism, gave place to rule and system: 'the monk must do nothing but what the common rule of the monastery and the example of the elders dictates,'[1]— 'ut in omnibus glorificetur Deus.'

The contrast between the *Rule* and the forms of Monasticism that had preceded it cannot be better illustrated than by the tale of the hermit near Monte Cassino, one of the products of the older ideal, who had shut himself up in a cave and bound round his foot a chain of iron, one end of which was fixed to a rock. 'If thou art truly the servant of Christ,' said Benedict, 'let not an iron chain be thy fetter, but the chains of Christ.'[2] But the chains of Christ are always the inner constraint of a heart which can do no other. 'When a man,' adds Benedict, 'has walked for some time in obedience and faith, his heart will expand, and he will run with the unspeakable sweetness of love in the way of God's commandments.'[3] It is in this emphasis of inner principle, rather than in any enforcement of a definite organization, that we find its secret of power. An organization would have waxed old and perished; an inner principle can adapt itself to changing needs. Hence the long life of the Benedictine Order, which has been, as Cardinal Newman claims, "rich rather than symmetrical, with many origins and centres and new beginnings, and the action of local influences. Instead of progressing on plan and system it has shot forth and run as if spontaneously, and has shaped itself according to events, from an irrepressible

---

[1] *Reg. Ben.* c. 7, ' the eighth degree of humility.'
[2] Greg. Mag. *Dial.* iii. 16 (*PL* 77).   [3] *Reg. Ben.* prologue.

fulness of life within, and from the energetic self-action of its parts." [1]

The opening words of the *Rule*, when thrown against the background of the rigid asceticism and reactionary laxness which they were designed to correct, and of which Benedict had had experience in the early spiritual ventures of his life, show us at once the secret of its influence. There is here not only sweetness and light, but that appeal to the individual conscience—not as yet merged in a Catholic Church but conscious of itself, its needs, and destiny—which forms so striking a factor in the rise of Monasticism. We realize here the chains of Christ, and not, as in the case of Stylites and others, the fetters of iron fastened to the rock. 'Listen, O son,' ('ausculta, O fili,' [2]), it runs,

'to the precepts of the Master, and incline unto Him the ear of thine heart; do not fear to receive the counsel of a good father, and to fulfil it wholly, that by thy labour of obedience thou mayst be led back to Him, from Whom by the sloth of disobedience thou hast departed. To thee, whoever thou art, who renouncest thy own will to fight under the true King, thy Lord Christ, and takest into thy hand the valiant and glorious weapons of obedience, are my words addressed.

'And in the first place, in all the good thou undertakest, ask of Him in earnest prayer that He will bring it to a good end; that having condescended to reckon us among His children, He may never be grieved by our evil actions. . . . With eyes open to the light of God, and attentive ears, let us listen to the daily cry of the Divine Voice ' (*Reg. Ben.* prologue).

Another secret of the success of the *Rule* lies in its consummate knowledge of the heart itself, and of the difficulties that hinder the yearning for renunciation.

[1] Montal. *MW* i. p. lv (Gasquet's preface).
[2] These words are familiar from many medieval pictures.

The *Rule* pursues self and pride into their most secret recesses.

> 'Our life in the world,' writes Benedict, 'is like the ladder which Jacob saw in a dream; in order to reach heaven it must be planted by the Lord in a humbled heart. We can only mount it by steps of humility and discipline' (*Reg. Ben.* c. 7).

But Benedict differs from his predecessors—and herein probably lies the great secret of his success—in the different emphasis that he lays upon the means for attaining their common end. Hitherto the monks had dwelt chiefly upon self-conquest; Benedict rather spoke of self-surrender—for this is really the meaning of 'obedientia.' To some the difference may appear slight; but in reality it is the difference between storm and peace, between the weakness of self, struggling to be free, and, alas, struggling in vain! and the strength of Christ manifesting itself in weakness.

The contrast between the *Rule* of Benedict and that of his predecessors has been drawn out in detail by Dom Butler.[1] The Egyptians reduced food and drink to a minimum—'an ounce or two of bread, and a little flask of wretched oil.' For others there was 'as much biscuit (*buccellatum*) as a man could grasp in one hand.'[2] Benedict took care only to avoid gluttony, and even allowed his monks a quarter of a litre[3] of wine a day as well as two cooked dishes and a third of fruits a day together with a pound of bread.[4] Abba Pambo laid it down that a monk's clothes should be such that if they

---

[1] Butler, *HL* i. 252–4.

[2] *HP* in *PL* 74, pp. 253, 270; *HL* (Gr.) 18 (2). (For the rare word βουκκελλᾶτον, *buccellatum*, see Rosweyd's *Onomasticon* in *PL* 74, p. 417.)

[3] *Reg. Ben.* c. 40. For the measure, '*emina*,' see Zöckler, *AM* 364 n.

[4] *Reg. Ben.* c. 39. Benedict's *pondus* is still preserved at Monte Cassino (Tosti, *op. cit.* 126).

were left on the road no one would think of taking them.[1] St. Benedict considered the requirements of cleanliness and warmth, and admonished the abbot to see to it that he supplied garments of suitable size.[2] In Egypt the monks, when not engaged in battling against sleep, slumbered in a sitting posture, or with stones for pillows, and regarded a blanket, according to Abba John, as 'a thing which I cannot mention without shame.'[3] Of the monk Dorotheus, Palladius tells us : 'Never did I see him stretch out his feet, or rest on a mattress or bed.'[4] St. Benedict allowed six to eight hours of sleep a night, and the use of blanket, straw mattress, and pillow, the monks, however, being required to sleep in their clothes.[5] Even in the matter of prayer Benedict was moderate compared with the continuous prayers of the Egyptian monks.[6] The common prayers are 'always to be short'; private prayer should be 'brief and pure unless it be prolonged by the inspiration of divine grace.'[7] Benedict in fact paid much attention to the systematization of worship. For this purpose he instituted the familiar canonical hours—Nocturns, Matins, Prime, Tierce, Sext, None, Vespers, and Compline.[8]

But the best testimony to the greatness of the *Rule* lies in its effect; and in nothing is this better illustrated than by contrasting the Monasticism of the East, which to this day has remained uninfluenced by it,[9] and the

---

[1] *VS* in *PG* 65, p. 369.
[2] *Reg. Ben.* c. 55.
[3] Cassian, *Coll.* xix. 6.
[4] *HL* (Gr.) 2. Cf. *supra*, 48.
[5] *Reg. Ben.* 55.
[6] Cassian, *Instit.* iii. 2 *et passim*.
[7] *Reg. Ben.* cc. 20, 52.
[8] *Ib.* 8–20.
[9] A few Eastern monasteries (Mount Sinai and some on Lebanon) follow the so-called *Rule* of Anthony; the majority that of Basil. But the Rule as such does not bulk large, nor are there in Eastern Monasticism any orders (*e.g.* " Basilians ") as in the West.

Monasticism of the West, which has grown up under its guidance and ideal. With Benedict, in fact, the Monasticism of the East and West split off for ever; and the ideals of renunciation henceforth run different courses.

In the East to this day Monasticism, untouched by the vivifying influence of Benedict, remains much as it was in the earlier centuries, only more formal and less an affair of the heart. It still lies, a stereotyped institution, outside the Church. In the East, in fact, the separation between the two ideals became complete, a married clergy [1] over against a celibate Monasticism; a divorce of ideals that in the West was prevented by Hildebrand.[2] In the East also the lower place of the Church ideal is sufficiently evidenced by the fact that the government of the Church is altogether reserved for the monks; [3] the married priests are the hewers of wood and the drawers of water. But in the West, monk and priest alike were under the control of one supreme head of the Church, who was, *qua* ruler, neither monk nor priest nor even bishop, but the representative, as it was held, of the Redeemer.

In the East, the breach of Monasticism with culture, and even with human society, became complete. Perched on the summits of precipitous rocks, to which the only access was by means of a windlass, as in the monastery of

[1] The reader should distinguish between a married clergy, *i.e.* married before ordination, and the marriage of the clergy. This last was prohibited in the East at an early date, *e.g.* Conc. 'in Trullo' (692), c. 6 (except for 'readers,' etc.), and the *Canons Apostol.* c. 27.

[2] See *infra*, p. 235.

[3] The Council 'in Trullo' (or Quinisext), c. 48, decreed that the wife of one raised to a bishopric 'must enter a monastery at a distance from the abode of a bishop.' This was the beginning of the Eastern custom.

Barlaam in Meteora, a handful of monks live out monotonous lives, ignorant of the treasures which the accidents of time may have left stranded in their libraries,[1] pushing their antagonism to sex to such a degree that female animals of every kind are excluded from every part of the peninsula of Mount Athos.[2] In the West, Benedictine monasteries became the centres of civilization and of education, the intellectual saviours of Europe, the ark of the Lord in which there took refuge from the flood of barbarism all that was best in the life and thought of the old world. In the East, Monasticism became a stereotyped institution, a barren asceticism without history or contribution to history, except in so far as its existence is the proof that mere asceticism is not a progressive factor and leads to no higher results of life and service. In the West, Monasticism was for centuries the bulwark and rampart not only of the Church but of society itself. Monasticism in the East retained its individualistic basis, and remained little more than an aggregation of units;[3] in the West, through the influence of Benedict, it became an organic whole wherein were maintained those fundamental virtues without which society itself must dissolve.

The changelessness of the East is one of the trite sayings of the day. Nowhere is this more seen than in its monastic life. The tourist may yet visit the monastery where lies the body of Macarius of Alexandria, and which still bears his name (Deir Mar Makar). There a handful of monks perform every evening their

[1] See the descriptions in R. Curzon, *Monasteries of the Levant* (1849), §§ 3 and 4.

[2] *Ib.* p. 369.

[3] Many monks, called ἰδιορυθμακοί, live apart from each other, receiving from a common centre their scanty supplies.

penance, making one hundred and fifty prostrations, falling flat on the ground with arms outstretched in the form of a cross. "The life," writes a recent traveller,

"in its outer guise at least, is scarcely altered since the dawn of Monasticism, though the high ideals of the early recluses are long since levelled with the dust, though their heroic enthusiasms have sunk down to a dull stagnation, though the lamp of their knowledge is extinguished, and the pulse of their devotion is still." [1]

With this changelessness contrast the fulness and richness of the monastic idea in the West, as we see it expanding and developing from Benedict to Loyola. But this theme demands a chapter in itself.

The greatness of Benedict is witnessed not only by the contrast between the Monasticism of East and West, but by the effect of his *Rule* on the life and thought of the Middle Ages. For, after all, the vast number of abbeys in every land that claimed him as their father was but the least effect of his inspiration. For the most part they have been swept away; forces that he set in motion still abide. For Benedict accomplished that most difficult of all tasks, a revolution in the moral attitude of man, and that in more ways than one. Compared to this profound issue a revolution in Monasticism is a small matter.

We see this moral revolution most clearly in the change which the *Rule* brought about in men's conceptions of the place of toil. In the degenerate Roman world manual labour had been reserved for slaves; nor had the Eastern monks succeeded in showing the way to a higher ideal. Their *Rules*, it is true, so far as they have

[1] A. J. Butler, *Ancient Coptic Churches of Egypt* (1884), i. 287.

come down to us, without exception make labour obligatory. 'If fasting hinders you from labour,' said St. Basil, himself the reputed author of a famous *Rule*, 'it is better to eat, remembering that you are athletes, workmen of Jesus Christ.'[1] So the day and night were divided into regular portions, the intervals between prayer and praise being filled with the systematic toil of the monks. By their labours " over wide desert tracts hopeless sterility gave place to golden harvests and abundant vintages."[2] Manual labour, chiefly sedentary, basketmaking, and the like, 'to the profit of spiritual meditation,' formed also one of the customs of Egypt,[3] though in the Antonian Monasticism of Lower Egypt work was looked upon as a form of penance. But in Upper Egypt there was a higher conception. According to Jerome no one was there received into a monastery unless he would work,[4] while the monasteries of Pachomius were organized on the basis of trades, the fullers living in one house, the carpenters in another, and so on,[5] in some convents no less than forty different trades being recognized. But too often the Eastern monks—and for that matter Western monks also before Benedict [6]—confused vagrant laziness with religious contemplation; while the latent Gnosticism of the whole movement often led them to despise all energy thrown away on the world around. Said Abba Abraham to Cassian:

'Those districts should be sought by the hermit which do not by their fruitfulness invite his mind to the trouble of cultivating

---

[1] Cf. St. Basil, *Ep.* 2 (6).   [2] *DCB* i. 285.
[3] Cass. *Instit.* ii. 14, x. 22.   [4] *Ep.* 125 (11).
[5] Jerome, *Pref. in Reg. Pach.* in *PL* 23, p. 63; Palladius, *HL* (Gr.) 32 (9); Butler, *HL* ii. 94.   [6] Cassian, *Instit.* x. 23.

them . . . or force him from his cell to go forth to some work in the open air, and so scatter to the winds all his concentration of mind.'

'Toiling day after day in the open air,' or, as Abba Abraham preferred to put it, 'moving about all day long in empty space,' tended, in his opinion, to 'discursiveness' of thought, instead of to concentration upon 'quelling its tempests.'[1] Even where work was enjoined it was almost wholly individualistic, 'making creels of reeds,' 'twisting lines for catching fish' and the like;[2] for the work of the community as a whole we must wait until Benedict.

But Benedict systematized labour as the rule of all monastic life. 'Indolence,' he said, 'is the enemy of the soul.'[3] So he laid down that in his 'school of divine servitude'[4] six hours each day should be given to manual toil, and two to reading. Even on Sundays 'any who shall be unable or unwilling to read or meditate shall have some work imposed upon him.'[5] The sons of Benedict, freemen be it remembered,[6] often men of high degree, as they laboured in the field clad in the dress familiar to the pagan world as the dress of slaves, or took their share in the work of the house, cooking the meals or cleaning the rooms,[7] sanctified industry by consecrating it to the lowliest tasks. 'This is a fine occupation for a count,' sarcastically exclaimed duke Godfrey of Lorraine when he found his brother Frederick washing dishes in the kitchen of a monastery. 'You are right, duke,' was the answer, 'I ought indeed to think

---

[1] Cass. *Coll.* xxiv. 3, 4. [2] Jerome, *Ep.* 125 (11).
[3] *Reg. Ben.* c. 48. [4] *Ib.* Prol. [5] *Ib.* 48.
[6] But this varied considerably in different centuries.
[7] The brethren for this purpose were elected weekly (*Reg. Ben.* 35).

myself honoured by the smallest service for the Master.'[1] 'In the monasteries,' writes Bernold in his *Chronicle* (1083), 'I saw counts cooking in the kitchens, and margraves leading the pigs out to feed.'[2] Such tales could be multiplied indefinitely. We may laugh at them, but their value is not the less great in the witness they give to the existence of a new ideal in the world. Facts such as these raised labour into new esteem, and aided in that development of industry which in centuries long after was to destroy feudalism itself, and to shift the centre of power to the producer and toiler.

The effects of this glorification of labour upon the history of civilization in Europe have been often described, and must not now detain us. Suffice to note the influence upon the spiritual life itself. The danger of Monasticism hitherto had lain in its tendency to degenerate into either Gnostic extremes or into an idle self-centredness, which instead of subduing temptation too often succeeded in creating it. The older Monasticism was too subjective, and had largely failed in consequence. By his emphasis of labour Benedict introduced objective remedies, and took the monk away from the thoughts which both chained him to himself and supplied him with an opposing host of powers of the air. Benedict did not see—the deserts in which they lived prevented the early monks from seeing—that the introduction of labour was destined, in the long run, to draw back the monk into the world from which he had fled, or, rather, to draw the world after him to the centres of light and peace which his labours created in the wilderness. This was, in fact, the first

[1] Free trans. of *Chron. Hugo Flavin.* in *MGHS* viii. 373.
[2] Bernold, *Chron.* in *ib.* v. 439.

step in an inevitable chain of evolution which was destined to change the whole character of Monasticism. To this evolution we shall return.

The mere glorification of toil—'laborare est orare,'—the religious significance which Benedict wished to give to all work, was not all. In one respect the modern world has swung back in its moral standpoint from the higher ideal of the monks. For theirs was toil from which they had eliminated the gain of the individual; from first to last it was toil for others; for a corporation, if you like, but after all toil for a corporation is more noble, because more altruistic, than toil for self. Toil was no mere scramble for pigs'-wash, to use the contemptuous phrase of Carlyle; it was not that feverish hustling of modern life—"each for himself and the devil take the hindmost, O!"—which is eating out and destroying the best elements of civilization. The toil of the monk was socialistic both in method and aim; though its socialism, it is true, in practice did not look beyond the corporation.

This socialism—an aim in all the *Rules*, however individualistic in other respects—Benedict, by his superior genius for organization, turned into a factor of immense importance in the history of civilization. For a thousand years Europe witnessed the spectacle of organized communities where the individual profited nothing, the community gained all; to the present writer a higher moral ideal than that which glorifies to-day the "Beef-kings," "Oil-kings," and other vultures of modern society, whose appetite for amassing, for the mere sake of amassing, is as cruel as it is insatiable.

In other directions also the effects of Benedictine Monasticism in the development of civilization cannot be exaggerated. In the dark ages of the world, when schools were few and learning almost extinct, the monasteries supplied the place. Probably this was the last thing that Benedict himself dreamed of, in spite of the provision that he made for daily reading 'for edification,' especially during meals.[1] The close connection which for so many centuries existed between the Benedictines and learning was really due, in the first place, to a contemporary of Benedict, Magnus Aurelius Cassiodorus. This remarkable man, at one time chief minister to the Ostrogothic princes of Italy, was born at Squillace in 470. His grandfather had delivered Sicily from the Vandal invaders under Genseric; his father had been employed by pope Leo in the embassy in 451 which diverted Attila from his purpose of marching on Rome. He himself for many years served Theodoric the Goth as tutor and minister, and on the death of that great prince in 525 did his best for his successors.

On the triumph of Belisarius, Cassiodorus, wearied out with his thankless task, finally withdrew, about 540, from public life and founded the monastery of Viviers in Bruttium. 'It is more noble,' he cried, 'to serve Thee, O Christ, than to reign over the kingdoms of the world.' But the energies of Cassiodorus were not to be satisfied with the ordinary pursuits of monastic life. As minister of the Goths he had watched, with the bitter grief of the Roman, the splendours of antiquity falling into hopeless decay; as a private man he would do what he could to save what he might. So, while on the summit of the mountain he built a home for his hermits, at the foot there sprang up, under his guidance, a colony of cenobites devoted to learning—a spectacle

[1] *Reg. Ben.* 38.

almost unique in that age of darkness. This colony he endowed with his own fine library, at the same time training the monks to the careful transcription of manuscripts. The date of his death is uncertain (? 575); itself a sign of the comparative neglect by posterity [1] of one of the greatest benefactors of civilization. For "the system of which he was the founder took root and spread beyond the boundaries of Italy, so that the multiplication of manuscripts became gradually as much a recognized employment of monastic life as prayer or fasting: nor is it too much to say that on this account alone the statue of Cassiodorus deserves an honourable niche in every library." [2] To Cassiodorus and the impulse he gave, more than to any other one man, must we give the credit for showing the new monasteries, which so rapidly sprang up all over Europe, the more excellent way of serving in the preservation and dissemination of such learning and culture as had survived the welter of the times. The story of their services to Europe in this matter, is an oft-told tale. The schools they founded, the libraries they gathered together, the writers on every branch of knowledge and culture then known to the world that they furnished, the manuscripts they copied, thus preserving to the world priceless treasures that would otherwise have been assuredly lost, the chronicles of contemporary history they compiled, the stately minsters, the envy and pride of later

[1] Heimbucher, *OKK*, for instance scarcely mentions him, and the account in Zöckler, *AM* 373, is slight.

[2] *DCB* i. 417. There is also a good sketch in F. Dudden, *Gregory the Great*; and a monograph by A. Franz (1872). But his real biography is in his own twelve books of *Variæ* (best ed. *MGH*, 1894; short Eng. trans. by T. Hodgkin, 1886). See also his *de institutione Divinarum literarum* (*PL* 70).

ages, that they built, all this is a familiar theme—by none told more eloquently or enthusiastically than by count Montalembert [1]—upon which we cannot dwell. Ignorance may scorn, but a more humble wisdom will ever realize the debt it owes to the medieval monks, especially in the early ages when the enthusiasm of their piety was as yet unspoilt by the world.

For it is a remarkable fact, the stress upon which cannot be exaggerated, that when once Monasticism ceased to be the handmaid of learning the hour of her fall was at hand. In the twelfth century, for various causes, the monastic schools began to close their doors to outsiders, and to receive only novices. A few years later we see the rise in Europe of the universities, which owed little or nothing to the monks, to whose whole spirit they were opposed and alien.[2] In the thirteenth century, it is true, the intellectual leaders of Europe were the friars; but the great wave of enthusiasm and culture of which they were both cause and result passed the older houses by. In the fourteenth century the monasteries contributed little to the intellectual work of the age; they neglected their chronicles; in some cases, even, they sold their libraries. The intellectual stagnation which characterized them, with rare exceptions, at the dawn of the Reformation, was only too sure an index of the loss of vitality and religious life. The monasteries fell, not so much because of crying scandals and rottenness, as because they had manifestly

[1] Mont. *MW* vol. 5. For a compressed survey, see Heimbucher, *OKK* i. 347–88. Cf. Krätzinger, *Der Benediktenorden u. die Kultur* (Heidelberg, 1876). On the great monastic libraries and their MSS. see Heimbucher, *OKK* i. 375 f.

[2] On this matter I may refer to my *Church of the West in the Middle Ages*, ii. c. 7; and my *Dawn of the Reformation*, i. c. 3.

outlived their usefulness and purpose. They had ceased to care for the highest things, whether of the mind or soul. But the cause of the Dissolution is a large theme upon which we cannot now enter.

III

Benedict's foundation was fortunate in its opportunity. It owed its success, not merely to its sanity and order as contrasted with the chaos in which Monasticism had hitherto found expression, but to its providential coincidence with two or three great movements in which it played no small part. These may be summarized as the rise of the medieval papacy, the beginning of the great missionary enterprises of the Western Church, and the consciousness in a re-awakened Christendom of the need of a new culture to take the place of the lost civilization of Rome. Upon the relation of Monasticism to this last matter we have already touched. A rapid survey is, however, desirable of the effect of the other two movements upon the fortunes of the Benedictine Order.

Of the medieval papacy the real father and founder was Gregory the Great; nor is it by accident that he was the first monk to ascend the papal throne. With the steps and processes whereby the see of St. Peter slowly secured its domination over the Western Church we are not here concerned; suffice that we point out the essential features of that primacy in their relation to Monasticism. First and foremost is the fact that this primacy was founded, whether rightly or wrongly, upon the suppression of nationalism in the Church. In the ordinary course of events the leaders of revolt against this oppression of nationalism would have been the great national primates, Canterbury, Arles, Rheims, Mainz, Hamburg, Lund, and the like. If they had been left to themselves the natural tendency of these great metropolitans would have been to turn the Church in the West into a federal republic under the lead rather than under the autocracy of Rome; much in the same way as we see in the early Church the great patriarchates of Antioch, Alexandria, Jerusalem, and, later, Constantinople, successfully claiming equality with Rome itself, save only that the successor of St. Peter was *primus inter pares*.[1] But this tendency in the West was defeated, in part by the need of these great metropolitans for papal support in their constant warfare with the civic authority, and in part by the endeavours of the Crown, especially in the Empire, in the constant struggle of Church and State, to divide the forces of the Church by securing the help of Rome against its own clergy, especially against its prince-bishops. Now in this struggle of Rome with nationalism, whether in Church or State, the monk was from the first the ally of the papacy.

The reasons for this alliance are so important as to warrant more detailed examination. Of the three elements in the ecclesiastical framework—bishop, pope, and monk—the place and power of the episcopal office was the first established. The means whereby this was accomplished fall without our scope. We may say, in brief, that it was, in part, the result of the con-

---

[1] Cf. Conc. Nicea (325) c. 6 (Hefele, *HC* I. i. 552; Mansi, *Conc.* ii. 669 ff.); Synod of Constantinople (381) cc. 2 and 3 (Mansi, *Conc.* iii. 560; Hefele, *op. cit.* II. i. 21 f.); Conc. Chalcedon (451) cc. 9, 17, 28 (Mansi, vii. 357, 369 f.; Hefele, *op. cit.* II. ii. 791 f.).

stitution of the primitive Church, but more largely due to the ruling ideas of the Roman Empire. Imperial Rome, characteristically, added little to doctrine, except, indeed, the emphasis of apostolic tradition as opposed to speculation; her work was to translate Christianity into the terms of her civil service, abandoning theology to the more subtle Greek. Even before the formal union of Church and State by Constantine, the Church had organized itself, especially in the West, on the lines of the Empire. " The conquering Christian Church took its weapons from the arsenal of the enemy."[1] In its hierarchy of religious pretors and pro-consuls, each in strict subordination to those immediately above them, in its rigidly defined ecclesiastical provinces, each divided into districts (bishoprics) and communes (parishes),[2] we have the civil organization adapted to religious purposes. So closely did the ecclesiastical organization follow the civil organization, and so firm was its hold upon society, that in the France of the present day, with hardly an exception, there is a bishop wherever there was a Roman municipality, and an archbishop wherever there was a provincial metropolis.[3]

[1] Mommsen, *Provinces of the Roman Empire* (1909), i. 349.

[2] The reader should not assume that the origin of the parish, even in France, is Roman. The Romans, in their territorial divisions, nearly always took an existing Teutonic or Celtic division. Especially in England was the parish of slow growth, intimately bound up with the *vicus* or *tun-scipe*. See article by Jessopp, *Contemporary Review*, February 1898; also Stubbs, *Constit. Hist.* i. 247.

[3] A more accurate though more technical way of expressing the same result would be to state that, so far as Gaul is concerned, every city which had a *flamen* to superintend the old State religion of the worship of Rome and Augustus (see *PEC* pp. 95 ff.) became the seat of a Christian bishop in the new State Church; whilst archbishops are to be found wherever there was a provincial priest

With the break-up of the civil administration under the onrush of the barbarians the ecclesiastical organization gradually tended to take its place. The bishop was not only an officer of the Church, he became one of the higher magistrates of the new State; by his race, speech, and legal training preserving its continuity with the vanished Roman Empire. A further development should be noticed. The rise of feudalism, the increasing wealth of the sees, above all the system of investitures, with its accompanying military services, its homage, its implied control by the sovereign, tended more and more to make the bishop a national prince. In general he owed his election to the sovereign; he became through his feudal relationships the king's man.

If, on one side of their work, the tendency of the episcopate was thus towards nationalism, on another the bishops and secular clergy were the representatives of individualism and wealth. When the enthusiasm or policy of Constantine first allowed the churches to hold property (321),[1] the Church became a kind of universal legatee. Hitherto the funds of the clergy had consisted almost wholly of voluntary offerings. They now received not only fixed revenues, in some cases charged on the land of municipalities, but also the ever-growing estates which superstition or piety bequeathed for their enjoyment. In the chaos of the times they alone were not troubled by forfeiture or violence, while alienation was rendered impossible by a perpetual curse. The lands of the conquered were divided by the barbarians,

---

of the imperial cult. See M. Desjardins, *Géog. hist. et administrative de la Gaule Romaine*, iii. 417, 418. Cf. Hatch, *DCA* s.v. Primate, &c.; Hatch, *OEC* 202 f.

[1] *Cod. Theodos.* xvi. 2, 4.

but the estates of the Church were guarded by the terrors of superstition. This wealth the bishop or incumbent regarded as his own. It was his for life; had it not been for the enforcement by Hildebrand of clerical celibacy, there was some danger lest it should have become his to bestow on his children as an hereditary possession.

As a consequence of the above, the natural tendency of the episcopate—to say nothing of the great metropolitans, to whose federal leanings we have already alluded—if the bishops had been left to develop on their own lines, would have been far otherwise than towards unyielding compliance with the dictates of Rome. Though they would have shrunk back from the thought of establishing national churches—for that matter the "nation," as distinct from the "race," "tribe," or Empire, was as yet an inchoate thought—they nevertheless unconsciously fostered their development, for every archbishop aspired to be a miniature pope within his own province. In that seething of the nations which led to the foundation of modern Europe, the bishop, as the count, would have drifted off into local or national independence but for two circumstances. The merely spiritual unity of the Church was to him unthinkable, as indeed it had ever been to the Roman mind; Church and Empire alike must be visible and concrete. The emperor, the head of the Holy Roman Empire, as the symbol of the unity of the secular world was oftentimes the shadow only of a great idea; but the popes ever made the bishops feel that both unity and orthodoxy, nay, the very existence of the Catholic Church, depended on the due recognition of their supremacy.

Furthermore, the lesser bishops were in perpetual revolt against their metropolitans. This latter office and power, after practically being swept away in Spain and Gaul by the decay of religious life or the whirlwind of conquest, had been revived by Charles the Great, as a check upon the growing disintegration of the Church, and as a political instrument for the administration of his vast realm. In their efforts to elude this metropolitan interference the bishops flung themselves at first into the arms of Rome. The purpose of the False Decretals, the responsibility for which later research has shown must be laid at their door,[1] was to provide an escape from the tyranny of local tribunals by an appeal to an authority to which they trusted that distance would give disinclination for vexatious interference. By a just retribution, this stupendous forgery delivered the episcopate from metropolitan tyranny only to hand it

[1] The consideration of the False Decretals lies outside our scope, and yet is so pertinent to our argument that some notice is needful. They were forged between the years 847–50, and attributed to Isidore of Seville. In reality, the work is an amplification, by means of interpolated forged decretals, of canonical collections of decretals in use in Spain in the 8th century, written in the interests of provincial bishops as against *chorepiscopi* and metropolitans. Though thus playing into the hands of Rome, the idea that the False Decretals were forged at Rome is now universally abandoned. The striking coincidences with the forged documents in the *Acta pontificum Cenomanis in urbe degentium*, first pointed out by B. Simson, *Die Enstehung der pseud. Fälsch. in Le Mans* (Leipzig, 1886), have led modern scholars to locate the forgery more exactly at Le Mans under the episcopate of Aldric (832–56). Of the many works on the False Decretals the following are the best : Wasserschleben, *Beiträge zur Geschichte der falschen Dekretalen* (Breslau, 1844; in favour of Mainz); A. Tardif, *Histoire des sources du droit canonique* (Paris, 1887; in favour of Rheims); and F. Fournier, *Étude sur les fausses décrétals* (in *Rev. d'hist. eccl. de Louvain*, 1906, 1907; in favour of Le Mans).

over to the stronger control of papal despotism. Nevertheless, the decentralizing forces of feudalism and race hatred would have proved stronger even than Rome, had it not been that in every land the leanings of the bishops towards independent national churches were more than balanced by the cosmopolitanism of the monasteries. To the monks, at any rate in their earlier enthusiasms, nationalism made no appeal. They were anxious to leave State and Church behind them, to flee beyond their bounds, not to develop their powers. From the first also the monasteries, as we have seen, were distrusted by the episcopacy, who ever sought to bring them under their visitation and control. Little, therefore, was needed of papal encouragement to turn the monks into the watchdogs in every land for the pope, ever ready to pick a quarrel with the bishop and to proclaim against him the supremacy of their papal overlord. So the lists were set: on the one side the individualism of wealth and the feudal localism of a semi-national episcopacy; on the other side the monks, by their very constitution socialists and cosmopolitans. Until the reforms of Benedict the political or ecclesiastical influence of the monks was but slight. But with the formation of the Benedictine Order we leave behind the age of individual monasteries each fighting for its own hand. Henceforth the monks formed a state within a state, an ecclesiastical internationalism whose head centre, under the subtle guidance of the papacy, was Rome. If the bishop was the king's man, the monk was the pope's —the course of events all tended to make him such— if the interests of the one were more national or local, the sole care of the other was the welfare of his monastery, the spread of his order, and the domination in the Church at large of his three vows, of community of goods, of obedience, and of celibacy.

If, in the principles of Monasticism as organized by Benedict, the papacy found an instrument already forged for the carrying out of its purposes, the first discernment of the fact must be credited to Gregory the Great, though, as was natural, he himself saw but as in a glass darkly the full issues of his policy. Gregory, the first monk to be elected pope, began the systematic linking on of Monasticism with Rome; its development became henceforth the settled policy of the popes. In 574 Gregory, at that time prefect of the city, resigned his office and became a monk. His vast wealth was devoted to the foundation of six monasteries in Sicily, and of the famous monastery of St. Andrew in his father's palace at Rome.[1] Of this monastery in 586, on his return from his position as resident ambassador at Constantinople, Gregory was elected, possibly, the abbot.[2] Under what precise rule Gregory's foundations were established is uncertain; there is no proof that in 574 Gregory was acquainted with the life and work of Benedict.[3] But in 589 [4] Monte Cassino was burnt by the Lombards under duke Zotto; whereupon the monks fled to Rome carrying their *Rule* with them, and were established by pope Pelagius II. in the monastery near the Lateran, which became for more than a century

[1] Greg. of Tours, *Hist. Franc.* xi.; Paul Diac. *Vita Greg.* 3, 4; John Diac. *Vita Greg.* i. 6, 7.

[2] So F. H. Dudden, *Gregory the Great* (1905), i. 187 n. But H. Howorth, *Saint Gregory* (1912), 11 n., doubts this.

[3] Dudden, *op. cit.* i. 108. Cf. Grützmacher, *op. cit.* 55–6.

[4] So Dudden, *op. cit.* i. 107, with the majority of critics. Heimbucher, *OKK* i. 213, dates in 585; Grützmacher, *op. cit.* 53, in 580 (basing his argument on *MGHS* vii. 580).

the headquarters of the Order. At what date Gregory came under their influence we cannot tell, but shortly after his consecration as pope (3 Sept. 590) we find Gregory devoting his energies to strengthening and developing the system of Benedict. As the letters of Gregory show, monachism in Italy was in sad need of reform—the disorder of the times reflected, as so often proved to be the case, in disorder in the monasteries. Lack of discipline, the accumulation of private property, purposeless wanderings from monastery to monastery, even grave immoralities were frequent.[1] To the task of putting down abuses Gregory addressed himself with zeal, his remedy being the strict enforcement of the *Rule* of Benedict.[2] Upon the Benedictine monasteries Gregory and his successors showered letters of protection and privilege which were assuredly not without their *quid pro quo* in devoted service and allegiance. How great was the number of these letters of privilege the student can judge for himself who turns over the pages of the early papal *Regesta*.[3] At first the papacy

---

[1] The instances have been carefully collected in Dudden, *op. cit.* ii. 174 f.

[2] *Ib.* 177 f. The supposed decree of Gregory placing the Rule ' inter canonicas scripturas et cath. doctorum scripta est teneri ' is not genuine, though believed to be so in the 9th cent. (See Jaffé, *RP* i. p. 172 ; it is dated 28 June 596 ; and cf. Labbé, *Conc.* ix. 266.) It is interesting to note that in Feb. 601 Gregory strongly condemned (Greg. *Reg.* xi. 30, ed. Ewald) the imperial law (*Novel.* 123, c. 40) which allowed a husband or wife to dissolve a marriage by entering a monastery.

[3] The standard ed. of the *Regesta*, or list of bulls, letters, briefs, and the like, a work indispensable for every medieval student, is P. Jaffé, *Reg. Pontif. Romanorum* (2nd ed., Leipzig, 1885, corrected and enlarged by P. Ewald and others). It is remarkable how many of these bulls and privileges, so far as monasteries are concerned, are forgeries. These are marked by Jaffé with a †.

contented itself with singling out individual foundations on which were lavished its favours. In the twelfth century this gave place to the system of privileged orders. But with this new development we shall deal in a later chapter.

Privileges, as history repeatedly shows, are dangerous gifts, even from the standpoint of the recipient. Of all the causes which led to the downfall of Monasticism none was more potent than the privileges which the monasteries had obtained from a long line of popes, whereby many had received exemption from episcopal control. The monks everywhere in later ages drew against themselves the ill-will of the secular bishops—as in fact they had done so, though from a different cause, in their first beginning—who only awaited a suitable opportunity for winning back their own. Of this policy of monastic exemption we can trace the beginnings in Gregory. Hitherto councils had aimed at protecting the rights of the bishop over the monasteries of his diocese,[1] though little attempt had been made to define the limits of that jurisdiction. Gregory severely abridged these rights, taking away from the bishop the choice of the abbot, or any interference in purely internal concerns. Though he did not grant to any monastery absolute exemption from episcopal authority, his charters and '*privilegia*' to such monasteries as Autun [2]

[1] Conc. Chalcedon (451) cc. 4, 8 (Hefele, *HC* II. ii. 780 n.); Conc. Agde (506) cc. 27, 38, 58 (see Hefele, *HC* II. ii. 999); 1st Conc. Orleans (511) cc. 19, 22; Épaone in Burgundy (517) c. 10 (Hefele *HC* II. ii. 1037); 2nd Conc. Orleans (533) c. 21 (*op. cit.* 1135); 5th Conc. Arles (554) cc. 2, 3, 5 (Hefele, *HC* III. i. 170).

[2] Greg. Mag. *Reg.* xiii. 11, 12, 13 (Nov. 602). These extensive '*privilegia*,' though sometimes questioned, are accepted as genuine by Hartmann, the editor with Ewald of the standard edition of Gregory's *Regesta*. They are alluded to by Gregory himself (Greg.

laid the foundations of a system that was afterwards to develop into the fixed policy of the papacy, with consequences that were disastrous both for the monasteries and for religious life. But for these later results Gregory can scarcely be blamed.

IV

The second great factor in the establishment of the Benedictine Order was the commencement by Gregory I. of the great missionary enterprises of the Western Church. For the record of these missions, as well as for the way in which their success built up the supremacy of the papacy, the reader should look elsewhere ; our present purpose is to draw attention to the close connection between their success and the spread of the Benedictines. The story of Gregory's conversion of Southern England is too well known to need repetition;[1] but it is important that the reader should note that

---

Reg. xiii. 7). It is scarcely correct to say that they are the first instance of exemption from episcopal control, for they do not go quite so far as that. They limited the rights of deprivation by the bishop of Autun to cases of crime proved before himself and six episcopal assessors. Gregory, however, insisted on the right of abbots to appeal to Rome, if necessary, and once went so far as to threaten exemption (Greg. *Reg.* vii. 40). The alleged 'constitution' (see *Reg. Greg. M.*, ed. Maur. App. vii.) of 5th Ap. 601 (so Bellarmine; but Jaffé, *RP* i. 168, dates 5 July 595 inasmuch as the signatures, &c., are the same as for the undoubted synod of 23 bishops of that date ; see Greg. *Reg.* v. 57*a*) in which Gregory exempts all monasteries from episcopal control is really forged by the combination of Greg. *Reg.* v. 49*a* and viii. 17—charters granted to the monastery of St. Thomas at Arimini, and of St. John and St. Stephen at Classis.

[1] In addition to the primary Bede (best ed. by C. Plummer) we may refer for good modern works to A. L. Mason, *The Mission of St. Augustine* (1897), with complete collection and Eng. trs. of documents; S. J. Brou, *St. A. et ses compagnons* (4th ed., Paris, 1900) ; W. E. Collins, *The Beginnings of Eng. Christianity* (1898).

ST. BENEDICT AND HIS ORDER 173

the first mission was wholly composed of monks. At the head of the mission was Augustine, the prior of Gregory's own monastery of St. Andrew, and under him there were thirty-nine other monks.[1] In June 601, in answer to the petitions of Augustine, a second band of missionaries was dispatched, again entirely composed of monks— unless indeed ' Lawrence the presbyter ' be an exception [2] —among them one named Paulinus. When on the eve of Whitsunday (1 June 597)—' dies Anglis et angelis solemnissimus '—there took place in the ancient church of St. Martin's, Canterbury, that scene of tremendous import, the baptism of the Kentish king Ethelbert,[3] it was not merely a victory for the Church but a triumph for Benedictine Monasticism. The first foundations of the new religion in Canterbury were both monastic— the cathedral, on the site of a ruined Roman church, dedicated to Christ, and the monastery first known as St. Peter's but afterwards by the name of Augustine himself,[4] this last probably the first Benedictine monastery established out of Italy. The importance for the future history of the English Church of the fact that for many centuries the 'archbishop of the English' was chosen by a chapter of Benedictine monks can scarcely be exaggerated. But the greatest event in the history of Benedictine Monasticism in England was the conquest of the Roman over the Celtic Church.[5] This was marked by the establishment of a long chain of

[1] Bede, *HE* i. 23, 25, 27.
[2] Bede, *HE* i. 27. Cf. Greg. *Reg.* xi. 41. On this question see especially Collins, *op. cit.* 161 ff. Lawrence succeeded Augustine as archbishop.
[3] Bede, *HE* i. 26. Place and time are conjectures, but very probable, as St. Martin's church was already there (*supra*, p. 109 n. 3).
[4] Bede, *HE* i. 29. [5] See *infra*, p. 206.

Benedictine mission-stations and schools which broke the silence of forest and fen with settlements which proved the forerunners of busy towns. In the great forest of Arden—to single out a few illustrations—we see the beginnings of the stately monasteries of Evesham (701) and Pershore;[1] on the edge of the fens the rise of Medeshamstead,[2] later known as the 'golden' burgh of Peter (Peterborough); in the heart of the fens the large community that gathered round the hermit Guthlac in Crowland;[3] while nearer London we mark the new enthusiasm in the foundation by Erkonwald, bishop of the East Saxons, of Chertsey and Barking.[4] In the West of England the most famous of Maildulf's[5] pupils, Ealdhelm, planted in the heart of the great woodland which stretched from the Cotswolds to the English Channel the four monasteries of Sherborne, Frome, Wareham, and Bradford-on-Avon — whose church still stands to-day as he built it, in almost perfect preservation.[6] 'Whereunto this will grow,' writes Bede in the closing lines of his *History*, as he recounts the extraordinary enthusiasm of his times for Monasticism, 'the future will show.'[7] There were, in fact, as Bede noticed, many signs of danger; ill-regulated monasteries established as comfortable refuges for old age, the loss of the fighting-men so needed in the troubled times, private monasteries where the founder lived as

[1] See *VCH* (Worcester) ii. 113, 127. Pershore, *c.* 689.

[2] *c.* 655 (Bede, *HE* iv. 6). For its history see *VCH* (Northampton) ii. 83 f.

[3] *c.* 714. But the origins of Crowland are obscure since F. Liebermann's exposure of pseudo-Ingulf's *Hist. Croylandensis*.

[4] Bede, *HE* iv. 6; about 666.   [5] See *infra*, p. 205.

[6] Ealdhelm (639–709). There is a good modern *Life* by bishop G. F. Browne (1903).

[7] Bede, *HE* v. 23.

a law unto himself.¹ The Danish invasions justified Bede's forebodings, and showed the weakness of much of the profuse monastic profession of the times. But the exposure of weakness itself led, when order was restored by Alfred the Great and Dunstan, to the growth of a stricter Benedictinism.

From England Monasticism was carried across the Rhine by the great missionary of Germany, Winfrith of Crediton, better known under his European name of Boniface. The work of Boniface ² lies outside our story. Few nobler heroes of the Cross have ever lived ; certainly none, by the toils of a lifetime, have added provinces so vast in extent and value to the kingdom of Christ. For thirty-five years we see this great apostle in labours more abundant and journeyings oft; now hewing down the sacred oak at Geismar amid the terror of the heathen ; now struggling with the opposition of the Irish, or the lack of discipline of the Hessian Christians ; preaching, baptizing, correcting heresies, founding schools, dividing into bishoprics his vast heathen territory from the Rhine to the Elbe, and finally in his old age setting off to preach to the pagans of Frisia, by whom he was murdered (5 June 754). For our present purpose it is important to remember that himself a Benedictine, brought up first in a Benedictine school near Exeter, and afterwards in the Benedictine

¹ See *infra*, p. 180.
² The best ed. of the *Vitae Bonifatii* is by W. Levison (Hanover, 1905). For the contemporary *Vita* by Willibald (priest at St. Victor in Mainz) see *MGHS* ii. 331 f. ; Jaffé, *BRG* iii. ; or critical text ed. A. J. Nurnberger (Breslau, 1895). See also *DNB* v., or *DCB*, and for Boniface's relations to Rome, his correspondence, ed. P. Jaffé in *BRG* iii. (Mainz, 1866), or better by Dummler in *MGH* (Berlin, 1892). There is a good *Life* by J. M. Williamson (London, 1904). For Sturmi, see *MGHS* ii. 366 f.

monastery of Nutsall, or Nursling, near Winchester, Boniface carried over into Germany not only the Roman obedience but the Benedictine *Rule*, and at a council in 742 made it the standard *rule* for Germany.[1] Of this we see the result in the rise on the other side of the Rhine of such stately Benedictine foundations as Fulda, founded by Sturmi, one of Boniface's companions, 'in a savage desert amidst a vast solitude' (744), and of other monasteries at Fritzlar, Utrecht, Amanaburg, and Ohrdruf. From these as the parent houses there sprang a number of Benedictine priories in the various dioceses of Germany. Nor must we forget the numerous English women who at this time accompanied Boniface and his missionaries across the Rhine, chief of whom were Walpurga,[2] Lioba, and Thekla, for whom we see the foundation of Benedictine nunneries at Kitzingen, Ochsenfurt, and other places. Thus powerfully through the aid of English missionaries did Benedictine Monasticism spread through Germany. From Germany, in turn, it was taken to northern lands, when in 829 Anskar, a monk of Corbey in Westphalia, another of the great missionary heroes of the Church, carried the gospel to Sweden.

Before we pass away from the English monasteries of the period one curious feature should be noticed. Many of them were "double monasteries"—the title goes back to the days of Justinian—in which the abbess ruled over the men, itself no small token of the high place assigned to the holy woman among the Teuton races. Double monasteries, in which a society of regular

---

[1] For the date (21 Ap. 742, rather than 743 or 744) of this first national German council see Hefele, *HC* III. ii. 815 n., 818 n.; for its decision *re* monks, c. 7 (*op. cit.* 824).

[2] See *infra*, p. 178 n. 1.

priests ministered to the spiritual needs of regular women, with the necessary association which this involved, were, in their main essentials, no new institution. At the very rise of Monasticism we find the sister of Pachomius establishing a community of nuns on the other side of the Nile opposite to her brother's monasteries,[1] while St. Basil and his sister Macrina presided over settlements of men and women separated only by the river Iris.[2] Though prohibited by the Council of Agde in Languedoc[3] and by Justinian,[4] the system of double monasteries flourished. Even in Rome itself, if we may trust a somewhat ambiguous statement of Bede, we find, in the middle of the seventh century, one institution of the kind,[5] while St. Radegund was head of a famous Frankish double monastery at Poictiers.[6] Thus before the advent of Columban double monasteries flourished in Gaul, while after his arrival we note the rise of some of the largest and most famous, though none of them owed their origin to the saint himself.[7] A further

[1] *Vit. Pach.* 28 (*PL* 73, p. 248); Ladeuzè, *ECP* 176 f.

[2] Basil, *Reg. brev.* 104, 108–11, 154, 220.

[3] Conc. Agde (506), c. 28. From this it was incorporated into Gratian's *Decretum*, causa 18, q. ii. c. 23.

[4] *Corp. Jur. Civ.* (ed. Krueger) I. iii. 43. Cf. *Novell.* 123 (36).

[5] Bede, *HE* iv. 1, 'monachum quendam de vicino virginum monasterio, nomine Andream.' Cf. Greg. Mag. *Dial.* i. 4 and Greg. *Reg.* xi. 13 (to Januarius, bishop of Cagliari).

[6] M. Bateson, "Origin and Early Hist. of Double Monasteries," p. 145 f. in *Trans. Hist. Soc.* (1879) vol. 13.

[7] Bateson, *op. cit.* 150 f. Examples are Remiremont, Soissons, Jouarre, Brie, Chellys, and Andelys—these last three especially favoured by English ladies (Bede, *HE* iii. 8)—also Marchiennes near Ghent, Nivelle, Maubeuge, and others. For the supposed early double monasteries east of the Rhine, see Bateson, *l.c.* 183 f. Two papers on double monasteries in the East are J. Pargoire, *Les monastères doubles chez les Byzant.*, in *Échos d'Orient* (1906) ix. 21–25; and S. Vailhé, *Les Stylites de Constantinople*, in *ib.* (1898) 303–7.

impulse to the establishment of double monasteries in Germany was given by the disciples of Boniface, many of whom had been brought up at the double monastery of Wimborne. Of these the most illustrious was Heidenheim, founded in 752 by Wunnibald, a native of Wessex, and ruled over by his more famous sister Walpurga.[1]

From the first double monasteries flourished in the Celtic Church, probably because they were a survival of the old clan system when men and women alike belonged to the same religious community.[2] In Ireland[3] the head of such monasteries was usually a man, as the head of the clan, but in the Scoto-Irish monasteries of England, especially in those founded by royal princesses, and in Columban's double monasteries in Gaul and Belgium, the monastery of clerks or priests placed at the gates of the nunnery was ruled over by the abbess. Of this we have a famous example in Hilda's double monasteries, first at Hartlepool (650) and later at Whitby, and queen Etheldreda's rule over the double monastery she had built at Ely. This singular inversion of the normal relationship is due, probably, to the fact that in such cases the real centre or original foundation was the nunnery,[4] but that for their spiritual needs, as well as for the oversight of their lands and estates, there grew up a smaller dependent monastery of priests and lay

[1] Bateson, *op. cit.* 184. Other double monasteries were Pfalzel near Treves, and Mauheim in Bavaria. For Walpurga, see *DNB* s.v. and *MGS* xv. 535 f.

[2] Willis-Bund, *CCW* 156, 167, and see *infra,* p. 192.

[3] Montalembert, *MW* iv. 422, denies that there were double monasteries in Ireland. St. Bridget's at Kildare may be cited as an example (Bateson, *l.c.* 165 f.), and for other cases see Plummer, *VSH* i. Introd. cxii. n. 5.

[4] Bede generally (e.g. *HE* iv. 25) calls a double monastery 'monasterium virginum.'

brethren. But in some double monasteries the monks were in the majority.

In his regulation of the monastic life of England the attention of archbishop Theodore was naturally called to this anomaly. In one of his canons he forbids all new foundations of this description, though forced to recognize those that already existed.[1] But his regulations were disregarded, and new double monasteries, *e.g.* Wimborne, were founded after his death. What the archbishop could not do the Danes accomplished by their general destruction at the end of the ninth century of the monastic life of England, though on the Continent we find double monasteries existing until late in the eleventh century.[2] In England, also, as we shall see later, there was an interesting revival in the twelfth century of double monasteries under Gilbert of Sempringham.[3] We may add that in most double monasteries, in England at least, the discipline seems to have been strict. Only in Coldingham, founded by the Northumbrian princess Ebba, does there appear to have been any scandal that should be credited directly to this curious anomaly.[4] In reality, monastery and nunnery were kept almost wholly distinct.

---

[1] Theodore, *Penit.* ii. 6 (8); H. and S. *Conc.* iii. 195. 2nd Nicea (787), c. 20, forbade future double monasteries, putting those existing under the *Rule* of Basil (see Leclercq's note in Hefele, *HC* III. ii. 790 f.).

[2] Bateson, *op. cit.* 196.

[3] For Gilbert, see *infra*, p. 263.

[4] Bede, *HE* iv. 25. Bede mentions the following double monasteries: Bardney (*HE* iii. 1), Barking (*HE* iv. 7), Ely (*HE* iv. 19), Whitby (*HE* iv. 23), Coldingham (*HE* iv. 25). Add also Wimborne, Repton, Wenlock, and Nuneaton, and possibly Carlisle (Bateson, *op. cit.* 176). That there were scandals in double monasteries on the Continent is, however, apparent from the terms of the canon of Nicea (*cit. supra*).

There is always a melancholy interest in tracing the stages whereby an idea or movement that at one time was full of the promise of good, becomes corrupted into an evil. The idea of the "double monastery" suffered a peculiar corruption, about as alien to the spirit of Monasticism as can be imagined. A custom arose, especially in Spain, of turning a private house into a monastery, in which the so-called monks and nuns were merely the family and their servants. Whole families could thus secure for their possessions the protection of the Church, and yet continue to live together with but few restrictions. Both in England and Spain in the seventh and eighth centuries it was found necessary to forbid the establishment of these monasteries falsely so called.[1] But in judging this, as all the other failures of Monasticism in the Dark Ages, the reader should remember the extraordinary evils of the times, and the difficulties, often overwhelming, with which every ideal had to wage unceasing warfare, oftentimes, alas! in the struggle suffering defeat and dishonour.

[1] Bateson, *op. cit.* 163, 191.

CHAPTER IV

THE IDEALS OF MONASTICISM
IN
THE CELTIC CHURCH

> No thoughts that to the world belong
>   Had stood against the wave
> Of love which sets so deep and strong
>   From Christ's then open grave.
>
> No cloister-floor of humid stone
>   Had been too cold for me,
> For me no Eastern desert lone
>   Had been too far to flee.
>
> No lonely life had passed too slow,
>   When I could hourly scan
> Upon His Cross, with head sunk low,
>   That nailed, thorn-crownèd Man!
>   M. ARNOLD, *Obermann Once More.*

ARGUMENT

§ I. Celtic Church and Monasticism—"Ephesian" legends—The "llans" of Wales—Germanus of Auxerre—Patrick—His life and work—"The Age of the Saints"—Monasticism and the Clan—The sept of the 'saint'—'Saints' and women—The abbots and bishops—Jurisdiction of the abbot—The struggle with Rome 183

§ II. Stability in Celtic Monasticism—Celtic restlessness—Brendan—The migration to Brittany—Wandering monks—The Celtic missions—Columba—His work in Northumbria—Aidan—Maildulf—Cuthbert—Synod of Whitby 196

§ III. Columban—Luxeuil—Kilian and Gall—Columban's *Rule*—Overthrow of Celtic Monasticism . . . 207

§ IV. Monasticism and the Penitentials—Theodore of Tarsus—Effect upon Europe of the Penitential System—Celtic asceticism—Flagellation—St. Elizabeth and Conrad of Marburg—The Flagellants . . . 212

pp. 183–216

CHAPTER IV

THE IDEALS OF MONASTICISM IN THE CELTIC CHURCH

I

HITHERTO we have confined our study to the fortunes of Monasticism among the various nations that made up the Roman Empire. There were, however, nations in the West, into which Monasticism was introduced at an early date, which either had never formed part of the Empire, or in which, at the date of the first proclamation of Christianity, the Celtic clan system was still in full vigour.[1] The form that Monasticism took in Ireland,[2] in ancient Wales, and in early Britain, with the record of its achievements, is of interest for every student not only in itself but because of the contrasts presented, through a changed environment, with the other developments of Monasticism in East and West.

On many of its sides the history of Celtic Christianity outside Gaul, where the Celt soon became lost in the Empire, is but the story of Celtic Monasticism. Of the

[1] Willis-Bund, *CCW* 94.

[2] It is perhaps necessary to warn the young student that the Latin Scotti=Irish. The 'Scots' under the sons of Erc invaded the S.W. portion of "Scotland" (Dalriada) from N.E. Ireland about 500 A.D. A convenient term for these invaders is 'Scoto-Irish.' It was only in the 11th cent. that the name Scotland came to be applied to Caledonia.

manner and date of the introduction of the gospel into Britain we know little,[1] but almost as soon as the British Church comes into clear light we find in it a strong tendency towards Monasticism. But the monachism of Britain was not the monachism of St. Martin or John Cassian, but another of a different, fiercer kind, with a discipline and vigour that has misled the unwary into supposing that it was derived from the East. Introduced from Southern [2] Gaul, Monasticism obtained a speedy mastery over Celtic minds not only by reason of its emotional appeal and its severe ideal of renunciation, but even more because of its perfect adaptation to the Celtic genius, and by its power of falling in with the clan or sept system under which the Celts were organized. In its eremite form also—probably, as usual, the first form [3]—where the recluse was brought face to face with

[1] What little is known is collected in H. and S. *Conc.* i. 3 f. and App. A. p. 22 f. See also W. E. Collins, *Beginnings of English Christianity* (1898); Williams, *CEB* 1–154, or in slighter form his article in *ERE* iii. 631 f.; bishop G. F. Browne, *Church in these Islands before Augustine* (1895).

[2] I have introducèd the adjective because of the evidence in L. Duchesne, *Fastes Épiscopaux*, i. 30–3, of the absence of organized Church life in Gaul elsewhere at this time. F. E. Warren, *The Liturgy and Ritual of the Celtic Church* (Oxford, 1881), 46–57, brings forward some confirmation, chiefly archaeological, in spite of exaggeration. But the inference of an " Ephesian liturgy " and general Asiatic origin, a theory once very popular, is groundless (H. and S. *Conc.* i. p. xix) and cannot therefore be used in explanation of the extreme asceticism of Irish Monasticism (*infra*, p. 214). It would be much better to trace the connection, through Cassian, Palladius, &c., between Ireland and Egypt. On the theory of its 'autochthonous' (druidical or bardic !) origin see Gougaud, *CC* 68 f.; Cabrol, *DACL* ii. 3075. On the whole matter of its origin Willis-Bund, *CCW* 149, seems to me needlessly sceptical.

[3] Willis-Bund, *CCW* 146, denies this, but without, as it seems to me, sufficient evidence. He maintains that Monasticism originated in the tribe, and developed onwards to the solitary (*ib.* 160).

the elemental facts of nature—ocean, river, or forest—there would be a certain congruity of sentiment between the new religion and the nature-spirits which formed the basis of the older Celtic religion.[1]

Celtic monachism has left imperishable marks of its presence. There is no word that meets the eye of the traveller in Wales or Cornwall more frequently than *llan*. But every *llan*—except the later place-names which indicate dedication to some saint (using the word in its stricter signification), every ancient *llan* in other words, especially in Brittany, where the word has retained its older meaning [2]—witnesses to the connection with a monastery, or to the presence of some primitive hermit, with his lonely cell destined, perhaps, to become the nucleus of a monastery, or, at any rate, the centre of worship for a whole district.[3] In Ireland the *kil* or *cil*

[1] See *ERE* iii. 278, 294.

[2] Williams, *CEB* 291. Cf. for Breton names Lan Sulian, Lan Aleth, Landevennic, Landerneau, Landeda, Lannillis, &c. See any good map of Brittany.

[3] There are in Wales 510 *llans* and 26 in Cornwall [E. J. Newell, *Welsh Church* (1895), 146–7]. Of these a minority, of later origin, are true dedications (*e.g.* to St. Michael, "Llanfihangel," 94 in number, or to St. Mary, "Llanfair." On their origin see Willis-Bund, *CCW* 330 f., 424). But the older *llans*, built in the days when "saint" was a wide word (*infra*, p. 190), do not imply dedication but foundation (H. and S. *Conc.* i. 203 dates the earliest dedication to other than founders in 717). The hermit origin of the *llan* accounts for the lonely situation of so many of them (*e.g.* llan Tudno, llan Paternus or Llanbadarn, or the llan Trillo, the small cell-chapel on the shore at Colwyn Bay—all three well known to tourists) and for the exceeding diversity of the names, often mistaken for an extensive calendar of "saints." Thus of 210 churches in Cornwall, Mr. Borlase has counted 117 still retaining names of British founders. (See also Williams, *CEB* c. 17, "British Terms indicative of Monachism.") *Eglwys* (i.e. *ecclesia*) as a church-name marks the victory of the Latin Church (Willis-Bund, *CCW* 338); *Bettws* (i.e. *Bed-hus*, "house of prayer") points to Saxon influence.

—Celtic forms of the Latin *cella*—still bear witness to the early prevalence of the hermit life, while the Welsh spelling of "Dyserth" scarcely conceals the *deserta* which attracted the recluses. As we might expect among a people that thus favoured the eremite form large monasteries were not numerous; nevertheless three Bangors (Ban-chor) at least bear their witness to the 'chief choir,' where the many monks were gathered together, possibly even a whole clan or sept.

The foundation of Monasticism in Southern Britain, while owing much to the inspiration of Martin, was largely the work of Germanus [1] of Auxerre. His two visits to Britain, the first at the instance of pope Celestine,[2] were primarily intended to put an end to the mischief wrought in the Celtic Church by the well-known heresy of the British monk Pelagius.[3] 'Committing themselves

[1] Modern Welsh, *Garmon*. In the Isle of Man we have St. Germain's; in Cornwall St. Germans.

[2] See Prosper Aquit. *Chron.* in *MGH Chron. Min.* i. 472.

[3] Zimmer, *CCB* 19–22, defends the statement of Jerome that Pelagius († c. 418) was 'progeniem Scotticae gentis' (*PL* 24, p. 758), *i.e.* Irish. But the majority of our early authorities call him 'Brito' (see Williams, *CEB* 202–3), and H. and S. *Conc.* ii. 290 refer the reference to Pelagius' coadjutor, Caelestius. Mansuetus, the first bishop of Toul (c. 350 ?), is also said to have been 'nobili Scotorum genere oriundus' (H. and S. *Conc.* ii. 289). These two names are of some importance in their bearing on pre-Patrician churches in Ireland (*infra*, p. 189 n.). For this mission of Germanus, see *infra*, p. 187, and for the narrative of the mission itself the curiously mixed work of Constantius of Lyons, *Vita Germani*, i. 19, 23 [written about 480. For Germanus and the *Vita* of Constantius, see W. Levison's masterly study in *Neues Archiv der Gesell. f. ält. deut. Geschichtskunde*, 29 (1) (1903)]. This work in its present form is sadly interpolated (Levison, *op. cit.* 112 f.), nor is there at present any good edition save that of Mombritius (Milan, 1480), reprinted by the Benedictines of Solesmes (Paris, 1910, 2 vols.). A new edition is in preparation for *MGH rer. Merov.* A few details are preserved in the *Vita Lupi*, c. 3 (ed. Krusch, *MGH rer. Merov.* iii. 120–4).

in the winter to the unexplored sea' and 'the waves of the terrible ocean,' Germanus and his companion, Lupus of Troyes, who had been brought up at Lérins, in 429 crossed the Channel, visited the grave of St. Alban, suppressed 'damnable unbelief' by their miracles, —chief of which was the famous Halleluiah victory over the Saxons and Picts in 429[1]—and returned, crowned with success. About the same time, unknown to Germanus, a great event occurred: the English began the occupation of the island. Some twenty years later (447), a second visit of Germanus, this time accompanied by Severus of Treves, was equally successful, in spite of the 'legions of demons' who met him on the sea—modern readers also may have met these demons—raising their violent storms 'to thwart the work of human salvation.' Through Germanus British monachism was brought into touch with the developments in Gaul. Once introduced it rapidly spread. "The early monachism of this island proved itself to be possessed of such a capacity for organic unity of purpose that it covered the whole land, almost appropriating to itself the functions and privileges of the corporate life of the Church."[2] But of one thing it seems to have been utterly incapable. Such was the hatred between the British and the Saxon invaders that the older inhabitants seem to have made no attempt whatever to Christianize the fierce new-comers. For this neglect of duty they were destined to pay a bitter price.

Greater even than Germanus was one who was for

[1] Bede, *HE* i. 20, from Constant. *Vita Germani*, i. 28. The traditional site of this victory, Maes Garmon near Mold, is impossible, whatever be the truth about the battle.
[2] Williams, *CEB* 307, 318.

many years an inmate of his monastery, the illustrious Patrick.[1] In his rude *Confessio*, a kind of *Apologia pro sua vita*, he tells us of his early history :

'I Patrick, the sinner, am the most rustic and the least of all the faithful, contemptible in the eyes of many. My father was Colpurnus (Calpurnius), a deacon, a son of Potitus, a presbyter, Britons both, who belonged to the village of Bannavem Taberniae.[2] He had a small farm close by, and here I was taken captive. I was then about sixteen years of age. I knew not the true God, and I was led into captivity in Ireland with many thousands of persons.'

In Ireland the slave—'freeborn once,' as he boasts in his *Epistle* to Coroticus (Ceretic) the British king of Strathclyde, 'born of a father who was a decurion '—was made a neatherd. In the land of captivity ' the Lord opened my understanding regarding my unbelief.' At length (410) he escaped in a vessel engaged in the

---

[1] Born about 389 (Zimmer, *CCB* 43, dates in 386). His British name of Sucat ("ready for battle") may seem to many to be strangely appropriate. His assumed name of Patrick (*patricius*) is an indication of Sucat's exaggerated estimate of his high birth as the son of a decurion or local magistrate (on 'decurions' see S. Dill, *RSWE* iii. c. 2).

The life of Patrick is a matter of much dispute. Students may consult J. B. Bury, *The Life of St. Patrick and his Place in History* (1905), the best life, excellent appendices and notes; H. Zimmer, *CCB*, too ingenious, needs care; W. Stokes, *The Tripartite Life of St. P.* (2 vols., *RS* 1907, badly edited) ; N. J. D. White, *Libri Patricii* (1905), with Introd., trans., and notes ; C. H. H. Wright, *The Writings of Patrick* (1889). The *Confessio*, *Epistola*, *Lorica*, &c., of Patrick are also in H. and S. *Conc.* ii. 296 f. For the Armagh *Vita S. Patric.* we have also the edition by E. Hogan in *Analecta Bollandiana* (1882), i. 531 f. The doubt of Plummer (Bede, *HE* vol. 2, p. 25) as to Patrick's existence is no longer tenable.

[2] Properly a posting house near Daventry. But this is too far from the sea for a raid of pirates (Bury, *op. cit.* 322 f.). So Banwen in Glamorganshire has been suggested. Kilpatrick near Dumbarton seems impossible for the residence of a 'decurion' at that date. Patrick also spoke a low-Latin dialect (Zimmer, *CCB* 52) that would seem to point to regions south of the Roman Wall.

MONASTICISM IN THE CELTIC CHURCH

export of Irish wolf-dogs, and after three days reached Gaul.[1] For twenty-eight days 'he journeyed through the desert'—a sufficient comment on the devastations of the age. But we cannot follow his wanderings in detail. Suffice that we find him an inmate of Lérins,[2] a monastery that was already attracting the religious from many lands, as also for at least fourteen years under Germanus at Auxerre. In these two monasteries he was brought under the ideals and discipline of Gallic Monasticism. So when in 432 [3] he was sent by pope Celestine to Ireland, the Christianity he introduced, or rather organized and developed—for there seem to have been a few Christian communities existing before his arrival [4]—was largely monastic in character,

[1] Bury, *op. cit.* 339 f.

[2] Bury, *op. cit.* 338, dates in 411–12, 414–5. But as Lérins was not founded until very shortly before 410 (*supra*, p. 121) this seems early. Possibly the visit to Lérins may have come after Auxerre.

[3] *Annals Ulster* (ed. Hennessy, 1887), i. 5.

[4] We touch here a very difficult matter. For Christian settlements in Ireland before Patrick we have the following evidence: (*a*) Pelagius was possibly an Irish monk; see *supra*, p. 186 n. 3. (*b*) Prosper Tiro of Aquitaine in his *Chron.* (ed. Mommsen in *MGH Chron. Min.* i. 473) speaks of pope Celestine in 431 sending Palladius as 'primus episcopus' 'ad Scottos in Christum credentes'. [quoted from Prosper in Bede, *HE* i. 13; cf. Prosper, *Cont. Collat.* 21 (2) ;'*Annals Ulster*, i. 3]. According to Prosper, *Chron.* (Mommsen, *op. cit.* i. 472), this same Palladius was responsible ('ad insinuationem Palladii') for Celestine sending Germanus in 429. The relation of Palladius to Patrick, whose mission took place the following year, is difficult. Zimmer, *CCB* 35 f., identifies the two; but this is not generally accepted (Gougaud, *CC* 39; Bury, *op. cit.* 343, 389; Willis-Bund, *CCW* 22). Bury, *op. cit.* 54–5, limits the mission of Palladius to one year and accepts the tradition of Nennius that he died in 432 among the Picts [*Hist. Brittonum* (ed. Mommsen in *MGH Chron. Min.*), iii. 195. Written about 679. Cf. also the Armagh *Vita Pat.* (ed. cit.) 553–4]. The existence of a few pre-Patrician churches seems demonstrated in any case (Bury, *op. cit.* 298, 349 f. Plummer, *VSH* i. Introd. xxx, lxi).

not only because of tribal exigencies, but because "the state of society rendered it practically impossible to maintain the Christian life except under some monastic rule."[1] In 440 Patrick visited Rome,[2] and on his return founded Armagh (444)[3] as the site of his see and the centre of his new authority. But after his death (461)[4] the Irish Church lost much of such episcopal authority as Patrick had imposed upon it, and, under the pressure of its tribal feuds, for some centuries continued to be predominantly "monastic," if indeed that is the right word to apply to these cases of the clan turned 'religious.'

With Germanus and Patrick we begin the era in Celtic Christianity known as the "Age of the Saints." But it should be noticed that the "saints," whether of the First, Second, or Third Order, almost without exception, were hermits and monks. Celtic scholars have not yet decided upon the elements of real history that lie hidden beneath the masses of Celtic hagiographic literature;[5] but sufficient is certain to show us a whole Christianity organized round Monasticism as its highest expression. The great names that have come down to us from the Celtic Christianity both of the earliest

[1] J. H. Todd, *St. Patrick* (1868), 505.

[2] Bury, *op. cit.* 367 f.; cf. *ib.* 159. It seems to have been his first visit (*ib.* 345).

[3] *Annals Ulster*, i. 11; Bury, *op. cit.* 308.

[4] *Annals Ulster*, i. 19; Bury, *op. cit.* 331 f. He was, probably, buried at Saul (Bury, *op. cit.* 380 f.).

[5] For a compressed account of the Welsh saints, see Williams, *CEB* 294–305; more succinctly still in *ERE* iii. 637; Loth, *EB* 38 ff. For the Irish saints reference may be made to the useful Plummer, *VSH* which takes the place of the scarce Colgan, *Acta Sanct. Hib.* or P. Fleming, *Collectanea Sacra*. For the character of these *Vitae*, see Plummer, *VSH* i. Introd. lxxxix f., cxxix f. (this last section a most valuable contribution on their relation to folk-lore).

ages and of the sixth and seventh centuries—Illtud (fl. 520),[1] David († 601), Daniel (Deiniol) of Bangor (c. 500), Gildas († 570) are the best known [2]—are all monks. But we must beware of confusing the Celtic " monk " or the Celtic " saint " with the monks and saints of the Latin and Greek Churches. We must not forget the vast influence on the Celtic Church of the tribal or rather " sept " system amidst which it was introduced, and of which blood-relationship was the basis.[3] So when Christianity taught that all men were capable of entering the " sept " of the " saint " by a mysterious re-birth, the conception of the " sept " and its blood-relationship still predominated. " Saintship," though never quite hereditary, came perilously near it ; it denoted blood-membership in the tribe of the " saint " ; this last, with the introduction of the new religion, a most important matter. For the preaching of the gospel had altered the whole social economy. Henceforth " no real Irish tribe, it was said, could exist, that is legally exist, without the two branches, the tribe of the ' saint ' and the tribe of the land." [4] Often the two branches were under one chief, and the " saintship " was regarded as almost as much hereditary,

[1] Illtud, the teacher of David and Gildas, had himself been under Germanus.

[2] For these, see the excellent accounts in Williams, *CEB* 316 ff., 366 ff. For Gildas, *DNB* s.v. or J. E. Lloyd, *Hist. Wales* (1911), i. 134 f., 160. His work, *de excidio Brit.*, was composed, probably, about 550 (Loth, *EB* 27 n.). Best eds. Mommsen in *MGH Chron. Min.* iii. 1 ff. or H. Williams with Eng. trs. in Cymmrodorion Soc. Records (1899, 1901).

[3] Willis-Bund, *CCW* 17, 19, 21, 30, 39 and c. 2, in special has brought out most clearly, though, possibly, with some exaggeration, the importance of the tribal system in the Celtic Church and its bearings upon Monasticism.

[4] Willis-Bund, *CCW* 39.

i.e. as the possession of the sept, as the land. Of the eleven immediate successors of Columba, for instance, nine were certainly of his kin; and elaborate rules have been left us for regulating the succession in any monastery so as to secure the founder's family or the "saint's" tribe. In Trim and Armagh, as well as in Iona, as Dr. Reeves has shown us, the office of abbot was confined to a single family.[1] The tie of the tribe was the strongest feature in Celtic Christianity.[2]

From this certain important consequences followed. Religion from the first adopted a clan or sept form, especially in Ireland. To this clan-form we may give the title of "monastic" provided we understand clearly the meaning of our word. Religion became "monastic" because in no other way could it so quickly claim the allegiance of the people as by thus basing itself upon the kinship of the sept. So we find whole sections of a tribe or clan adopting a spiritual or semi-monastic life, with the head of the clan as the abbot of the monastery or monasteries—for the clan could not all dwell in one building or place, especially with the growth of years. This abbatial government by the chief of the clan, a survival in Christian times of the old Celtic king-priesthood,[3] was so much a matter of course that early exceptions seem to have been of the rarest. Of such a spiritual sept the male members were known as "saints,"

[1] Willis-Bund, *CCW* 195 f., and cf. *ib.* 426 f.

[2] Reeves, *AC* 342; Willis-Bund, *CCW* 45, 185 f. We may compare the attempt of the Church of Jerusalem to limit its bishops to the kinsmen of Jesus (*PEC* 122 f.), and the hereditary character of saintship with the Moors. In England certain monasteries in Saxon times were kept strictly in the government of the family of the founder (M. Bateson, *Origin and Early History of Double Monasteries*, 173, 177).

[3] On this king-priesthood see *ERE* iii. 294.

a word that had none of the close significance that it acquired in the Roman Church.[1] In accordance with Celtic usage of descent through the mother,[2] for such "sainthood" illegitimacy, as we should now term it, importing ideas that were then alien, was no bar; it was sufficient that the 'saint' was the child of a tribal maiden. Nor at first were the women and children driven from the "monastery";[3] only with greater piety or increased regulation did this become the rule. But only rarely, in the case of high birth, were women reckoned among the 'saints,' at any rate in earlier and ruder times.[4] Another consequence was the enormous numbers who were members of these clan-monasteries— 2000 at Bangor, 3000 at Clonard, 3000 at Clonfert, and so on. But such figures, apart from all the deductions necessary for medieval inexactitude, are really the figures of the clan at large.

There was another result of this system, round which there has raged much controversy. In consequence of the predominance of the clan, diocesan episcopacy, such as we find early developed in Italy and Gaul, did not exist, or, rather, existed only in a subordinate tribal form. The clan or monastery was supreme. Bishops there

[1] *ERE* c. 9. The word began to be limited, under Latin influence (Willis-Bund, *CCW* 421). We see this change of significance in the commencement in 717 of the dedication of churches to St. Michael, St. Mary, and other "real" saints (see *supra*, p. 185 n.). The earliest known papal canonization is that of Ulrich of Augsburg by John xv. (3 Feb. 993; Jaffé, *RP* i. 488).

[2] For the survivals of the matriarchate among the Celts, see *ERE* iii. 298.

[3] Willis-Bund, *CCW* 156, 160. We are expressly told of the first order of 'saints,' 'mulierum administrationem et consortia non respuebant' (H. and S. *Conc.* ii. 292).

[4] Willis-Bund, *CCW* 438 f. Bridget (on whom see *DNB* or *DCB*) is a later elaboration.

were in abundance, but they were incidental rather than essential. As Mr. Willis-Bund puts it, though in a somewhat exaggerated way, " every monastic establishment had among its officials a bishop, just as it had a porter or any other officer." " The ecclesiastical jurisdiction was in the hands of the abbots of the great monasteries who administered the districts subject to them, the bishops being merely members of the monastic bodies, and as such subject, even as regards the exercise of their episcopal functions, to the authority of the abbot, in virtue of the vow of monastic obedience." Ordinations and other episcopal functions were, of course, performed by the bishop alone, but "under the direction of the abbot and convent"; while the bishop as such had no voice in the affairs of the convent, or in the administration of the district. The abbot, in fact, "represented the tribe of the saint; the bishop did not."[1] In the cases where the abbot might chance to be a bishop, "he exercised his jurisdiction not as bishop but as abbot."[2] For "the head of a Celtic monastery

[1] Willis-Bund, *CCW* 205.

[2] See Bede, *HE* iii. 4 with Plummer's excellent note, and cf. Reeves *AC* 335; Plummer, *VSH* i. Introd. cxi ff. Bede speaks of this system as 'ordine inusitato,' as it was in his day, and. H. and S. *Conc.* i. 142 n. maintain that it never existed among the British Celts. Their chief evidence for diocesan episcopacy in Britain would appear to be the list of the three British bishops present at Arles (314 or ? 316). But there is little to prove that these were diocesan, while the evidence against is overwhelming, *e.g.* the 118 Welsh bishops present about 569 at the synod of Llanddewivrevi (Willis-Bund, *CCW* 36), and especially the whole structure of the early Celtic Church (*supra*, p. 192; Willis-Bund, *CCW* 208 f.: the argument of Willis-Bund on p. 221 is founded on an error; the true reading is 'ipsi monachi,' not 'episcopi monachi.' See Bede, *HE* iv. 5 with Plummer's note). Stubbs, *Constit. Hist.* i. 240, speaks more guardedly; while Loth, *EB* 207-9, maintains that originally in Britain the "episcopal dignity was abbatial" (cf. Williams,

admitted no superior; he considered himself, like Henry VIII., 'supreme head next after Christ.'"[1] The later conflicts of Roman and Celtic Christianity, from the abortive conference in 603 or 604 between Augustine of Canterbury and the Welsh bishops at 'Augustine's Oak,'[2] down to the Synod of Whitby and the repressions that followed, are often represented as if they had turned on matters of ritual, the date of Easter,[3] the kind of tonsure, and the like. These may have been the external occasions; the real struggle arose from radical differences in Church organization, especially in the relation of bishop and abbot, of clan and of diocese. Nor must we forget that rigid uniformity, the mark of Rome, has never been a distinguishing feature of the Celtic temperament.

CEB 316, 394–5; Newell, *The Welsh Church*, 57; Willis-Bund, *CCW* 190), or, as it could be more accurately put, the "bishop was a monastic official under the control of the abbot" (Willis-Bund, *CCW* c. 5; caution needed at times. With this dictum, Cabrol, *DACL* ii. 3213, agrees). In the time of Gildas (550) we see the beginnings of diocesan episcopacy (H. and S. *Conc.* i. 143; Willis-Bund, *CCW* 215), and in the seventh century greater fixity was given to the system. In Ireland Patrick probably intended an episcopal organization (Bury, *op. cit.* 375). But the tribes were too strong for him, and as a matter of fact bishops without sees were common (Todd, *St. Patrick*, 1 ff.; Willis-Bund, *CCW* 35). Not until the Synod of Rathbreasail (1120) was Ireland definitely divided into 24 dioceses with Armagh at the head, as the issue of a long struggle one result of which was the evolution of the modern Patrick legend (Zimmer, *CCB* 92–105; for opposite view, cf. Bury, *op. cit.* 389).

[1] Willis-Bund, *CCW* 206.

[2] Bede, *HE* ii. 2. The traditional site is Aust on the Severn, which is, however, probably *Trajectum Augusti*, not *Augustini*. A better site is Down Ampney near Cricklade (Collins, *Beginnings Eng. Christianity*, 87 f.). At the second conference 'learned men' were present from the monastery of Bangor-is-y-Coed on the Dee.

[3] Those interested in this matter should consult *ERE* ("Calendar") iii. 88 f.

II

In Celtic Monasticism there appears from the first another feature of remarkable interest and influence. In the Monasticism of the West there was no law upon which greater insistence was placed, especially after Benedict, than that of 'stability,' *i.e.* the fixed domicile of the monk. The wandering monk was sternly suppressed—until, indeed, he reappeared with papal sanction in the wandering friar. But in Celtic Monasticism we are struck from the first with its extraordinary restlessness [1]—in many respects, no doubt, the reflection of the general restlessness of the Celtic populations, especially in Ireland. A nomad at home, the Scot or Irish colonized the northern parts of Scotland in the fifth and sixth centuries, and traces of his wanderings a thousand years before the Christian era are found in the burial mounds of Scandinavia. Of this restlessness the typical hero in song and romance is the monk Brendan († 577) of Clonfert, who crossed the ocean 'through a thick fog' that he might find an earthly paradise 'beyond which shone an eternal clearness.' [2] From the greater monastic settlements of Wales and Ireland—for instance, from the monastery of Illtud, on the small island of

---

[1] Walafrid Strabo noticed this 'consuetudo peregrinandi' (see *MGH* ii. 30).

[2] The tale of the two voyages was worked up into a popular romance before 1050 (Plummer, *VSH* Introd. xli n. 2) by Irish monks on the Lower Rhine (*DNB* vi. 260). As this *Navigation* (*Peregrinatio*) became very popular in Spain (Plummer, *VSH* i. Introd. xli n.) it may have inspired Columbus. Its popularity in Germany was such that no less than three vernacular texts of it have survived. See C. Schröder, *S. Brandan* (Erlangen, 1871), for Latin and other texts with notes. Cf. Reeves, *AC* 211 n.; Plummer, *VSH* i. Introd. xxxvii n.; and for the *Vita Brendani, ib.* i. 99 ff.

Caldy or Ynys Pyr, for twenty years at the commencement of the sixth century the rival of Lérins itself;[1] from the great monasteries of Bangor-is-y-coed near Chester, and of Bangor in Ireland—there poured forth a succession of Celtic enthusiasts who carried their religion and their monasticism to far-off places the names of which still preserve their memories. Chief of these we may instance St. David, by whom, it was believed, twelve monasteries in succession were founded; to whom, above all others, has gone forth the reverence of the Welsh.

In this restlessness Celtic Monasticism was powerfully assisted by a current political movement. In the fifth century, owing first to Pictish and Irish[2] invasions, followed at a later date by pressure from the Saxons[3] and from the distress caused by a great plague in 547,[4] we find a steady emigration of the British to Armorica, a land henceforth to be known under its new name of Brittany.[5] The leaders in this emigration were monks,

---

[1] Williams, *CEB* 325. Caldy is not far from Tenby. A second monastery of Illtud was at Llaniltud Fawr or Llantuit Major. Illtud is commemorated in Brittany in the names of Lanildut near Brest and of S. Ideuc near Malo (de la Borderie, *Hist. de Bretagne*, i. 275 n.).

[2] Bury, *Patrick*, 325 f.

[3] Gildas, *de excidio Brit*. c. 25, ' alii transmarinas regiones petebant.' Cf. *ib*. c. 23 and Loth, *EB* 168. For date of the first Saxon invasions, about 446, see Bede, *HE* i. 15, with Plummer's note. The presence of a British bishop without diocese at the council of Tours in 461 (Hefele, *HC* II. ii. 899, Mansi, *Conc*. iv. 1053) may point to this emigration (Loth, *EB* 153). According to Cabrol, *DACL* ii. 1256, the earliest emigrant monastery founded in Britain was by St. Budoc before 470 on the island of Lavré. The last British emigrant that we know of was Yvi of Lindisfarne, a disciple of Cuthbert at the commencement of the 8th cent. (Loth, *EB* 160). Loth distinguishes three main groups of emigrants (Loth, *EB* 200 f.).

[4] Williams, *CEB* 286, 411.

[5] The older theory of E. Freeman, *Hist. Geog. of Europe* (ed.

and the witchery of their lives—that constant witchery of Monasticism, to us, perhaps, so inexplicable, to the early and medieval Church so réal—drew others after them. "The emigrating saints," [1] writes M. Loth, "were usually accompanied by numerous followers." [2] They found Armorica largely a desert, almost wholly heathen, its cities burned without inhabitant,[3] "made desert by the Empire itself, owing to many years of crushing imperial taxation extorted by selfish officials, and because of the ravages of barbarian hordes." [4] In the dense forests that ran down to the coast the British monks established their clearings or *lans*, in which their rude huts [5] and chapels of wood or stone mark the beginning of later villages that bear to this day the

J. B. Bury, 1903), 93, that we have in Britain the persistence of the old pre-Roman Celts is now abandoned owing to recent researches into Celtic philology (see especially Loth, *EB* 82–94). As Loth points out, p. 92, " at the commencement of the 5th century Armorica was a Romanized country like the rest of Gaul. By the middle of the sixth century all was changed " (cf. de la Borderie, *op. cit. infra*, i. 247, and the two maps, *ib*. i. 593). The two chief works on the subject are J. Loth, *EB*, and A. de la Borderie, *Hist. de la Bretagne* (4 vols., Paris, 1896, of which vol. i. deals with our subject and has good maps). The reader may content himself with the summaries of results in Williams, *CEB* c. 18, or Gougaud, *CC* c. 4.

[1] For a list of leaders, see Loth, *EB* 161–3, 202–5.

[2] Loth, *EB* 166; Williams, *CEB* 288. From these followers (*plebs*) we get the Breton word *plou* or *plwy* (Williams, *CEB* 289–91; Loth, *EB* 228–9; de la Borderie, *op. cit.* i. 281–3), for illustrations of which see any good map of Brittany.

[3] " It is remarkable that almost everywhere the ruins (of the cities) are covered with a thick layer of cinders " (de la Borderie, *op. cit.* i. 224; and for the desert character, i. 261).

[4] Williams, *CEB* 289 and, at length, de la Borderie, *op. cit.* i. 212–28. For the extensive Roman civilization of Brittany, see Loth, *EB* 65 f. ; de la Borderie, *op. cit.* i. 78–155. The revolt of Armorica against the Romans began in 408 (Loth, *EB* 72).

[5] The Breton monks, like the Irish, lived, as a rule, in separate huts (de la Borderie, *op. cit.* i. 508).

names of these first settlers. Nor were these wandering monks confined to Brittany alone. In the see of Bretoña near Lugo in Gallicia, with its Welsh bishop Mailoc, perhaps the brother of the better known Gildas, we find evidence of their presence in Spain.[1]

Even more conspicuous than Britain in its missionary and monastic enterprises was the Celtic Church in Ireland. In the sixth century we find the Irish Church, untroubled by the disasters which were overwhelming the sister island, full of activity and resource. Embracing Christianity with Celtic ardour, the Irish monasteries became, for a while, the centres in the West of the ancient civilization and learning, retaining even some knowledge of Greek, a language almost unknown elsewhere.[2] In the middle of the sixth century, especially, we note a wonderful outburst of monastic enthusiasm. In 520 Finnian († 548) founded Clonnard on a strict monastic rule that was afterwards largely used and developed elsewhere. In 546 Columban established the monastery of Derry, and that of Durrow before 560. In 541 we see the foundation of Clonmacnoise by Ciaran, while Comgell founded Bangor (in Ulster) either in 554 or 558. In 552 Brendan established Clonfert in Longford,[3] while in 563 Columba set off for Hi, 'desiring to go into exile for the sake of Christ'[4]—a momentous step, to the consequences of which we shall return. From these monasteries there poured out a succession

[1] A. W. Haddan, *Remains* ("Scots on the Continent"), 262.

[2] Bede, *HE* iii. 27, speaks of Irish learning in high praise, and gives names of English students who journeyed to Ireland.

[3] Zimmer, *CCB* 64, 70 for the above dates.

[4] Reeves, *AC* 9. For the idea that Columba's journey to Hi was a penance, see *ib.* 247 f.

of daring missionaries. In their flimsy coracles they crossed the stormy seas to Brittany, where, among the Breton saints of the sixth and seventh centuries, we find more than a dozen whose names are Irish.[1] As late as 818 the Breton monasteries as a whole still followed the Irish rather than the Roman usages.[2]

Others sought for seclusion from the world by escaping to the numerous islands off the western coast where the roar of the Atlantic and the screams of the gulls alone would disturb their devotions. When these became too crowded with devotees drawn by their fame, they put out into northern seas that they might find some desert in the ocean. The Hebrides, the Orkneys, the Shetlands, even lonely St. Kilda and distant Iceland [3] itself were all reached by these adventurous wanderers, who carried everywhere their Irish monasticism as well as their Irish culture and their Irish manuscripts. In the early years of the ninth century whoever knew Greek on the Continent was either an Irish monk or taught by an Irish monk.[4] The last representative of the Greek spirit in the West and one of the earliest torch-bearers in the long line of Christian mystics, by his very greatness unintelligible to the men of his

[1] Loth, *EB* 164–6.

[2] de la Borderie, *Hist. de Bretagne*, i. 508. See *infra*, p. 211.

[3] The Irishman Dicuil (on whom see *DNB* s.v.), writing in 825 his treatise *de mensura orbis terrae* (ed. A. Letronne, Paris, 1814, p. 39), gives details of Iceland which he had received from Irish monks about 795 (see Gougaud, *CC* 136 f.).

[4] Zimmer, *CCB* 92. Besides the MSS. in the Vatican and Nat. Lib. Paris, Zimmer points out that there are 117 early Irish MSS. in Continental libraries. Of the culture of the Irish Church there is a good account in Gougaud, *CC* c. 8, or G. T. Stokes, *Ireland and the Celtic Church* (6th ed., 1907), c. 11.

generation, was John Scotus the Erin-born,[1] who about the year 847 drifted from Ireland and settled at the court of that patron of scholars, Charles the Bald.

Some of these wandering Irish missionary-monks deserve the passing tribute of our mention. From the Faroe islands (725) and Iceland (795) to the plains of Italy, from the shores of the ocean to the sources of the Rhine and the Danube we find them everywhere, working with an enthusiasm that must not be judged by the absence of permanence in their results. The reputed pioneer of the host was Fridolin, whose Irish birthplace is unknown, and whose existence is not beyond dispute. "From Poictiers, his first halting-place, he passed by the Moselle and Strasburg, founding churches dedicated to St. Hilary, first to Glarus [2] which still retains in its name the trace of his presence, and finally to Seckingen, near Basle,"[3] where he built a double monastery of the usual Celtic type.

Towards the close of the sixth century we come across

[1] For John Scot Eriugena (*i.e.* Erin-born), see my *Development of Christian Thought* (1911), c. 6, § 5; Alice Gardner, *Studies in John the Scot* (1900); or R. L. Poole, *Medieval Thought* (1884), c. 2.

[2] There seems no authority for this save Haddan's inference from the name Glarus, the truth of which seems doubtful. All that Balther tells us is that Fridolin founded churches dedicated to Hilary in Chur and the district round (*op. cit. infra*, 363). According to A. Bellesheim, *Gesch. der kath. Kirche in Irland* (Mainz, 1890), i. 137, Fridolin has left his mark " in the coat of arms of Glarus."

[3] Haddan, *Remains*, 269. Date, 6 March, probably about 511 rather than 695 (see *DCB* ii. 565). For Fridolin we are dependent on the *Vita* by Baltherus of S. Gallen (*c.* 1050) (ed. B. Krusch in *MGH rer. Merov.* iii. 350). Out of much that is legendary the bare facts may be taken as genuine (see Krusch's note, *op. cit.* 351). There is a full study in J. Ebrard, *Die iroschottische Missionkirche* (Gütersloh, 1873), 285–304. See also J. Schuler, *St. Fridolin, sein Leben u. seine Berehrung* (Säckingen, 1884); or H. Leo, *Der hl. Fridolin* (Freiburg, 1886). Nothing in *DNB*.

the greatest of these missionaries, Columba and Columban, whose monastic systems for a while struggled in competition with that of Benedict. Columba,[1] the descendant of Irish kings, in whose character we see at all times the imperiousness of his high birth,[2] was born at Gartan, among the mountains of Donegal (7 Dec. 521). On his baptism he changed his name of Crimthann or "wolf" for that of Colum or "dove." He was brought up by St. Finnian on the shores of Strangford Lough; on his ordination he lived the life of a 'religious' at Glasnevin. After founding sundry monasteries in the north of Ireland,[3] Columba set off in 563 with a band of twelve companions to preach the gospel to the emigrant Scots in Dalriada. Crossing the seas in a currach of wickerwork covered with hides, Columba finally landed on the barren shores of Hi or Iona,[4] on the border-line between the kingdoms of the

---

[1] The classic authority for Columba is Reeves, *AC*. This has also been published by W. F. Skene (Edin. 1874) abridged and re-arranged. Of Adamnan there is another ed. by J. T. Fowler (Ox. 1894). Adamnan, who was abbot of Iona from 679–697 (*AC* liii.), incorporates in his third book sections from an earlier *Vita Columbae* by Cuimene Ailbe († 669) ('Cummeneus Albus'), extant in Mabillon's *AS. Ben. Ord.* (1733) i. 342–9 (Reeves, *AC* 199 n.). Of modern lives, Montalembert, *MW* iii. 1–168, is eloquent and enthusiastic, and for his facts follows Reeves.

[2] Reeves, *AC* lxxvii. 255; Willis-Bund, *CCW* 25.

[3] For list, see Reeves, *AC* 276–98.

[4] Hi is the original name (in Gaelic='island,' cf. ey) and is still prevalent in the monumental records of the island (Reeves, *AC* 261): I-coluim-cille, *i.e.* 'island of Columba's cell,' is the Scoto-Irish; Iona, which Adamnan (Reeves, *AC* 5) rightly claims is Hebrew for 'dove' (*columba*), is the usual English name. Columban in his letters [ed. *MGH* (1892) 156, 169, 176] makes similar play on the identity of meaning of the Hebrew Jonah (Iona) and Columba. In reality Iona is the softened adjectival form (Io-na) agreeing with *insula* formed, by monks, from Hia or Hio. See Reeves, *AC* 259.

Scots and Picts. There he founded the famous monastery which was destined to become the centre and source of Christian missions in the north, from Inverness and Deer—'the monastery of *tears*'[1]—in the north-east corner of Aberdeen, down to the Humber. There, after thirty years of arduous life, the call came. As Columba climbed for the last time the little hill above the monastery he lifted up his hands in blessing. 'This place,' he said, 'is small and of no reputation; yet even the rulers of strange nations with their subjects shall confer great honours on it.' During the brief watches of the night he gave to his disciples his last message 'to be at peace and have sincere love one to another.' At daybreak he arose with the rest, and on his knees before the altar passed quietly away amidst a blaze of summer light.[2] A week before his death, the baptism of the Kentish king Ethelbert, away down in the far south, marked the success of the Roman mission of Augustine.

From Hi the Irish monks carried the gospel as far south as the Humber. Their organization, as usual, was monastic rather than episcopal, the various monasteries they founded all looking up to Iona as their head.[3] The beginnings of Christianity in the north of England, it is true, were due to the Roman mission, when, in the Easter of 627, Paulinus at Goodmanham near Market Weighton persuaded the Witan of Eadwine, the overlord

[1] Montalembert, *MW* iii. 67.

[2] 5, 8 or 9 June 597. The recent attempt to date in 580 contradicts Bede, *HE* iii. 4 (see Plummer's note). Reeves, *AC* 309 f., dates Sunday, 9 June 597.

[3] As Iona was so frequently ravaged by the Danes (801, 805, 877), the headship of the Columbite monasteries in Britain was transferred to Dunkeld (Skene, *Celtic Scotland*, ii. 304-5).

of every English realm save Kent, to abandon their idols and be baptized into the new faith.[1] But the overthrow of Eadwine at the battle of Hatfield Chase near Doncaster (12 Oct. 633) by the heathen Penda led to the triumph once more in Northumbria of the old gods, until the victory of Oswald the son of Eadwine at Heavenfeld near Hexham gave to Christianity a new and more vigorous life.[2] But the re-awakened Christianity of Northumbria was not that inherited from Paulinus but from Hi, within whose walls Oswald and twelve of his nobles had received baptism while still in exile.[3] At the heathen reaction Paulinus and his band had fled southwards, all except the deacon James, who remained behind in 'a village near Catterick, still to this day called by his name,' and 'plucked much prey from the old enemy by teaching and baptizing.'[4] The place of the deserters was more than taken by missionaries from the Scoto-Irish stations. In 635 their leader Aidan[5] fixed his bishop-stool on the island-peninsula of Lindisfarne. From this monastery monks journeyed far and wide over Northumbria, and even the triumph of heathenism once again, by Penda's victory at Maserfeld or Oswestry,[6] was not able altogether to undo their work. Burnt and harried by the heathen, Bernicia still clung to the Cross; and the reconstruction of the

---

[1] Bede, *HE* ii. 9–14.   [2] *Ib.* ii. 20, iii. 2.

[3] *Ib.* iii. 3.

[4] *Ib.* ii. 20. According to bishop G. F. Browne, *Conversion of the Heptarchy*, 218 f., the village is Aikburgh (=Jacobusburgh), now a farm called Aikbar, eight miles S.W. of Catterick.

[5] Aidan died 31 Aug. 651 (Bede, *HE* iii. 15, 17). For his character, see Bede, *HE* iii. 5, 14–17.

[6] *Ib.* iii. 9. Date, 5 Aug. 642.

Northumbrian kingdom under Oswiu ended in the overthrow and death of Penda, in his unfaith true to the end, at the battle of Winwaed.[1] As with this battle "all active resistance on the part of the older heathendom came to an end,"[2] the Scoto-Irish once more found their opportunity.

For a few years the spell which Ireland cast over England, especially in the North, was almost irresistible. One Scoto-Irish monk, Dicul, made his way with five comrades to where the South Saxons still clung to their paganism, severed by the dense forests that clothed the Wealds from the forces that were redeeming the rest of England.[3] Another, the son of a prince of Munster, established amongst the East Saxons the monastery, Fursey, the village of which still bears his name.[4] A third Irish scholar, Maildulf or Maelduin,[5] set up his hermitage and school in the midst of the forest that cut off the latest conquests of the West Saxons from the then borders of Welsh-land. His name is still preserved in the 'Maildulf's burgh' (Malmesbury) which gathered

---

[1] 15 Nov. 655. See Bede, *HE* iii. 24. The site of Winwaed is unknown.

[2] Green, *Making of England*, 310.

[3] His little monastery was at Bosham. See Bede, *HE* iv. 13; date, before 678.

[4] Bede, *HE* iii. 19. Fursa's chronology is very doubtful; all we can say is that he arrived in England about 637 (see Plummer's note, Bede, *HE* vol. 2, p. 173. Krusch, *op. cit. infra*, 423, dates before 635). He died at Péronne on the Somme on 16 Jan. year uncertain. Péronne was for many years a Scoto-Irish settlement (L. Traube, *Perrona Scottorum*; Munich, 1900). His *Vita* by a contemporary has been published, ed. B. Krusch in *MGH rer. Merov.* (1902) iv. 423 f. For the habitats of Fursa in England, Ireland, and France, see M. Stokes, *Three Months in the Forests of France* (1895), pt. 2.

[5] See Plummer's note, Bede, *HE* vol. ii. p. 310.

round his monastery. It was from the Irish mission-station of Old Melrose (Mailros) that Cuthbert, himself a peasant of the Lowlands, than whom no saint has left a deeper impression on the memory of the northern English, set off to proclaim the story of the Cross in the remoter villages of the Cheviots, as yet unreached in their heathenism.[1] Though in his later life he loyally accepted the Roman usages, yet, both as prior of Melrose and afterwards of Lindisfarne—both of them Scoto-Irish foundations—he showed that all his tendencies, as were those of all the Scoto-Irish mission, were towards the monastic ideal. So when, as the result of the work of Wilfrid of Ripon and Benedict Biscop, the Synod of Whitby, under the presidency of Oswiu (664), decided for St. Peter and the power of his keys as against the authority of Columba,[2] though Colman and the Irish returned in dudgeon to Hi, they yet left behind them as one result of their labours a network of monasteries throughout Northumbria. These the great archbishop Theodore of Tarsus,[3] himself an Eastern monk, in his reduction of the English Church to Roman usage and order slowly brought into general line with the Benedictine movement. Among other canons of the Synod of Hertford (673) special stress was laid upon the Benedictine vow of 'stability,' or permanence of domicile,[4] the absence of which had rendered possible the Celtic

---

[1] Cuthbert entered Melrose in 651. He was consecrated bishop 26 March 685; died 20 March 687.

[2] Bede, *HE* iii. 25. Northern Ireland conformed to Rome in 697, south Ireland in 636, the Columbite monasteries in Scotland in 717 (Zimmer, *CCB* 106).

[3] Theodore was consecrated 26 March 668. He died 19 Sept. 690 (Bede, *HE* v. 8).

[4] Bede, *HE* iv. 5, canon 4.

restlessness. But though by this and other means the monastic foundations of the Celtic Church were thus supplanted, the pioneer work they accomplished should not be forgotten.

III

What Columba did for Britain, Columban attempted to do for Gaul; and for Columban as for Columba the final result was the same. Columban was born in Leinster in 543, the same year in which Benedict died, and was brought up in the great monastery of Bangor in Down. At the age of forty he was inflamed with missionary zeal, and with twelve companions crossed over to Gaul (585). There after several years of wandering he built a monastery, first in the ruined Roman fort of Anagrates (591)—the present village of Anagray—where oftentimes the monks had nothing to eat save grass and the roots of trees. But soon the numbers so grew that he was forced to build a larger monastery amid the extensive ruins of the old Roman Luxovium (Luxeuil) in the Vosges. Within a few years his followers had become so many that it was necessary to build other houses, over each of whom he placed a superior who was yet subordinate to himself, and for whose management he drew up his *Rule*. 'Obedience unto death,' with entire suppression of all personal will or thought, is the basis of his system. Great emphasis is laid on the confession of sin at all times, and on a life lived out in every detail by the practice of some religious observance. Columban's *Rule* simply bristles with punishments—six stripes for failing to say Amen after the grace before meat, six stripes for unnecessary talking, twelve stripes for forgetting to pray before or after work, two hundred stripes for speaking to a woman without the presence of a third party, and the like. Only by this means, so Columban thought, shall the brother 'find the higher way and cling to God' ('carpere iter tendens ad alti fastigia summa').

As Columban—'traditionum Scoticarum tenacissimus consectator'—naturally maintained the Celtic usages against the Roman, the jealousy of the Frankish bishops was furnished with a suitable weapon of offence. But his enemies could have accomplished little had not Columban lost the favour of the royal house of Burgundy by his outspoken rebukes of the infamous queen-grandmother, Brunhild, as well as of the licentiousness of Theodoric II. So in 610 he was banished from Luxeuil, and after a vain attempt to ship him back from Nantes to Ireland he wandered up the Rhine to Zug in Switzerland. Banished thence by the people for setting fire to one of their temples, Columban established himself at Bregenz. There we see him, assisted by St. Gall, with characteristic impetuosity, breaking the vats in which the heathen prepared their beer for Woden and throwing the gilded idols into Lake Constance. When driven thence by the fury of the priests, or by the revenge of Brunhild, his faith did not falter. 'The God Whom we serve,' said he, 'will lead us elsewhere.' So Columban crossed the Alps (612) to Milan, and spent the last two years of life in building his monastery of Bobbio in the Apennines, where he died and was buried (23 Nov. 615).[1]

[1] For Columban (in reality a useful variant only of the name of Columba) the chief authority is the *Vita S. Columbani* by Jonas, a monk of Bobbio, almost a contemporary. This can be read in Patrick Fleming's *Collectanea Sacra seu S. Columbani opera* (Augsburg, 1621) or in the critical ed. of B. Krusch [*MGH rer. Merov.* (1902) iv. 65 ff.]. For Columban's *Rule*, see Holsten, *CR* i. 166–78,

The labours of Columban were followed up by those of other evangelists. From their great monastery of Luxeuil, which became for a time the monastic capital of Gaul, the Irish missionaries spread everywhere. One of these, Dichuill—Latinized into Deicolus—found his way through the forests of Burgundy to where now stands the town of Lure, the outgrowth of the cell that he first established. Not far away another monastery, under the modern form of St. Diè, still preserves the name of this Irish saint. Another monk, Rupert, whether Irish by birth or Frank of the royal house brought up under Columban is uncertain, after settling for a while at Worms, struck across the Danube and established himself at Salzburg,[1] while another Irishman, Kilian, crossed the Rhine to Würzburg, and was there murdered with his two companions[2] (8 July 689). Dysibod or Disen, an Irish abbot-bishop, after preaching for some time down the Rhine, settled near Mainz in a monastery that has given its name to the present town of Disemberg.[3]

or Fleming, *op. cit.* As there printed, it consists of two separate treatises, the first of ten chapters whose authenticity is incontestable. The best critical ed. is by O. Seebass in *Zeit. f. Kirchg.* xvii. 218–34, xv. 366–86, xviii. 58–76, with copious notes. Cf. Seebass, *Ueber Columbas von Luxeuil Klosterregel* (Dresden, 1883). For Columban in general the best critical study is by A. Hauck, *Kirchengesch. Deutschlands* (1904), i. 262 f., and the good short study in Zöckler, *AM* 381 f. Krusch has also prefixed a biography in Latin to his ed. of Jonas. See also *infra*, p. 210 n. (authorities for St. Gall). Good popular accounts of Columba and Columban will be found in G. T. Stokes, *op. cit.* cc. 5–7.

[1] *DCB* iv. 562; Heimbucher, *OKK* i. 183.

[2] The *Passio Kiliani*, the outlines of which are historical, has been edited with good Introd. by B. Krusch (1910) in *MGH rer. Merov.* v. 711 f. If we can trust the reference to pope Conon in *op. cit.* c. 5, the date of Kilian's mission to Franconia was in 687.

[3] Dysibod died about 674. His *Vita* by the abbess Hildegard († 1180) is in *A.SS*, July, ii. 581–99.

No monastery of the Middle Ages was more noted than that of St. Gallen,[1] whose library still remains unsurpassed for the wealth of its old manuscripts. Its name commemorates an Irishman, the friend of Columban, brought up in the same monastery of Bangor, who accompanied him to Luxeuil, and followed him, when driven out thence, to Zug and Bregenz. Before his preaching, in the native dialects of Swabia, the spirits of flood and fell fled wailing up the mountains, crying, as with the voices of women, 'Where shall we go? for he prays continually, and never sleeps.' When in 612 Columban left Bregenz Gall remained behind, for he was sick of a fever. On his recovery he commenced once again his missionary journeys in Swabia. One evening he arrived at the place where the torrent of the Steinach hollows for itself a bed in the rocks. As Gall was about to kneel in prayer, he was caught by a thorn bush, and fell. The deacon ran to his assistance. 'No,' said the saint; 'here is my chosen habitation, here is my resting-place for ever.' So he arranged two hazel boughs in the form of a cross, passed the night in prayer, and began the next day to build the monastery which in later times gave its name to a Swiss canton.

A list of the Irish monasteries on the Continent that were established at this time [2] would be of great interest

[1] For the life of St. Gall, in addition to Jonas' *Vit. Columbani* (see *supra*, p. 208 n.), we have the *Vita Galli* by Wettin (fl. 771). Best ed. in *MGH rer. Merov.* (1902) ed. B. Krusch, iv. 257 f. Wettin was the master of Walafrid Strabo, who about 833 wrote a *Vita Galli* (also ed. Krusch, *op. cit.* iv. 281; also ed. in *PL* v. 114, p. 975). For Dichuill we have the *Vita Deicoli* in *A.SS*, Jan. ii. 563 f. See also *DNB* s.v. Gall died on 16 Oct., but the year is uncertain, either 627 or 645. St. Gallen was founded in 614.

[2] A partial list will be found in Haddan, *op. cit.* 275–8; more critical lists in Gougaud, *CC* 148 f.; Heimbucher, *OKK* i. 182–4; and

MONASTICISM IN THE CELTIC CHURCH 211

and would confer immortal lustre on the annals of the sister island. Ireland indeed at that time, as one of its own chroniclers puts it, was 'full of saints.' But, unfortunately, the enthusiasm of these Celtic missionaries was not combined with equal resources of administration. Within less than a century of their establishment all but a few of the Irish monasteries had been driven to adopt the rival *Rule* of St. Benedict. In 818 Louis the Fair forced those which still clung to Celtic usages to fall into line with the others.[1] The austerity of Columban's *Rule*, its system of punishments, its lack of all the higher elements that made the success of the *Rule* of Benedict, were fatal to it—let alone that it was the mark of a Church that attempted to put itself into competition with Rome, and against which, therefore, the whole resources of the papacy were brought to bear. Both in England and on the Continent the work of Columba and Columban was not so much lost as merged in a rival form of a higher nature. The fate which thus attended Celtic monasticism was followed by the disasters of the Viking invasions. Plundering hordes of Norse and Danish heathen marked down the monasteries of Britain and Ireland as their prey, the more easily inasmuch as, especially in Ireland, the greater number lay within easy access from the coast. With untiring

for later Irish monasteries (Benedictine) *ib.* i. 258-61. See also Pflugk-Harttung, "Old Irish on the Continent" (in *Transactions of the Royal Hist. Soc.*, 1891, pp. 75-102), and L. Gougaud, *L'Œuvre des Scotti dans l'Europe continentale* in *Rev. hist. eccl.* (1908) ix. 21-37, 257-77. There are also two interesting, chatty, illustrated books by Margaret Stokes, *Three Months in the Forests of France in Search of Vestiges of Irish Saints* (1895) (deals with Luxeuil, Lure, and the abodes of Fursa), and *Six Months in the Apennines in Search of Vestiges of Irish Saints* (1892).

[1] de la Borderie, *op. cit.* i. 385-6, 507-8, ii. 252-3.

patience the monks again and again rebuilt their monasteries, only once more to see them destroyed by fire. When at length in 943 Christianity was once again nominally introduced into the Norse kingdom which the Vikings had established round Dublin, it was too late. The golden age of the Irish Church had passed away in an era of blood and fire. Her libraries had been burnt, her education ruined, and the highly cultured monks of the seventh and eighth centuries displaced by a clergy inferior both in ability and enthusiasm. Such monasteries as survived had become the centres of fierce tribal feuds. The promise of the early morn had passed into the storm-clouds that have ever since overshadowed the " ancient land of saints and sages."

IV

One effect of Celtic Monasticism long survived the absorption or destruction of its monasteries by the victorious Latin Church. We refer to the elaboration of Penitentials. This great system for Christianizing barbarian tempers, the doctrinal basis of which may be found in the acts and teaching of Ambrose, was probably in its origin the creation of the Irish Church, and in especial of Columban. Thence through the English archbishop Theodore of Tarsus the Penitentials passed into the general Church of the West.[1] An attempt

[1] For the British, Irish, and Anglo-Saxon Penitentials the best works are F. W. H. Wasserschleben, *Die Bussordnungen der abendländischen Kirche* (Halle, 1851), pp. 101–352; ib. *Die irische Kanonensammlung* (2nd ed., Leipzig, 1885); H. and S. *Conc.* iii. 173–213 (Theodore's Penitential), 226 (Judicium Clementis), 326–34 (the so-called Penitential of Bede), 413–31 (Egbert's Penitential); B. Thorpe, *Ancient Laws* (2 vols., 1840, in *RS*. The Penitentials of

at codification of the different systems in vogue formed part of the reforms of Charles the Great; this was one of the forces on which he relied for reducing his empire to order. In time the older Penitentials gave place to the scholastic sacrament of penance, though many of the earlier prescriptions were embodied in the text-books of canon law of Gratian and Gregory IX.

In condemnation of the principles and methods of the penitential system, historians and theologians are now substantially agreed. "The penitential literature is in truth a deplorable feature of the medieval Church. Evil deeds, the imagination of which may perhaps have dimly floated through our minds in our darkest moments, are here translated and reduced to system. It is hard to see how anyone could busy himself with such literature and not be the worse for it."[1] And yet such a view, though perfectly correct, may be an instance of the difficulty of thinking historically. For the student should never forget the law, illustrated on every page of ecclesiastical history, "that those beliefs or institutions which seem irrational, or absurd, or unworthy of the Christian spirit, came into vogue in order to kill some deeper evil, not otherwise to have been destroyed."[2] The Penitentials were, perhaps, necessary if the Church was to bring the masses, that had nominally passed into the kingdom of Christ, yet

Theodore and Egbert are uncritically printed in ii. 1–62, 170–239). For Celtic Penitentials, see H. and S. *Conc.* i. 113–5, 117–20, 127–37. For the Penitential of Gildas, the best ed. is by H. Williams, *Gildas* (Cymmrod. Series, 1901), 272 f.

[1] Plummer's Bede, *HE* Introd. vol. i. p. clviii. Cf. illustrations in H. and S. *Conc.* iii. 178. The Penitentials, besides dealing with deadly sins, descend to instructions as to what to do when a mouse is found in the food (H. and S. *Conc.* iii. 429).

[2] Allen, *Christian Institutions*, 408. Cf. H. Williams, *Gildas*, 273.

remained in many respects heathen in heart and practice, into a working acquaintance with the elementary laws of decency and hygiene, let alone into any real experience of religion. They were a rough method of enforcing obedience to moral law upon a rough people, and of holding down the usages and reminiscences of heathenism.

Any attempt to trace out, even in barest outline, the effects of this system upon the history of Europe would lead us too far afield. Suffice that we point out that we have in the Penitentials the revival, or rather the continuance, of the same spirit of mortification that we see in the excesses of the Syrian monks, and which comes out so markedly in the *Rule* of Columban. The punishment of the body was always a strongly marked feature of the Celtic Church. One Irish monk, Adamnan of Coldingham, would only touch food twice a week, on Thursdays and Sundays; another, Drythelm of Melrose, would stand up to his neck in winter in the Tweed reciting prayers and psalms, and even Cuthbert and Kentigern are said to have done the same. We are told of one monk-bishop in the ninth century who broke the rule and ate meat. He was killed by the Danes. After death his ghost appeared to an Irish bishop and said: 'I ate meat, and so I have become meat.'[1] From asceticism

---

[1] Bede, *HE* iv. 23, v. 12; *Vita Cudbert*, c. 10; Plummer, *VSH* i. Introd. cxx.; E. J. Newell, *The Welsh Church* (1895), 85–6. Immersion up to the neck was a favourite Celtic custom. The practice seems to have been an extension of the idea of purification with the idea of asceticism, however, predominant. Thus, whereas in hot countries, where the bath would have been a luxury, it was denied (see *supra*, p. 64), in cold countries the idea of purification was allowed play, as it involved asceticism as well. (See the excellent article, s.v. *Bains* in Cabrol, *DACL* ii. 94 f., with full sources and notes. Also cf. Gougaud, *CC* 100.)

of this order it was but a step to the imposition of these penances for the sin of the soul. And yet in one sense the theoretical basis of the system was changed. For in the Penitentials, at any rate in their later developments into penance, the emphasis is not so much on the Gnostic conceptions of the body as the root of all evil, as upon the sin—regarded, it is true, as something arbitrary and external—for which atonement or commutation must be paid, this last an imported Teutonic idea [1] that was grafted onto and finally changed the whole character of penance. At their worst the Penitentials were but an injury to the individual; under their later developments into indulgences and the like they became a danger to the moral bases of society.[2]

But, perhaps, the worst effects of the system were seen in the development of the penance of flagellation and the sudden apparition in the middle of the thirteenth century of the Flagellants. Of the former the classic example is St. Elizabeth of Thuringia († 1231), a woman of the rarest self-abnegation and spiritual aspirations, whom the fanaticism of Conrad of Marburg sought to break into perfect obedience by constant scourging, stripped to her shift. Conrad, whom the Dominicans have falsely claimed as one of their number,[3] is the supreme embodiment of the method which regarded torture, mental or physical, as the most efficient aid to salvation, as also of the priestly arrogance which in the treatment of sin and weakness could act as if possessed

[1] Cf. for illustrations such Teutonic codes as the Laws of Ethelbert (604) in H. and S. *Conc.* iii. 42–50, where all sins are assessed, and the later Laws of Ine (690) in *ib.* iii. 214–9.

[2] See further Workman, *History of Christian Thought up to the Reformation* (1910), 136–9.

[3] H. C. Lea, *Inquisition in Middle Ages*, ii. 325.

of the omniscience of an avenging God. In the outbreak of the Flagellants (1259), this rude form of penance became a dangerous, contagious disease. Tens of thousands of all ranks and ages in the cities of Northern Italy walked in solemn procession scourging themselves until the blood ran. Thence the movement spread to the Rhinelands and Germany, but disappeared as rapidly as it had arisen. A century later, as the result of the Black Death, Europe was again covered with bands of Flagellants, stripped to the waist, scourging themselves with thongs knotted with iron spikes. They believed that this torture, continued for thirty-three days and a half, would deliver the soul from all taint of sin.[1]

[1] H. C. Lea, *Inquisition in Middle Ages*, i. 272, ii. 382 f.

CHAPTER V

THE DEVELOPMENT OF MONASTICISM
FROM
ST. BENEDICT TO ST. FRANCIS

All we have willed or hoped or dreamed of good, shall exist;
Not its semblance, but itself; no beauty, nor good nor power
Whose voice has gone forth, but each survives for the melodist
When eternity affirms the conception of an hour.
The hard that proved too high, the heroic for earth too hard,
The passion that left the ground to lose itself in the sky,
The music sent up to God . . . .
Enough that he heard it once: we shall hear it by and by.
BROWNING, Abt Vogler.

ARGUMENT

§ I. The effect of Benedict's *Rule* in the evolution of Monasticism—The struggle to escape wealth—Chaise Dieu—Bec—Lanfranc and Anselm—Constant repetition of the same tale 219

§ II. Benedict of Aniane—His *Concordia Regularum*—His mistake—The rise of Cluny—Its influence—Hildebrand's dream—Its daring—Degeneracy of the secular Church—Damiani—Farfa—The effect of Hildebrand's ideal 225

§ III. Fall of Cluny—The Cistercians—Robert of Molesme—Stephen Harding—St. Bernard—Origin in England—Characteristics—Architecture and hymns—Episcopal independence—Poverty gives place to obedience—Cistercian wool-trade—Cistercians and education . 236

§ IV. The return to Eastern methods—Camaldulians—Vallombrosians—Carthusians—Wesley and the Charterhouse 248

§ V. Canons—Eusebius of Vercellae—St. Augustine—Chrodegang of Metz—Austin Canons—English monastic cathedrals—Rahere—Brethren of the Common Life—St. Bernard of Menthon—Gilbert of Sempringham—Premonstratensians 253

§ VI. Military Orders—St. John of Jerusalem—The Templars—Teutonic Knights—The change of the ideal . . 266

pp. 219–268

CHAPTER V

THE DEVELOPMENT OF MONASTICISM FROM ST. BENEDICT TO ST. FRANCIS

I

BENEDICT'S success in linking on Monasticism with labour was the first step in a long evolution upon whose details we cannot dwell, but whose main features demand attention. The first change, common both to East and West, had been that from monachism to cenobitism, from the hermit to the brethren of the common life. The value of this change, especially when in the West it received the inspiration given to it by Benedict's *Rule*, we have already noticed. But the change itself would have been of little value, at any rate viewed from the standpoint of social development, had it not been accompanied by the glorification and systematization of toil. With this addition the change lay at the root of all that was best and most progressive in Monasticism. Instead of the dervish of Eastern fancy, we have a colony of workers. Instead of the hermit crushed by the horror and loneliness of Nature in her most terrible aspects, we have the organized community, in its beginnings as anxious as the hermit to escape the haunts of men, but whose axes and spades cleared the densest jungles, drained pestilent swamps, and by the alchemy of industry turned the sands into waving gold, and planted centres of culture in the hearts of forests.

This change, invaluable as it was from the standpoint of the history of civilization, proved fatal in the long run to the principles of Monasticism, at any rate as first enunciated. For Monasticism was founded upon renunciation; but renunciation became impossible for a Monasticism whose remunerative toil forced upon it a wealth from which there seemed no escape. No rules or regulations which the wit of man could devise seemed capable of saving a brotherhood of saintly toilers from entering into their labours. The passion for solitude, the desire to reform Monasticism by a return to primitive poverty, might drive the monks into wastes and forests; but within a generation or two at most the lonely hermitage would become a crowded monastery, surrounded by a thriving dependency of serfs and tenants. The illustrations of this law would be almost as numerous as the monasteries themselves. Two must suffice for all. Few abbeys were more famous than Chaise Dieu (Casa Dei). This monastery, one of the many results of the reform movements of the eleventh century, was founded in 1046 by a certain Count Robert of Aurillac († 1067), who with two companions sought to find a holier life in the forests of Auvergne, forests so vast that it would have taken a strong horse four days to traverse them at a gallop, so dense that horror and silence reigned alone. 'Robert, Robert,' cried the demons, 'why dost thou try to chase us from our dwellings?' Well might they be alarmed, for within a few years Robert was joined by three hundred monks whose axes and spades opened up to civilization regions hitherto inaccessible. In process of time Chaise Dieu counted three hundred dependent priories united to it by origin and service.

Another monastery, even more famous, was Bec. Its beginnings were but humble. In 1034 Herlwin († 26 Aug. 1078), a knight of Brionne, under the influence of the great revival which turned the Normans from a race of pirates into the foremost defenders of the Church, had at the age of forty sought a refuge from the world in a valley edged with woods of ash and elm, through which a tiny stream—called then, as now, by the old Norse name of Bec—finds its way to the Risle. There, with two companions, he built his humble house of God, labouring during the day at the foundation of his church, and spending the night in learning how to read. At length the church, such as it was, was finished, and Herlwin was ordained the first abbot of the new monastery, 'it being so poor that no one else would take the government.' It was to no sinecure that he was thus elected. When the daily office in the church was finished, abbot and monks alike turned out to the field. 'They hoed, they sowed, no one ate his bread in idleness, and at each hour of prayer they assembled in the church.' In the poor chapter-house it was with difficulty that the taller monks could stand upright. The dormitory was a bare attic, access to which was gained by a steep ladder. Cloisters there were none; the first rude attempts had tumbled down the night after they were completed. Such was the poverty that the same candles had to serve for kitchen and altar. As Herlwin was one day building an oven of mud with his own hands, a stranger greeted him. "God bless you," said the abbot, looking up; and then, struck with the foreign look of the man, added, "Are you a Lombard?" "Yes," was the reply; and, praying to be made a monk, the Italian knelt down at the mouth of the oven and kissed Herlwin's feet. That stranger was Lanfranc of Pavia, a scholar of noble family, skilled in Roman law, who had crossed the Alps to seek his fortunes in the North. Herlwin, though himself a rough soldier, knew well the value of scholarship, and the dangers of the fanaticism into which religion without learning soon degenerates. He set Lanfranc to teach (1042). In a few years, under his lead and that of his greater successor Anselm of Aosta, Bec became the most famous school of Christendom. Gifts of tithes and manors poured in, enabling Herlwin to replace the first rude structures by a stately abbey worthy of its wealth.[1] In Normandy a jingling refrain was long current—

> "De quelque part que le vent vente
> L'Abbaye du Bec a rente."

When Lanfranc became the Conqueror's archbishop of Canterbury, he did not forget his old Benedictine home. Dependent priories or cells of the abbey were founded in sundry counties in England, most of which were swept away at the suppression of alien priories in 1414. But the names of Weedon Bec and Tooting Bec still survive as witnesses to this former connection,

[1] Its site is about a mile farther up the valley than Herlwin's first abode. The standard history of Bec is A. A. Porée, *Hist. de l'abbaye de Bec* (Evreux, 1901, 2 vols.). The history of Monasticism in the days of decay forms no part of my plan. Suffice to point out that Chaise Dieu in 1640 was held *in commendam* by cardinal Richelieu. The *commendatory* abbots of Bec in the three centuries before its destruction (1791) were a disgrace.

while the chief dependent priory of Bec, St. Werburgh's at Chester, became at the Reformation the cathedral of a new diocese.

Everywhere it was the same, whether by the slopes of the Jura, in the forests of Bavaria, or amid the wastes of Northumbria. The saint who fled from the haunts of men that he might the better save his soul, drew after him, against his will, a brotherhood of disciples and settlers, who laid the foundations of towns, broke the silence of moor and fen with a chain of religious houses, established agricultural colonies in the midst of the forests, or planted on some dreary coast, as at Whitby, the forerunner of a busy haven. The brotherhood of toiling renunciants, flee as they might, could not escape the pursuing curse of wealth, as they

> " Wrought to Christian faith and holy order
> Savage hearts alike, and barren moors." [1]

The history of Monasticism in the Western world is, in fact, the constant repetition of the same tale, the same ideal, with what would seem the same inevitable corruption of success. First we have the burning enthusiast, seeking salvation in a more perfect renunciation, plunging into the wilderness that he may find a solitude where he may pray alone. There his reputation for renunciation draws to himself others of like mind, who place themselves under his direction. Or if he is already a monk, by profession a renunciant, in reality an inmate of some lordly abbey rich in its vineyards and granaries, we see him, pricked to the heart by the memory of the poverty of Christ, setting off to found some new convent where he may carry out

[1] Kingsley, *Saint's Tragedy*.

in stricter fashion the primitive *Rule*, with the good seed no longer choked by the multitude of riches. In a few years his humble abode becomes too strait for the multitude who have sought out this Jacob's ladder with its vision of the angels. Wealth pours in; the rude huts of wattle and mud give place to the stately abbey; the humble church becomes the soaring minster. By their care and toil the desert blossoms as the rose, the fats overflow, while serfs and hinds, attracted by the security and greater freedom which the Church affords, build up outside its walls the town which perpetuates its name. The first dreams of poverty are once more forgotten; all things are ripe for some new saint to make a new effort towards that primitive renunciation, the dream and despair of Monasticism during the long centuries of its existence.

For eight hundred years the ebb and flow of the monastic tide centred round this rock of offence. For eight hundred years after Benedict men tried to achieve the impossible, to attain simplicity and poverty by renunciation, through means of an organization that must inevitably produce wealth. To this conflict of ideal and actuality we owe the various congregations, orders, and reforms the mere names of which would demand a volume in themselves, for whose history the reader must seek in the great works that the devotion of the Orders has produced. But we shall do well, without losing ourselves in endless details, to notice, though in broadest outline, the various methods which were employed in the struggle of reformers with an evil for which, however, as experience showed, there was no permanent cure; noting also the consequent change of outlook which came over the monk's ideal.

II

The first of the great Benedictine reforms originated with Benedict of Aniane, "the second founder" of Western Monasticism. Benedict [1]—the name was assumed on his 'conversion' in place of his first name Witiza (Euticius)—was the son of a noble of Maguelone in Languedoc, a cup-bearer in the court of Pepin. While serving in Italy with Charles the Great in 773, a narrow escape from drowning led the young soldier, without his father's knowledge, to enter the monastery of St. Seine (Sequanus) in Burgundy. He found the Benedictine monasteries in a deplorable state. Many had been alienated, because of their wealth, to laymen; while in most the monks were a law unto themselves, though ofttimes cruelly oppressed by their superiors. Monasticism had ceased to possess an ideal that lay outside the Church; she had become dependent on the bishops, with a few ceremonies to distinguish the regular from the secular clergy. In no small measure the disorder was due to the disorder of the age; to some extent it arose from the struggle in the monasteries of the Franks between the *Rules* of Benedict, of Columban, and of Caesarius of Arles for the mastery.[2]

At first Benedict, though he had spent some years in a Benedictine monastery, or perhaps because of this training, sought to obtain a cure by a return to the more primitive and rigid Eastern type, and collected together in parallel columns, with other intention than

---

[1] For Benedict of Aniane the primary source is the *Vita* by his scholar Ardo or Smaragdus († 843), in *MGH* xv. 198 ff. or *PL* 103, p. 354 f.

[2] See *supra*, pp. 123, 211.

that of the historian, the various rules of the East and West.[1] Refusing the invitation of the monks of St. Seine to be their head, he had retired in 779 as a hermit to the gorge of the Aniane in Aquitaine. But he now realized that salvation was not of the East. Never again could the West look to the hermit to save the life of the Church; that ideal was for Latin Christianity a thing of the past, destined to survive only in a fragment of an idea. Before 782 his lonely cell on the Aniane had become a stately abbey, with over a thousand monks under his rule, attracted to him by the fame of his piety, by the diligence with which he acquired books for the library, and by his zeal as a reformer. On the death of Charles the Great (814), the emperor Lewis the Pious, who had been attracted to Benedict when ruler of Aquitaine, persuaded him to transfer himself to the monastery of Cornelimünster near Aachen, that he might be near his court. At his direction Benedict presided over the important Council of Aachen (10 July 817), one of whose objects was to secure more thorough Monastic discipline. Under Benedict's influence the Council sought, in the stricter enforcement of the *Rule* of Monte Cassino, the lost ideal of renunciation.[2] Four years later he passed away (11 Feb. 821).

In his efforts to secure reformation Benedict of

[1] The *Concordia Regularum* of B. of Aniane contains extracts from twenty-six different *rules*: seven from Egypt, one from Syria, one from Cappadocia, one from Italy, one from Africa, four from Spain, and eight from Gaul. It was first published in 1638 in Paris by the French Benedictine F. H. Ménard, and can be studied either in Holsten, *CR* vol. i.; or Migne, *PL* vol. 103. There is a critical study of it by O. Seebass in *ZKG* xv. 244-60.

[2] Hefele, *HC* IV. (1) 25 f.; *MG leg.* i. 202.

Aniane made one fatal mistake : he sought a renunciation which should express itself in rigid uniformity. Meat, drink, the cut of the dress, the order of services, were to be exactly alike, the products of an almost mechanical mill. Even prayer and praise did not escape his machinery. Offices were multiplied until they became almost continuous. The issue could not be in any doubt. The activity which for the moment blazed up in the monastic systems of Europe was bound from the first to flicker down into even more sombre ashes. The mechanical can never be anything else than short-lived ; the swaddling-clothes of a rigid uniformity never fail in time to crush out the new-born enthusiasm and power.

Within a century of Benedict of Aniane's reforms, matters were worse than ever ; the renunciation, discipline, and ideal of Monasticism lost. The age was out of joint. A contemporary bishop, Heriveus of Rheims, compared mankind to 'the fish of the sea who live by devouring each other.' The inroads of the Danes and Huns, the uncertainties of the times, the seething of the nations, all this had affected for evil the existing monasteries. In many places the old monasteries had disappeared—burnt, destroyed, or appropriated. In others the ancient rule had given place to the law which seems to come uppermost in times of insecurity : 'Let us eat and drink, for to-morrow we die.' To counteract this decay, Duke William IX of Aquitaine founded about the year 910 his new monastery of Cluny in Burgundy.[1] Its rule

---

[1] For the vast literature on the Cluniac reform, see Heimbucher, *OKK* i. 242 n. We may single out F. Cucherat, *Cluny au XIe Siècle* (Autun, 1886, 4th ed. ; not in B.M.) ; A. Bernard et A. Bruel, *Recueil*

was the strictest interpretation of the *Rule* of Benedict. But more important than the mere revival of old *Rules* was the new aim of the Cluniacs, under the lead of a series of able abbots. Monasticism as an organization had been ruined not merely by the disorders of the age but by the covetousness of the world obtaining a stronghold in the Church, its wealth appropriated, its morals corrupted by the great ones of the earth, too often acting hand in hand with secular bishops. Things would be better if the secular Church were beneath the feet of the monk. So the Cluniacs—or rather the master-mind who took hold of the Cluniac idea, developed it and made it his own—set before themselves the dream, if it were possible, to impress upon the whole Church the ideals of the cowl.

The logic of Cluny was the logic of conviction. On all sides it was agreed that Monasticism was the highest ideal of Christianity; but hitherto this ideal had lain outside the Church and beyond the world as the dream of the few. But the highest ideal of Christianity ought by rights to be the rule of all, at any rate in the Church if not in the world. Instead, therefore, of seeking to realize the monastic ideal as heretofore by fleeing from the world, it were better to infuse the ideal into the world. Such infusion must, of course, begin with the Church itself. A corollary followed, at any rate in the clear brain of Hildebrand: the government of the world would then pass to a Church fitted rightly to discharge its duties. This at any

des Chartes de Cluny (Paris, 1876, 6 vols.; for detailed study only); G. F. Duckett, *Charters and Records of Cluny* (2 vols., 1888; continuation of the above); also E. Sackur, *Die Cluniacenser* (Halle, 1892-4, 2 vols.; this last a serviceable general history). The 'Consuetudines' of Cluny may be studied in Holsten, *CR* ii. 176-91.

rate was the dream that presented itself to the greatest mind in the annals of the papacy. Though himself no monk, Hildebrand so deliberately adopted as his own the monastic ideal, especially in the form and practice expounded by Cluny, that until recently historians were misled into supposing that he had taken the cowl and had been at one time an inmate of Cluny.[1] This supposition was not only false in fact; it tended to throw out of perspective the whole Cluniac reform. Valuable as it proved in the reformation of Monasticism itself—to this point we shall return later—the importance of the Cluniac reform, after all, lay outside itself in the use made of it, both before and after he became pope, by one who was himself an outsider, Hildebrand, pope Gregory VII, the master-builder of the papacy. With Hildebrand the monastic ideal reaches its highest development; its contents become almost one with that of the Catholic Church itself.[2]

[1] The only contemporary source for this statement is the worthless Bonizo of Sutri, *Liber ad amicum* (in Jaffé, *BRG* ii. 630). In the next century this was amplified by Otto of Froising (*Chron.* vi. 33) into the statement that Hildebrand was prior of Cluny. But this was a confusion with another Hildebrand who was a prior in the 10th cent. (Sackur, *op. cit.* s.v.; see *EHR* Jan. 1911, pp. 30–1; also W. Martens, *Gregor VII* ii. 281 ff., for exhaustive study of the matter).

[2] The main sources for Hildebrand consist in his letters and decrees collected in the *Registrum* [ed. P. Jaffé in *BRG* vol. 2, "Monumenta Gregoriana" (Berlin, 1865)]. With these should be studied the *Libelli de lite imperatorum et pontificum sæc. xi. et xii. conscripti* (in *MGH*, 2 vols., Hanover, 1891–2) to understand the ideals of Hildebrand and the controversies they caused. These have been analysed in C. Mirbt, *Die Publizistik im Zeitalter Gregors VII* (Leipzig, 1894). A good life of Hildebrand has yet to be written. Critical materials for it are found in W. Martens, *Gregor VII* (2 vols., Leipzig, 1894), from which A. H. Matthew, *Life and Times of Hildebrand* (London, 1910), has borrowed wholesale. Older lives are inaccurate and misleading.

The daring of Hildebrand's conception was extraordinary, not only in itself but by reason of the age in which it was formed. To the historian looking back on the years immediately preceding, no century would have seemed less adapted to accept this ideal. The tragedy of pope Formosus, the ghastly trial of his corpse by his successor Stephen (Jan. 897), had been the commencement of a period of shame unequalled in the annals of the Church, relieved by few gleams of better things, and which lasted for nearly a century and a half. At one time the papacy itself was in the gift of two remarkable women, Theodora and her daughter Marozia, of whom Baronius can believe nothing too evil. By the order of Marozia, John X, whose skill had delivered Southern Italy from the scourge of the Saracens, was seized in the Lateran and finally smothered in prison (928).[1] By the justice of destiny Marozia perished at the hands of her son Alberic, under whose able rule successive pontiffs were but puppets, whose sole use was to lend their names to bulls that they did not originate. Of one pope, Marinus II († April 946), we read in a contemporary that 'he did not dare to touch anything without an order from his prince, Alberic.'[2] The son of Alberic, Octavian, secured his own election to the papal chair (16 Dec. 955) and exchanged his secular name for that of John XII—the first instance of this custom in papal history. The change of name was the only preparation that he made for his spiritual duties. He turned the Lateran into a brothel, and in a drunken brawl bestowed consecration upon a

---

[1] *MGH* iii. 312, 378.
[2] Benedict of Soracte, c. 32 in *MGH* iii. 716.

deacon in a stable. Becoming involved in difficulties with the national party, of which his father had been the head, in an unwise moment John invited Otho to take the imperial crown. So Otho crossed the Brenner and made a solemn entry into Rome (2 Feb. 962). No satire on the condition of the papacy could be more bitter than Otho's attempt to excuse John's immoralities : ' He is still a lad, and will yet learn to control himself by the example of nobler men.'[1] But at length Otho was driven to John's deposition. ' Charges so disgraceful,' ran the writ of citation, ' are laid to your account that were they insinuated even against a comedian they would make us blush with shame.'[2]

For the next forty years the Roman see lay at the feet of secular princes. The usual fate of the puppet-popes was to be thrown by some insurgent faction into St. Angelo, and there strangled or starved to death unless rescued by some counter-revolution. One pope, Boniface VII, literally stepped to the throne across the body of his dying predecessor. He ruled by a reign of terror, tearing out the eyes and tongues of opposing cardinals. On his fall in 985 his corpse was dragged through the streets and thrown under the statue of Marcus Aurelius ; a picture whose irony suggests many reflections. With the dawn of a new century matters became still worse. For nearly half a century the turbulent nobles of the Campagna, especially the counts of Tusculum, turned the papacy into a mere addition to their family possessions, as if it were some robber castle or broad champaign. In

[1] Liutprand, *Hist. Otton.* 5 in *MGH* iii. 341.
[2] *Ib.* 12 in *MGH* iii. 343.

Benedict IX (1033) the circle of time brought back the age of Nero. A thousand years had gone by since the Crucifixion and Resurrection, and as the thoughtful looked round on the world and counted the results, they sighed for the end. The chair of St. Peter was a count's fief; a youth,[1] more criminal than Heliogabalus in his shameless debauchery, was the head of the Church. 'What his life was after his taking the priesthood,' wrote pope Victor III at a later date, 'I shudder to relate.'[2] In despair of his crimes, the Romans tried to strangle him at the altar as he said high mass. The conspiracy failed; the superstition of the accomplices quailed before an eclipse of the sun.[3] At length Benedict grew tired of the papacy; he was desirous of marrying his cousin. So he sold his rights to a rich priest, John Gratianus (Gregory VI), for the revenue of Peter's pence from England—about £1500.[4] As a result, whatever be the truth in Bonizo's tale, three popes struggled together in Rome for the mastery. In despair, clergy and people sent an

---

[1] The incredible statement, repeated in all the histories, that at his ordination he was but twelve years of age, rests merely on the authority of Ralph Glaber, iv. c. 5 and v. c. 5 in *MGH* vii. 68. But Glaber is by no means a contemporary, and is often worthless. Even more important is the silence of that bitter opponent of the papacy, Beno, in the account he gives of the doings of Benedict IX in his *Gesta Rom. Eccl.*

[2] Desiderius, *Dial.* iii. Cf. Beno, *Gest. Rom. Eccl.* ii. 4 in *MGH de lite Imper.* ii. 376.

[3] 29 June 1033; see Gregorovius, *Rome in Middle Ages*, iv. (1) 43 n., for the astronomical calculations as to the date; for the incident, see Glaber, iv. 9 in *MGH* vii. 69.

[4] Bonizo, *Lib. ad amic.* in Jaffé, *BRG* ii. 626. [Better ed. in *MGH Libelli de lite imper.* (1892).] Date 1 May 1045. But Bonizo is a worthless authority, as Jaffé, *BRG* ii. 577 ff., has shown, and I doubt the tale.

urgent message to the emperor Henry III begging him to save the papacy from utter ruin. 'We admit,' said they, 'that we have been so thoughtless as to appoint idiots as popes.' Henry came, and at the Council of Sutri Henry secured the deposition of the three, and nominated as pope a bishop of his own.[1]

Outside the papacy things were as bad, or worse. Peter Damiani, the friend of Hildebrand and one of the leaders of the reformers, has pictured the age for us in his work *Gomorrhianus*, the title of which is as suggestive as it is true.[2] The book was published with the approval of pope Leo IX. His successor judged, not without reason, that its faithful description of existing vices was too polluting to be given to the public. So he carried it off and locked it up within a casket. But it was not possible to lock up the sins themselves. It was an age in which men blasphemed God because of the plague, for the plague was exceeding great. We are told by a contemporary that in Rome in the year 1040 'it would have been very difficult to find a single priest who was not illiterate, simoniacal, or had not a concubine.' Of the priests of Milan we read: 'they struggled together who should have the most sumptuous dresses, the most abundant tables, and the most beautiful mistresses.' In the monasteries matters were as bad. Take, for instance, this picture from the celebrated imperial monastery of Farfa. In 936 two of the monks murdered the abbot and seized the abbey. For years they ruled as joint heads, carrying on a perpetual struggle with each other, squandering the convent's estates on their followers

---

[1] 20 Dec. 1046; see *MGH* iii. 6. [2] In *PL* 145, pp. 159 ff.

and soldiers. One of them was the father of seven daughters and three sons, whom he ostentatiously brought up in princely luxury. Like abbot, like monk; each had a mistress with whom he lived openly. That these women might not be without bravery, the consecrated vestments were turned into dresses, the altar vessels melted down into earrings and brooches. In spite of all attempts at reform by brethren from Cluny, this state of things went on for fifty years.

The picture that we have given is, no doubt, in many respects exaggerated. The reader must not forget that even in the darkest night there are stars of hope; not all the popes were the sport of faction or monsters of depravity. Nevertheless, in its broad outlines the picture is true. Moreover, only by setting forth without extenuation the horrors of the age can we realize the daring of Hildebrand in the use he made of the Cluniac ideal. In the midst of an age that seemed hopeless in its depravity, he did not lose hope, but set to work deliberately to mould the secular Church after the monastic type, and as far as possible subject it to the principles of its rules. And, what was more, Hildebrand succeeded. The essential virtues of the monk are celibacy, poverty, and obedience. The first of these Hildebrand secured by stamping out, through a cruel persecution, the marriage of the priesthood, then so prevalent. In this struggle the monks everywhere were the pope's allies, stirring up the people against the seculars. Against the enemy of poverty—the curse of simony—the great pope waged incessant war; while he enforced obedience by subjecting all—reluctant archbishops, rebellious kings, and princes alike—to the will of Rome.

The originality of Hildebrand's schemes has been

conclusively established by modern research. But originality, daring, and genius would have profited nothing had not Hildebrand and the reformers had on their side the moral consciousness of Europe awaking from the long night of barbarism to a new life and larger hopes. The result was, in some respects, the most wonderful fact in the history of the Church. For a while the world lay at the feet of the monastic ideal; no longer an ideal outside the Church, but dominating the Church itself. For in the tenth and eleventh centuries the hope of Christendom lay in the monastery. The monk and not the secular represented all that was vital and progressive. The ultimate failure of this movement to bring the Church within the monastic mould was inevitable, but should not blind us to the measure of its then success. In the celibacy of the Roman priesthood to-day, a persistent instinct round which has gathered with the lapse of the centuries the conviction of custom, we see the results of a movement as daring in its aims, as thorough in its methods, as any that history can record.

Nor must we overlook the effect of the Hildebrandine ideal upon the monasteries themselves. For if the monastic ideal was to govern the world, the ideal itself must be more strictly watched and guarded. The weakness of the monasteries, hitherto, had lain in their isolation and individualism. Each was a law to itself, chiefly dependent for character upon the character of the head. There was a lack of responsibility to outside authority; for, from the first, the idea of subjecting the monastery with its ideal outside the secular Church to the control of the bishop, the representative of a Church that neither regarded poverty nor despised marriage, was repugnant to every true monk, one of the pricks against which he unceasingly kicked, though not always with success. As a consequence there were few checks to prevent the fall of a convent into evil, when once the inner enthusiasm for renunciation had been lost. The Cluniacs remedied this by the introduction of what we should call to-day the connexional principle. They formed congregations under the leadership of Cluny, monasteries united to guard the common maintenance of the *Rule*, though at the same time they sought exemption for Cluny from the control of the bishop. Thus Monasticism passed into the third stage of its history. The solitary monk had long since given place to the solitary community; the solitary community now became an affiliation of communities in one international organization that looked to the pope for support, and, in return, gave him their aid.

III

The Cluniac reform in its turn proved inefficient; nor is the cause far to seek. The whole burden of discipline of the united order rested upon the abbot of Cluny. He was the "general" of the order—to use the later term associated with the Jesuits and Salvation Army—the absolute ruler of the whole system, and of the thousands of monks whom it embraced, every one of whom was only professed by his permission. The priors of dependent monasteries—by the middle of the twelfth century numbering over three hundred [1]—how-

[1] At the end of the 15th cent. there were 825 Cluniac houses (Duckett, *op. cit.* i. 39).

ever great, were but his deputies and nominees.[1] If he fell into evil ways, this over-centralized system made the result the more appalling. By the beginning of the twelfth century, Cluny had followed the common round, and showed signs of falling from its high estate. Hitherto it had been ruled by a series of great abbots; now there was a disastrous change. A straw will show the direction of the wind: instead of the 138 Psalms which, at one time, the whole body of monks sang every day, the number was now reduced to but fourteen. In part this decay was the result of Cluny's enormous wealth; in part because of the rule of the evil Pontius[2] (1109-22), who, when deposed by pope Calixtus II, scrupled not to make war on the monastery itself, and to melt down its gold and silver plate that he might pay his hirelings.

The successor of Pontius, Peter the Venerable (1122-57),[3] made an effort to revive once more the ancient discipline and fervour by a revision in seventy-six statutes of the whole Cluniac life and obedience.[4] But the effort was vain, nor was the subsequent curtailment of the arbitrary powers of the abbot by the appointment of a permanent council more successful.[5] The internationalism of Cluny was fatal to it; not, of course, because of its internationalism—this was afterwards the basis of every successful order—but because of the centralization of the wealth of the several parts.

[1] For an interesting account of a visitation of English Cluniac houses in 1279, see Duckett, *op. cit.* ii. 131-45, ii. 208 f.

[2] Pons de Melgueil. For his life, see *PL* 166, pp. 835 f.

[3] To Peter was due the first translation of the Qurân into Latin.

[4] For these, see Holsten, *CR* ii. 176-91.

[5] After 1528 Cluny became held *in commendam* by the dukes of Guise.

From the forty Cluniac dependencies in England alone over £600 a year in tribute—equal to £20,000 to-day—was dispatched to Cluny,[1] a drain of gold intolerable at all times, more intolerable when England and France were at war. The dissolution or sequestration of these " alien priories "[2] became a national necessity, and showed the way at a later date for a more wholesale spoliation.[3]

By the decay of Cluny all things were ready for a new reform. The initiator of this reform—for we can scarcely call him the leader—was one Robert, a nobleman of Champagne.[4] At one time, about 1060, Robert had been abbot of the Burgundian monastery of S. Michel de Tonnerre. Driven thence by the bad lives of the monks, he had accepted the invitation of seven hermits of Colan to be their head. On the increase of their numbers, Robert saw fit, in 1075, to remove their habitation to Molesme in the bishopric of Langres. There, in the heart of the forests, they carried out St. Benedict's *Rule* to the letter. With the increase of

[1] See Duckett, *op. cit.* i. 199; the actual sum about 1400 was ' six hundred gold " scuta," ' *i.e.* écu d'or, 13 f. each.

[2] Of Cluniac houses in England the first foundation was at Barnstaple; the chief were Lewes (1077), Montacute, Wenlock, Bermondsey (1082), and in Scotland Paisley. See lists in Duckett, *op. cit.* i. 196. At the Dissolution there were 8 great and 30 lesser Cluniac houses.

[3] The various steps in the sequestration of alien priories are set out in Duckett, *op. cit.* i. 31. Cluny tried in vain to sell its estates (*ib.* i. 180 f., 256, &c.).

[4] Born about 1027; died 17 April 1110. For the origin of the Cistercians I have followed the account in the *Exordium parvum* of Stephen Harding, drawn up in 1119, printed in Ph. Guignard, *Les Monuments Primitifs de la Règle Cistercienne* (Dijon, 1878), 61–75. The *Exordium magnum*, compiled about 1221 (in *PL* 185, p. 996 ff.), gives the history down to 1206. For Cistercian bibliography, see Heimbucher, *OKK* i. 420 f.

wealth there came the usual degeneration; so Robert with some twenty companions retired in disgust to Citeaux,[1] not far from Dijon, one of the wildest places in the then stubborn desert of Champagne, and which took its name from its stagnant pools or *cisterns*. Robert himself was compelled in the following year by the command of Urban II[2] to return to the convent at Molesme; the refractory monks had found that his secession had brought them into disrepute. But before he left Citeaux he freed its monks from the obedience that they owed to him, thus giving to Citeaux complete independence.

Among those who had accompanied Robert to Citeaux, if indeed he did not prompt the migration, was an Englishman, Stephen Harding of Sherborne,[3] who had wandered as a pilgrim to Rome, but could not there satisfy the hunger of his soul for complete renunciation. At last he found what he desired first at Molesme, then later in desolate Citeaux, of which monastery he became the third abbot. Stephen was the real founder of the Cistercian order, though, apart from his formation of its usages, his success was due not so much to himself as to another. While he was yet abbot, at the moment when the fortunes of the monastery were at their lowest through a long visitation of sickness, there knocked at the door of this austere monastery a youth of twenty-two with thirty companions (1112). That youth was the great medieval prophet and preacher, St. Bernard,[4]

[1] Founded 21 March 1098. [2] 28 April 1099; Jaffé, *RP* i. 701.
[3] Abbot from 1109 to his resignation in 1133. He died 28 March 1134. For his life, see *DNB* xxiv. 333 (not always accurate). His *Life* by J. B. Dalgairns (1844) has been reprinted by H. Thurston with notes (1898).
[4] For St. Bernard (1090–20 Aug. 1153), see my article in *ERE* ii,

—for many years the uncrowned pope of the Church, almost the dictator of Europe—by whose influence and enthusiasm the order so grew that within forty years it had founded one hundred and sixty daughter-houses, sixty-eight of which were filiations of the most illustrious offshoot of Citeaux, Bernard's own foundation at Clairvaux.[1]

From Burgundy and Champagne the 'White monks,' as the Cistercians were called from the colour of their indoor robes—for they looked upon dyeing as a needless refinement [2]—soon spread over Europe.[3] In 1128 they were introduced into Stephen Harding's native land by the foundation of Waverley in Surrey.[4] In 1131 Rievaulx was established in the heart of the Yorkshire Wolds, and in the same year Tintern in the Welsh Marches. Fired by the new enthusiasm, thirteen brethren from the wealthy monastery of St. Mary at York determined to go forth into the wilderness that they might find the lost art of following a 'naked Christ.' 'With nothing but their clothes on their

530 f. The best life is by E. Vacandard, *Vie de S. Bernard* (2 vols. Paris, 1895). For complete bibliography, see L. Janauschek, *Bibliograph. Bernardina* (Vienna, 1891).

[1] Founded 25 June 1115. For the numbers of the Cistercian abbeys, usually much exaggerated—the maximum number was 728—see the lists in L. Janauschek, *Origines Cistercienses*, vol. i. 286 ff. (Vienna, 1877), and E. Vacandard, *op. cit.* ii. App. C. The Cistercian nunneries, chiefly in France and Germany, numbered 900 (see lists in Heimbucher, *OKK* i. 453 f.).

[2] On a journey they seem to have worn grey.

[3] For a list of German Cistercian houses, see Heimbucher, *OKK* i. 428. The extent of the revival of Monasticism in France in the 12th cent. may be estimated from the following figures. Down to the year 1000, 1108 monasteries had been founded; in the 11th cent. there were added 326, and in the 12th, 726.

[4] See *VCH* (Surrey) ii. 77 f. For their rise in England, see A. M. Cooke, *Eng. Hist. Rev.* xxxii. 625 ff.

backs,' they journeyed in the depth of a Yorkshire winter to a lonely valley called Skeldale near Ripon 'full of thorns and enclosed by rocks,' where, however, a great elm tree gave them the needed shelter.[1] Amid many privations they there established a rude house that later grew into the stately Fountains. From Fountains daughter-houses soon covered the land, or rather the waste places, for it was in the wilderness that the Cistercians resolved to dwell, if possible alone. To secure this end, their *Rule* forbade the erection of a house of their own order within a certain distance of another, an isolation that has resulted in England in the preservation of their ruins. When the Dissolution came there were, as a rule, no neighbouring towns to use the abbey as a quarry, nor did the wilds in which they were planted tempt the harpies of Henry's court to turn the abbey into a residence.

So far as discipline was concerned, the keynote of the Cistercian reform, as set forth by Stephen Harding, was a return to the literal observance of the *Rule* of St. Benedict. Stress was laid once more on manual labour, especially upon work in the fields. At Cluny, on the contrary, it was considered indecent that monks should be begrimed with dirt, or bent down with rustic labours.[2] For the spiced meats and costly wines of Cluny—' the eggs now fried, now roasted, now stuffed, made hard or soft, or chopped fine '[3]—the Cistercians

---

[1] The elm was still standing when Leland visited Fountains (K. Norgate, *Angevin Kings*, i. 73 n.).

[2] Peter Venerab. *Ep.* i. 28 in *PL* 189.

[3] See the invective of St. Bernard against Cluny in *Bern. op.* i. 526 f. (in *PL* 182, p. 895 f.). Considerable extracts are given in C. Morison, *St. Bernard*, 124 f.

had nothing but contempt; at Citeaux even the use of fish was restricted. Cluny loved to welcome high-born guests; even popes were sheltered within its walls. Stephen Harding gave the dukes of Burgundy to understand that their presence was not desired. The possession of tithes by Cistercian monasteries was forbidden—at Cluny over one hundred churches were in the gift of the abbot. The vast church at Cluny was the largest [1] and most beautiful in Christendom, with its carved stalls in the choir for 220 monks, its candlesticks, which St. Bernard called 'great trees of brass, glittering as much through their jewels as their lights,' its cloisters where 'before the very eyes of the brethren when reading' there were distracting sculptures of 'disgusting monkeys, spotted tigers, or fighting soldiers.' The Cistercians insisted on the plainest architecture and refused to allow any ornaments in their churches except crucifixes of wood; the candlesticks must be iron, the censers of brass, the garments of the priests of common undyed stuff, and even the chalices must not be of gold, only of silver gilt [2]—usages, we may add, which were also observed by the contemporary reformers, the Carthusians.[3] At Cluny the ritual was splendid and elaborate; at Citeaux all accretions to the divine offices were cut away to make room for work. Most remarkable of all, the Cistercians emphasized the simplicity of worship by refusing to allow the use of hymns that were written

---

[1] But see Prior, *Gothic Art in England*, 34. The abbey was 555 feet long. Details in Duckett, *op. cit.* i. 16 f.

[2] On Cistercian architecture see Heimbucher, *OKK* i. 442 f.; also E. Sharpe, *The Architecture of the Cistercians* (1874 and 1876); F. Bond, *Gothic Architecture in England* (1912), 16.

[3] See *infra*, p. 251-2.

in rhyme,[1] an ordinance that reminds us, with a difference, of the Highland Presbyterians.[2]

The revival by the Cistercians of the primitive discipline is, however, of less importance than their polity.[3] The Cistercians represent the fourth development of the Monastic ideal. The Cluniacs had fallen because they had centralized authority in the abbot of Cluny. With the Cistercians each foundation was an independent abbey, and not a subject priory of its parent. But they kept up the connexional spirit by enforcing everywhere a unity of usage, and by an annual congregation or conference in September at Citeaux of abbots,[4] while discipline was maintained not only by this conference but by giving to the abbot of Citeaux a prevailing voice in the congregation of which he was the president, with also the right of visiting any monastery at will. To his position of pre-eminence in the order itself successive popes add high place in the

[1] See the statement of Nicholas of Clairvaux (*Ep.* 15) in *Bib. Max. Pat.* xxi., and cf. Mabillon's remarks in *Op. Bernard.* v. 891, also Vacandard, *op. cit.* ii. 101–5. Bernard therefore cannot be the author of the famous hymn "Jesu, dulcis memoria"; see my remarks on this matter in *ERE* ii. 532.

[2] For the sources of this section, see the *Consuetudines* or *Instituta* passed by the Chapter in 1152, really the work of abbot Raynard († 16 Dec. 1151). They are printed in Guignard, *op. cit.* 245 ff. Cf. *ib.* pref. xv.

[3] This is set out in the so-called *Carta Caritatis* of Stephen Harding sanctioned by Calixtus II on 23 Dec. 1119 (Jaffé, *RP* i. 791), reaffirmed by the Cistercian pope Eugenius III, 1 Aug. 1152 (Mansi, xxi. 669). For this *carta*, see *PL* 166, p. 1377 f. or Guignard, *op. cit.* 79 f. or Sharpe, *op. cit.* (II.) App. The differences between the ordinances of the Cistercians and Cluniacs are set out in parallel columns in Zöckler, *AM* 408–13.

[4] Considerable resemblance to the Methodist polity might here be pointed out. On this see my remarks in *A New History of Methodism* (1909), i. 43.

hierarchy of the Church.[1] Independent almost from the first of all episcopal authority,[2] the Cistercians bound themselves to the pope by oaths of direct obedience. They were thus the first of the militant spiritual orders, whose object was to bring the world under the government of Rome, nor is it without value in this connection to note that the Templars were supposed to have received their constitution from Bernard.[3]

But this very fact of papal dependence marks the real fall of Monasticism. When the monk became the auxiliary of Rome, with the control of its organization centred in the pope, it was plain to all that Monasticism had outlived its first purpose. She no longer held up an ideal of renunciation higher than that of the Church, to some extent even outside the Church: the ideal had become materialized as a tool in the hands of the Church to be used for their common aggrandizement. The Church had shown her usual astuteness. She had seemed to yield her claims, to recognize the greatness of the monastic ideal, and to elevate it to a higher plane than her own. In reality she had stooped to conquer, and after yielding homage had annexed to her own service the very ideal that at one time had successfully claimed to be her superior. The question, in fact, had long since ceased to be one of ideals, and had passed into the struggle of two orders, the pope and the regulars as his allies, over against the bishops and the seculars. At the back of the bishops and seculars we may also see the rise of the national con-

[1] See Heimbucher, *OKK* i. 432.
[2] This exemption was finally confirmed by Innocent II (18 Feb. 1132; see Jaffé, *RP* i. 854, also *PL* 179, pp. 122–6).
[3] See *infra*, p. 266 n.

sciousness, the fatal rock upon which both pope and regulars were destined to break. Benedict's conception of the monastery as separate families of renunciants had given place to the idea of an organized international corporation with its head centre in Rome seeking the dominion of the nations of the world. And this the new nations were determined not to allow.

There was another aspect of the rise of the Cistercians in which we see the germs of the final form that Monasticism assumed. By the transfer of the order to the control of the pope we see that the centre of emphasis in renunciation was being slowly changed. Hitherto 'poverty' had been supreme, but the experience of centuries had shown that poverty as an ideal defeated itself. But 'obedience' had in it latent possibilities as yet little exploited.[1]

With the rise of the Cistercian, Monasticism on the lines laid down by Benedict became exhausted. The Cistercians had once again sought the wilderness and the solitary place: in England, for instance, their houses are to be found in what were formerly the wildest and least cultivated districts, the great valleys of Yorkshire and Lancashire. The usual result followed, the more quickly because of their insistence on manual labour. The Cistercians amassed enormous wealth by the improvement of the virgin soil they had acquired, and by their skill in the breeding of horses and cattle. In Yorkshire, especially, they soon became famous for their wool-growing—in fact, the export of wool by the monks became a feature in the commerce of the country.[2]

[1] See *infra*, p. 268.
[2] On this matter there is an interesting contemporary document quoted in W. Cunningham, *Growth of English Industry*, vol. i. (5th ed. 1910), App. D. See also *infra*, p. 294.

At Citeaux they soon owned the most famous vineyards of Burgundy. The results were not altogether advantageous. At first these Cistercian colonies were missionary centres, which did much to Christianize and civilize the surrounding peoples. This was especially the case in the marches of Prussia.[1] But in time a commercial spirit invaded the monastery, and wealth and splendour produced the inevitable decay. Nor was this lessened by the fact that farming and commerce led to the association with the monks of an excessive number of lay brothers, especially on the Continent. These lay brothers were a feature of the system from the first. They were inferior men, often peasants, with their own rooms and round of prayer. But with the loss of the primitive simplicity their introduction tended to a class separation which ministered to pride, especially when wealth poured into the coffers of the abbey. In England by the end of the twelfth century "as an element in the nation's spiritual life the order of Citeaux, once its very soul, now counted for worse than nothing."[2] The later history of the Cistercians follows the same dreary path as its predecessors; it is the record of the repeated attempts at revival and reform,[3] beginning in 1335 with a series of regulations by the Cistercian pope Benedict XII. Solitude had once more failed as a defence of poverty. It was reserved

[1] Heimbucher, *OKK* i. 440.

[2] K. Norgate, *Angevin Kings*, ii. 435. See also especially Girald. Cambrensis, *Speculum Eccl.* (in *RS*) iv. 29 ff., 54, this last the famous answer of Richard I to Fulk as to the marriage of his 'tres filias'— 'Superbiam Templariis, Luxuriam nigris monachis, Cupiditatem albis monachis:'

[3] Of these the best known are the Trappists (1664). For these reformed orders, which lie outside my limits, see Heimbucher, *OKK* i. 433 f. and for the Trappists *ib.* i. 460 f.

for St. Francis of Assisi to attempt some other method.

One matter in connection with the Cistercians should be noted. They do not seem to have contributed in any way to the education of the country. In Cistercian abbeys there were no schools except for novices.[1] This was so not merely because the primitive austerity was unsuitable for boys, but because in this matter the Cistercians followed the drift of the age. Nothing, in fact, more marks the later degeneration of Monasticism, when contrasted especially with its earlier enthusiasm, than the poor part it played in the education of the people. The defect of Monasticism at all times was its essential aloofness from the life of the outside world. Educational usefulness, except for its inmates, was no part of its real programme; and though by the accident of the times the monasteries were driven into providing schools, monastic education always bore the stamp of an "extra." Even in the palmy days the schools for the monks and outsiders were kept apart, and of course the first concern of the monastery was for its own inmates. So in the twelfth century the monasteries one by one closed their gates to outsiders and seculars—a course for which they might seek justification in the rapid rise of more unrestricted schools, whether " grammar " or schools of cathedral or collegiate foundation. The rapidity of the change was remarkable. In Anselm we have the greatest of monastic teachers; half a century later, in Abailard,

---

[1] This is expressly stated in *Consuetudines* No. 78 (Guignard, *op. cit.* 272). For the theological and literary writers of the Cistercians, see Heimbucher, *OKK* i. 446 f.; for the 26 universities in which in time there arose Cistercian colleges, *ib.* i. 445.

education, both higher and lower, had deserted the monastery for the cathedral. In the rise of the universities at the end of the twelfth century we see how completely the monks had abandoned their once proud position as the intellectual leaders of Europe. No university was ever the offspring of a monastery, and in the internal life of any medieval university the older orders of monks took but a limited interest, chiefly confined to their need for some study of canon law.[1]

IV

The Cistercians had sought in solitude and the revival of the *Rule* of St. Benedict in its primitive austerity the secret of reform. There were other movements that arose about the same time as Cluny and Citeaux in which we see a tendency to go back to the discipline of the East, and to the eremitical life from which Benedict had delivered Europe. Possibly the cause of this retrogression may be found in the number of Greek monks who in the tenth century found a refuge in Calabria and Sicily; possibly, also, it is sufficient to point to the evils of the age from which men in their despair sought escape in the solitary life. In all these returns to primitive type, though

---

[1] I cannot enter into the authorities for this section, but must refer the student to my chapter in the *Church of the West in M.A.* ii. c. 7 "Rise of the Universities," or the exhaustive work of H. Rashdall, *Univs. of Europe in M.A.* For schools, the works of A. Leach, both the sections on schools in the *VCH* and his monographs, are indispensable, though perhaps his main contention is a little exaggerated. For the small part played by the monasteries at Oxford, see my *Age of Wyclif*, 125 f.

differing widely in their plan, we discern certain common elements: rigorous bodily austerities, the contemplative life, and a tendency to neglect the factor of work. As our subject is the evolution of the monastic ideal and not the details of its history, we need not dwell at any length on movements which looked for salvation to methods which the experience of the past had demonstrated as of little value for permanent uplifting.

The first of these eremitical orders was the Camaldulian, founded by Romuald of Ravenna († 1027) at Campo Maldoli—whence the name—near Arezzo in the Apennines in 1012. Romuald had atoned for his wild early life by first reforming the monastery of St. Apollinare in Classe at Ravenna, and then by founding numerous hermitages in Venetia and elsewhere, modelled on the 'lauras'[1] that had once existed in the 'deserts' of Egypt and Syria—'deserts,' in fact, was his favourite name for his own creation. A wave of mystic enthusiasm swept over Italy, and pious penitents made their lonely dwellings on mountains and in woods and caves. Princes sat at the feet of Romuald; the emperor Otho III prostrated himself before him, and kissed his cowl, homage the more easy to understand when we remember the degradation at this time of the papacy and secular Church.[2] The eremitical life did not prevent the Camaldulians from missionary enterprise to the heathen in Prussia,

[1] See *supra*, p. 130.

[2] *Supra*, p. 231. For Romuald we have the *Vita* by Peter Damiani († 1072) in *PL* 146, p. 955 f. For the Camalduli and their later history, see Heimbucher, *OKK* i. 402 f. Their *Rule* or *In regulam Benedicti declarationes* is in Holsten, *CR* ii. 191 f. Camalduli still exists, with strict observance of the *Rule*.

Poland, and Russia ; some, in fact, obtained the martyr's crown.[1] St. Romuald himself in extreme old age set off for Hungary and died on the journey.

Another order, the Vallombrosian, founded by Gualbert [2] in a leafy vale of the Apennines, though maintaining a cenobite form of life, gave themselves up chiefly to contemplation in the fifty cloisters that had followed Gualbert's lead.[3] A third order, the Grandmontines, was practically confined to France. It was founded by a nobleman of Auvergne, Stephen of Thiers, as the result of his pilgrimage to the hermits of Calabria. In 1076 [4] he established himself in the desert of Muret near Limoges, and there gathered a few disciples round him. By these he was called not 'abbot' but 'Corrector'—a fair summary of the general severity of the discipline. In 1124, after Stephen's death (8 Feb. 1124), the *Rule* of the order was reduced to writing; it was modelled upon that of Camalduli. Compelled in 1150 to leave Muret, the hermits settled in Grandmont—whence the name of the order—and by 1170 had established sixty houses in France. The 'Bons Hommes' of Grandmont, as the brotherhood was popularly called, though special favourites of Henry II [5] never took root [6] in England. The management of the

---

[1] *e.g.* Benedict of Benevento in Poland (11 Nov. 1003); Bruno of Querfurt in Prussia, with 18 companions (14 Feb. 1009).

[2] *Vita* by Azzo († 1155) in *PL* 146, pp. 671 ff. Gualbert died in 1073; he founded Vallombrosa in 1038.

[3] Later history in Heimbucher, *OKK* i. 410 f.

[4] According to Heimbucher, *OKK* i. 415, followed by all historians, he received in 1073 the permission of Hildebrand. The date should be 1 May 1074, but the bull is marked by Jaffé, *RP* i. 606, as spurious.

[5] See K. Norgate, *Angevin Kings*, ii. 436. Henry had desired to be buried at Grandmont (*ib.* 270).

[6] See *VCH* (Yorks), iii. 194.

secular affairs of the order was left largely in the hands of numerous lay brethren; in consequence, the history of the order was one of constant friction owing to the "airs" which the lay brothers assumed.[1]

The best known, if not the most important, of these hermit-orders was that of the Carthusians.[2] In 1084 St. Bruno of Cologne and six companions established themselves in a desolate place called Chartreuse—whence the name of the order, and the English "charter house"—near Grenoble, and there, amidst snows that were almost perpetual, gave themselves up to prayer and silence. In 1091 Bruno, being summoned to Rome by Urban II, found the opportunity of establishing other houses in Calabria, in one of which Bruno died (6 Oct. 1101). Of the severity of the discipline of these hermits, whose religious duties, even, were usually discharged apart, we have a description by Peter the Venerable, much of which is true to-day:

'.Warned by the negligence of many of the older monks they adopted for themselves greater precautions against the artifices of the Evil One. As a remedy against pride they chose for themselves a dress more poor and contemptible than that of any other religious. . . . To mortify the flesh they wear hair shirts; their fasting is well-nigh continuous. They always eat bread of unbolted meal; they never eat meat whether well or ill; they may eat cheese and eggs only on Sundays and Thursdays. On Tuesdays and Thursdays they eat cooked vegetables; on other days they take only bread and water. . . . They live in separate little houses like the monks of Egypt and occupy themselves continually with reading, prayer, manual labour, especially the

---

[1] For the Grandmontines, see Heimbucher, *OKK* i. 415 f.; Holsten, *CR* ii. 303.

[2] For the Carthusians, see Heimbucher, *OKK* i. 477 f. For the Life of Bruno (*b.* 1030) the main authority is H. Löbbel, *Der Stifter des Carthäuserordens* (Münster, 1899, in Knöpfler, *Kirchges. Studien*, vol. 5); good abstract in Heimbucher.

writing of books. On fast-days they eat twice and sing all the offices in the church.[1]

The history of the Carthusians is remarkable for its changelessness. For eight centuries they have lived according to the same *Rule*[2] cut off from the outer world, "never reformed because never deformed," untroubled by either revivals or lapses. To-day, in the countries where they are suffered to remain, they still present much the same type of monastic life as was current in Egypt in the days of Anthony—whom, in fact, the Carthusians held in special honour, claiming to possess some relics of his body.[3] Of such an order, in a world that dared not thus linger in the past, the numbers were necessarily few, let alone that the severity of its discipline was too much save for the strongest. At the time of their greatest extension, in 1360, they numbered in all about 170 charterhouses, the greater number of which were in France.[4] In Italy the magnificence of some of the "Certosas," though witnessing to the magnificence of the princely patrons of the order, was scarcely in keeping with its primitive austerity. In England the "charterhouses" never numbered more than eleven, the first of which, Witham in Somerset,[5] was founded in 1178 by Henry II in expiation of his murder

[1] Peter Venerab. *de miraculis*, ii. 28 (in *PL* 189, p. 943). For modern usages, see Heimbucher, *OKK* i. 486 f. or P. Kauffmann, *Les Chartreux* (Meudon, 1898)—this last not in B.M.

[2] First reduced to writing by Guigo, 5th prior of Chartreuse, in 1130 (*PL* 153, p. 631; also in Holsten, *CR* ii. 312 f.). The order as such was constituted by Alexander III, 2 Sep. 1176 (*PL* 200, p. 1080; Jaffé, *RP* ii. 299).

[3] On these relics see H. Thurston, *St. Hugh of Lincoln* (1898), 467 f.

[4] Though outside my theme, it were well to record their expulsion from the Grande Chartreuse after 800 years' residence on 29 April 1903.

[5] For Witham, see E. M. Thompson, *Somerset Carthusians* (1895).

of Thomas Becket. To this priory there came in 1180,[1] from the Grande Chartreuse, the saintly Hugh of Avalon, afterwards known as the great bishop of Lincoln. But "the stern loneliness of the Carthusian rule was hardly endurable by ordinary Englishmen."[2]

V

The attempt of Hildebrand to impose the principles of Monasticism upon the whole body of the secular clergy as apart from its hierarchy [3] does not stand alone. It was the last and most successful of a series of efforts in this direction, for the most part dealing with 'canons.'[4] For the origins of this movement we must go back to Eusebius of Vercellae († 371), who a few years after his appointment as bishop made the clerics of his cathedral live together according to a rule (363).[5] When St.

[1] For this correction of the usual date (1175) see Thurston, *op. cit.* 90 n. I may point out that John Wesley's knowledge of the Charterhouse at London, where he was at school, and the traditions of the Charterhouse at Epworth, led to his wild identification of the monastic life with "cells," a popular delusion that it is difficult to destroy. Few save the Carthusians lived in "cells," the majority of monks in cloisters.

[2] Thompson, *op. cit.* 356.

[3] For the celibacy of the hierarchy, see *supra*, p. 152.

[4] According to Hatch, *OEC* 206–10, espec. 207 n., the signification of 'canon' in late Latin was the fixed contribution of corn paid by a province to Rome (cf. Vopiscus, *Vit. Firm.* c. 5), hence the total amount of such contributions available for distribution to the Roman people (Lamprid. *Vit. Elagab.* c. 27; Spart. *Vit. Sever.* c. 8). For the history of the word the reader should also consult Westcott, *Canon of NT*, App. A.

[5] Ambrose, *Ep.* 63, c. 66; Serm. 56; S. Spreitzenhofer, *Entwick. des alt. Mönchtums in Italien*, 13–17. In 328 Eusebius went to Egypt as a legate of pope Silvester I. He may there have gathered the idea, which he developed on somewhat oriental lines (Cabrol, *DACL* iii. 232).

Augustine returned from Italy in 388, though he does not seem to have known of the work of Eusebius,[1] he established a similar community at Tagaste, and on his becoming bishop of Hippo (396) he introduced the custom into several sees of Africa.[2] The usage was part of a larger movement which was slowly driving the clergy into a separate caste of the community, with a different dress, different method of trimming the hair (tonsure), different civil status, in a word, with altogether different habits of life from the laity.

But such differentiation was of slow growth. Neither in dress, tonsure, nor community life was the change rapidly effected. Not until the sixth and seventh centuries did it become the custom in Gaul and Spain for the clergy in a town to live together in the bishop's house, in part for the sake of discipline, in part for the concentration of resources, in part to secure the better training of the younger clerics.[3] The members of this community were called 'canons,' a title originally applied to all, whether clerics or poor laymen, who were entered on the church-roll (*matricula*) as in the receipt of church funds.[4] The portions or specified victuals which such 'canons' received were called *praebendae*. In course of time those 'praebends' or funds for the

---

[1] In his *de moribus eccles. cath.* 33, written in 388, he only mentions houses of laymen at Rome and Milan. See *PL* 32, p. 1340.

[2] Possidius, *de vit. August.* 3, 5, 11 (in *PL* 32, pp. 33 ff.); St. August. *Serm.* 355, 356; and cf. H. Leclercq, *L'Afrique chrétienne* (1904), ii. 70–7; Cabrol, *DACL* iii. 226 f.; ii. 3225–6.

[3] Conc. Toledo, II. (531) cc. 1, 2, III. c. 7, IV. c. 23; Conc. Tours, II. c. 12; Conc. Orleans (538), c. 11. See *DCA* i. 281; Hatch, *OEC* 207 n. 27.

[4] The word is used in Greek in this sense at an early date (Cabrol, *DACL* iii. 235) and includes women as well (*ib.* iii. 249, and cf. Soc. *HE* i. 17, where a virgin is spoken of as the κανών of the church).

support of the canons and their common table were separated altogether from the general funds under the bishop's control.[1] In the seventh century great disorders arose, and the whole institution drifted far away from the simple ideas laid down by Eusebius and St. Augustine.

At the close of the eighth century efforts were made to bring the 'canons' into line with the monastic ideal. The leader in the movement was Chrodegang, bishop of Metz († 766). Chrodegang,[2] whose rugged German name assumes strange forms in the Chronicles, was the scion of a noble Frank family of Brabant. In the court of Charles Martel he rose rapidly until he attained the office of chancellor. By the favour of Pepin in 742 he was appointed bishop of Metz, though still retaining his civic dignity. As a bishop he set himself to correct the worldliness and laxity of the clergy by forcing them to live together under monastic discipline. In this effort he received the constant support of Charles the Great, who intended to make these colleges of clergy educational centres. One of the canons was designated chancellor (*cancellarius*) or schoolmaster for this very purpose. In 817 the Council of Aachen, encouraged by the Emperor Lewis the Pious, went so far as to extend to all the clergy [3] the canonical dis-

[1] Hatch, *OEC* 208 n. 29; Cabrol, *DACL* iii. 238.

[2] For Chrodegang, see *DCB* i. 499 ff.; Zöckler, *AM*, 422 f. The main source of his life is in Paul the Deacon, *Gesta Episc. Metens.* (in *MGH* ii. 276 ff.), written in 783. Chrodegang's *Rule* in its original form is in Mansi, xiv. 313 f. It was drawn up about 760; a longer form of later date in *ib.* 332. See also Holsten, *CR* ii. 93 ff., and *PL* 89, p. 1097 f. For medieval secular canons reference for advanced students may be made to H. Bradshaw and Ch. Wordsworth, *Statutes of Lincoln Cathedral* (3 vols., 1892, 1894, and 1897).

[3] Attempts in this direction had already been made by Pepin in

cipline, and a *Rule* based upon that of Chrodegang.¹ From the first the attempt was doomed to failure. In England, for instance, in 786 an effort was made to introduce the *Rule*, but like all other later attempts without result.² The only effect so far as the clergy was concerned was "to change the name of secular clerks into canons and to turn secular abbots into deans"; ³ though greater success followed the establishment of houses of canonesses.⁴ In the towns and populous parishes it was possible to force the clergy to live together under the control of a bishop or dean the more easily, if, as in Harold's foundation at Waltham, sumptuous provision was made for their common life,⁵ but in the thinly peopled country districts such a step was neither desirable nor practicable.

The attempt of Chrodegang and of those who continued his work is, however, of considerable interest. The canons, or clergy living a corporate life, were placed

---

789, in 802 by Charles the Great (*Capitul*, c. 22 in *MGH Leg.* i. 94), at the synods of Arles, Mainz, Rheims, and Tours in 813 (Mansi, xiv. 60, 67, 78, 86).

¹ Commonly ascribed to Amalarius of Metz († c. 857). For this council and the *Rule* of Amalarius in 145 chapters, see Mansi, xiv. 147 ff.; *PL* 89, p. 1098 f.; Cabrol, *DACL* iii. 245 f.

² Cf. Freeman, *Norman Conquest*, ii. 85.

³ Stubbs, *de invent. cruc.* (1861), introd. pp. ix, x. In France in 789, in the *Capitularies* of Aachen, we see the names of canon and of priest become synonymous (Cabrol, *DACL* iii. 243; *MG Leg.* i. 65).

⁴ Cabrol, *DACL* iii. 253.

⁵ For the significance of Harold's college of secular canons at Waltham (3 May 1060), see Freeman, *Norman Conq.* ii. 438 f. In 1067 Leofric, who had been educated in Lorraine, when he transferred the bishop's stool from Crediton to Exeter, placed the new cathedral under Chrodegang's *Rule* (Freeman, *op. cit.* ii. 84). Gisa, the Lotheringian bishop of Wells (1061-88), forced part of the *Rule* of Chrodegang upon the secular canons of Wells (Freeman, *Ch. of Wells*, 33; *Norm. Conq.* ii. 449). Both efforts were short-lived.

under a rule; in the main, the *Rule* of Benedict with two fundamental differences. The obligation to poverty was relaxed. Instead of all wealth lapsing to the common fund the canons were allowed a life interest both in their real property and in such fees and offerings as they might receive. Nor was the vow of unquestioning obedience so rigid as in the monastery. In other respects also the wind was tempered for the shorn seculars. Each canon was allowed his own cell or dwelling room. They did not wear the monk's cowl nor bear his name. Better provision was made for sleep by placing the singing of the vigil at midnight instead of two o'clock in the morning. Meat was customary; more wine was allowed at meals; fasting is less rigorous; manual work less peremptory. Instead of the democratic equality of all inmates of the monastery under the abbot, Chrodegang brings in distinctions of rank within the one common life, with perquisites and privileges accordingly; a priest has three glasses of wine for dinner, a sub-deacon only two, and so on. In one respect, however, we mark a development of idea. The abbey-church was built solely for the spiritual wants of the inmates; only by accident or special arrangement, generally of a pecuniary kind, did outsiders acquire either consideration or rights. But from the first the canons existed for the service of cathedral or church, and of the multitudes of whose spiritual life it was the centre.

Chrodegang's reform was short-lived. Mild as was his *Rule* it was too severe to be acceptable to the seculars, many of whom, especially in England, were married men, who naturally resented the effort to break up their homes and curtail their liberty. " The secular had no mind to be entrapped into becoming a sort of half monk, while still nominally retaining the secular character."[1] Even where his *Rule* or that of Amalarius was adopted its deviations from Benedictine simplicity were fatal. Luxury and self-indulgence were the inevitable outgrowth, together with increasing aloofness from all the interests of the other seculars. So in England the reformers of the tenth century, with Dunstan at their head, drove out the canons from nine cathedrals, replacing them by Benedictine monks.[2] In places where they were retained the canons gradually developed into bodies distinct from, often antagonistic to, the clergy of the diocese, while all that they held of their common life was the name.

In the eleventh century, as part of the general revival of discipline, Ivo of Chartres († 1117) attempted once more, about the year 1078, to bring cathedrals and collegiate churches under monastic discipline. Following in this matter the lead given by Hildebrand in the Lateran Council of 1059[3] a stricter rule was intro-

---

[1] Freeman, *Norman Conquest*, ii. 450.

[2] The English monastic cathedrals were Bath, Canterbury, Carlisle, Durham, Ely, Norwich, Rochester, Winchester, and Worcester—all Benedictine; also Carlisle (Austin Canons) and Coventry. At the Reformation these became cathedrals of the " *new* foundation " —Bath was merged, Coventry destroyed—as distinct from the " old foundation " of secular canons. To the above were added, also of the "new foundation," the abbey-churches of Bristol, Chester, Gloucester, Oxford, and Peterborough. I may add here that the word " minster " is most loosely used in English, and by no means is an accurate guide to whether a church was in any way monastic, though of course its derivation points to such connection. Cf. *VCH* Somerset ii. 6, for illustrations.

[3] Mansi, xix. 897; *PL* 143, p. 1316. For the decrees of Hildebrand *re* canons drawn up in an undated (? 1074) Roman council, see Leclercq's note in Hefele, *HC* v. i. 94–8 n.

duced, drawn in part from the works of St. Augustine, in part from spurious writings attributed to him.[1] The Austin Canons, as they were thus called—Canons Regular of St. Augustine, to give them their fuller title—differed from monks by being also clerics, with singular powers of adapting themselves to work of any sort, whether pastoral in the churches they served,[2] educational, or philanthropic, as in the hospitals attached to their houses; also by their greater simplicity and elasticity of organization. For the Austin *Rule*, as was natural from the circumstances of its origin, was not an elaborate code but a casual summary, confining itself to fundamental principles. Unlike the canons of Chrodegang, the Augustinians were obliged to renounce private property, while they differed from the secular canons both by their community life and by their monastic vows. At first they were without connexional organization, but in 1339 Benedict XII established a system of provincial chapters and visitations, while by their natural growth they became divided in process of time into some thirty different congregations.

Early in the twelfth century Austin Canons were

[1] The so-called *Rule* of St. Augustine is based in the main on part of a letter (*Ep.* 211 in *PL* 33, p. 958) written by him, probably in 423, for the guidance of a nunnery in his diocese of Hippo; also on *Serm.* 355, 356, in which Augustine describes the common life he lived with his clergy at Hippo (see *supra*, p. 254). From these sources were compiled three *Rules*,—the *First Rule* and the *Second Rule*, both mere fragments; the *Third Rule* (the Rule that commonly goes by the name of the *Austin Rule*) being in 45 sections. [For the three *Rules*, see Holsten-Brockie, *CR* ii. 121 f., or Dugdale, *Monasticon*, vi. 42; and for a study of the *Rule* and its effect, *Owens College Hist. Essays* (1902), 57-75.]

[2] It has been shown by the Rev. J. Hodson (*Archæol. Journal*, vols. 41 and 42) that 37 out of 254 Austin Churches in England were parochial.

introduced into England. Their first priory was founded in 1108, at the instance of Anselm, by the English Queen Maud, in the soke of Aldgate, and was dedicated to the Trinity. Its first prior, Norman, a native of Kent who had studied the new *Rule* at Chartres and Beauvais [1] lavished all his funds on the building of his church and the shelves of his library. When Sunday came the starving brotherhood set out a row of empty plates to attract the attention of the citizens taking their stroll in the suburbs. How the burghers' wives peeping in curiously at the windows of the new building were moved to sympathy and vowed each to bring a loaf every Sunday, is an oft-told tale. Fifteen years later (1123), Rahere, the king's minstrel, threw up his post at court and built another Austin priory, dedicated to St. Bartholomew, in the marshes of Smithfield, the mutilated fragment of whose church is to-day one of London's most cherished shrines. To this he attached an hospital for the sick and needy, for whose support the master Alfhun went daily begging in the shops and markets. Another famous Austin house was that of Merton in Surrey. There the brotherhood devoted themselves to educational work. One of the most illustrious of their early pupils was the son of a citizen of London, Thomas Becket.[2]

[1] In *VCH* (Essex), ii. 148, it is shown that Norman was first at St. Botolph's, Colchester, which he took steps to turn into a regular house, but whether Colchester as an Austin house is before 1108 or not is not quite certain.

[2] For these Austin priories, see Dugdale, *Mon.* vi. pts. 1 and 2. Another famous Austin priory in London, still existing, was St. Mary Overy (*i.e.* over the river), now St. Saviour's Cathedral. A good deal as to Austin Canons may be learned by the English reader from J. W. Clark, *The Observances in Use at the Augustinian Priory of Barnwell* (1897).

Of the different congregations of the Canons Regular [1] the most illustrious was the congregation of St. Victor, founded by William of Champeaux (c. 1110), the opponent of Abailard, famous for its renowned teachers Hugh († 1141) and Richard of St. Victor († 1173), and for the mystical school they established; the congregation of Windisheim, established in 1386 under the influence of the preaching of Gerard Groot, the Wesley of the fourteenth century, the founder of the " Brethren of the Common Life." [2] Into one of the houses of this congregation, Mount St. Agnes, there entered in 1400 a monk who had been educated at the schools of the Brethren of the Common Life at Deventer. There, " in this silent motionless centre of a whirling and incomprehensible world," [3] for seventy-one years lived Thomas Haemerlein of Kempen, whose mystical work, *Imitatio Christi*, "remains to all time a lasting record of human needs and human consolations, the voice of a brother who, ages ago, felt and suffered and renounced."[4] Historically the work of Thomas is the last, as it is the best, expression and defence of the ideals of the monastic world; it is the swanlike song of a system whose effective work in the world was in reality finished, and whose days, therefore, were numbered. For us its chief importance in this study is to note its abandonment of the mere negative side of self-renunciation. The negative side, it is true, is there; for that matter, there can be no spiritual life where it is not found. At

[1] These congregations are exhaustively dealt with by Heimbucher, *OKK* ii. 21–49.

[2] For Gerard Groot, see Rufus Jones, *Studies in Mystical Religion* (1909), 314 f.

[3] de Montmorency, *Thomas à Kempis*, 89.

[4] George Eliot, *Mill on the Floss*, bk. iv. c. 3.

times also this negative side appears in a mischievous form, illustrations of which will readily occur to every reader of the *Imitation*. But the core of the message of Thomas is that no mere abandonment, self-mortification, self-crucifixion, without a holy passion of love can bring us to our goal. Such a belief is fatal to all quietism, its logical issue is the advice of Thomas: ' Never be idle or vacant. Be always reading or writing or praying or meditating, or employed in some useful labour for the common good.' But this ' common good ' could no longer be restricted to the monastic community.

Another congregation of Austin Canons should be mentioned, if only because of its interest for the tourist. About the year 962 St. Bernard of Menthon[1] († 15 June 981), who in his younger days had joined in a military expedition against the robbers whose raids rendered the roads into Italy so dangerous, founded amid the snows of the Alps, on the highest and most dangerous points of two Roman passes that then were both dedicated to Jove, the hospices which still bear his name. As in time the discipline of these 'Brothers of St. Bernard's Mountain' became somewhat loose, Innocent III in 1212 put them under the *Rule* of the Austin Canons, and in 1438 they were constituted a separate congregation. As might be gathered from their arduous services their numbers were never large.

In another congregation of Canons Regular, the Gilbertines, we may take a special interest, inasmuch as it was the only congregation or order directly established

---

[1] For this St. Bernard, Heimbucher advises students to consult L. Burgener, *Der hl. Bernard* (Lucerne, 2nd ed. 1870), or A. Durand, *Le vrai conquérant des Alpes* (Paris, 1905). Neither volume seems to be in the Brit. Mus. (1912).

by an Englishman, for as such we may claim Gilbert of Sempringham,[1] the son of a Norman baron by an English mother. Gilbert, on his return to England from Paris, where he had gained considerable reputation as scholar and teacher, set up a school at Sempringham, a village in Lincolnshire, of which he was the rector, for the instruction of boys and girls on severe monastic lines. Afterwards, about 1131,[2] he erected against the north wall of his church simple cloisters for seven maidens whom he had taught in his school, their daily necessaries being passed in to them through a window by some village girls. Soon these serving maids requested that they too might have a dress and rule of life, and the needs of the estate forced him to add lay brothers, to whom also he gave a dress and a *Rule*. As his numbers grew, in 1139 Gilbert was forced to build a larger house, with double cloisters and monastic buildings, but with church in common, for his nuns and for the canons whom, a few years later, he added as chaplains and teachers, following in this the example of Fontevrault,[3] which would have come under his notice when in France, to say nothing of earlier usages of which he was probably ignorant.[4] In 1147, after attempting in vain to transfer his nuns to the care of the Cistercians, he

[1] For Gilbert and his order, see *VCH* (Lincolnshire), ii. 179–99; Dugdale, *Monast.* vi. (2), pp. v–xxix (for text of his *Vita*, written by one who had known him personally); R. Graham, *St. Gilbert of S.* (1901); or *DNB* xxi. 315 f. His *Rule* is in Dugdale, *op. cit.* xxix–xcvii; Holsten, *CR* ii. 466–536; or, briefly, in Graham, *l.c.* 48–77.

[2] For this date, as against the usual 1139, see *VCH* (Lincolnshire) ii. 179 n.

[3] Fontevrault was founded in 1100. For this "double" Benedictine monastery, see Heimbucher, *OKK* i. 417 f.

[4] See *supra*, p. 176 f.

obtained, through the help of St. Bernard, the sanction of Eugenius III for his congregation and for the *Rule* which he drew up ; a mixture of the *Rules* of the Austin and Premonstratensian Canons, and of the Cistercian *Rule*, with certain adaptations necessary for a dual foundation. The nuns, for instance, who lived under the *Rule* of St. Benedict, as interpreted by the Cistercians, had the control of the expenditure ; the administration of the estate was in the hands of the canons ; and the manual labour entrusted to lay brethren of menial station who followed the *Rule* of the Cistercians. As might be expected from the influence of St. Bernard, the connexional idea was emphasized, a general Chapter meeting once a year at Sempringham on Rogation Days, under the direction of the ' Master of Sempringham,' as the head of the order was called, who, however, was not attached to any one house, but went from one to another on visitation. The local government of each house was in the hands of a committee of four seniors, two canons and two nuns. The Order, which like the Cistercians was wholly exempt from episcopal control and under the papacy alone, was especially strong in Lincolnshire, where they possessed ten houses in all. Except for a brief existence in Scotland it was confined altogether to England.[1] When the founder died in extreme old age, as a humble inmate in one of his own monasteries (4 Feb. 1189), the congregation contained 700 canons and 1500 sisters. At the Dissolution it numbered twenty-two houses. Like the Cistercians the Gilbertines were at one time great wool-

---

[1] At one time there was a Scots house at Dalmulin, near Ayr. This was abandoned in 1221. See J. Edwards, *The Gilbertines in Scotland* (1904), p. 7.

growers and wool-staplers, a trade into which they were tempted by their exemption from all tolls and customs. Nor were they always sufficiently careful to keep their business within legitimate bounds.[1] In 1320, for instance, Sempringham was in debt £1000, due to speculations in wool with an Italian merchant. The priory of St. Catherine outside Lincoln had "plunged" even more disastrously, and only with difficulty met their bonds. But after the Black Death of 1349 they were forced to abandon the cultivation of their own lands and to let their estates on leases, a change that led to the disappearance of the lay brothers.

One branch of Austin Canons, established in 1120 by St. Norbert [2] at Prémontré,[3] a lonely valley near Laon in France, was called Norbertine, or Premontratensian, or White Canons. Though under the Augustinian *Rule*, they differed from the Austin Canons as then constituted by the emphasis laid upon the connexional idea, a development that synchronized with the similar change among the Cistercians.[4] The monasteries of the order were grouped in provinces—at the time of the order's highest extension numbering thirty—with a 'corrector' or president at the head of each, and over all as 'first father of the order,' the abbot of Prémontré'; where every year a general

[1] Details in *VCH* (Linc.), ii. 182, 183, 184, 189.

[2] Norbert (for whose *Vita* see *MGH* xii. 663 f.) was born c. 1080 at Xanten on the Rhine. He was the second son of Count Heribert of Gennep, and related to the Emperor Henry IV. In 1126 he was elected archb. of Magdeburg, and so was enabled largely to introduce his order into Germany. He died at Magdeburg, 6 June 1134. On this German order Heimbucher, *OKK* ii. 50 f. is very full both as to its bibliography and history.

[3] *i.e.* Praemonstratum, "the place shown to him by God."

[4] *Supra*, p. 243.

chapter was held on the ninth of October.[1] Though very strong in Germany, and among the Wends, to whose Christianization they devoted themselves as missionaries, they never made much headway in England. At the Dissolution there were but thirty-four houses of this order, the chief of which were Welbeck and Shap, and in Scotland Dryburgh.

VI

Nothing is more remarkable than the elasticity of the so-called *Austin Rule*, and the variety of service to which it led. We have an illustration of this in the rise of the military orders, nominally, at least, enrolled under this *Rule*.

When, in 1119,[2] Hugues de Payens and eight French knights devoted themselves to the task of keeping the roads to Jerusalem clear of robbers, and thus established the famous Templars,[3] or when in the previous year Raymond du Puy reorganized the 'Poor Brethren of the Hospital of St. John at Jerusalem,'[4] they opened out a new conception of holiness. Their idea was to unite under the banner of the Cross the two strongest

[1] Not held at Prémontré since 1736.

[2] For date, see Hefele, *HC* v. ii. 669 n., where also is given the latest literature.

[3] The real start was not made until Jan. 1128, when at the Synod of Troyes Bernard gave them his advocacy. To Bernard was assigned their *Rule*, the greater part of which is by a later hand (Mansi, *Conc.* xxi. 360; *Op. Bernard*, ii. 543 in *PL* 182, p. 919; Hefele, *l.c.*; Vacandard, *Vie de Bernard*, i. 227).

[4] The date of the foundation of this hospital at Jerusalem is not known; see R. Röhricht, *Erst. Kreuz.* (Innsbruck, 1901), 11 n. W. Heyd, *Gesch. d. Levantehandels in MA* (2 vols. Stuttgart, 1879; Fr. trans. Paris, 1885), i. 103–6, argues against the accepted view that it was founded by merchants of Amalfi (*Recueil des Crois.* v. 401).

impulses of the age, the impulse to fight and the impulse to watch and pray. Hitherto in Europe the two motives had been at variance, the knight and the monk had nothing in common. Henceforth, under the pressure of the Paynim, they become one; feudalism passes into the service of the Church. In the days that were gone her typical hero was Achilles, sulking in his tents over personal wrongs ; her new ideal is the warrior who shall have approved himself most in the service of man. A further step was taken when in 1190 German democracy, under one Walpot von Bassenheim, a trader of Bremen, established the third great order of Teutonic Knights, originally a union of ship captains from Lübeck for the succour of the sick and the dying at Acre. 'This Walpot,' we read, 'was not by birth a noble, but his deeds were noble.' The new order obtained vast possessions in Germany, and in 1228 drew their swords against the heathen Prussians, who, since their massacre of St. Adalbert, had steadily resisted all attempts at conversion. Henceforth their history is " a dim nightmare of unintelligible marching and fighting," [1] but the results at any rate are luminous still. From their head centre at Marienburg they slowly subdued the pagans, and laid the foundations of modern Prussia.

The establishment and growth of these military orders is of considerable importance in any study of the development of the monastic ideal. They form the middle stage in a slow but organic process. In the original conceptions of Monasticism, if a man would serve God he must quit the world. Even Abailard, in one of his letters to Héloise, tells with approval of a monk who said he had fled from his fellows because it was impossible

[1] Carlyle, *Frederick the Great*, i. 82.

to love both God and man at the same time. With the military orders, to serve God was to fight the world. St. Francis, as we shall see in our next section, changed this into the nobler formula: to serve God we must serve the world. In this progress we mark a shifting of the centre of gravity of the three fundamental ideas. In the solitary hermit the central thought is asceticism; celibacy is a corollary, while obedience is impossible. In the monastery, in spite of all the intentions of its founder, poverty becomes a counsel of perfection, and celibacy and obedience the distinctive marks. In the friar, the thought of 'our Lady Poverty' is again uppermost, and a rule of life is framed in order to guard her, but on principles very different from any that had yet appeared in Monasticism. But the military orders anticipated the Jesuits by laying the emphasis on obedience. The applicant for admission begged that he might become the serf and slave of the 'House' for ever, and was warned that he must surrender his will irrevocably. Now of all the three virtues it is obedience that would prove most serviceable to the papacy. For the realization of the dreams of Hildebrand poverty is an incumbrance (it must be expelled, as we shall see later, even from the friars [1]), sins against celibacy were often too lightly pardoned, but unswerving obedience is vital. In the great papal orders, therefore—the Cistercian, the military, and the Jesuit—this is the central idea; changed only by Loyola from its first rude military form to that more subtle obedience which claims not merely the will but the intellect and imagination.

[1] *Infra*, p. 302 f.

CHAPTER VI

THE COMING OF THE FRIARS

> Fac me plagis vulnerari
> Cruce hac inebriari.
>
> JACOPONE DA TODI.

> He stood before the sun
>   (The peoples felt their fate)
> "The world is many,—I am one;
>   My great Deed was too great.
> God's fruit of justice ripens slow;
> Men's souls are narrow; let them grow.
>   My brothers, we must wait."

> Qui Minor es, noli ridere, tibi quia soli
> Convenit ut plores; jungas cum nomine mores.
> Nomine tu Minor es, minor actibus esto, labores
> Perfer, et ingentem nuntiat patientia mentem.
> Umbra Minoris erit, qui nomen re sine quaerit.
>
> ECCLESTON, *de adventu Minorum in Angliam.*

ARGUMENT

                                                                                     PAGE

§ I. Decline of Monasticism—The new ideal of the Friars—Gloomy state of the Church—Jacques de Vitry's description—Dante on St. Dominic and St. Francis—Life of St. Dominic—His missionary activities—His death . 271

§ II. St. Francis—Sources of his Life—Recent criticisms—Francis' writings—His early life—The Poor Clares—Growth of his order—The mission of the friars—Saracens and Moors—Their sermons—Extravagances—The Children's Crusade—Last years of Francis—The Stigmata—*Canticle of the Sun* 278

§ III. Secret of success—Durand of Huesca—Connexionalism and internationalism—The 'watchdogs' of the papacy—Organization of the orders—Democratic significance—'Brothers Minor'—Tertiaries—Discovery of the laity—Brother Giles and King Louis—Ardent missionaries—Raymund Lull—Place of poverty—'Zealots' and 'Moderates' 293

§ IV. Francis and Nature—Sermon to the Birds—Francis and Art—Unity of Francis' character—Francis and Learning—The Schoolmen—Roger Bacon—English Franciscans—The contradictions of the Franciscans—Carmelites and Austin Friars 305

                                                                            pp. 271-316

CHAPTER VI

THE COMING OF THE FRIARS

I

WITH the opening years of the thirteenth century Monasticism, which had once more passed into a period of decay and death—the old fires burning out, the old usefulness gone—entered upon the greatest revolution it had as yet experienced. Without changing its basal principle of poverty, celibacy, and obedience it sought to work out its ideals, no longer by shunning men, but by seeking them, following, in this matter, but with greater completeness, the lead already given by the Austin canons, with their attention to education, parish duties, the care of the sick and needy,[1] the building of bridges[2] and the like. The coming of the friars, under the inspiration of St. Dominic and St. Francis, was the rise, in fact, of a new conception of Monasticism so completely different that friars were forbidden to enter within the walls of any monastery.[3] Hitherto the highest religious life had identified itself with a retreat from the world, the retiring like St. Bruno to some Grande Chartreuse, where in a rarer air, far from its noise and whirl, men could save their souls and rule into their

---

[1] *Supra*, p. 260.

[2] The Fratres Pontifices, an Augustinian brotherhood (Heimbucher, ii. 258), were founded by Benezet of Avignon († 1184).

[3] See the *Reg. Bullata* of St. Francis, c. 11 (see *infra*, p. 282 n.).

characters the fine lines. But the friars were essentially an order of social labourers. In the dream of their founders they would go about doing good. They must find their Grande Chartreuse in the wretched slums of overcrowded cities, their mountain-tops of contemplation in the haunts of plague and fever. They should save themselves by losing themselves in saving others. "Live," said the monk, "as if you were alone in this world with God"; and it was from the following out of this advice that, as we have seen, the chief difficulties of Monasticism arose. "Live," said both St. Francis and St. Dominic, "as if you only existed for the sake of others." Their whole lives were illustrations of this doctrine. In his youth, in a time of famine, Dominic had sold his books and all he possessed to relieve the distress. At a later date he spent ten years in Languedoc going about barefoot and in extreme poverty, in villages and castles alike preaching to the Albigensian heretics, despising both threats of death and actual persecution. 'Our order,' wrote Humbert de Romanis († 1277) in his commentary on Dominic's *Rule*,

'has been founded for preaching and for the salvation of our neighbours. Our studies should tend principally, ardently, above everything, to make us useful for souls.' [1]

So with St. Francis. The most ecstatic joy of the Umbrian saint was when he heard the voice of God

'that it behoved him by preaching to convert much people. Thus saith the Lord: "Say unto brother Francis that God has not called him to this estate for himself alone, but to the end that he may gain fruit of souls, and that many through him may be saved."' (*Little Flowers*, c. 16).

---

[1] The best edition is by J. J. Berthier, *Opera de vita regulari Humberti* (2 vols., Rome, 1888).

The reader should note that, as usual, this revival of monastic piety was the reaction from the despair of the preceding age. It would be difficult to paint in colours too gloomy the state of the Church at the close of the twelfth century; nor do we intend to essay the task.[1] Suffice that we point out that once more in this hour of her need the Church was saved, not so much by either the genius and energy of her popes—great as the pontiffs of this evil time undoubtedly were—nor by the self-sacrifice of her secular bishops and clergy, as by the labours of two regulars. 'Master Dominic and his Preaching Brothers' revived the forgotten duty of preaching, while Francis and his 'Little Brothers' showed an astonished Europe how to remove mountains by faith wedded to love. In a letter written at Genoa in Oct. 1216 by Jacques de Vitry, shortly before he sailed for Damietta, we read—

> During my sojourn at the imperial court I have seen many things which deeply saddened me. They are so busy there with temporal affairs, with quarrels and lawsuits, that it is almost impossible to speak about religious matters. I have nevertheless found in these countries one subject of consolation; it is that many persons of both sexes, rich and living in the world, leave all for the love of Christ. They are called Friars Minor. . . . They disentangle themselves completely from secular things, and make every day the most energetic efforts to snatch perishing souls from the vanities of this world, and draw them into their ranks. Thanks to God their labour has already produced much fruit, and they have conquered many souls. . . . I think it is to put to shame the prelates, who are like dogs incapable of barking, that the Lord wills before the end of the world to raise many souls by means of these simple and poor men.[2]

---

[1] For this, see my *Ch. of West in MA* ii. c. 5; Sabatier, *St. Francis*, c. 3.

[2] This *Epistola* has been printed by Boehmer, *Analekten zur Gesch.*

In Dominic, the apostle of faith, and Francis, the apostle of love, 'the bridegroom of Lady Poverty,' the Latin Church will ever recognize the most successful of her champions, the two of whom Dante sings, by Providence

> ordained, who should on either hand
> In chief escort her : one seraphic all
> In fervency ; for wisdom upon earth,
> The other splendour of cherubic light.
> I but of one will tell ; he tells of both,
> Who one commendeth, which of them soe'er
> Be taken ; for their deeds were to one end.[1]

Following the advice of the poet we shall restrict ourselves for the most part to the more original of these two heroes of God.

Nevertheless some sketch should be given of Dominic's life.[2] Though not very familiar to Protestant readers

des Franciscus [II. (6) 1904], p. 94 f. ; also by Sabatier, *Spec. Perfect.* (Paris, 1898), 278 f. For its correct date, see Felder [*op. cit. infra* (p. 309 n.), p. 7 n.] and cf. *infra*, p. 289 n.

[1] Dante, *Par.* xi. (H. F. Cary's trans.).

[2] For Dominic, who still lacks his English interpreter, we are reduced to the panegyrics of H. D. L. Lacordaire (1840, 8th ed. 1882, trans. Hazeland) and A. T. Drane (1891 ; American Ultramontane nun), both uncritical and historically worthless. On a higher plane is the Introduction by the Bollandists (*A.SS* Aug. 4th, 359 f.). The best Eng. work is the trans. by K. de Mattos (1901) of J. Guiraud's life (5th ed. Paris, 1905 ; excellent bibliography). The most trustworthy original source is the record of Jordan of Saxony († 1237), the successor of Dominic (best ed. J. J. Berthier. Freiburg, 1891 ; or in *A.SS* Aug. 4th, 541 ff.). Other sources for the early history of the order may be found in F. Balme et Lelaidier, *Cartulaire de St. D.* (3 vols. Paris, 1892); the valuable *Chronica ordinis* and the *Vitae Fratrum* of Gerardi di Fracheto, both in B. M. Reichert, *Monumenta ord. Praed.* (Louvain, 1896) ; J. Quétif and J. Echard, *Script. ord. Pred.* (2 vols. Paris, 1719) ; especially the *Vita Dom.* by Bernard Guido (*op. cit.* i. 44 f.); the *Vita* by Constantine of Orvieto, written c. 1245 (in *op. cit.* i. 25 f.); and the record of the depositions at

"Dominic was a noble personality of genuine and true piety. . . . In the purity of his intention and the earnestness with which he strove to carry out his ideal, he was not inferior to Francis."[1] Domingo de Guzman—his right to this noble surname is not above suspicion—was born at Calarvega in Old Castile (5 April 1170). The country of his birth influenced his whole life. The fairest provinces of Spain were still in the grip of the Muslim, and Dominic from his earliest days was brought up to think of heresy as the great foe that must be overcome. Nor must we forget that not far from his home was the tomb of the Cid. After ten years of training in the schools of Palencia Dominic entered, about 1195, the chapter of Osma, whose canons a few years later were induced by their bishop to take up the *Austin Rule* (1199). In 1203 Dominic set off with his bishop, Diego, to 'the Marches,' *i.e.* probably to Languedoc, a land overrun by the heretical Cathari or Albigensians. There, while the country was deluged with the blood of a crusade, he spent the next ten years in preaching. He further showed the drift of his endeavours by his founding in 1206 a school at Prouille, under the shadow of the Pyrenees, for women of gentle blood, for the most part converts from the Albigensians.[2]

Round the ardent evangelist there gathered a little band of kindred souls—the first two to join him being burghers of Toulouse—to whom in 1215 the archbishop

the official enquiry with reference to D.'s canonization (in *A.SS* Aug. 4th, 629 f.). For complete bibliography, see Heimbucher, *OKK* ii. 93–101. (A great number of the works there mentioned are not, so far as I can discover, in the British Museum.)

[1] Grützmacher in Herzog *PRE*³ iv. 773. Cf. also Heimbucher, *OKK* ii. 105.

[2] The school soon became indistinguishable from a convent.

of Toulouse assigned a house and church. With his archbishop Dominic set off for Rome to the Lateran Council that he might obtain formal sanction for his new community. The journey was not successful. Innocent III would not allow the introduction of a new Rule. So, on Dominic's return, the brotherhood at Toulouse enrolled themselves as Austin Canons (10 April 1216). But a few months later Dominic succeeded in obtaining from Honorius III sanction for the new order (22 Dec. 1216), though without express sanction of any Rule. This was followed two years later by a bull recommending to the whole world 'the order of Brothers Preachers' (21 Jan. 1217). At two general chapters, held at Bologna in 1220 and 1221, a formal constitution was adopted—for as yet the brethren were still Austin canons—the new *Rule* being based upon the severest interpretation of that of St. Augustine with supplementary regulations from the Premonstratensian code and from the use of Cluny.[1] In 1218—or possibly in 1215 in Rome—Dominic had met Francis, and from him adopted the idea of corporate poverty.[2] This, after considerable opposition, Dominic succeeded in making one of the regulations of his order.

The last years of Dominic's life were taken up in a series of journeys in Italy, into Spain, and as far as

[1] We do not possess the constitution of Whitsuntide 1220, the oldest we have being that set out in 1228 by Jordan of Saxony, revised in 1238 by Raymond of Peñaforte († 1275). On these see Deniffe in *Archiv. f. Lit. v. Kg. d. MA.* 165–228, 530 ff.; Holsten, *CR* iv. 17–127.

[2] For this meeting, see Heimbucher, *OKK* ii. 103. The whole story, if put down to 1215, seems to me a later myth (cf. Zöckler, *AM* 495), but may well have happened in 1218, possibly at the Portiuncula at the Whitsuntide chapter-general (cf. Sabatier, *St. F.* 218), or at Rome in March 1218 (*ib.* 214, 215).

Paris, for the organization of his order. Dominic's work was now finished. His missionaries were at work in almost every country of Western Europe. Sixty friaries divided into eight provinces witnessed within his lifetime to the extraordinary success of his idea. He determined that he would end his days in carrying the gospel to the East; he would realize the dream of his youth and preach to the Kuman Tatars of the Volga. But the end was at hand. Worn out with his austerities he was unable to leave his friary at Bologna. So he gathered the brethren together, and for the last time exhorted them to fear God and to hold fast to the *Rule*. 'As my parting legacy I leave to you this: Have love; guard your humility, and continue to live by voluntary offerings.' As he had no cell of his own they placed the dying man on a bed of ashes in the cell of friar Moneta. They wished to change his garments, but having none save those which he wore, Moneta gave him one of his own tunics. Friar Rodolfo supported the saint's head, wiping the death-sweat from his brow, the rest of the friars looking on weeping. In order to comfort them, Dominic said, 'Do not weep; I shall be of more use to you where I am going than I have been here.' One of the friars asked him where he desired to be interred. He replied, 'Beneath the feet of the friars.' They then commenced the prayers for the departing, in which, from the movement of his lips, Dominic appeared to take part. When they came to the words, 'Let the holy angels of God come forth to meet him, and conduct him to the city of the Heavenly Jerusalem,' his lips moved for the last time.[1] His splendid monument at Bologna

[1] For the last scenes we have the deposition of Rodolfo and others who were with him (in Quétif & Echard, *op. cit.* i. 51 f., or *A.SS*,

still witnesses to the devotion of his children, but his abiding memorial is in the world-wide order that he established.

II

In dealing with St. Dominic the task of the historian is not difficult. He has merely to clear away the manifest accretions and legends of later generations. Very different is the case with St. Francis. Here the historian has to pick his way through the rival versions of two different schools among the Franciscans themselves, each hating the other with a hatred that nothing could assuage, each anxious to claim the sanction of their founder for their tenets,[1] each of which has sought to establish his narrative with the customary legends and miracles. In addition he has to meet—a rare matter in the case of a medieval saint—what may fairly be described as a modern Protestant legend, in some respects as anachronistic and fanciful as any medieval story, and which has obtained an abiding hold upon cultured England that it will be difficult for German criticism to shake. Nevertheless, through all fogs and uncertainties the character of St. Francis himself stands out luminous and clear. Moreover, though the time has not yet come for the writing of an authoritative and accurate life, the chief matters of doubt turn, not upon the man himself and his work, but upon the date and value of our

Aug. 4th, p. 635). Dominic died 6 Aug. 1221, but, as that day was already occupied by the feast of the Transfiguration, on his canonization (13 July 1234) his day was transferred first to the 5th, then the 4th of August. Hence the date in the *A.SS.*

[1] See *infra*, p. 304.

primary sources, and, in special, upon the relation of St. Francis to the ecclesiastical authorities.[1]

[1] The first intelligent appreciation of St. F. in English was J. S. Brewer, *Monumenta Franciscana* (2 vols. in *RS*. 1858 and 1882, with valuable introduction). Then followed Mrs. Oliphant, *F. of A.* (1889, of some value still); A. Jessopp, *The Coming of the Friars* (an excellent sketch). Interest in St. F. was, however, aroused by the publication of P. Sabatier, *St. F.* (Paris, 1893; 31st ed. 1905); Eng. trans. by L. S. Houghton, 1896, unfortunately stereotyped. Readers of early editions must beware, and should, if possible, obtain the latest French ed. The value of this work cannot be exaggerated. ("Others may have compiled; M. Sabatier has interpreted.") Nevertheless it must be used with caution as regards its view of the relation of St. F. to Rome (see *infra*). Sabatier's work led on the Continent to the publication of a vast Franciscan literature, and to the critical editing of many of the sources; and of this vast literature, ancient and modern (fully set out in Heimbucher, *OKK* ii. 307–22), the student should, at least, read the following "sources":—

(1) Thomas of Celano († 1255, author of '*Dies irae*'), *Vita Prima*, and *Vita (Legenda) Secunda*, the first written between July 1228 and Feb. 1229 at the command of Gregory IX, the second in 1248. Critical eds. by E. d'Alençon (Rome, 1899, 1906); Eng. trans. by A. G. F. Howell (1908). (2) *Legenda trium sociorum*, composed in 1246, according to its own statement (see *infra*), ed. M. Faloci-Pulignani (Foligno, 1898); Eng. trans. by E. G. Salter (1902). (3) *Speculum Perfectionis*, discovered by P. Sabatier and edited in 1898 in *Coll. d'études sur l'hist. rel. du MA.*; also ed. L. Lemmens in *Doc. antiq. Francis* (Quaracchi, 1901 f.); Eng. trans. by S. Evans (*Mirror of Perfection*, 1899). (4) *Legendae* of Bonaventura, both the *Leg. Major* (1260) and the *Leg. Minor* (in *A.SS*, Oct. ii. 742 ff.; also ed. by the Franciscans of Quaracchi). This was made the official *Vita*, all others being forbidden on the triumph of the "Moderates" (see *infra*, p. 304). (5) *Floretum* (Italian, *Fioretti*; Eng. *Little Flowers of St. F.*). See *infra*, p. 287 n. (6) The existing writings of St. Francis himself. See *infra*, p. 282 n. Their importance cannot be exaggerated for the insight they give into his character.

Now it is upon the date of (2) and (3), and the relative value of each to the other and the whole, that the Franciscan controversy at present turns. Sabatier in his edition of the *Spec. Perf.* contended that this was the first life, written by Brother Leo, as the colophon states, in 1227; he further maintained in his *St. F.* (App. on

Born at Assisi, as the twelfth century was running out (1182), Francis was the child of the middle classes. His father, Pietro Bernardone, was a wealthy cloth

" Critical Study of the Sources "), that the *Leg. 3 Soc.*, a fragment, as he claimed, of a larger work (on this see Heimbucher, *OKK* ii. 317 n.) was composed, as it claimed, in 1246 by Leo, Angelo, and Ruffino, and that the *Vitae* of Thomas of Celano, and, *a fortiori*, of Bonaventura, were written on behalf of the " Moderates." For a critical examination of Sabatier's views the student may consult H. Tilemann, *Spec. Perf. u. Leg. 3 Soc.* (Leipzig, 1902); W. Goetz, *Die Quellen zur Gesch. des hl. F.* (Gotha, 1904); A. G. Little, *Eng. Hist. Rev.* (1902); van Ortroy in *Anal. Boll.* xix. 119 ff.; H. Boehmer, *Analekten zur Gesch. des F.* (Leipzig, 1904); A. Barine, *St. F. et la légende de 3 Comp.* (4th ed. Paris, 1905); H. Thode (*op. cit. infra*, p. 307 n.), ii. 266–97 (who sums up strongly against Sabatier), and, in defence, P. Sabatier, *De l'authenticité de la lég. de 3 Comp.* (Paris, 1901). The drift of critical opinion at the present time would seem to be against Sabatier [cf. the summary against Sabatier of Goetz's arguments by Dom Butler in *Encyc. Brit.* (11th) vol. x. p. 939]. Boehmer (*op. cit.* p. 68) maintains that the *Spec. Perf.* was written in 1318 (cf. Tilemann, *op. cit.* 105 f.). Goetz, *op. cit.* 158 f., has carefully analysed its contents and attempted to disinter the more primitive from its later accretions. Van Ortroy (*Anal. Franc.* i. p. 5 f., cf. Tilemann, *op. cit.* 56 f.) has pointed out impossible anachronisms in the *Leg. 3 Soc.*, and has somewhat discredited the date of 1246. With any discredit of the *Spec. Perf.* and the *Leg. 3 Soc.* as the primary sources, the value of Celano's *Vita* becomes greater, and there will be less tendency to depreciate Bonaventura's *Legenda* (cf. Goetz, *op. cit.* 243 f.). But this involves some distrust of Sabatier's exaggerations of the relation of Francis to cardinal Ugolini, pope Gregory IX, and to the Church in general (cf. *infra*, p. 290 n.).

MODERN LIVES.—In addition to Sabatier and the others mentioned at the beginning of this note the following may be selected out of a vast number: B. Christen, *Leben des hl. F.* (2nd ed. Innsbruck, 1902, also in French), R.C., with good illustrations; J. Herkless, *Francis and Dominic* (1901, popular); and the popular G. Schnürer, *F. v. Assisi* (Munich, 1905), with excellent illustrations; also Canon Knox Little, *St. Francis of Assisi* (1897), inclined to edification. For other literature on the Franciscans, see *infra*, pp. 282, 287 n. I regret that my references to Sabatier, *St. F.*, are for the most part to the Eng. trs., though, possibly, to some this may be an advantage. But I have taken care to point out later corrections.

merchant. The education that his lad received had the usual limitations of the times. Francis wrote with difficulty, and in later years signed all his letters with the simple sign of the Cross. In one respect, however, the boy had an advantage. Owing to his father's business journeys to the fairs of France, he acquired familiarity with the language (the " langue d'oil ") and songs of the country to which, in fact, he owed his name. For to the father the little lad born in his absence was not Giovanni, as he had been baptized, but his little " Frenchman," a nickname that has ever since been borne by millions in honour of the saint. This connection with Provence is of importance ; it was the height of the age of chivalry, when the troubadours were a power in Europe. Francis would be the troubadour of the people, singing to them, sometimes in French, the songs of the Divine Love.

There was nothing in the early life of Francis to foreshadow his future. Conversion was for him a radical change ; not the slow breaking of the day, but the opening of the blind eyes. Nevertheless, it had its stages. At twenty-one his dissipations brought him face to face with death. From a second fever, contracted on a military expedition to Apulia, he arose a new man. A divine restlessness possessed his soul. His conflicts were intense. He spent his days in a cave, from which he came home at night pale with his struggle. Once, on a pilgrimage to Rome, he borrowed the rags of a beggar and stood for a whole day in the Piazza of St. Peter's with outstretched hands (Nov. 1205). Francis was in a fair way of becoming a saint after the usual monastic pattern. From this he was saved by his heart of love, his redeeming feature in his days of dissipation. Francis was troubled by no subtle questionings of outward things, no wonder where to find the wicket-gate and the narrow way. To Francis all was objective and clear. The command came to him as to one of old : This do and thou shalt live. He did not even ask, Who is my neighbour ? the interpretation was exceeding broad ; it was also very plain. Untroubled by any difficulties of exegesis, he took Christ literally. A more complex nature would have passed by on the other side ; Francis, in the simplicity of love, did the duty of love which lay next to hand. After one sharp struggle with his natural repulsion, love gained the victory. Ministering to the outcasts in the lazarettos, Francis found, as did Sir Launfal, in the least of these His brethren the Christ Himself.

The growth of his religious life was not without its difficulties. In the opening words of his last *Testament*,[1] a document in which we find the clearest account of the stages of his conversion, Francis tells us—

> See in what manner God gave it to me Brother Francis to begin to do penitence ; when I lived in sin it was very painful

---

[1] For this and the other writings of St. F. see Sabatier, *St. F.* 351 f. ; Heimbucher, *OKK* ii. 452. They have been published in the *Bib. Franc. ascet. MA* by L. Lemmens (Quaracchi, 1904) ; also by L. Wadding, but with many spurious additions, *Op. S. Franc.* (Antwerp, 1623 ; reprinted 1658). My references are to the convenient ed. by H. Boehmer in *Analekten zur Gesch. des Franc.* [II. (6) 1904]. The *Rule* of St. F., one of the most important of these documents, passed through three forms. Sabatier, *St. F.* 89 n., thought he detected four forms ; cf. K. Müller, *Die Anfänge des Minoritenordens v. d. Bussbruderschaften* (Freiburg, 1885), 185 ff. Of the 1st *Rule* (*Regula Primitiva*) of 1210, chiefly quotations from the Gospels, we have fragments in Boehmer, *op. cit.* 88–9. The *Rule* of 1221 (*Regula prima non bullata* in Boehmer, *op. cit.* 1–26) is a lengthy document, which gives, however, a valuable picture of St. F.'s character. This was simplified in the *Regula Bullata*, ratified by Honorius III on 29 Nov. 1223, by leaving out the edificatory passages (in Boehmer, *op. cit.* 29–35 ; also in

to me to see lepers, but God Himself led me into their midst. When I left them that which had seemed to me bitter had become sweet and easy.[1]

But his chief foes were his former companions and his own household. No doubt the doings of Francis were more than trying. He went about dressed in rags. He would sell all that he had to repair a ruined roadside chapel, or would give his last coin to the beggar. So his father sought to restrain him, cast him bound into his cellar, and applied to the magistrates to deal with the madman. This last step might have had serious consequences had not the magistrates referred the case to the bishop. On the day appointed, in presence of a great crowd of curious townsmen, the bishop gave his decision. He advised Francis to give up all his property. This was what Francis was longing to do. So, then and there, he made solemn renunciation of all, stripping himself even of his clothes.

'Listen, all of you,' he said, 'and understand it well. Henceforth I desire to say nothing else than this, "Our Father which art in heaven."'

Henceforth he was free, free as the birds who seemed to him to live the perfect life; they build no barns and yet they sing unceasingly.[2] So full of a new joy he set off

German in Heimbucher, *OKK* ii. 337 f.). That the differences between the *Regula prima* (1221) and the *Regula Bullata* have been exaggerated by Sabatier seems to me clear, both from the arguments of Goetz, *op. cit.*, and from a study that I have made of the two side by side. The differences formed part of Sabatier's theory as to F.'s relations to the Church. But in all churches practical necessities lead to a hardening tone in official documents, from which, apart from other evidence, little can be inferred. (In an App. Boehmer, *op. cit.* 83, gives a useful collection of the most ancient references to the *Regulae* of St. F.).

[1] Boehmer, *op. cit.* 36.
[2] Date probably in the spring of 1206.

from Assisi,[1] singing a song of chivalry, clothed only with an old garment which the bishop's gardener had thrown over his nakedness. In the forest some robbers suddenly attacked him. 'Who are you?' they asked. 'I am the herald of the Great King,' he answered. 'Lie there, then, poor herald of God,' they sneered, as they stripped him of his mantle and flung him naked into the snow. The robbers gone, Francis resumed his singing, and set off to visit his friends the lepers. In ministering to them, or in rebuilding with his own hands ruined shrines, he found work that he loved. In one of these, St. Mary of the Angels—its former name was Portiuncula, or 'The Little Portion'—there came to him, after three years of poverty and toil, the final call. It was the 24th of February 1209, date ever memorable as the birthday of the Franciscan order. The gospel for the day was this:

"Wherever ye go preach, saying, The kingdom of heaven is at hand. Heal the sick, cleanse the lepers, cast out devils. Freely ye have received, freely give. Provide neither gold nor silver nor brass in your purses, nor scrip for your journey, nor two coats, neither shoes nor yet staves, for the workman is worthy of his meat" (*Matt.* x. 7).

To Francis these words were the voice of Christ Himself: 'This is what I want,' he cried. 'This is what I am seeking. Henceforth I will set myself with all my strength to put it in practice.' The next morning he set off for Assisi, and began to preach.

We must leave the reader to search out for himself the record of how one by one other eleven joined themselves to Francis, drawn by the same desire for complete

[1] For an excellent picture-map of Assisi at this time, see Schnürer, *op. cit.* 137.

consecration—' nudi nudum Christum sequi';—how in the summer of 1210 Francis went with his companions to Rome that he might obtain from Innocent III the sanction of his simple *Rule*;[1] how from these humble beginnings the new order spread with marvellous rapidity to every land; how he invested Clara his sister († 1253) with the Franciscan habit and so instituted the "Second Order," that of the nuns;[2] and how Rome, wise, as ever, in her generation, was quick to bring the new enthusiasm under her sanction and control. But the order itself, its ideal and place, cannot be so lightly dismissed. It forms one of the great spiritual epochs of mankind. That a company of men, many of them laymen too, or at most in minor orders,[3] renouncing all that the world held dear, should wander barefoot over all Europe, penetrating even to the Soldan's country, everywhere preaching the gospel to the poor, and, what was more, living it out as men had never seen it lived before; that these men, accepting insult and persecution, making their refuge for the night in haystack or lazarhouse, choosing for their

[1] See *supra*, p. 282 n. For date, see Sabatier, *St. F.* 88 n.

[2] 18 March 1212. For the "Poor Clares," see Heimbucher, *OKK* ii. 475 f.; and for the sources of Clara's life, *ib.* ii. 476 n.; Sabatier, *St. F.* 147 n.; ib. *Franciscan Essays* (1912), 31–49; also *St. Clara and her Order* (London, 1912; R.C., uncritical). Francis did not originally give them a formal Rule, only a short *Forma vivendi*. This was followed in the last year of his life by his *Ultima voluntas* (both in Boehmer, *op. cit.* 35). Meanwhile cardinal Ugolini had taken them under his protection, and during Francis' absence in Palestine turned them into Benedictines, and gave them privileges (1219). The wrath of Francis, on his return, seems to have led to the writing of a new *Rule*, verbally sanctioned by Honorius in 1224 and formally approved in Aug. 1253. [See Zöckler, *AM* 488; E. Lempp, *d. Anfänge des Clarissen Ordens* in *ZKG* xiii. 181 ff. (1892). For the *Rule* itself, see the (German) analysis in Heimbucher, *op. cit.* 482 f., and the original text in P. Sabatier, *Regula Antiqua* (Paris, 1901).]

[3] On this see Sabatier, *op. cit.* 131 n.

homes the poorest and most neglected quarters—in London, the Stinking Lane and shambles of Newgate—should find the highest joy of life in the meanest drudgery that only love would undertake,—this was indeed the bringing back the living Jesus from His grave of centuries, this was also the restoration of His teaching.

At first, as might be expected, especially when we remember how saturated was Italy (for that matter all Europe) with heresy — Cathari, Albigensians, Patarins, and the like [1]—the Little Brothers were exposed to no small measure of persecution. When Brother Bernard came to Bologna the very children, 'seeing him in poor and threadbare habit,' made mock of him, 'while the men of the city plucked at his hood and pelted him with dust and stones,' all which Brother Bernard 'bore with patience and with joy for the love of Christ.' Of the first missionary journey of the three Companions we read that 'some listened willingly, others scoffed, the greater part overwhelmed them with questions : Whence come ye ? Of what order are ye ? And they, though sometimes it was a weariness to answer, said simply, We are penitents, natives of the city of Assisi.' [2] When the authorities threatened to hang certain of their number as vagabonds they offered their own rope girdles as halters. Their first missionaries to Germany [3] were roughly handled and expelled,

[1] On all this read the short account in Sabatier, *St. F.* c. 3, or the monumental work of H. C. Lea, *Inquisition in MA* (3 vols. New York, 1897)—a vast storehouse of recondite medieval lore.

[2] *Leg. 3 Soc.* 36, 37.

[3] For the first expeditions to Germany we have the *Chronicon f. Jordani a Jano* (*i.e.* Giordano di Giano) and the *Chron. Anòn.*, both in *Anal. Franc.* i. (Quaracchi, 1885). For England we have the delightful story of Eccleston (in *Anal. Franc.* i. 217 f. or in J. S. Brewer, *Mon. Franciscana*, i. 1–72. The readings in the *Analecta*

—they were, in fact, totally ignorant of the language of the country—in France they were mistaken for the heretic Cathari; while in Morocco five of them were tortured to death by the Saracens.[1] But whether accepted or rejected they everywhere made common life with the poor, helping the labourers to gather the olives or to strip the vines, singing the while their hymns of joy, or making merry, like children at a feast, over the broken scraps tossed to them from the rich man's table.

And then their sermons! Let the reader through the mist of centuries discern the following:—

Ye must needs know that St. Francis being inspired of God set out for to go into Romagna with Brother Leo his companion; and as they went they passed by the foot of the Castle of Montefeltro; in the which castle there was at that time a great company of gentlefolk and much feasting. . . . And St. Francis hearing of the festivities that were holden there . . . spake unto Brother Leo, Let us go up unto this feast, for with the help of God we may win some good fruit of souls. . . . Coming to the castle, St. Francis entered in, and came to the courtyard, where all that great company of gentlefolk was gathered together, and in fervency of spirit stood up upon a parapet and began to preach, taking as the text of his sermon these words in the vulgar tongue—

So great the joys I have in sight
That every sorrow brings delight.[2]

---

are more critical). Of this there is a trans. by Fr. Cuthbert, *The Friars and how they came to England* (1903).

[1] An account by an eyewitness of their death was published by K. Müller, *Anfänge des Min.*, p. 207 f.

[2] *Little Flowers*, App. on "The Stigmata" (first reflection). About the year 1322 there was published by Hugolin of Monte Georgio a work entitled, *Actus b. Franc. et soc. ejus*. [Ed. by P. Sabatier in *Collection d'études* (Paris, 1902); also a smaller ed. without notes &c., entitled *Floretum S. Franc* (Paris, 1902).] Of this *Floretum* or *Actus* there was an early Italian trans. entitled *Fioretti*, of which an Eng. trans. by T. W. Arnold (*Little Flowers*, 1898). Though the work is

There was nothing remarkable in the preaching itself, no grace of oratory, no profundity of the thought, only men preaching Christ with burning love and conviction. 'Francis had not the manner of a preacher' —so writes one who heard him in 1220 at Bologna—'his ways were rather those of conversation.'[1] Those who tried to repeat the sermons found it was impossible— they were so artless, so simple; yet as they listened the downtrodden realized that God was their Father, robbers became honest men, the enemies of years were reconciled, and, strangest of all, the cities of Italy forgot the feuds of centuries. Wherever St. Francis went it was the same; the pent-up enthusiasms of Europe were let loose. Men of wealth renounced their wealth that they might live among lepers—'God's patients' as Francis called them—and wash their sores; the scholar abandoned his books that he might the better study the Perfect Life. Of course, here and there, there were extravagances. Women appeared naked in the streets; fifty thousand children set off to conquer Palestine and were sold into slavery by two merchants of Marseilles.[2] But for these excesses Francis was not

really a collection of edifying legends it may fairly claim to give a correct portrait of St. Francis and of the impression he produced among the common people (cf. Sabatier, *St. F.* 416). Much that the book supplies is incorporated from earlier sources. The success of the *Fioretti* as originally published led to later additions.

[1] From the narrative of Thomas of Spalato, archdeacon of Bologna, conveniently printed in Boehmer, *Anal. Franc.* 106.

[2] The story of the two Crusades by the children, the German (1212) under a lad of twelve, Nicholas of Cologne, and the French under a shepherd lad, Stephen of Cloyes, is one of the most pathetic incidents of the Middle Ages. It is told in popular fashion by G. Z. Gray, *The Children's Crusade* (New York, 1898). The student may consult the narrative of Alberic in *MGH* xxiii. 893; cf. also the *Annales* of Ogerius Panis in *MGH* xviii. 131.

to blame. They were in fact part of the new enthusiasm of the age.

History tells us that this early enthusiasm did not last. As Innocent III had foretold, in his first interview with Francis, the primitive rigour of the *Rule* was beyond human strength. Though the differences in the order, due to growing laxity, did not come to a head until later, even in his own lifetime Francis had to mourn that the first simplicity had become perverted. Hundreds had joined the order, the majority of whom, unlike the early disciples, had no chance of coming under the personal spell of the master. At times, also, Francis was away from Italy for the greater part of each year. In 1212 he set off for Palestine, but was shipwrecked in the Adriatic, and so returned. Then in 1214 he set off to preach to the Moors in Spain, but was forced by sickness to come home (1215). After four years spent in the consolidation and extension of the work in Italy, Francis embarked for Egypt from Ancona (June 1219), was captured, preached before the sultan, and was sent back by him to Damietta, of whose surrender to the crusaders (5 Nov. 1219) he was an eyewitness.[1] Thence he passed to Palestine. On his return in the early summer of 1220 he found a vast increase in the numbers of the friars, and in their missions, accompanied by corresponding friction between the two sections into which the movement was already dividing. The two vicars whom he had left in charge in his absence had also attempted unwise

---

[1] We owe these details to Jacques de Vitry in a letter written to his friends in Lorraine from Damietta in March 1220. (Conveniently printed in Boehmer, *op. cit.* 101, as is also the fuller account of the friars by de Vitry from his *Hist. orientalis*, ii. c. 32.)

changes, chiefly in the direction of assimilation to other monastic orders. So Francis journeyed to pope Honorius III at Orvieto, and placed his order under the protection of cardinal Ugolini, the later pope Gregory IX. Nor was this all. Honorius definitely recognized the order, giving leave to Francis to compose a more elaborate *Rule*, but insisting on the need of a year's noviciate.[1] Whether because he felt unequal to the control of so vast an organization, or because of weariness of spirit due to growing laxity, a week later, at the Chapter-General held at Portiuncula (29 Sept. 1220), Francis resigned, whether voluntarily or under pressure is uncertain. He knelt at the feet of Peter di Catana,[2] the new minister-general, and became a private brother.

'Lord Jesus,' he said, 'I give Thee back this family which Thou didst entrust to me. Thou knowest that I have no longer the strength or the ability to take care of it. I entrust it therefore to the ministers. Let them be responsible before Thee at the day of Judgement if any brother by their negligence or bad example or by too severe punishment shall go astray.'

'From henceforth,' he significantly added, 'I am dead to you.'

Francis was not blinded by his obedience. Though he spent the next few years in the development of his Tertiaries,[3] and in the revision of his *Rule*, he was conscious of a lost ideal. Though, probably, he recognized that changes were inevitable, there were times when he passionately longed for the simplicity of the early days. In one of his dreams he saw the brothers, ' with loads upon their backs,' swept away by a ' mighty

[1] 22 Sept. 1220. [2] Or dei Cattani († 10 March 1221).
[3] See *infra*, p. 298.

river, broad and rushing furiously.' The great river was the world. 'The time will come,' he said again, 'when our order will have so lost all good renown that its members will be ashamed to show themselves by daylight.'[1] 'We must begin again,' he murmured, as he lay stricken with mortal sickness, 'to create a new family who will not forget humility, who will go and serve lepers, and, as in the old times, put themselves always, not merely in words but in reality, below all men.' Almost his last act was to exhort the friars in his *Testament* to keep to the old paths and to reject all glosses on his *Rule* 'under pretext of explaining it.' 'Ah!' he added, 'if I could once again go to the Chapter-General.'

But this was not to be. Though not quite forty-five, Francis' work was finished. In June 1224 he attended his last chapter. The new *Rule*, the confirmation of which had been received (25 Nov. 1223), was adopted; a mission to England inaugurated. In the following autumn he retired to La Verna—" the freezing mountain "—in the upper valley of the Arno, and there, in a forty days' fast, received his famous 'Stigmata,' the theme in later ages of art and poetry.[2] Exhausted by his trances, and by his attempt to evangelize Southern Umbria, by slow stages he was brought home to Assisi, to the joy of the people, who had feared that by his death elsewhere they should lose a priceless relic. Conscious that the end was near, he poured out his whole soul in an epistle to all Christians (*Opusculum com-*

---

[1] *Spec. Perf.* 73.

[2] For a critical study of the Stigmata, see Sabatier, *op. cit.* App. Boehmer, *op. cit.* 90 f., gives a useful collection of the primary sources that have reference to the matter.

monitorium). The close of this *Nunc Dimittis* is a strain of pure music—

I, Brother Francis, the least of your servants, pray you by that Love which is God Himself, willing to throw myself at your feet and kiss them, to receive with humility and love all words of our Lord Jesus Christ, to put them to profit and carry them out.

This was followed by his last *Epistle to the Chapter-General*, which closes with a prayer that rings like an apostolic benediction :

God Almighty, eternal, righteous, and merciful, give to us poor wretches to do for Thy sake all that we know of Thy will, and to will always what pleases Thee, so that inwardly purified, enlightened, and kindled by the fire of Thy Holy Spirit we may follow in the footsteps of Thy well-beloved Son, Jesus Christ.[1]

As the last days dawned, all pain became lost in joy and song. 'Father,' said a physician, trying, after his kind, to conceal the incurable nature of the disease, ' all this may pass away if it please God.' ' I am not a cuckoo,' replied Francis, smiling, ' to be afraid of death. By the grace of His Holy Spirit I am so intimately one with God that I am equally content to live or die.' He then bade his companions sing his own *Canticle of the Sun*. When they had sung the last verse, St. Francis added a new strophe—

Be praised, O Lord, for our sister, the death of the body,
Whom no man may escape.
Alas for them who die in mortal sin !
Happy they who are found conformed to Thy most holy will,
For the second death will do them no hurt.

Thus in the beautiful words of Thomas of Celano, ' he

[1] For these two works, see Boehmer, *op. cit.* 49–62. For the *Canticum solis*, *ib.* 65.

went to meet death singing.' On Saturday, October 3, 1226, towards sun-down, the end came in his beloved Portiuncula. 'I have done my duty,' he said to the brothers as they knelt around him, 'may Christ now teach you yours.' His last smiling word was this: 'Welcome, Sister Death.' Stripped of his clothing and laid on the bare ground, he died in the arms of his Lady Poverty. As his spirit passed away, without pain or struggle, innumerable larks alighted singing on the thatch of his cell.

III

From this brief survey of the lives of these two great saints we pass to the consideration of the orders they established—not, of course, in any detail, or with reference to their later history, for with the coming of the friars we must bring this work to a close, but from the standpoint of our theme, the special part they played in the development of the monastic ideal. To one aspect of the matter we have already drawn attention.[1] There are, however, others which should not be neglected.

At the outset, however, it were well to warn the student lest he suppose that the secret of the success of St. Francis lay in any novelty of idea. The most striking external feature, his dream of poverty, was "in the air." In his boyhood he would hear of the Poor Men of Lyons. Two years before Innocent III had blessed the design of Francis he had accorded approbation to the attempt of Durand of Huesca, a converted Waldensian, to enroll a mendicant order under the name of 'Poor Catholics.'[2]

[1] Life for the sake of others: *supra*, pp. 271–2.
[2] On these see Heimbucher. *OKK* ii. 185; Sabatier, *St. F.* 100 n.

Even the lepers had not been without their friends. Before the days of Francis the Cruciferi[1] (a congregation under the *Austin Rule*, to whom in 1169 Alexander III had given a constitution) had established over two hundred houses in Europe and Palestine devoted to their care, one of which was at Assisi. Nor were the Tertiaries —the most original of Francis' organizations—altogether without precedent, for in 1201 Innocent III had approved a somewhat similar movement on the part of a religious association called the 'Humiliati,' whose enterprise gave them in Northern Italy almost a monopoly in the wool-trade.[2] With their manner of life St. Francis must have become acquainted at Assisi. What was new was a love that turned the aspirations of the few into the life experience of thousands in every country of Europe.

We would note, in the first place, that the connexionalism, to whose slow growth in Monasticism we drew attention in our last chapter, has now been completely established. With the Dominicans the supreme power, subject, of course, to the pope, rests with the master-general, who dwells at Rome. One of his duties was to preside over the chapter-general, in early days held annually, one year in Bologna, the other in Paris. The order is divided into provinces, each of which is governed by a provincial, elected for four years, who holds provincial chapters. Every friary is governed by a prior or warden—again elected for a limited period. Finally the old law of 'stability,' which gave to the Benedictine monasteries their intense localism and indivi-

---

[1] On these see Heimbucher, *OKK* ii. 33 f. ; Sabatier, *St. F.* 108 n.

[2] On these Humiliati see Sabatier, *St. F.* 158 n. ; Zöckler in Herzog, *PRE*³ s.v.

dualism, has disappeared; so has, also, all local control by the episcopate. The friars belong not to any one house or province but to the whole order, and can be told off by the master-general to live in what friary or province he pleases.[1] All is international and connexional —localism in any form becomes impossible.[2] The organization of the Franciscans was similar. Two chapter-generals were, however, held each year, one at Michaelmas, the other and more important at Whitsuntide. Over these there presided the 'minister-general,' as the chief of the order was called. It is characteristic of the differences of the two orders that that of Dominic was governed by 'masters,' that of Francis by 'ministers.' Each province under its provincial-minister was further divided into 'custodies,' the exact organization of which it is now difficult to determine.[3] That the 'custodian,' one of whose duties was to admit novices to profession, had a certain right of enforcing bye-laws in his 'custody' is evident from the fact that in the Oxford 'custody'—which included Reading, Bedford, Stamford, Nottingham, Northampton, Leicester, and Grantham[4]—the use of pillows was at one time prohibited, in the custody of Cambridge, mantles.[5]

One effect of this complete connexionalism should not be overlooked. With the decay of their first enthusiasms the friars became in every land the 'watch-

[1] On Dominican organization, see Heimbucher, ii. 106. For the absence of 'stability,' see *ib.* ii. 338.

[2] In *A New History of Methodism*, i. 43, I have pointed out the striking similarities to the Methodist organization.

[3] For 'custodies,' see Heimbucher, *OKK* ii. 346. The student will find a list of the 'custodies' for about 1390 in *Anal. Francis.* iv. 503 f. (Quaracchi, 1906).

[4] For English 'custodies,' see list in *Anal. Franc.* iv. 545 f.

[5] Brewer, *Mon. Franc.* i. 27; Little, *GFO* 68.

dogs' of the papacy, a fact due to their highly centralized organization, to their complete independence of all episcopal control, and especially to the international character of their brotherhood with its lack of any vow of 'stability.' Of this internationalism we have a remarkable illustration, in itself prophetic of the future. When in 1216 St. Dominic assembled his friars at Notre Dame de la Prouille they were sixteen in number, but among them were Castilians, Navarese, Normans, natives of Languedoc, and even English and Germans. This internationalism, so marked in the start of the orders, characterized them throughout their history, and, combined with the system of mendicancy, led to a strange social feature. The Benedictine monk shared the outlook and instincts of the local landowner; the Carthusian was tied down to his cell; but the friar journeyed everywhere—the constant wandering of the friars was one of the most noteworthy features of the age [1]—with no other tie than the interests of his order, and his duty of obedience. The effect of this wandering, in cases far too many, was a return to a state of things similar to that in the days of the 'Gyrovagi,' 'Sarabaites,' 'Messalians,' and other pests of early Monasticism.[2]

Organization—however centralized, international, and complete—would not of itself explain the extraordinary success of the friars. We must not overlook as a strong contributory force the democratic significance of the movement, especially of the Franciscans. Hildebrand's attempt to impose Monasticism on the world had been essentially the effort of an aristocrat.[3] He had used as

[1] J. J. Jusserand, *Eng. Wayfaring Life*, 304.   [2] *Supra*, p. 134.
[3] I do not, of course, refer to his birth. Hildebrand was the son of Bonizo, a goatherd of Rovaco, near Saona.

his fulcrum the chair of St. Peter, and worked, so to speak, from the highest downward. The attempt had failed; the friars now renewed it in an effort to work from the lowest upward. Hitherto monks had belonged, as a rule, to the upper classes; only for the aristocrat was there open the refuge of the cloister.[1] The poor, except in the towns, were serfs tied down to the soil; the heavenly walks were not for them, save possibly as lay brothers. But in the brotherhood of St. Francis caste distinctions were unknown; the men whom feudalism had despised took the world by storm. The very title of the Franciscan order is almost untranslatable because of its democratic significance. In all the towns of Italy the people were divided into 'majores' and 'minores,' the nearest equivalent would be "guilded" and "unguilded." Francis deliberately changed the name of his disciples from the 'Penitents of Assisi,' and enrolled himself with the unguilded; his was the company of the 'Brothers Minor.'[2] The coming of the friars was one of the few great spiritual movements that have arisen direct from the people. Benedict and Bernard were both of noble descent; Luther and Wesley belonged to the university; the fathers of Puritanism were the doctors of Geneva, but the Brothers of Assisi sprang from the common soil. Throughout its history the Franciscans, on the whole,

[1] See the learned study of A. Savine, *Eng. Monasteries on the Eve of the Dissolution* (Oxford, 1909), 265–7.

[2] In England the more familiar title, from their dress, is Greyfriars, as that of the Dominicans was Blackfriars. In France the Dominicans, from the site of the house in which they were first installed (6 Aug. 1218) at Paris, were called Jacobins, or Jacobites (as in Wyclif), a name changed to other significance on the seizure of their house at the Revolution.

have ever been true to their democratic origin; they have been the leaders in popular movements; their recruits, for the most part, have come from the middle classes.[1]

Francis, in fact, enrolled on the side of Monasticism forces greater than Hildebrand or Bernard had dreamed of. The coming of the friars was an effort to reform Monasticism on a democratic basis. For the moment it seemed as if democracy would accomplish what the saint and the statesman had failed to complete. The friars swept all before them; in bishopric, parish, and university, their ideal reigned supreme, while the uneasiness of the older monasteries at the rapid spread of their rival showed itself in many ways very early in their career. Nor had the friars conquered the Church alone. By his foundation of the Tertiaries or Third Order, Francis claimed the allegiance of the laity for his ideal.[2] In an age when all men were seeking to become guilded

[1] See, for proof, the vast number of middle-class benefactions. Little, *GFO* 101, and cf. *ib.* 111.

[2] For the Franciscan Third Order the best account, with full bibliography, is in Heimbucher, *OKK* ii. 489–527 (with full details of the vast extension, especially in the nineteenth cent., and numerous subdivisions of this order). The reader may also consult J. G. Adderley and C. L. Marson, *Third Orders* (1902). The *Rule* of the Tertiaries, professing to date from May 1221, in its present form is full of additions (Boehmer, *op. cit.* 73 f. prints it among the 'spuria'). It was first printed by Sabatier in the *Opuscules de crit. Historique* (Paris, 1901). The *Rule* now followed (see Heimbucher, *OKK* ii. 493 f.) is that of 1221, altered in 1289 by Nicholas IV and extended by Leo XIII (1883). There were Tertiaries among the Dominicans, *e.g.* Catherine of Siena, originally called the 'Brothers of the Militia of Christ '—the modern title, 'Brothers of Penitence,' is not found before 1286. If instituted by Dominic—a matter of extreme doubt (Zöckler, *AM* 498) —they were an imitation of the Franciscans. For their history, see Heimbucher, *OKK* ii. 169 f.; Helyot, iii. 245 ff.; J. Kleinermanns, *Der dritte Orden v. d. Busse d. hl. Dom.* (Dülmen, 1885). Their *Rule*, drawn up in 1285 by Munio of Zamora, was first sanctioned by Innocent VII in 1405. It may be found in Holsten, *CR* iv. 140–9.

in some form or other, Francis sought to enroll all classes within his great guild of the 'Brothers and Sisters of Penitence.' Though celibacy was necessarily dropped in thus accommodating the ideal to the world, the monastic virtues of poverty and obedience were not neglected. The obligations of this lay fraternity were peace and charity, while the rich were to distribute their surplus wealth to the poor. The first member was Lucchesio, a merchant of Poggibonzi, who had made a fortune by " cornering " wheat in a time of scarcity, but who now turned his house into a hospital.

The founding of this order (soon imitated by all the other Mendicant orders, as also by older societies, *e.g.* the Premonstratensian),[1] to-day far exceeding in its numbers every other fraternity,[2] was the beginning of a social revolution, the depth of which was hidden from our older historians. For centuries the laity had had little place in the organization of the Church. Now Europe was filled with a host of earnest laymen, bound together in social service and church work, most of whom earned their own living, like St. Paul, by the labour of their hands. Francis realized that his own life could never be the life of all; it was the life of the apostles of the Gospel, not of the multitude of believers. But the life and labour of love was open to every Christian. Of this call for fraternity we see the influence in the rapid rise in France alone of the number of leper hospitals from a few to over two thousand,[3] as also in

[1] On this see Heimbucher, *OKK* ii. 58.

[2] In 1905 the Franciscan Tertiaries numbered nearly two millions (Heimbucher, *OKK* ii. 494).

[3] For the medieval hospitals of England, for the most part swept away at the Reformation, the student should consult Miss R. M. Clay, *Medieval Hospitals of Eng.* (1909).

the formation of other societies for social work. But by nothing is the success of Francis' attempt to bring the classes together more clearly brought out than in the famous tale—

'*How St. Louis, King of France, went in person in the guise of a pilgrim to Perugia for to visit the holy Brother Giles.* . . . So the porter went to Brother Giles and told him that at the door was a pilgrim that asked for him. . . . And being inspired of God it was revealed to him that it was the King of France: so straightway with great fervour he left his cell, and ran to the door, and without further questioning, albeit they ne'er had seen each other before, kneeling down with great devotion they embraced and kissed each other, with such signs of tender love as though for a long time they had been close familiar friends; but for all that they spoke not, the one nor the other, but continued in this embrace in silence ' (*Little Flowers*, c. 34).

Upon this let us hear the comment of one of our own prophets.

"Of all which story not a word of course is credible by any rational person. Certainly not: the spirit nevertheless which created the story is an entirely indisputable fact in the history of mankind. Whether St. Louis and Brother Giles ever knelt together in Perugia matters not a whit. That a king and a poor monk could be conceived to have thought of each other which no words could speak . . . this is what you have to meditate on here." [1]

From the outset the friars, both Dominican and Franciscan, were ardent missionaries. They did not flee the world; on the contrary, the world was their parish. To the desire of St. Dominic to preach to the Kuman Tatars, to the efforts of St. Francis to convert the Sultan, we have already referred. Nor did the leaders stand alone. In the *First Rule* of St. Francis there is a whole chapter on the duty of going 'inter

[1] Ruskin, *Mornings in Florence*, p. 89.

Saracenos et alios infideles.'[1] The Brothers were consumed with the passion for souls. During the lifetime of their apostle the Dominicans spread to almost every country of Europe, including the heathen Wends and Letts of Prussia and Livonia. The missionary activities of the Franciscans were even more remarkable. The growth of the order was amazing. At the 'Chapter of the Mats' in 1221 three thousand Brothers attended, and delegates were received from France, Germany, Greece, Spain, and Portugal. Two years previously two missionaries had been sent to the Saracens of Tunis, and six to Morocco, Francis himself with twelve others setting off for the East. The missionaries to Morocco were beheaded, and their bodies mutilated; the friars had received their baptism of blood (16 Jan. 1220). From that day to this neither Dominicans nor Franciscans have ever counted the cost if by any means they could convert some. In journeys over pathless deserts and prairies or through untrodden forests, amidst savages thirsting for blood, surrounded by the devotees of superstitions that were hoary before Christianity was born, or exposed to the fanaticism of the Muslim, they have ever been true to the missionary call of their Lord and to the ideal of their founders, paying the penalty of their fidelity, if need be, with their lives.[2] Long before the end of the thirteenth century both the Dominicans and Franciscans had preached the Gospel to the Mongols of Northern China, and in 1308 they reached Pekin itself. Shortly after 1265 the Dominicans entered Abyssinia, and in

[1] *Reg. Prima*, c. 16 (Boehmer, *op. cit.* 14).

[2] For the missionary labours of their orders, see Heimbucher, *OKK* ii. 111, 118, 154 f., 328, 427–46.

1326 reached Ceylon. The Holy Land was from the first a special object of care for the Franciscans. The Muslim of Northern Africa, the Franciscans regarded as peculiarly their own, bought with the blood of their earliest martyrs. In 1227 seven other Brothers Minor laid down their lives for their faith at Ceuta in Mauretania, and in 1275 Raymund Lull established in Mallorca a missionary college in which the Franciscans might be trained in Arabic and Chaldee for service in the East. A few years later (30 June 1315) Raymund died as a martyr at Bougie in Algiers. Throughout life, in spite of his intellectual vagaries, he was true to his own motto:

> He who loves not, lives not:
> He who lives by the Life can never die.

Some note must be taken of the place of 'poverty' in the system of St. Francis; for in this connection Dominic may be ignored, as he borrowed the idea and its workings from the Umbrian saint.[1] We have seen the struggles of successive monastic reformers to escape from corporate wealth, and the impossibility, as experience showed, of securing 'poverty' by the negation of individual possession. Francis, though his first intentions seem to have been to insist on the Brother's following their regular calling, and in cases of necessity falling back on mendicancy, made this 'poverty' not as heretofore individual but corporate also. The friar must, of course, possess nothing himself—that obligation would have been acknowledged by the

---

[1] In 1425 Martin V relaxed the law of poverty for the Dominicans, and in 1475, under Sixtus IV, the order ceased to be mendicant, and became, like other orders of monks, the holders of property and fixed sources of income.

wealthiest Benedictine monastery—nor must his friary have any possessions or property, save only the bare monastic building and its church. Now this was the rock of offence on which Monasticism had hitherto foundered, but on which there were sirens ever singing that drew monks and friars, in spite of themselves, into the dangerous swirl. For to the natural man, even if subdued by grace, the consequences of corporate poverty are not pleasant to contemplate. For one thing—to leave out of account the loss of all the ignoble results of wealth, its pomp and power—corporate poverty means a livelihood only to be gained by mendicancy, the daily begging from door to door. So certain brethren called 'limitors'[1] were appointed in every friary by the warden to 'procure' food for the convent during some fixed period by begging, two by two, from door to door.[2] Among minor discomforts we may note that the friar, when on a journey, must set off without money, nor was he allowed a horse.

Once again poverty, even in this new form, failed as a protection of Monasticism. In spite of the example of St. Francis, in spite of his *Rule*, and of the solemn injunctions of his last *Testament* against all glosses or interpretations which would alter its literal meaning, in spite also of all the arguments and struggles of the more 'zealous' of his followers, Francis was scarcely dead before the friars began to whittle away the obliga-

[1] Cf. Chaucer, *Prologue*, 209.

[2] *Mon. Franc.* i. 10–11; Little, *GFO* 91. See the picture of the friar in Chaucer's "Somnoure's Tale":

> Yeve us a bushel whete, malt or rye.
> A goddes kechil (a small cake), or a trip of cheso
> Or elles what yow list. . . .
> Or yeve us of your brawn, if ye have eny.

tions of his precept, and to teach that his words were but counsels of perfection. Far be it from our purpose to enter into the dreary annals of the long conflict between Zealots and Moderates. The quarrel has long since burnt itself out into ashes which we would not lightly disturb. Nevertheless the blaze had in it once the fire of life; the struggle was something more than a quarrel over the precise number of rags that could be patched on to an old garment, as in the famous case of Fra Corrado da Offido, who for fifty-five years wore the same gown.[1] Put in a word, the quarrel was this: Should the friars descend from the ideals of their founder to the common dreams of common day? Francis had held before the world the vision splendid. Gregory IX, Brother Elias of Cortona, and the Moderates maintained that it was unattainable, and attempted to reconstruct, or rather interpret, the *Rule* on the lines of the possible. In 1230 Gregory IX pointed out that Francis could not bind his successor.[2] In 1279, after forty years of controversy, Nicholas II attempted to settle the quarrel by his bull *Exiit qui seminat*. The *Rule* of Francis was declared to be the inspiration of the Holy Ghost; absolute renunciation of possession had been practised by Christ and His Apostles. But while ownership or *dominium* was thus denied, usufruct or use might be permitted. The proprietorship of all that the Franciscans enjoyed must be vested in the Roman pontiff as the trustee of the order. Thus the friars would have all the benefits of property, and yet keep the *Rule*, at any rate in the letter.

The subtle evasions of this bull did not end the

[1] Lea, *Inquis. in MA* iii. 41.
[2] By the bull *Quo elongati* of 28 Sept. 1230 (Potthast, 8620).

controversy. The consciences of the spiritual Franciscans were not satisfied. Poverty, they claimed, as Wyclif claimed in the next generation, was an indispensable note of the true Church. But into the details of this struggle we cannot now enter.[1] Nevertheless, we cannot, in parting, withhold our admiration from the hundreds of spiritual Franciscans who chose to rot in chains, as Jacopone da Todi, or to endure death at the fire rather than to surrender the ideal of their founder.

IV

In a previous chapter we pointed out that Monasticism, which " began with an almost Gnostic hatred of the created world, as the medium of temptation and the abode of sin, oft-times ended in the identification of the man with nature itself."[2] Of this tendency nowhere have we a more complete illustration than St. Francis. With him Monasticism ends in an absolute joy in the created world the like of which had never been seen before, the consequences of which upon civilization cannot be over-estimated. Francis felt himself one with Nature, for everywhere he realized the presence of love. In his passionate verse he claims the moon for his sister, the sun for his brother. He loved the purity of a drop of water; it was an anguish to him to see it sullied. He sometimes wished to see the Emperor. I

---

[1] I purpose at no distant date to deal with this matter more fully. Meanwhile I may refer the reader to my *Dawn of the Reformation*, i. c. 2. There is a full account of the spiritual Franciscans in Lea, *op. cit.* iii. 1–180. For the literature dealing with the controversy, see Heimbucher, ii. 356 n. The '*dominium*' or trustee idea is set out in brief in Little, *GFO* 76.

[2] *Supra*, p. 34 f.

would ask him,' he explained, 'for the love of God to publish an edict against catching my sisters the larks.' He had a special interest in bees, and as for flowers he could not see them without bursting into praise. They were the one luxury he allowed his disciples. Of his tenderness for all created things the sweet and simple stories are almost numberless, and seem absurd to a generation that impales birds for the adornment of a hat. His sermon to the birds is well known, and forms one of the gems of the *Little Flowers*. The story suffers much from being isolated from its context. For it is in the same chapter that we read that there came to Francis the great joy of souls. Thereupon, 'Let us be going,' he cried; and forthwith set out, 'taking no thought for road or way':

'And as with great fervour he was going on the way, he lifted up his eyes and beheld some trees hard by the road whereon sat a great company of birds; whereat Saint Francis marvelled, and said to his companions: "Ye shall wait for me here upon the way and I will go to preach unto my little sisters, the birds." . . . The sermon that Saint Francis preached unto them was after this fashion: "My little sisters, the birds, much bounden are ye unto God, your Creator, and alway in every place ought ye to praise Him, for that He hath given you liberty to fly about everywhere, and hath also given you double and triple raiment; still more are ye beholden to Him for the element of the air which He hath appointed for you; beyond all this, ye sow not, neither do you reap; and God feedeth you, and giveth you the streams and fountains for your drink, the mountains and the valleys for your refuge, and the high trees whereon to make your nests; and because ye know not how to spin or sew, God clotheth you, you and your children; wherefore your Creator loveth you much, seeing that He hath bestowed on you so many benefits; and therefore, my little sisters, beware of the sin of ingratitude, and study always to give praises unto God'" (*Little Flowers,* c. 16).

In this sympathy with nature Francis stands out almost alone among great reformers. Even St. Paul, with all his intense breadth, seems, like the majority of the ancients, to have been blind to the mysteries of nature. At Athens his eye cared nothing for the surpassing loveliness of the landscape; he was arrested rather by an altar to an Unknown God. Francis could never have written St. Paul's amazing allegory: 'Doth God take care for oxen?'[1] As the Italian walked the lanes he felt that God so cared even for worms that he would stop and pick them up lest he should tread upon them. Nor could the saint of Assisi ever have ridden for a whole day, as did St. Bernard, by the shores of Geneva, and at the end of the journey, when his companions spoke of the lake, ask to what lake they referred, he had seen none.[2] But because of this love of nature Francis has justly been called "the Father of Italian art." Materialism kills art; money cannot buy it; it is the child only of centuries stirred by mighty ideals, and penetrated with the conviction of the unity of nature. So in a later age Giotto and Fra Angelico of Fiesole († 1455)—a Dominican it is true[3]— painted in blue and gold the angels that Francis had seen everywhere ascending and descending upon the sons of men, while architecture inspired by love won its noblest triumphs. If we want to estimate his in-

---

[1] *1 Cor.* ix. 9.   [2] C. Morison, *St. B.* 68.

[3] With the exception of Fra Angelico the Dominican contributions to art (fully set out in Heimbucher, *OKK* ii. 152 f.), have not been of importance. For the relation of Francis to art, see the important work of H. Thode, *F. v. Assisi u. d. Anfänge d. Kunst d. Renaissance in Italien* [2nd ed. 1904. I have used the Fr. trans. (2 vols. Paris, 1909), with fine illustrations]. In vol. i. will be found a full description of the great churches at Assisi.

fluence in this matter we must look around at the peerless cathedrals which the reawakened piety of the thirteenth century built for God. 'The earth,' writes a Benedictine monk, ' woke from its slumber, and put on a white robe of churches.' But all this lies beyond our limits. Our immediate purpose is to note the complete abandonment by Monasticism of the principles with which it had started. The cycle of time and of evolution had brought back the monk to the world from which he had fled.

This sympathy of St. Francis with nature was the result of the essential unity of his character. This unity, again, was to some extent the product of the times. Frederic Harrison has pointed out that the thirteenth century was the last age " when one half of the world was not engaged in ridiculing or combating what the other half was doing ; nor were men absorbed in ideals of their own while treating the ideals of their neighbours as matter of indifference and waste of power." [1] From the Atlantic to the Black Sea the consciousness of Europe, if we may so express it, was still one. Francis reflected this unity in his complete freedom from all intellectual conflict. Unlike the Protestant reformers, he waged no battles of the pen ; as you study his life you are not disturbed as you are, alas! in the study of Luther or Wesley, with the pother and dust of vanished controversy. He was, in fact, profoundly unconscious both of the difficulties of his teaching and of the dangers that threatened it. He taught that men should seek a higher perfection than that set forth by the Church, without realizing that this involved the reformation of the Church on lines

[1] *The Meaning of History*, c. 5.

that the Church, with its vast legal, almost commercial, certainly secular, interests would not have welcomed. He preached that society should go back to the Sermon on the Mount, at the very time when Innocent III was making the Chair of the Fisherman into the most powerful throne since the days of the Caesars. In an age when a dominant sacerdotalism had established impassable gulfs between clergy and laity, he attempted a revolution whose ideal, at any rate in its earlier forms, was the priesthood of all believers. But of all this antagonism between the real and the ideal this Francis seems to have been profoundly unconscious until the very close of his life.

In one respect only does the unity of Francis' character fail: in his dread of the influence of learning. Though in his last years he modified his position, there was a time when he was not even willing that the Brothers should become men of one book; his ideal was men of one life. 'When you have a psalter,' he said to one of the novices, 'you will want a breviary, and when you have a breviary you will seat yourself in a pulpit like a great prelate.' Then taking up some ashes, Francis scattered them over the head of the novice, saying, 'There is your breviary, there is your breviary.'[1] Francis was right in so far as he saw that dialectics and canon law monopolized too much the thought of the

[1] *Spec. Perf.* 4. Too much may be made of this incident. It should really be interpreted by Francis' undoubted statements, 'ut bona operatio sequatur scientiam' (in his *Verba admonitionis*, 7; see Boehmer, *op. cit.* 44). For the relation of the Franciscans to knowledge and culture the students should consult the monumental work of H. Felder, *Gesch. d. Wissenschaftl. Studien in Franziskanerorden* (Freiburg, 1904). For Francis himself, see *op. cit.* 29–30. For the friars and the schoolmen I may refer to my *Hist. of Christian Thought*, c. 9.

secular clergy. But Francis—possibly because, as do so many Evangelicals to-day, he exaggerated "results" as the test of knowledge—failed to see that by laying the foundations of life in love, even the less practical branches of knowledge—judged, that is, as St. Francis would have judged them from their effect upon moral life— would become true helpmates to work. Nor was Francis, in spite of his emphasis of their practical side, conscious of the theological value of his own writings.[1] Nevertheless, to Francis Europe owes, to some extent, the rise of science. He really taught men, though he knew it not, to turn from verbal quibblings to the study of nature, while the care of the friars for men's bodies, their loving service among the lepers, soon developed among the order the medical and physical studies for which they became celebrated.[2] Within a few years the brethren became the intellectual leaders of Europe. They learned the great truth repeated in every revival, that no Church can be built up on mere experience, or by descending to the social condition of the outcast. They set out to win the towns for Christ; they found the towns in a ferment of unbelief. To obtain a hold they must enter into the intellectual as well as the moral difficulties of their flocks. They revived the almost forgotten art of preaching, but they discovered, as preachers have discovered in every age, that to preach effectively they must first study deeply.[3] The Domini-

---

[1] See *supra*, p. 282 n. ; Heimbucher, *OKK* ii. 451.

[2] Felder, *op. cit.* 390 f.

[3] For a list of the great Dominican preachers, see Heimbucher, *OKK* ii. 144 f. ; for Franciscan, *ib.* ii. 462 f. The reader will remember that Savonarola († 1498) was a Dominican. An English Dominican, John of Bromyard († 1390), published one of the earliest "Preacher's Helps," his *Summa Praedicantium* (some early printed eds. in B.M.).

cans, to their credit, from the first perceived this, and eagerly sought out the centres of learning. Their leader's first effort to fight the heretics of Toulouse had not been, as his supporters have ignorantly claimed, the establishment of an Inquisition,[1] but the founding of a large school for girls at Prouille. His followers speedily captured the rising universities. Their headquarters were at Paris, Montpellier, and Bologna; in England their earliest convent was at Oxford;[2] in Germany at Cologne. To one or other of these universities every Dominican friary sent its ablest sons that they might study theology. The Franciscans were not slow to follow. Their first English Provincial 'built a school in the fratry of Oxford, and persuaded Master Robert Grosseteste of holy memory to read lectures there to the brethren.'[3] The revival of religion was followed by a revival of learning, but the great teachers of the age drew their inspiration from the Cross. The five great doctors of the later scholasticism all belonged to the Mendicants; Albert the Great († 1280), and Albert's greater scholar, Thomas of Aquinas († 1274), the glory of the Roman Church ('doctor angelicus'), were followers of Dominic—the greatness of Aquinas so overshadowing all others that the order has done little since except guard and expand his writings;[4] Bonaventura († 1274), Duns Scotus († 1308), and William of Ockham († 1347) were Franciscans. To these

[1] Lea, *Inquis. in MA* i. 299, ii. 180. The claim has the support of infallibility in the bull *Invictarum* of Sixtus V.

[2] For the Dominicans at Oxford, see *Dublin Review*, iv. (5) 84 f.; *EHR* xxxi. 519 ff.

[3] *Mon. Franc.* i. 37.

[4] For a list of the Dominican theologians, mostly but second-rate, see Heimbucher, *OKK* ii. 135 f. The Franciscan in *ib.* ii. 454 f.

add Alexander of Hales († 1245), Adam Marsh († 1258), Raymund Lull, Nicholas de Lyra († 1340)—whose glosses become a recognized part of every Bible—and a long list of distinguished names, among whom we may single out for their interest in science, Berthold Schwarz, the inventor of gunpowder (c. 1313), and the Englishman, Thomas of Bungay († c. 1300). But greatest of all was Roger Bacon († ? 1292). As a man of science his achievements have perhaps been exaggerated; certainly his antagonism to scholastic thought. But it is impossible to exaggerate the zeal with which this martyr of science pursued his way amid difficulties that would have crushed others. 'Unheard, forgotten, buried'—to quote his own sad verdict on his life—Bacon struggled for a century with the ignorance of the times, pleading that truth cannot be attained by syllogisms built up on *a priori* premisses to the neglect of experiment and observation. He did not despise authority; but authority, he insisted, must not rest, if we may so put it, like the world in the Hindoo cosmogony, on the back of the tortoise. With equal daring he carried this principle into theology. He died in poverty and neglect—where he is buried no man knows [1]—leaving to future ages to roll away the obscurity that has gathered round his memory, and to place first in the roll of modern science the name of Roger Bacon.[2]

Our national pride will note that with the exception

[1] Little, *GFO* 26 n.

[2] For Bacon, out of a vast literature I select the following: Felder, *op. cit.* 397 ff.; J. S. Brewer, *Op. hactenus inedita* (1859); R. Steele, *Op. hactenus ined. R. Baconi* (London, 1905); S. Vogl, *Die Physik R. Bacos* (Erlangen, 1906); and for an older enthusiastic estimate E. Charles, *R. Bacon sa vie, &c.* (1861). Little, *GFO* 191 f., gives a useful summary.

of Bonaventura the great schoolmen of the Franciscan order hailed from England.[1] We are proportionally scanty in the roll of great Dominicans.[2] The teaching of Francis seems to have suited our national temperament; and the heroic period of the movement, on its migration from Italy, to have found its home among us. By their enthusiasm, their democratic tendencies, their emphasis of practical holiness, their insistence, in the words of Grosseteste, 'that ordinary law and right must give place to the salvation of souls,' the stress they laid on the human side of our Lord's life and sufferings, their insistence that for the preacher all other studies must come second to that of the Bible and of theology, the Franciscans touched a sympathetic chord in our character that the Dominicans, with their greater fidelity to the teaching of their great doctors, their stern insistence on orthodoxy and authority, failed to reach. But we must beware lest we flatter ourselves overmuch. If throughout the Middle Ages, as Dr. Rashdall well puts it, "Franciscanism was the fruitful parent of new philosophies and new social movements, of new orthodoxies and new heresies," the cause will be found, probably, in the far greater emphasis of individualism by its founder, and in his fear of crippling the spontaneity of life by overmuch red-tape.

To the remarkable success of the friars, even in the lives of St. Dominic and St. Francis, we have already

[1] I have not dwelt on the familiar story of the coming of the friars to England. See *supra*, p. 286 n. For the contrast of the Franciscan and Dominican philosophies, see Rashdall, *Univs. in MA* ii. 526 f.; Brewer, *Mon. Franc.* pp. liii.–lix.

[2] Of English Dominicans of the second rank we may mention William of Alton († 1265). There is an excellent list of Eng. Franciscans with details in Little, *GFO* 125 ff.

referred. For five hundred years that success, though not without its vicissitudes, has been continued. To-day the Franciscan order is still the most numerous in the world. But upon the history of the friars, their times of decay and reform, the civil war between the Franciscans over 'evangelical poverty,' we cannot dwell. We must content ourselves in conclusion, in accordance with our limits and aims, in pointing out the contradiction the success involved between the ideal and the real—a contradiction more striking, it is true, in the case of the Dominicans than the Franciscans, if only because of the greater nobility of St. Francis' ideal. For Francis would have been the first to own, as in fact we have seen that he owned, with deepest sorrow, in his own lifetime, that the organization he founded has not fulfilled in its history his aims, or realized its true self. A movement which in its origin was anti-monastic added another to the long family of monkish orders. The devotion of the early friars to 'Lady Poverty' gave place to the repudiation by Gregory IX of Francis' last *Testament*, and to the ingenious dialectics by which friars were henceforth enabled to accept the wealth that poured in upon them from every quarter. Their simple preaching of the Cross ended in a disastrous Mariolatry [1]—in part, no doubt, the outcome of their democratic instincts, in part their answer to the Manichaean tendencies of the Cathari—against which, to their honour be it said, the Dominicans protested. A revival, whose starting-point was the value of the individual layman, bequeathed to the papacy, as the champion of sacerdotalism, a standing army, speaking all languages,

[1] For the causes of the Franciscan exaltation of the Virgin, see *Mon. Franc.* pref. xxxviii f.

scattered through all nations, maintained without cost, and sworn to unhesitating and exclusive service. Exempt from all jurisdiction, save that of their own superiors, the friars became Rome's network of irresponsible police. Their power overshadowed the bishop; their papal Inquisition, under the control of the Dominicans, extinguished liberty of thought in a deluge of blood. Even their good qualities were not without drawbacks. By their energy and popular favour they still further degraded the secular clergy into whose parishes they intruded, whose function they usurped, whose worshippers they drew away, building stately edifices that would have made St. Francis weep. To the long quarrel between secular and regular they now added the more bitter struggle between secular and friar, nowhere more bitter than in the universities, the mutual hatred of the rival mendicants, and the dreary civil war among the Franciscans between the 'Spirituals' and 'Moderates.'[1]

We must be careful lest we paint the later degeneracy of the Mendicants in colours too dark. That they had not entirely lost the self-abnegation of their early days, even after more than a century of slow decay, was abundantly shown during the Black Death of 1349.

[1] I have not thought it needful to deal with the other orders of friars of later growth, as they do not illustrate any new ideas. Of these orders the chief were the Austin Friars, originally an order of Augustinian Hermits (on whom see Heimbucher, *OKK* ii. 177–211), and the Carmelites (Heimbucher, *OKK* ii. 535–80) or White Friars. Of later Carmelites the most illustrious member was St. Theresa. On one branch of Austin friars, the Friars of the Sack, see A. G. Little in *EHR* Jan. 1894. The four orders are easily remembered by Wyclif's frequent jest on the word Caim (the older spelling of Cain) as equal Carmelites, Austin Friars, Jacobites (Dominicans), and Minorites (Franciscans).

The friars stayed by the sick, and were swept away in their thousands. But even if the order had ever become as vile as some later writers would have us believe, the Church of Christ should never forget the debt that she owes to St. Francis. For a few years the Sermon on the Mount became a realized fact. But the dream passed away, as other dreams had passed away before, the inspiration vanished, as other inspirations had vanished before; once more men slept in the dust of the earth, for the times were not yet. Yet at the end of the days Francis shall stand in his lot. The seed sown so many years ago in the fields and lanes of Italy shall still bear its hundredfold. Seekers after God will ever feel his gentle influence, and follow in flight the white wings of St. Francis as he soared toward the Infinite Love.

> The Master whisper'd
> 'Follow the Gleam.'
>
> . . . .
>
> There, on the border
> Of boundless ocean,
> And all but in heaven,
> Hovers the Gleam.

CHAPTER VII

THE MESSAGE OF MONASTICISM

> What though, about thy rim
> Scull-things in order grim
> Grow out in graver mood, obey the sterner stress?
> Look not thou down but up!
> To uses of a cup,
> The festal board, lamp's flash and trumpet's peal,
> The new wine's foaming flow,
> The Master's lips a-glow!
> Thou, heaven's consummate cup, what need'st thou with earth's wheel?
> BROWNING, *Rabbi Ben Ezra.*

ARGUMENT

	PAGE
§ I. Lessons of Monasticism—Nature and the pitchfork—Tormenting dreams—Jérome—Cassian—St. Bernard—Beautiful devils of both sexes—The salvation of the whole man—Sins of the Spirit—Gnosticism—Monasticism and self-sacrifice	319
§ II. Accidie—Analysis by Cassian—Modern accidie—With the worldling and the cleric	326
§ III. The unimportance of environment for self-conquest—The safety-valve of spiritual energy—The norm—'Eagles' and 'sparrows'—Contrast in this of Protestantism and Romanism—The importance of renunciation as a condition of work—Monasticism and Milton—Luther's attack—Monasticism and silence—The value of *askesis*—The peril of cheapness in religious vocation	331
§ IV. The contradictions of Monasticism—The sacrifice of praise and thanksgiving—The continuance of its spirit	342
§ V. Monasticism and joy—The gladness of renunciation—Macarius—Francis of Assisi—The 'jugglers' of God—Brother Leo and Brother Ruffino—Jacopone da Todi—St. Bernard—The possibilities of victory . .	345
§ VI. The conclusion of the whole matter—'Sub specie aeternitatis'—The furrows of His Cross . .	351

pp. 319–352

CHAPTER VII

THE MESSAGE OF MONASTICISM

I

FROM this survey of the development and history of Monasticism we shall do well to turn to the lessons we may learn from its story. In the intercourse of the saints, upon what special aspects of spiritual life, as consciously apprehended in his own soul, would the monk have dwelt ? to what factors would he have pointed as of importance ? to what special temptations would he have acknowledged that he was liable ? Such an inquiry, it is evident, cannot be treated save on the broadest lines. We can only touch the fringe of a subject the materials of which are almost bewildering in their vastness, and, in some respects, as varied as the individuals themselves. But in the case of spiritual life the main factors are independent of the external garb with which the varying centuries clothe them. There are, therefore, certain general laws which reveal themselves, and which may fairly be labelled the common experience of the system.

We shall do well, inverting the usual method, to begin with the lessons we may gather from the failures of Monasticism. You may drive out nature with a pitchfork, wrote Horace, nevertheless it will return—the more so, perhaps, because of the pitchfork. Monachism in all its forms found this to be true. The hermit could fly from his fellow men; but, fast as he ran, self could keep up with him. If in the monk we see

> "A hunter hunting out the beast in man,"

we often see the beast turning and attempting to rend its too venturesome foe. The monk tried to violate Nature with impunity; Nature revenged herself by wrapping round his soul a mist, half disease, half the true self, through which he saw devils, not men, as trees walking. He made a desert of the heart and called it peace, but often found that the wilderness asserted itself, strident with the roar of diverse beasts. The very passions that the monk hated and trampled beneath his feet seemed to regain new strength, like the iron men whom Jason mowed down in his pursuit of the Golden Fleece. The fires of purity, or rather of the yearning for it, too often scorched the hearts that were laid on its altar.

'Go to the Thebaid,' said Chrysostom, 'and you will find there a solitude more beautiful than Paradise, a thousand choirs of angels under human form, nations of martyrs, armies of virgins, the devil chained, Christ triumphant!'[1]

But in life the cell of the monk, instead of being the abode of 'angels' and of the 'triumphant Christ,' was too often peopled, as indeed we see on almost every page of the *Historia Lausiaca*, with innumerable demons ever on the watch to destroy the souls of the inmates. 'Ah, how sweet it is,' cries Jerome, in one

---

[1] *In Matt. hom.* 8 (*PG* 57, p. 87). The student anxious to see the views of Chrysostom on Monasticism should look up the numerous passages in the index of *PG* 64 *s.v.* 'Monachus.' They are often very exaggerated.

of his panegyrics of Monasticism, 'to lay aside the weight of the body and to soar into the pure bright ether.'[1] More accurate is the description he gives of actual experience:

'How often in the desert, in that vast solitude which, parched by the sultry sun, affords a dwelling for the monks, did I fancy myself in the midst of the luxuries of Rome. I sat alone, the companion of scorpions and wild beasts, and yet was in the midst of dancing girls. My face was white with fasting, but the mind in my cold body was hot with desires. The fires of lust burned up a body which was already dead. Destitute of all succour I cast myself at the feet of Jesus, washed them with my tears, dried them with my hair, and subdued the rebel flesh by a whole week's fasting' [*Ep.* 22 (7)].

The experience of Jerome could be multiplied a hundredfold. Jerome himself tells us the story of Hilarion, who first introduced Monasticism into Syria, but whose nights were tortured by visions of naked girls, whose fasts were spoiled by dreams of sumptuous feasts.[2] When Anthony began his hermit life he saw every night 'beautiful women.'[3] Cassian tells us that in some of the monasteries, such were the temptations of the devils, the monks dare not all go to bed at once, but took turns, some sleeping, others reciting psalms 'to ward off their attacks.'[4] The experience of St. Benedict was the same.[5] A fair face haunted him; at last, flinging away the skin which was his only dress, he flung himself naked into a thorn bush, and rolled himself in this bed until he had extinguished the lure of the senses. Of Evagrius, who in early life

---

[1] *Ep.* 14.   [2] Jerome, *Vit. Hilarion*, 7.
[3] 'Nulla omittens figmenta lascivia.' *Vit. Ant.* 4. Cf. the story of Pachon in *HL* (Gr.) 23 (5).
[4] Cassian, *Coll.* vii. 23.   [5] Greg. Mag. *Dial.* ii. 1.

had suffered much from the pursuit of a woman of high rank, we read that 'at one time the devil so multiplied fornications upon him, during the night scourging him with leather whips,' that henceforth 'he spent the whole night standing in a well praying.' Under this treatment 'his flesh dried up like a stone.' At another time, 'when the spirit of blasphemy troubled him for forty days, he did not enter under the roof of a cell, until all his body was full of ticks like a beast's.'[1] St. Bernard, tormented by impure thoughts, rushed into an icy pool and stood neck deep until he had subdued his body.[2] St. Nilus fought with a sensuous temptation until the sweat rolled down his face.

The experiences of these heroes of renunciation were repeated in thousands of nameless individuals. Temptation by visible devils forms one of the commonest incidents in monastic life. These devils appear under all shapes, but the beautiful youth of both sexes—this last point is worthy of note, and significant of the moral society from which the monk sought escape—is the most frequent. They vanish with the sign of the Cross, or the Gloria Patri—always, however, leaving a smell behind them.[3] Here and there we may find a man

---

[1] *HL* (Gr.) 38; Amélineau, *HL* 115-6.

[2] William of Thierry, *Vita Bern.* 3, in *PL* 185, p. 230. This was before he became a monk.

[3] Rosweyd in his Index to the *VP* (*PL* 74) gives two columns of instances. Luther and the ink-pot was no new thing. See also my *PEC* 127 ff. For the moral temptations of monasteries see Augustine, *Ep.* 78. Among the monastic rules bearing on morals it is interesting to note the emphasis (e.g. *Conc. Aachen*, 817, c. 136) on each monk or canon having his own bed, and that a lamp shall burn all night in the dormitory. In some monasteries young monks were sandwiched between old ones to lessen temptation. Sodomy, however, often prevailed, if we may judge from the regulations against it.

of stronger will or more burning enthusiasm than his fellows, who could succeed in destroying all his natural instincts, and who was content to mistake the desolation of his heart for the peace of God. But such men were rare. If experience is of any value, one thing may be regarded as settled by centuries of trial : that in all save rare exceptions, who are born not made, Christian life must be built up on the clear recognition that the social instincts of man are divine in their origin—not a demon to be crushed, but a power of the soul of the highest value. The salvation of the unit cannot be isolated from the salvation of society.

Furthermore, the salvation of the man must be the salvation of the whole man, not of a soul artificially divorced from mind and body:

> "the music
> Of man's fair composition best accords
> When 'tis in concert, not in single strains."

The whole history of Monasticism teaches us that man is not built in water-tight compartments, with bulkheads and automatic doors whereby we may cut off the waters from one part, indifferent whether the rest is under flood. No experiment has been more carefully tried than this, under a variety of conditions, and in a variety of ages. The issue has been the clear demonstration that the experiment is one that ought never to have been made. The universal verdict of history is against it : ' securus judicat orbis terrarum.'

There was another consequence of this failure to consider the whole man. The mistake of Monasticism in the matter of discipline lay in its tendency to consider that the conquest of self lay in the conquest of two passions which they singled out from the rest—the pride of life, and the lust of the flesh. This exaggeration threw all life out of perspective, and the result, even in the stricter sphere of the soul, was disastrous. There grew up in certain circles a comparative indifference to sins of the spirit, while the morbid introspection and concentration of thought upon sins of the flesh often produced diseases of the soul as deadly as the sins themselves. The student of the pages of the *Historia Lausiaca*, and other human documents of the same order, must often feel that if the victims of the flesh had found less time to think about their temptations they would not have suffered so severely from them.

The neglect of this great truth of the essential unity of human nature—that in one sense there is neither body nor soul, but the *ego* only—has produced a multitude of errors. Throughout its career, whether in the East or the West, there has been one aspect of Gnosticism from which Monasticism has never been able to free itself. Monasticism has always failed to realize the noble conception of St. Paul, that the body is the temple of the Holy Ghost, and that, as such, it possesses a continuity which defies the withering touch of death. On the contrary, not only the wilder hermits of the East, but monks of culture and influence—for instance, St. Bernard—sought to reduce it to a ruin. They made pain an end in itself; they gloried in tribulations, but they were not the tribulations which 'God worketh together for good,'[1] but, too often, tortures which, after the manner of Red Indians, they had inflicted upon their own bodies. They believed that thorns in themselves will make a crown. 'He that is near me,' said Jesus, in one of the most familiar of

[1] *Romans* viii. 28, *RV* marg.

the *agrapha*, ' is near the fire,'[1] but that fire is not the fire which destroys, but the fire which purifies.

Gnosticism was not the only influence at work in producing this indifference to and contempt of the body. There was another cause for the self-tortures of the early monks. We have seen that Monasticism arose when the age of martyrdom had ended,[2] but the glory of the martyrs had begun. In the dim religious light that followed the adoption of Christianity by the State, men began to look back and idealize the spirit of the age that had preceded. Sacrifice was dead, but self-sacrifice was the highest form of human aspiration. Worthier souls still counted it all joy to suffer for His name's sake. If they could not be martyrs in act, they would make the nearest approach to it that was possible. Even in the old days there had been men and women not a few who had sought out martyrdom for its own sake, in spite of the official discouragements of the Church.[3] Little wonder that ardent souls "tortured for themselves the flesh which lictors would no longer scourge, and constructed for themselves the prisons which no longer kept Christian confessors for the lions."[4] Said Palaemon, the early guide of Pachomius, when urged to take food : ' If of the martyrs of Christ some were tortured, some beheaded, some burnt, and yet bravely endured to the end for the faith, why should I because of my small pains throw aside the rewards of suffering ? '[5] No better illustration of how fully this view underlay much of Monasticism can be

[1] Orig. *Hom. in Jerem.* iii. 778. [2] *Supra*, p. 6.
[3] See my *PEC* 343. Cf. Euseb. *Mart. Pal.* 3 (3); Tertullian, *ad Scap.* 5. Synod of Elvira, *c.* 60, denounced the matter.
[4] Hatch, *OEC* 160. [5] *Vit. Pach.* 13.

given than the comment of Sulpicius, when he heard of the death of his hero Martin:

'He now follows the Lamb as his guide free from all stain. For though the character of our times did not allow him the honour of martyrdom, nevertheless he will not be without his glory, inasmuch as by his vows and character he was able to be, and indeed longed to be, a martyr. . . . For what agonies of human suffering did he not endure in the hope of eternal life?'[1]

II

In all ages men have found that it is impossible to play fast and loose with the laws of nature, which, because they are laws of nature, are also laws of God, without suffering the consequences. One of the results of this defiance of physical law was the familiar state of reaction called by monastic writers "Accidie."[2] The use by Chaucer and by others of this old English word—now almost entirely dropped out of use—as well as the careful analysis they give of its meaning, shows that the idea was more familiar to our fathers than it is to ourselves, or rather that they more carefully diagnosed, from the spiritual side, a form of temptation or disease common to every age, but which was reckoned by them among the seven deadly sins. Of "accidie" we have a full analysis by Cassian, doubtless the result of his own experience. 'Accidie,' says Cassian:

'is heaviness or weariness of heart. This is akin to dejection, and is especially trying to recluses, and a dangerous and frequent foe to dwellers in the desert; and especially disturbing

---

[1] Sulp. Sev. *Ep.* ii. (ed. *CSEL* 144).

[2] Accidie, Gk. ἀκηδία, "heedlessness." See *Ps.* cxviii. 28, LXX ἐνύσταξεν ἡ ψυχή μου ἀπὸ ἀκηδίας. For the history of the word see Murray's *New Eng. Dict.* s.v.; for its place among mortal sins see S. Schiwietz, *Das morgenländische Mönchtum*, 266 n. 4.

to a monk about the sixth hour, like some fever which seizes him at stated times. . . . Some of the elders declare that this is the "noontide demon" spoken of in the ninetieth Psalm.'[1]

He then goes on to describe at length its effects:

'When accidie has taken possession of a man it produces dislike of the place, disdain and contempt of the brethren, as if they were careless or unspiritual. . . . He complains that he is cut off from spiritual gain, and is of no use in the place. . . . He cries up distant monasteries and those which are a long way off, and describes such places as more profitable and better suited for salvation. He paints the intercourse with the brethren there as sweet and full of spiritual life. On the other hand, he says that everything about him is rough and unedifying. . . . Besides this he looks about anxiously this way and that, and sighs that none of the brethren come to see him, and often comes in and out of his cell, and frequently gazes up at the sun as if it were too slow in setting. So a kind of unreasonable confusion of mind takes possession of him like some foul darkness, and makes him idle and useless for every spiritual work, so that he imagines that no cure for so terrible an attack can be found except in visiting some of the brethren.'[2]

The effect of accidie, according to Cassian, is twofold. In the soul it produces sleep and idleness; in the body a restlessness which drives the monk away from his cell,[3] and which makes him 'anxious about the people's affairs.'[4] The cure for accidie, according to Cassian, is manual labour, the remedy which Benedict applied more fully at a later date. In this connection Cassian relates an old saying of the monks of Egypt: 'A man who works is attacked by but one devil: an idler is tormented by countless spirits.'[5]

[1] *Instit.* v. 1, xi.; cf. *Ps.* xci. 6.

[2] *Ib.* x. 2. Bk. x. of Cassian's *Instits.* is devoted to the analysis of accidie.

[3] Cf. *HL* (Gr.) 21 (1), where Cronius relates that he fled from his monastery, ἀκηδίας χάριν.

[4] *Instit.* x. 7. [5] *Ib.* x. 14, 23.

For the monk the daily death of the individual will was not without its perils, "especially in the long hours of obscurity and silence which succeed to the effort and impulse of sacrifice."[1] The routine of the abbey, the continuity of its religious exercises, the lack of variety in them, all tended to produce accidie, especially when it was the *Rule* that became uppermost in the mind, and not the delight of the heart itself in its voluntary service. Among other symptoms, such accidie manifested itself in great sorrowfulness or gloom, and in the absence of gentleness. Accidie, says Chaucer, in his analysis of this sin in "The Persone's Tale," 'maketh a man heavy, thoughtful, and wrawe'[2]—but the sorrow is the 'sorrow of the world that worketh death.'[3] From this sorrowfulness, as St. Gregory puts it, come forth malice, grudging, faint-heartedness, despair, torpor as to that which is commanded, and the straying of the mind after that which is forbidden.[4] This sluggishness in all good works manifests itself now in talkativeness, now in yawning, and now 'in the flagging of voice'[5] because the soul is absorbed and taken up with its own indolent dejection. Its final effect is a despondent renunciation of all care, hope, and effort concerning its true calling and its highest good, the forfeit of a great vocation through a faint heart and lack of faith and

---

[1] Montalembert, *MW* iv. 434.

[2] *i.e.* peevish. For Chaucer on Accidie, see the prose sermon, "Persone's Tale"; §§ 53–61 [*Works of Chaucer* (ed. Skeat), iv. 612 f.].

[3] *2 Cor.* vii. 10.

[4] Greg. *Reg. Past.* iii. 3. *Moral.* 30 (*PL* 75, p. 546).

[5] S. John of Damascus, *de orth. Fide*, ii. 14 [quoted in Bp. Paget's illuminating essay on "Accidie," in his *Spirit of Discipline* (12th ed. 1912), 13].

courage—' like to the coward champion recreant, that seith creant (flieth) withoute need.' [1]

The translation of accidie into modern thought is not difficult. Accidie is ennui—we have no word of our own that translates it, now that we have lost the older term—and our difficulty in recognizing it as one of the seven deadly sins of the cloister arises from the fact that to-day we rather associate accidie with the worldling than the religious. In the old days accidie was not so associated, and for a good reason. The life of the man of the world was too full of stirring incident, we might even add too self-satisfied in a rude coarseness, for him to feel ennui. He could only maintain himself in his position by a ceaseless activity, aimless, uncivilized, perhaps even deadly in its results, but which left no place for accidie. The modern worldling has changed all that. He has become the parasite of a social system; he toils not, neither does he spin, but lives upon the toil of others. He spends his life about town, in a ceaseless whirl of pleasure and self-indulgence. He contributes little or nothing to the social well-being, and because of that is never tired of opposing every movement that makes for the general welfare. When not slaughtering grouse in battues, he is shooting pigeons at Hurlingham, flinging away his money at Monte Carlo, or racing at Newmarket. The people—that many-headed beast which supplies for him the sinews of his pleasures—die at his doors, herded like beasts, spending their lives in ceaseless toil,—but of that he recks little. The moan of the sweated cannot penetrate the double windows of his club. Yet there is one thing he cannot escape: that which Carlyle in one of his finest passages has

[1] Chaucer, *l.c.* § 56 in *ed. cit.*

called "the inexorable, all-encircling ocean of ennui. If you could mount to the stars and do yacht voyages under the belts of Jupiter, or stalk deer on the rings of Saturn, it would still begirdle you."[1]

The accidie of the worldling has formed the commonplace of the pulpit in all ages, from the writer of *Ecclesiastes* downwards. But there is a religious accidie not the less dangerous because the more subtle. The "desultory, listless, nerveless languor of the acciduous," "the self-indulgent, unaspiring resignation to one's moral poverty,"[2] which can no longer understand that "it is the prerogative of human nature to force and compel the most adverse circumstances to give new firmness to integrity and new fire to enthusiasm,"[3] which, with growing dimness of vision, no longer greets the promises from afar, or goes on from strength to strength—this accidie, the phases of which are many and yet one, is perhaps the deadliest foe with which men devoted to a religious vocation, whether as ministers or teachers, have to contend; especially when the enthusiasms of youth are past, and the road that must henceforth be trodden is one that will have no turn before the end. Accidie is the great moral snare of middle life; as deadly to-day, though in different ways, as in the old days when it attacked the men who wore the cowl and tonsure.[4] Accidie is the opposite of all that is expressed by Browning in his swan-like song, when he speaks of himself as

[1] Carlyle, *Latter-Day Pamphlets*, p. 286.
[2] Paget, *op. cit.* 27, 40.
[3] R. W. Dale, *Nine Lectures on Preaching*, 195.
[4] Cf. Paget, *op. cit.* 33 f. for analysis of accidie in modern poetry. The bishop seems to me perfectly correct in his claim (p. 38) that one of Browning's great charms is his total freedom from accidie.

One who never turned his back, but marched breast forward,
    Never doubted clouds would break;
Never dreamed, though right were worsted, wrong would
    triumph;
Held we fall to rise, are baffled to fight better,
    Sleep to wake.

III

One of the lessons that Monasticism, or rather its failure, has to teach us is the comparative unimportance of environment, its futility in producing true self-surrender. The lesson is one of special importance for an age which too often confuses a favourable environment with the root of the matter, and imagines that salvation is the result of transplanting to new streets, a larger hinterland, brighter skies, and purer airs. The monk, like the twentieth-century socialist, exaggerated the spiritual value of environment. He denied that the highest life was possible save in certain favoured conditions. He surrounded the soul with walls to keep out all evil. He prepared for its abode fretted cloisters and soaring minsters. Life for the monk was one ceaseless round of praise and thanksgiving. Everything was done to make the path to Calvary the natural road of the soul. And yet, in cases all too many, this spiritual environment proved useless. In some instances—no doubt a vast number—it succeeded in producing a noble type. The wonder would have been if it had not, though even here—in the case of St. Bernard, for instance—the critic may well doubt whether it was so much the monastic environment which produced the result as what Dr. Chalmers has finely called " the expulsive power of a new affection." At any rate, it is to this last that many would point as the secret of life; nor is it contradicted by anything in the history of Monasticism. The power of environment to change a soul, to produce the true spirit of self-surrender, is limited; the power of a soul on fire with love to change an environment is as limitless as the might of God. But such souls need neither the security of the desert nor the peace of a cloister. They are above such artificial aids. The traveller, whether in the tropics or penetrating the solitudes that guard the secret of the Poles, is enabled to do his work because he carries his temperature with him, and can therefore defy heat and chill alike. So with the child of God. He carries his temperature with him. The pure in heart see God, nor is the vision caused by the things that are without.

We should err if we supposed that this was altogether a modern discovery. Nowhere has it been better expressed than in the *Epistles* of Ivo of Chartres:

'I approve the life of those anchorites for whom solitude is a paradise, and the city a prison; who live by the labour of their hands, and seek to renew their souls by the sweetness of a life of contemplation—men who drink with the lips of their heart at the fountain of life, and forget all that is behind them in gazing at that which is before. But neither the secret places of the forests nor the peaks of mountains can give happiness to a man if he has not within himself the solitude of the soul, the sabbath of the heart, tranquillity of conscience, ascensions within his spirit. Without these there is no solitude which does not produce accidie, curiosity, vain-glory, and the other perilous storms of temptation.'[1]

There is another lesson which we may learn from the history of Monasticism of supreme importance for the ecclesiastical statesman as well as for the historian of

[1] *Ep.* 192 in *PL* 162, p. 201. Cf. *Ep.* 256, *op. cit.* 261.

the Church. Throughout the Middle Ages Monasticism supplied, if we may so express it, the safety-valve for the energy of the Church. For it seems to be a law of the life of the Church, whether rightly or wrongly we need not now discuss, constantly to set before herself a certain form of character, conduct, and zeal, departures from which are regarded with frowns and disapprobation. This norm or standard will vary with different ages, as for instance the norm of the eighteenth century, both of the Anglican Church and of the older dissenters of the period, with its dread of all enthusiasm, becoming the byword of the next generation. The larger also a Church the larger also the possible variations in the same age in the standard norm. Nevertheless, the presence of a norm is one of the most constant phenomena of Church life. This it is that so often crushes the reformer with that sense of opposition within the camp, worse than any opposition from without. This it is that so often leads to a species of civil war within the Church itself, when the swords of the normalist and the enthusiast are turned against each other rather than against the common foe. In this also, more than anything else, we may see the source of the schisms and splits which have furrowed deep both the Anglican and Nonconformist Churches.

But in the case of Rome it has been otherwise. Monasticism has always enabled her to retain the norm in the Church itself conveniently low—we use the term without any disrespect—so as to suit the many, while yet providing for those elect spirits who were minded to reach a higher standard. In the striking phrase of St. Ambrose, due provision was thus made 'for the soaring of the eagles,' as well as for 'the fluttering of the sparrows.'[1] Protestantism, on the other hand, has too often driven out the 'eagles' to save the 'sparrows,' or sought to exterminate the 'sparrows' because of their inferiority to 'eagles.' The Church of Rome would have used Wesley and Booth to found new orders within herself, whose zeal and enthusiasm would have strengthened rather than weakened the Church. Nor would Rome have allowed a small clique of stern and "peculiar" Christians to arrogate to themselves the title and merits of the Church, in contempt of the weaker brethren who could not rise to their heights; she would have constituted such a congregation or society for the development of whose special tenets, or the attainment of whose special standard, due provision must be made—thus securing the proper cultivation of ideals that lie beyond the normal idea of the Church at that moment, and yet conserving for the use of the Church forces that might otherwise be lost, or even become a source of weakness and mischief.

To many this proposition will seem to be a truism. But it is one of those truisms which history teaches us has been systematically forgotten. By some writers of repute, exception, even, has been taken to the doctrine. They have urged that Monasticism really stands condemned because it encourages the belief "that there are two classes of believers, with two standards of conduct,"[2] whereas in the Christian Republic there can be but one rule of life for all : Be ye therefore perfect even as your Father which is in heaven is perfect. They maintain

[1] Ambrose, *de fuga sec.* c. 5, 'Qui non potest volitare ut aquila, volitet ut passer' (*PL* 14, p. 584). Cf. R. Thamin, *S. Ambroise* (Lyons, 1891),416,"Le christianisme offrit alors deux voies : l'une étroite, l'autre large. Il y eut deux Églises : l'Église de tous, et l'Église des saints."
[2] Black, *Culture and Restraint*, 273 ff.

that the perfection which all must seek is a perfection which is possible for all. If this last were true, Monasticism could have no further defence, for it set forth a perfection always impossible except for a minority. 'Consider,' wrote Cassian, 'that you belong to the few and elect,'[1] words which show how far the Church had moved in the direction of what may be called spiritual specialization since the plea of Tertullian: 'We are under a delusion if we believe that what is not permitted to the priests is permitted to the laity. Are not we laics also priests?'[2]

Is this theory true either in daily life or in the Church? Is the conscript army, with its ideal of military service obligatory for all, the only defence of a country? Must all serve their time in the navy? If it is pleaded that these are duties that we all discharge vicariously by means of our support of the few to whom the actual duties are assigned, the same reasonably might be alleged —or, rather, would certainly have been alleged in medieval times—on behalf of Monasticism. The monks were looked upon as the soldiers on actual service,[3] by whose prayers the safety of the people was provided.

But it is in the Church that the theory is even more conspicuously at fault. Are all called to be ministers? Are all called to be missionaries? Is the same measure of self-sacrifice demanded from every child of God? Are there no special centres of danger, no forlorn hopes in the King's army? Is the sacrifice of Abraham—'thy son, thine only son Isaac'—an incident in every life?

---

[1] *Instit.* iv. c. 38.

[2] Tert. *de Exhort. Cast.* 7. Tertullian was pleading against digamy. Cf. *Apoc.* i. 6, "He made us to be priests."

[3] Cf. *supra*, p. 65.

Is the command : Go sell all that thou hast and give to the poor, of universal application ? Are there no martyrs, whose glorious end we could no longer imitate however much our desire ? When put in this form, the question answers itself.

There is another lesson that we may learn from Monasticism, the value of which is for all time. The whole history of Monasticism is the emphasis of the importance of the conquest of self—in other words, of renunciation—as the one condition of effective work in the world. As we run through the record of the leaders that Monasticism produced, as we realize their supreme importance in the history of the Church, as we ponder over the work that they effected in their day and generation, we discern clearly that they best will help to subjugate the world who have first obtained the victory in their own souls, that they are best fitted for work in the world who have succeeded in freeing themselves from its clasp. Not by coming down to lower levels, but by living on the mountain-tops, will men influence their fellows most powerfully. De Tocqueville, in another connection it is true, hit upon the secret of monastic success when he claimed "that to become master of his own fate and to rule his fellows a man has only to overcome himself," whatever may be said of de Tocqueville's limitation of this truth to the aristocratic ages.[1] Throughout its career Monasticism utters its protest against the idea that an accommodated Christianity will ever influence the age to whose supposed needs it has been adapted. "If the ideal of the Gospel is Christ crucified, it is an ideal which will never perish." [2] The

---

[1] A. de Tocqueville, *Démocratie en Amérique*, iii. 173, Fr. ed. (1842).
[2] Abbot Tosti, *St. Benedict* (trs. Wood), p. 5.

fall of the system, when men pronounced it worldly, when the monastery had become little more than a club of celibate landlords under a *Rule*, but emphasizes the secret of its strength and its message for to-day.

The attack upon Monasticism has sometimes been made from an altogether different quarter: not that it called men to a higher standard of life, a fiercer conflict, but that it provided a path to heaven of inglorious ease. Milton's noble words have often been quoted, as if specially applicable to Monasticism :

"I cannot praise a fugitive and cloistered virtue, unexercised and unbreathed, that never sallies out and seeks her adversary, but shrinks out of the race where that immortal garland is to be run for, not without dust and heat. Assuredly we bring not innocence into the world, we bring impurity much rather; that which purifies us is trial, and trial is by what is contrary." [1]

But in reality our chief objection to Monasticism is that it exposed virtue to too great a conflict, and to all the dust and heat of a struggle with self ten times the more fierce because of the absence of objective life. "Monasteries," writes Montalembert,[2] "were never intended to collect the invalids of the Church." The remark is true; a feeble religious life could not stand the strain to which the monk was exposed. In that arena the strong could grow stronger; but the weakling, driven in upon himself, became the sport of diverse temptations. Solitude, it has been finely said, can never be the mother country save of the strong. Christian's conflict with Apollyon—the representative of the temptations that come from without—was far less formidable than his struggle with Giant Despair, when imprisoned from the outer world; it was his own

[1] *Areopagitica* (ed. Bohn, ii. 68). [2] Montal. *MW* i. 18.

thoughts sweeping up behind him in the Valley of the Shadow of Death that threw his soul into misease, at a time when he was alone, with no Hopeful to help him. Only of the Miltons of life can we safely sing:

> "Thy soul was like a star and dwelt apart."

Luther was right when in his rough way he laid his finger upon the weakness of Monasticism in the greater temptation to which it subjected the soul:

'It is a perilous thing for a man to be alone. Wherefore they that ordained that accursed, monkish, and solitary life gave occasion to many thousands to despair. If a monk should separate himself from the company of others for a day or two to be occupied in prayer (as we read of Christ that He sometimes went aside alone into the mountains and by night continued in prayer), there was no danger therein. But when they constrained men continually to live a solitary life, it was a device of the devil himself: for when a man is tempted and alone he is not able to raise himself up, no, not in the least temptation that can be.' [1]

Closely allied with this conquest of self there was another lesson which Monasticism teaches, not without value for this generation. The ideal monk was the man who had learned the value of a life of silence. He was not afraid, as so many are to-day, to be alone with himself. With Tennyson's "Ancient Sage" he would have said:

> "If thou would'st hear the Nameless, and wilt dive
> Into the Temple-cave of thine own self,
> There, brooding by the central altar, thou
> May'st haply learn the Nameless hath a voice,
> By which thou wilt abide, if thou be wise."

---

[1] I have unfortunately mislaid the reference to this passage. It is not in his *de votis monasticis judicium* of 1521.

He realized that only by withdrawing can one draw nigh to the Presence :

> "From the world of sin and noise
> And hurry I withdraw,
> For the small and inward voice
> I wait with humble awe."

In the same way, for the more reasonable monk asceticism was but a means to an end, rather than an end in itself. A St. Benedict or St. Bernard strove to get this world beneath his feet that he might the better see the other world above his head.

'What is the reason,' asks Thomas à Kempis, 'why some of the saints were so perfect and contemplative ? Because they learned to mortify themselves wholly to all earthly desires, and therefore they could with their whole hearts fix themselves on God, and be free for holy retirement.'

We in these latter days would do well to remember the words that follow : 'We are too much led by our passions, and too solicitous for earthly things.'[1]

> "The world is too much with us, late and soon,
> Getting and spending, we lay waste our powers."

Monasticism was also the emphasis of a truth, too often forgotten to-day, the need of discipline for any effective conquest of self. The very word asceticism brings this truth prominently before us, for in ancient Greece the word ἄσκησις indicates the discipline through which athletes must pass in the course of their training. From Stoic philosophy the word passed into Christian thought,[2] the more easily because of the familiarity of the early Christians with the Isthmian games. In Greece this *askesis* was always regarded as a means to an end,

---

[1] *Imit. Christi*, i. 11.
[2] In NT once only, *Acts* xxiv. 16, as a verb.

perfect harmony or beauty. Naturally, also, it was characteristic of Greek Ethics, with its watchword of μηδὲν ἄγαν, its central position that virtue lies in the mean, to avoid turning this asceticism or training into an end in itself. But for the untutored mind there is nothing more difficult than to avoid the confusion between means and end. We need not be surprised, therefore, that in early and medieval times monastic zealots not a few, as we have already seen, mistook the distinction, and made discipline a good in itself, rather than viewed it from the standpoint of result.

Nevertheless, when all deductions have been made for aberrations and extravagancies, Monasticism was the emphasis of the great truth of the need of discipline, and that without discipline there can be no holiness. Monasticism further insisted that the discipline which costs nothing, which is not renunciation in some form or other, must be valueless. If a man would master himself, he must pay the price. Only by patient endurance can a man win his own soul.[1] There is no remedy for the soul's disease which will enable us to avoid the use of the knife. Monasticism (and for our present purpose we include under this head Puritanism and Methodism, its lineal descendants) refused, in the glow of their first enthusiasms, to accommodate the higher life to modern, materialistic ideas. The monks preached, in tones perhaps more strident and repellent then gentle and persuasive, that there is a higher, more inspired gospel than that of comfort. The words of St. Paul, 'Mortify, therefore, your members which are on the earth,'[2] did not seem to them an out-of-date command. If the pruning-knife played too great a

[1] *Luke* xxi. 19 R.V.   [2] *Col.* iii. 5.

part in the culture of their hearts, better at any rate the pruning-knife than the rank growths of modern self-indulgence, many of which, we fear, find a congenial soil in the Church itself.

Another lesson of Monasticism, not without value for this generation, is the emphasis that it laid upon not making the spiritual vocation too cheap, or too easy of access. The early monks were keenly alive to the dangers of spasmodic renunciation founded upon impulse rather than upon settled conviction. The would-be renunciant was never received at once. 'To him that newly cometh to change his life' (*ad conversionem*), writes St. Benedict, 'let not an easy entrance be granted.'[1] He must give 'an evidence of his perseverance by lying outside the doors for ten days or more, of set purpose scorned and repelled by all the brethren.' Only after a certain probation

'is he brought forward into the midst, stripped of his clothes,[2] and clad by the abbot's hand in the vestments of the monastery, that so he may know that he has laid aside all earthly pride and come down to the poverty of Christ.'[3]

Even then he was not permitted to mingle with the brethren at once, but was left in the guest-house, at first, according to Cassian, for a whole year,[4] a period soon reduced to a few months, and finally to a few days. But Benedict compensated for this lesser period by ordering a year to elapse before the would-be monk

[1] *Reg. Ben.* 58.

[2] The clothes were kept by the steward. If the postulate was unworthy, they were returned. If worthy, they were given to the poor (Cassian, *Instit.* iv. 6).

[3] *Reg. Pachom.* 26 ; Cass. *Instit.* iv. 3; St. Basil, *Reg. fus. tract.* Interrog. 6, 9. See at length *PL* 103, pp. 1261-1302.

[4] Cass. *Instit.* iv. 7.

was allowed to register his vows.[1] During this time 'the hard and rugged paths by which we walk toward God' were duly set before him.

IV

Nothing is more instructive to the student of Christian life than to note the contradictions of its own ideals into which Monasticism was driven in spite of itself. For in Monasticism, as in life in general, the simple ideal is one thing; the ideal, incarnated in activities and subject to human limitations, from the very necessities of the case, can scarcely avoid becoming another. This truth, too often forgotten, might be illustrated in diverse ways from modern as well as ancient times. Puritanism as an ideal of government is one thing in the lofty dreams of Milton; another in its actual working, whether under Cromwell's lieutenant-generals, in the kirk-sessions of Scotland, or subject to the rigours of New England. Ideals and Utopias are not difficult to construct; the attempt at their realization, which after all is their sole test, often reveals strange contradictions, or lines of development that few would have suspected. In the case of Monasticism the study of these contradictions is not the least valuable of the lessons we may learn.

Monasticism began with the belief that the world and all it contains lies under the Evil One; but the noblest of its pages are those in which it showed that there is nothing human which is not capable of higher use and meaning. Monasticism, in its original outlook, despised learning as one of the vanities to be eschewed;

[1] *Reg. Ben.* 58.

THE MESSAGE OF MONASTICISM

yet it exalted learning as it had never been exalted before, and preserved it amid all the assaults of the barbarians. The monk started with leaving the world behind him; nevertheless in the earlier Middle Ages it was the monasteries which did more to bind men together than any other agency. But for the solidarity which they gave to Europe, localism would have reigned supreme. Monasticism was the emphasis of the value of the individual;[1] nevertheless it enslaved the individual, robbed him of his will, degraded him into a cog in a machine, and ended by denying his rights as an individual to settle for himself the bounds and claims of his own self-denial. Monasticism began with the consciousness of an ideal that lay above and beyond the recognized ideal of the Catholic Church; but ended with the imposition of the fetters of the Church upon souls struggling otherwise to be free, with monks as the watch-dogs and police of a centralized hierarchy. The last phase of a movement which originated in the protest of the individual asserting his place in spiritual life was the absolute grip of the Jesuit upon the soul of the individual.

Viewed on its inner side as the expression of personal relation of the soul to God, the influence of Monasticism was as great as it was lasting. The monk, in his origin, was the protest of the laity against an encroaching sacerdotalism; the emphasis that the laity also are kings and priests unto God. Though the monk was forced by circumstances, as we have seen,[2] to join the priesthood, nevertheless Monasticism never forgot that personal holiness is something higher than any succession can bestow. Throughout its career, instead

[1] See *supra*, p. 23.   [2] See *supra*, p. 17 f.

of the intermediate communion of the soul and God through priests and sacraments—the ideal of the Catholic Church—we find Monasticism upholding the ideal of direct intercourse of the soul with its Maker. We are not surprised, therefore, to find in the Middle Ages that it is to the monasteries we must turn for the rise of the Mystics.[1] Now in all ages the Mystics have witnessed—sometimes, it is true, by their exaggerations —that 'the dwelling in the Inner Kingdom of God,' to use a favourite phrase of Tauler, is not 'something that can be learned from the Masters of Paris,' or the result of an external organization, but is imparted direct to 'the Ground of the Soul.' Thus it was in the monasteries, in days when Pentecost was forgotten, that we find men waiting for the coming of the Holy Ghost. Richard of St. Victor, Eckhart, Tauler, Gerson, and Thomas à Kempis are a few names in the great roll of monastic mystics that will readily occur to the reader.

In another way also has Monasticism outlived its dissolution. 'Our first and most important duty'— so ran the *Rule* of the Austin Canons—'is to serve God in Church.' But that service was not usually the adoration of the Mass. It was rather a perpetual 'sacrifice of praise and thanksgiving,' the realization of the Kingdom of God upon earth by means of continual intercourse with the Creator in the choir. In an age when religion was tending more and more to the external, the monks laid emphasis upon prayer. 'What the sword is to the huntsman prayer is to the monk,' claimed Chrysostom,[2] and, certainly, the intercession of the monks was

---

[1] For the Mystics I may refer the reader to chapter viii. of my *Development of Christian Thought*.

[2] Chrysostom, *Comparatio regis et monachi*, c. 4 (*PG* 47, p. 391).

unceasing. The keynote had been struck in the earliest document. Anthony spent long nights in prayer, and still was not satisfied. 'O sun,' he cried, 'why dost thou arise already, and turn me from contemplating the splendour of the true Light!' There were monasteries not a few in which, if the Master of the House had come at midnight, or at cockcrow, or at even, He would have found the inmates still engaged in prayer, in the round of vigils, primes, tierces, sexts, nones, vespers, and complines which marked for the monk the division of the day. 'To occupy oneself with God,' said St. Bernard, 'is not to be idle ; it is the one occupation of all occupations.'

Monasticism was dissolved, but its spirit survived. We see it reappearing in the Puritan, to whom the Bible became the living voice of God. Though banished for a while by a dominant Sacerdotalism to the lowly conventicle, or to the gathering of Covenanters on the moor-side, the genius of Monasticism in this matter emerged triumphant again, though perhaps in an exaggerated form, in the Nonconformity of England and America, with its consistent protest against any sacerdotal conception of the Church. Little does the member of some humble Methodist class-meeting, the wayside preacher of the Salvation Army, or the head of his family as he gathers his children around him for worship, realize that he is perpetuating in new ways the characteristic motive of a system that, possibly, he despises and contemns.

V

We should err greatly if we imagined that the life of the monastery was one of unrelieved gloom. The opposite is rather the truth. Though it would not be correct to state with St. Chrysostom that 'the monks have no sadness, for they wage war with the devil as if they were playing,'[1] nevertheless for many the way of the Cross was the way of light:

> "Via lucis via crucis,
> Per angusta ad augusta."

The great renunciation always brings sunshine. No fact in the history of spiritual life is better established than this; nor has its truth been limited to one age alone. The quiet joy of Martin was one of the things that struck Sulpicius. 'No one,' we read,

'ever saw Martin either angry, disturbed, gloomy, or breaking out into laughter. He was always one and the same. He seemed to bear on his face, somehow or other, a gladness of heaven that came from no human source' (*VM* c. 27).

Sulpicius himself was not slow to follow this example. The pages of his writings glow with gladness. "Sin might sadden him, bishops might worry him, but the dominant character of his work is his joyousness and brightness."[2] In the *Life of Anthony* we read: 'From the joy of his soul his face, too, was bright. . . . He was never disturbed, for his soul was at peace; he was never gloomy, for his mind rejoiced.'[3] 'In Anthony's presence,' continues the writer, 'who did not exchange sadness for joy, anger for peace, the sense of crushing poverty for the consciousness of wealth?' The criticism that this is an extract from a novel, even if it were true, would not be to the point, for the whole purport of the novel, if such it be,[4] is to explain the

---

[1] In *Matt. Hom.* 68 (*PG* 58, p. 646).
[2] Glover, *LLFC* 286. [3] *Vit. Ant.* c. 55 (in *PL* 73, p. 165).
[4] This idea is sufficiently exposed, *infra*, p. 354.

power and charm of Monasticism. Evidently in the writer's mind joy was one of the results.

The tales of this joy are numberless. We have noted the austerities of the two monks named Macarius. The two were once crossing the Nile with two Roman tribunes who were attended by a great train. 'You are happy,' said one of the tribunes as he gazed from their old rags to their tranquil faces, 'for you despise the world.' 'It is true,' replied the hermit, 'we despise the world, while the world makes a mock of you. You have spoken rightly. We are both called Macarius.'[1] We have an illustration of this sense of joy in the generic title given to all works concerning the Egyptian monks. To the confusion of later students, they are all at times called '*Paradise*.'[2] We see the same consciousness of joy in the endearing names which monks gave to their monasteries—" Sweet Valley," " Valley of Hope," " Vale of Peace," " Peace of God," " Gate of Heaven," " Beautiful Peace," and the like—meanings which have long since become petrified and lost in the place-names they have supplied.[3]

Most of all do we find this sense of joy in the story of the early friars, above all in the saintly Francis. Foremost in renunciation Francis stands out among religious

---

[1] μακάριος, *i.e.* "Blessed." For these two worthies, see *supra*, p. 45 n. For this incident, see *PL* 73, p. 1112.

[2] The title is applied to the *Hist. Monachorum* of Rufinus, to the *Verba Seniorum*, to the original *Hist. Lausiaca* of Palladius, the common title for which is *Heraclidis Paradisus* (*infra*, 356). The *Pratum Spirituale* of John Moschus is also called *Novus Paradisus* (in Rosweyd *VP* or *PL* 73, p. 44).

[3] *e.g.* Clara Vallis (Clairvaux, also Zwettl), Curia Dei (la Court Dieu), Carus Locus (Chairlieu), Bellus Locus (Beaulieu), Bellus Beccus (Welbeck), Vallis Paradisi (Valparayso), Vallis Lucis (Glenluce), &c. &c.

leaders by his gaiety of spirit. The servants of God, he said, are really 'jugglers' ('joculatores Domini'), and 'must revive the hearts of men' and lead them to spiritual joy. He called himself 'God's troubadour'; he deemed perfection and joy equivalent terms. The astonishing thing is that he made thousands feel this truth of a transcendent idealism. A sour religion Francis could not endure. 'My brother,' he said, 'if thou hast some fault to mourn over, do it in thy cell, groan and weep before God, but here with thy brethren be as they are in tone and countenance.' Above all let the reader, who would understand in this matter the secret of St. Francis, turn to the record of the ever-memorable walk from Perugia, when Francis, 'grievously tormented by the very bitter cold,' discoursed of 'that wherein is perfect joy'—

O Brother Leo, thou little sheep of God, if with patience and with gladness we suffer all things, thinking on the pains of the Blessed Christ, the which we ought to suffer for the love of Him, O Brother Leo, write that here and herein is perfect joy—in sola cruce est perfecta laetitia.[1]

Well did the early Brothers Minor learn the lesson. When men 'threw mud upon them, or put dice into their hands and invited them to play,' despoiling them of their only tunic, 'in the midst of their tribulations they still rejoiced.' When Brother Bernard, the first disciple to join St. Francis, drew nigh unto death (1245), 'Sursum corda, Brother Bernard, sursum corda!' cried Brother Giles with joyfulness. The face of the dying saint 'grew bright and joyful beyond measure' as he replied, 'O brothers most dear, this I find within my soul, that for a

---

[1] *Little Flowers*, c. 8. This chapter is one of the great pages of spiritual biography.

thousand worlds the like of this I would not have served any other Lord.' [1]

Brother Ruffino, of whom we are told that 'whether asleep or awake his mind was always with the Lord,' narrates that when he saw the Saviour His sign to him was this: 'As long as thou shalt live thou shalt no more feel sadness nor melancholy: he that made thee sad was the Devil.' [2] Brother Masseo, another of the earliest converts, was so filled with

'the light of God that from thenceforward he was always joyful and glad; and oft-times when he prayed he would break forth into sounds of joy, cooing like a dove U U U.'

Brother Jacopone da Todi († 1306)—the author of the *Stabat Mater*, over whose tomb is written the touching epitaph, 'Stultus propter Christum'—was thrown into a dungeon.

'A cesspool,' he writes, 'opens on it, hence a smell not of musk. . . . I am tripped up of my irons, and wound round in a big chain. I have a little basket hung up on high, so that the mice may not injure it; it can hold five loaves, . . . while I eat them I suffer great cold.'

Nevertheless, such was his joy, which many waters could not quench, that he fills a volume with love songs to Jesus. [3]

One other illustration must suffice. No one ever practised deeper austerities of self-surrender than St. Bernard. 'Good Lord,' he cried, 'what happiness Thou procurest for Thy poor!' 'Gracious Lord,' writes

---

[1] *Little Flowers*, c. 6.   [2] *Ib.* c. 29.
[3] For the remarkable outburst of song that accompanied the Franciscan revival see A. F. Ozanam, *Les poètes Franciscains en Italie* (Paris, 1852, 6th ed. 1882).

his biographer, William of St. Thierry, who was fortunate enough to fall ill at Clairvaux,

'what good did not that holiday do for me ? For it happened that during the whole of my sickness *he* also was ill. Thus we two, laid up together, passed the whole day in sweet converse concerning the soul's spiritual physic.' [1]

Closely allied with the joy in self-surrender to which the history of Monasticism witnesses is the testimony that it bears to the possibilities of victory. As we turn over its annals, in spite of all the failures which it were folly to disguise, we hear the shouts of triumph, the exultant cry of warriors who, even in this life, have got Satan beneath their feet. 'I have been assailed by three usurers,' said the "wandering fakir" [2] Sarapion: 'avarice, sensuality, hunger. Of the first two I am rid, having neither money nor passions.'[3] Hugh of Lincoln, at the age of forty, came face to face with a temptation so violent that he said afterwards that he would rather face the pains of hell than encounter it again. But he wrestled in prayer until he felt the cursed thought, like a fiery mass, driven from his bosom. Henceforth he was strong for life.[4]

The stories of complete victory are endless, and have oft-times a rare beauty of their own. We must content ourselves with but one only. "Let us have one quarrel like other men," said an old hermit who had lived for years in the same cell with another but without a disagreement. Quoth the other: "I do not know what a quarrel is like." Quoth the first: "We will put this brick between us, and each say 'It is mine,' then have a

---

[1] William of St. Thierry, *Vit. Bern.* c. 12 (*PL* 185, p. 259).
[2] Apt title given by C. H. Turner in *JTS* (1905) 346.
[3] *HL* (Gr.) 37 (7). [4] Froude, *Short Studies*, ii. 69.

squabble over it." So they put the brick between them.
" It is mine," said the first. " I hope it is mine," said the
other. " If it is yours, take it," said the first—and so
the poor attempt at a quarrel came to an end.[1]

VI

We must bring this short, inadequate study of a
great subject to a close. Monasticism as the one great
expression of renunciation has passed away, nor were its
latter days days of success. Into the causes of this
downfall we cannot now inquire; any adequate discussion would demand a volume in itself. Suffice that,
whether merited or otherwise, the downfall, in England
at least, was complete. We stand on another shore,
and watch the " tired waves " of a different ocean
here and there gain some " painful inch." For us
other suns of hope, a different night of darkness.
The world moves on for good or ill, yet every age
has some lesson for all time, some souls in whom there
glowed the eternal fire. That the dead should bury
their dead is a sound rule of life; nevertheless, we
should be careful lest, in the pride of life, we reckon as
dead

> " The choir invisible
> Of those immortal dead who live again
> . . . in scorn
> For miserable aims that end with self."

So for this latter generation. The gospel of work is
in our marrow; we are hitched on to a mighty flywheel; rest and contemplation are vanished arts.
We look down, sometimes, from our superior heights

[1] *VS* 96 in *PL* 73, p. 777.

upon the coarse forms of self-sacrifice and self-surrender to which Monasticism led men in other days ; and, to some extent, we do well so to look down. When I was a child I spake as a child, I thought as a child ; nor can the world go back in its manhood to childish things. On the other hand, there is no greater folly than to judge the past by whether it saw things as the twentieth century sees them. To estimate a man's true worth, he must be viewed, as Spinoza would have said, *sub specie aeternitatis*. That which is merely the inevitable outcome of his age in the soul's warfare with the time-spirit must be separated from him, and the true soul as God sees it, his real effort upwards, the Yes or No that he gives to good and evil, will then shine forth. Let us beware, then, lest we confuse the essential fact of self-sacrifice with the strange and bizarre manifestations in which it has sometimes expressed itself. Our superior heights are right enough, but if at the last day Christ shall search in our souls for the marks of His Cross and the furrows of His passion, and find them not, it were better then, perhaps, to have erred with some of old—foolishly, even, to have cut off the hand or plucked out the eye—than to be right with those who have never known what self-denial means. For the Christian of to-day, as for St. Gregory of Nazianzen, the test of life must be the willingness ' to lay all things, wealth, birth, authority, glory, and all possessions . . . yea the one sole object in the world which has possessed my heart, the glory of eloquence . . . at the feet of Christ, under the empire of that divine word which effaces and throws into the shade the perishable and changing form of all human thought.'

APPENDIX A

ON THE SOURCES OF OUR KNOWLEDGE OF EARLY EGYPTIAN MONASTICISM

It is of the utmost importance for the student of early Monasticism that he should weigh carefully the historical value of the primary documents upon which our knowledge depends. In the following pages we have indicated the main sources, with their modern editions, and attempted to estimate their value. Upon the estimate thus formed the worth of the narrative we have given in cc. 2 and 3 largely depends.

I. THE *VITA ANTONII*

The *Vita Antonii* was assigned to Athanasius and generally regarded as history until Weingarten (*UM* 21 f.) declared that it was a romance fathered on Athanasius. Weingarten's view was widely accepted in England, e.g. H. Gwatkin, *Studies of Arianism* (2nd ed., 1900), 102–7; *Arian Controversy*, 48; F. W. Farrar, *Lives of the Fathers*, i. 451; T. R. Glover, *LLFC* 384–6. The chief argument in its favour, as it seems to me, is the difficulty of reconciling Anthony's ignorance of Greek (γράμματα μὲν μαθεῖν οὐκ ἠνέσχετο in *VA* 1; cf. Sozomen, *HE* i. 13) with the story of his coming to Alexandria to help Athanasius, and by his logic and eloquence discomfiting the Arians. But this ignorance seems exaggerated, and to refer rather to ignorance of Greek literature (cf. Bury's Gibbon, iv. 59 n., and Rosweyd's note, *VA* c. 1 in *PL* 73, p. 171); while Butler allows [*HL* i. 227, as against A. Robertson, *Athanasius* (in *Post-Nicene Fathers*), 189] that the long disputations with Greek philosophers (*PG* 26, cc. 72–80, *PL* 73, cc. 44 ff.) may be interpolated—or put into Anthony's mouth by Athanasius, after the manner of the age,—and this seems likely from the shorter redaction in the Syriac version and from the fact that, as we told, Anthony needed an interpreter (*VA* c. 44), who seems to have been a certain Isaac (Jerome, *Vit. Hilar.* 25). Similar pious additions may have been made at an early date as regards the contest with the Arians.

That the work is in the main historical seems to me proved by the arguments of A. Robertson (*op. cit.* 188 ff.); Butler, *HL* i. 215–28; Zöckler, *AM* 188 ff., as against Weingarten's scepticism. More might be said against the Athanasian authorship. An argument of weight is the complete silence elsewhere of Athanasius, who only once mentions Anthony, *Hist. Arian.* 14, with which cf. *VA* (Greek) 86. The *argumentum ex silentio*—and the authorship of the *Hist. Arian.* has been disputed—may be fortified by the silence of Eusebius, especially as regards Constantine's letter to Anthony (*VA* 81). The *VA* is also more credulous in tone than is common to Athanasius (A. Robertson, *l.c.* 192). But the positive evidence in favour seems to prove that Athanasius was responsible at any rate for editing it—possibly the analogy would be with the modern practice of books published "With an Introduction by Archbishop X," &c.—The work is definitely ascribed to Athanasius by Evagrius († 393) in his translation [This must have been written within a year of Athanasius' death in 373 (Robertson, *l.c.* 189)]; by Palladius (420) in *HL* 8, or *HP* 2 (*PL* 74, p. 259); by Jerome (391) in *Vir. Illust.* c. 88 [cf. the indirect evidence in *Ep.* 127 (5)]; by Greg. Nazianzen, *Orat.* 21 (5)—a direct encomium of the 'great' Athanasius, delivered about 380; by Rufinus (c. 400) in *HE* i. 8; by the *Vit. Pachom.* (see *supra*, p. 89) c. 1 (*PL* 73, p. 231), not to mention Socrates, *HE* i. 21, whose testimony is second-hand. But though the work may thus be assigned, at least in part, to Athanasius, "it stands on a lower level of historical value" (Butler, *HL* ii. Introd. xii) than the *Hist. Lausiaca* (see *infra*, § II). The phrase of Greg. Nazianzen [*Orat.* 21 (5) in *PG* 35, p. 1088] that 'Athanasius set forth in the form of a narrative the laws of the monastic life' may point to his consciousness of a certain "tendency-narrative." The date of publication is uncertain, possibly 357.

The *Vita Ant.* will be found in the original Greek in *PG* 26, pp. 835 ff. For a Latin version, translated by Evagrius about 373, see Rosweyd's *VP* or *PL* 73, p. 126. Except where something depended on the original, I have made my references to the Latin version as more accessible to students. Large fragments of the *VA* will be found translated in C. Kingsley's *Hermits*, and the Greek is translated in A. Robertson's *Athanasius*, 195 ff. For the so-called *Rule of Anthony*, see Heimbucher, *OKK* i. 95–6, or *PL* 103, p. 423. It is followed by the Maronites, Heimbucher, *OKK* i. 101 f.

II. THE *HISTORIA LAUSIACA* OF PALLADIUS

This most important work was written by Palladius about the year 420. The work—so called from Lausus, a chamberlain at the court of Theodosius II, to whom it is dedicated (*PG* 34, p. 1001 f.)—

APPENDIX A

gives a series of sketches of monks and nuns whom Palladius had known personally or through report. Palladius, a native of Galatia [*HL* 35 (5)], born about 363, became a monk in his twentieth year with Innocent (*ib.* 44)—possibly the later pope Innocent I; see Wittig's conjecture in Butler, *HL* ii. 219—lived for three years on the Mt. of Olives (386–8), where he met Rufinus and the elder Melania, and in 388 arrived at Alexandria (*HL* 1). After a sojourn there of two to three years he withdrew to the Nitria in 390 [*HL* 7 (1), 35 (3)] and a year later to the more remote desert of the "Cells" where he spent nine years [*HL* 18 (1); Butler, *HL* ii. App. VII. But Amélineau, *HL* 7, inclines to think there is here some error.]. On the breakdown of his health he left Egypt for Palestine, spending a portion of 399–400 with Posidonius at Bethlehem [*HL* 36 (1)]. Early in 400 he was consecrated bishop of Helenopolis in Bithynia, and flung himself with ardour into the cause of John Chrysostom who, possibly, had consecrated him (Preuschen, *RP* 241) and for whom in 405 he went to Rome. In 406 he was exiled to Syene, visiting the disciples of Pachomius at Panopolis. In 412 he returned to Galatia [*HL* 45 (1)]. In 417 he was translated to Aspuna (Soc. *HE* vii. 36) and died about 425. (For the above chronology, see Preuschen, *RP* 233–46; *DCB* iv. 173 f.; and Butler, *HL* i. 186 and App. V. The traditional chronology will be found in Rosweyd, *PL* 73, pp. 1066 ff.)

The *Historia Lausiaca* exists in no less than nine different forms :—

(a) A Greek text, first printed at Paris in 1624 by Du Duc, and to be found in *PG* 34. This has been considered by scholars from Rosweyd to Weingarten as the original.

(b) A Latin translation of this made by Gentian Hervet and published at Paris in 1555. Printed by Rosweyd in *VP* bk. viii.

(c) A short Latin redaction, corrupt and incomplete, to be found in *VP* App. II. (*PL* 74, pp. 343 ff.). No Greek text of this is known.

(d) A Greek version printed by Meursius at Leyden in 1616.

(e) A Latin version of (d) first printed at Paris in 1504 under the title *Paradisus Heraclidis*; to be found in *VP* App. I. (*PL* 74, p. 243 f.).

(f) Several Syriac versions and redactions. On these see Butler, *HL* i. 77–95.

(g) Certain Armenian versions and redactions. On these see Dean Robinson in Butler, *HL* i. 97–106.

(h) A Coptic version published by Amélineau in his *HL* (Paris,

1887), with preface and Latin translation. The views of Amélineau are contested by Butler, *HL* i. 107-55.

(*j*) Certain Ethiopic and Arabic fragments. See Butler, *HL* i. 155-71.

Now Dom Butler in his remarkable volume has shown, in my opinion conclusively, cf. C. H. Turner in *JTS* April 1905—

(1) That (*a*) and (*b*)—the Long Recension, as it is called—is not, as Weingarten and others supposed, the original, but is a mere fusion of the original *Hist. Lausiaca* with the *Historia Monachorum* (see *infra*). See Butler, *HL* i. 15-51.

(2) That the original work of Palladius is the same as (*e*) of the above, the Latin so-called *Paradisus Heraclidis*. On this Heraclides see Butler, *HL* ii. 183, and on the *Par. Herac.* Butler, *HL* i. 58-69. It may be pointed out in confirmation of the Latin original that the monks on the Mt. of Olives, where Palladius resided (*supra*), were Latins (cf. Schiwietz, *MM* 81 n.).

(3) That there is no ground for supposing that Palladius made use of Greek documents which were translated into Latin by Rufinus (the theory of Grützmacher, *Pachomius*, pp. 1-4) or which were the originals both of the *Hist. Laus.* and Sozomen (the theory of Dr. Lucius and of Zöckler, *AM* 213, 220). See Butler, *HL* i. 51-8.

(4) That the theory of Amélineau (*HL* 71), accepted by Bury (in his ed. Gibbon, iv. 526 App.) that for Upper Egypt at any rate this work depends on Coptic sources, is not proven (Butler, *HL* i. App. III.).

As regards the historical value of the *Hist. Laus.* there are two opposite views, largely dependent on the view taken in the previous section as to what we deem to be the original form. Weingarten in his *UM*, and later in his article "Mönchtum" in *PRE*², considered the work [the original form of which he identified with (*a*) and (*b*) above] a mere romance. Weingarten has been followed by many others. Amélineau, *HL* 44, was of the opinion that in the five chapters in which he treats of Upper Egypt, Palladius was copying Coptic writings [see (*h*) *supra*] and that in these his narrative must not be implicitly followed. But Butler has demonstrated that the *HL*, in its original short form, is an authentic and veracious document, and Dr. Preuschen agrees that, apart from incidental errors, it gives a true picture of monachism [Butler, *HL* i. 191; Preuschen, *PR* 260]. Amélineau, *HL* 6-10, is of the same opinion (" Si auctori quidam fides est adhibenda, haud dubium mihi videtur quin Palladius pleraque suis oculis ipse perspexerit," &c.), especially for Lower Egypt, largely because of its minute and accurate local colouring, a matter on which Amélineau was well qualified to judge.

III. *HISTORIA MONACHORUM IN AEGYPTO*

Dr. Preuschen (*PR* 196 f., cf. 170 ff.) is of opinion that this work is rightly attributed (as by Rosweyd, *VP* Proleg. iv. in *PL* 73) to Rufinus of Aquileia. The ascription in certain Greek and Latin MSS. to Jerome only shows uncertainty of authority (cf. Schiwietz, *MM* 80 n.). He considers that the Latin version (in *PL* 21, pp. 387–402, or Rosweyd, *VP*) is the original, written about 402–3 (see *infra*). Amélineau (*HL* 60–1), on the other hand, rejects Rufinus. Dom Butler [*HL* i. 12–5, 198–203 and App. I. (i.)] argues for the Greek original published by Dr. Preuschen in 1897 (*PR* in *TU*).

The historical value of the book has been variously estimated, and depends somewhat on the view taken of date and authorship. Weingarten (*UM*) and Gwatkin (*Studies in Arianism*, 93) regard it as " past defence save as a novel," Preuschen as an historical novel of substantial truthfulness. The geographical accuracy of the itinerary is a strong point in its favour (Butler, *HL* i. 200–3).

According to Rosweyd and Baronius (see *PL* 73, Proleg. iv. § 10 and *ib.* 707 ff.) Rufinus visited Egypt probably in company with the lady Melania about 372, returning to Rome about 397. Probably, however, he left Egypt not later than 385. In 402–3 (Preuschen, *op. cit.* 203–5) he set himself to draw up for the benefit of his brethren in the monastery of the Mt. of Olives an account of the Egyptian monasteries. For this purpose he seems to have used, or at any rate purports to use, a personal narrative of a journey of inspection made by seven tourists in the winter of 394–5. Dr. Preuschen (*op. cit.* 178) considers this a mere literary device; Butler pleads that "the journey was a real one," and that the story was written by one of the tourists and merely translated into Latin by Rufinus from the original Greek (Butler, *HL* i. 198–203), and hazards the conjecture [App. I. (5). See also Rosweyd, *VP* Proleg. iv. § 1] that it was written, as Sozomen affirms, by one Timotheus, archdeacon of Alexandria (not ' bishop,' as Sozomen, *HE* vi. 29). Butler's views certainly meet many difficulties.

IV. PACHOMIUS

The chief sources of our knowledge of Pachomius—apart from certain Latin letters preserved for us in Benedict of Aniane's *Concordia*

Regularum (*supra*, p. 226), on whose genuineness see Ladeuze, *ECP* 111 f.—are two : (A) *Vita Pachomii*, (B) *Regulae Pachomii*.

(A) *Vita Pachomii.*—The *Vita* is preserved in various recensions :—

(1) An incomplete version in the Coptic of Lower Egypt (Memphitic). But this really depends on

(2) An incomplete version in the Coptic of Upper Egypt (Theban). Both these versions will be found with French translations in Amélineau, *MG* xvii. (1889).

(3) A 13th-century Arabic version.

(4) A Syriac version published at Paris in 1895 by P. Bedjan.

(5) Three Greek recensions (see *A.SS* iii. May 25 ff.), one of which has not yet been published. On these see Ladeuze, *ECP* 6 f.

(6) A Latin translation made from an unknown Greek text by Dionysius Exiguus († 556) published by Rosweyd in *VP* (in *PL* 73, pp. 230 ff.).

The relation of these various recensions has been investigated by several scholars : Grützmacher, *PAK* 6 f. ; Amélineau, *MG* xvii. Introd. ; followed by Zöckler, *AM* 193, argued for a Coptic (Theban) original written within twenty years of the death of the saint. But Ladeuze, *ECP* 5-108 (see espec. 37, 101)—followed by Butler, *HL* i. 108 n. ; Schiwietz, *MM* 119-48—claims that the Greek is the original and that the Coptic and Arabic versions are 'tendency-versions' written for edification. The accuracy in detail of the Greek original shows that it was written by a Pachomian monk shortly after the death of the saint.

(B) *Regula Pachomii.*—The *Regula* exists in the following forms :—

(1) Ethiopic ; first published by Dillmann in his *Chrestomathia Aethiopica* (Leipzig, 1866), 57-69 and translated by König and Basset in *Studien u. Kritiken* (1878), 333 ff. This was held by Weingarten, *UM* 51, to be the primitive, but its many Greek words show that it is a translation from the Greek (Ladeuze, *ECP* 262).

(2) Two Greek redactions : one short (*PG* 11, pp. 947-52 ; also in a different form in *A.SS* iii. May 62 ff.) ; one long [Pitra, *Analecta Sacra* (1888), i. 113].

(3) Two Latin redactions: the first in Gazaeus, *Cassiani Opera* (1628), App. ; also in Holsten, *CR* ii. 40, cf. *PL* 50, p. 271 ; the second in Holsten, *CR* i. 32. Of these the text in Gazaeus is less like the Latin

translation made by Jerome in 404 (Ladeuze, *ECP* 267 f.).

(4) The Latin version of Jerome in *PL* 23, pp. 61–86. As Jerome did not know Coptic he must have used Greek versions. Possibly he obtained his knowledge at the Pachomian monastery of Canopus near Alexandria (Schiwietz, *MM* 173). Date, about 410.

(5) A Greek form found in Palladius, *HL* 38, and Sozomen, *HE* iii. 14. According to Butler, *HL* i. 157; Grützmacher, *PAK* 117–29; Zöckler, *AM* 200–5; Ladeuze, *ECP* 262–72, this is the nearest to the original form, which was probably Coptic. (For this Coptic form, see Amélineau, *MG* xvii. p. cxi.)

V. JOHN CASSIAN

According to Gennadius (*de vir. illust.* 62) Cassian was a Scythian, the child of lowly parents. Petschenig in his standard edition of Cassian (*CSEL* 2 vols., 1886) argues (*op. cit.* i. pref. pp. i–iv, cv) that this is a mistake, but, as Gennadius was a native of Marseilles, it is difficult to see how he would not have known if Cassian had hailed from Gaul. The Dobrudscha, therefore, has been proposed for his birthplace (Heimbucher, *OKK* i. 175 n.); date about 360 (Petschenig, *op. cit.* i. pref. viii). He was brought up in a cloister at Bethlehem, and in 385 made his first journey to Egypt, where he seems to have spent the greater part of the years between 385–400, in which year he visited Constantinople. He died on 23rd July, shortly after 435.

Cassian's *Institutes* must have been written before 426, the year in which Castor, to whom it is dedicated, died. His *Conferences* or *Collations*, written in three parts, the second for the benefit of the monks of Lérins, would be written a little later. (For the *Regula* of Cassian, see *supra*, p. 123, n. 2.) No works were more popular in the Middle Ages than these of Cassian. This is evidenced by (*a*) the *Epitomes* of the *Institutes* made at an early date, e.g. by Eucherius, bishop of Lyons, in 434 (*PL* 50, pp. 867 ff.). (*b*) By the translations into Greek (see on these Petschenig, *op. cit.* i. pref. pp. iic ff.). (*c*) His numerous citations in such writers as Wyclif and Hus [see my *Letters of Hus* (1904), *passim*]. See also *infra*, the case of Savonarola.

Weingarten, *UM* 62, considered the works to be unhistorical, theological polemics. Some of the *Conferences* (e.g. No. 13) may be idealized and unreal (cf. Gibson, *op. cit. infra*, 188, 191), but that Cassian was a witness of much that he narrates can scarcely be doubted (cf. Butler, *HL* i. 203–8).

The standard edition of Cassian before Petschenig was that of Gazet (Gazaeus) (Douai, 1616, 2nd ed., Arras, 1628), still useful for its commentary. According to Petschenig the first printed edition of the *Institutes* is Venice, 1481, of the *Conferences*, Basel, 1485. But in the B.M. there is a black-letter edition assigned to 1476 (without colophon or title), issued from the press of the Brothers of the Common Life at Brussels. There are also in the B.M. two free German translations, the one printed at Augsburg in 1472, the other possibly in 1470 (s.d. and s.p.). The copy of the Venice edition in the B.M. formerly belonged to St. Mark's, Florence, and has marginal notes in the handwriting of Savonarola. There is a good English translation of Cassian's works by Dr. Gibson (*NPN* Ox., 1894).

VI. *VERBA SENIORUM* (= *VS*) OR *APOTHEGMATA PATRUM*

This work exists in three main redactions :—

(1) In Greek, arranged alphabetically (*PG* 65, pp. 71–440), and more completely, as Butler points out, in the Brit. Mus. in the unpublished *Burney MS*. 50.

(2) In Latin : in Rosweyd, *VP* v. and vi. (Migne, *PL* 73, pp. 851 ff.). The two, as Rosweyd pointed out (*op. cit.* p. 991), really form one book of about twenty sections or booklets arranged according to subject-matter.

(3) Another collection arranged topically in forty-four chapters, and forming bk. vii. of Rosweyd [Migne, 73, pp. 1025 ff.], according to its prologue was translated from the Greek by Paschasius the deacon (*c.* 500). See Rosweyd, *Prolegomen.* xiv. in *PL* 73. Part of bk. vii. of Rosweyd, *VP* is also found in bk. iii. of Rosweyd (where it is erroneously attributed to Rufinus of Aquileia) and another part in Rosweyd, *VP* App. III. (Migne, 74, pp. 382 ff.).

These collections of anecdotes and sayings of the Hermits were formed in the main during the 5th century (Butler, *HL* i. 211–4, and cf. Socrates, *HE* iv. 23, where we see a collection of apothegmata already in use). Though containing many added elements, and some that are clearly unhistorical, the work may be regarded as giving a true picture in the main, though at times written somewhat too much for edification.

VII. OTHER SOURCES

Of these the most important is Sozomen, whose work, written between 439-50, is of value for Asia Minor and Syria (*HE* vi. 32-4). Elsewhere his account of monks is derived, according to Butler, *HL* i. 51-8, from the *Historia Monachorum*.

APPENDIX B

ADDITIONAL BIBLIOGRAPHY

In addition to the list of works frequently cited—see *supra*, pp. xv.-xxi.—the student may welcome the following short bibliography of the most important of the other works, to which reference has been made in the text and notes. For the sake of convenience and to save repetition, subject-matters are printed in small capitals, and the bibliographies under these headings are indicated by the place in the notes where details may be found.

H. Achelis	*Virgines Subintroductae* (1902).
Amélineau	*Vie de Schenoudi* (Paris, 1889).
ANTHONY	*Supra*, p. 353.
ST. AUGUSTINE OF CANTERBURY	*Supra*, p. 172 n.
ROGER BACON	*Supra*, p. 312.
M. Bateson	*Origin and Early History of Double Monasteries* (*supra*, p. 177, n. 6).
BEC (Abbey of)	*Supra*, p. 222 n.
A. Bellesheim	*Gesch. der kath. Kirche in Ireland* (3 vols., Mainz, 1890).
BENEDICT OF ANIANE	*Supra*, pp. 225 n., 226 n.
BENEDICT OF NURSIA	*Supra*, pp. 140 n., 142 n.
BERNARD OF CLAIRVAUX	*Supra*, p. 239 n.
J. M. Besse	*Les Moines de l'ancienne France* (Paris, 1906).
BONIFACE OF GERMANY	*Supra*, p. 175 n.
A. de la Bordorie	*Hist. de la Bretagne* (4 vols., 1896).
H. Bradshaw, and C. Wordsworth	*Statutes of Lincoln Cathedral* (3 vols., 1892 f.).
BRENDAN	*Supra*, p. 196 n.
E. A. W. Budge	*Thomas of Margâ, Book of the Governors* (1893).
L. Bulteau	*Essai de l'Histoire Monastique d'Orient* (Paris, 1680).
L. Burgener	*Der hl. Bernard* (Lucerne, 1870).
F. Burkitt	*Early Eastern Christianity* (1904).
A. J. Butler	*Ancient Coptic Churches of Egypt* (1884).
CAESARIUS OF ARLES	*Supra*, p. 123 n.
CASSIAN	*Supra*, p. 359.
CELTIC CHURCH	*Supra*, p. 184 n.
CHILDREN'S CRUSADE	*Supra*, p. 288.

APPENDIX B

CHRODEGANG	*Supra*, p. 255.
CLARA AND THE CLARISSES	*Supra*, p. 285.
J. W. Clark	*The Observances in Use at the Augustinian Priory of Barnwell* (1897).
R. M. Clay	*Medieval Hospitals of England* (1909).
CLEMENT (Pseudo)	*Supra*, p. 82 n.
CLUNY AND THE CLUNIACS	*Supra*, p. 227 n.
COLUMBA	*Supra*, p. 202 n.
COLUMBAN	*Supra*, p. 208 n.
F. Conybeare	*On the Contemplative Life* (1895).
R. Curzon	*Monasteries of the Levant* (1849).
DOMINIC AND DOMINICANS	*Supra*, p. 274 n.
F. Dudden	*Gregory the Great* (2 vols., 1895).
A. Durand	*Le vrai conquérant de Alpes* (1905).
J. Edwards	*The Gilbertines in Scotland* (1904).
H. Felder	*Ges. der Wissenschaftl. Studien in Franziskanerorden* (Leipzig, 1904).
FRANCIS OF ASSISI AND THE FRANCISCANS	*Supra*, pp. 279 n., 280 n., 282 n., 286 n., 287 n.
FRIDOLIN	*Supra*, p. 201 n.
FURSA	*Supra*, p. 205 n.
GALL	*Supra*, p. 210 n.
F. A. Gasquet	*English Monastic Life* (1904).
GERMANUS	*Supra*, p. 186 n.
GILBERT OF SEMPRINGHAM	*Supra*, p. 263 n.
GREGORY VII	See *s.v.* Hildebrand.
GREGORY THE GREAT	*Supra*, pp. 169 n., 120 n. 3.
G. Grützmacher	*Hieronymus* (1901).
Ph. Guignard	*Les Monuments Primitifs de la Règle Cistercienne* (Dijon, 1878).
HARDING, STEPHEN	*Supra*, pp. 238 n., 239 n.
HILARION OF GAZA	*Supra*, p. 111 n.
HILDEBRAND	*Supra*, p. 229 n.
HUGH OF LINCOLN	*Supra*, pp. 35 n., 252 n. 3.
L. Janauschek	*Origines Cistercienses* (Vienna, 1877).
JOHN SCOTUS ERIUGENA	*Supra*, p. 201 n.
JOVINIAN	*Supra* p. 16 n.
P. Kauffmann	*Les Chartreux* (Meudon, 1898).
H. Koch	*Virgines Christi* (in *TU* v. 31, 1906).
Krätzinger	*Der Benediktenorden u. die Kultur* (Heidelberg, 1876).
H. Lake	*Early Days of Monasticism on Mt. Athos* (1909).
H. C. Lea	*An Historical Sketch of Sacerdotal Celibacy* (1867).
"	*Inquisition in MA* (3 vols., 1887).
J. Leipoldt	*Schenute v. Atripe* (in *TU* xxv.).
H. Löbbel	*Der Stifter des Carthäuserordens* (Münster, 1899).
F. Loofs	*Eustathius v. Sebaste* (Halle, 1898).
"	*Antiquae Britonum Scotorumque Ecclesiae* (Leipzig, 1882).

J. Mabillon	*Annales ordinis S. Benedicti.* See *supra*, p. 145 n.
MARTIN OF TOURS	*Supra*, pp. 101 n., 104 n.
J. Meyer	*Die Christliche Askese* (Freiburg, 1894).
Abbé Nau	*Histoire de Thais* (see *supra*, p. 51 n.).
E. J. Newell	*The Welsh Church* (1895).
T. Nöldeke	*Studies from Eastern History* (1892).
A. F. Ozanam	*Les poètes Franciscains en Italie* (Paris, 1852, 6th ed., 1882).
PACHOMIUS	*Supra*, p. 358.
J. Pargoire	*Les monasteres double chez les Byzantines* (Paris, 1906).
PATRICK	*Supra*, p. 188 n.
PAUL (the hermit)	*Supra*, p. 96 n.
PENITENTIALS	*Supra*, p. 212 n.
PILLAR-SAINTS	*Supra*, p. 41 n.
H. Plenkers	*Untersuchungen zur überlieferungsgeschichte der alt. latein. Mönchsregeln* (Munich, 1906).
E. Preuschen	*Mönchtum u. Serapiskult* (2nd ed. Giessen, 1903).
SCHENOUDI	*Supra*, p. 126 n.
SCOTS MISSIONS	*Supra*, p. 201 n.
SCOTS ON THE CONTINENT	*Supra*, p. 210 n.
E. Sharpe	*The Architecture of the Cistercians* (1874, 1876).
E. Spreitzenhofer	*Die Entwicklung des alt. Mönchtums in Italien* (Vienna, 1894).
G. T. Stokes	*Ireland and the Celtic Church* (6th ed., 1907).
M. Stokes	*Three Months in the Forests of France in Search of Vestiges of Irish Saints* (1895).
,,	*Six Months in the Apennines in Search*, &c. (1892).
SULPICIUS SEVERUS	*Supra*, p. 101 n.
E. L. Taunton	*English Black Monks of St. Benedict* (2 vols., 1898).
TERTIARIES	*Supra*, p. 298.
THERAPEUTAE	*Supra*, p. 90 n.
H. Thode	*F. v. Assisi u. d. Anfänge d. Kunst d. Renaissance in Italien* (2 vols., 1904).
E. M. Thompson	*Somerset Carthusians* (1895).
H. Thurston	*St. Hugh of Lincoln* (1898).
Abbé Tosti	*St. Benedict* (see *supra*, p. 140 n.).
E. Vacandard	*Vie de S. Bernard* (2 vols., Paris, 1895).
S. Vailhé	*Les Stylites de Constantinople* (1898).
VIGILANTIUS	*Supra*, p. 16 n.
WELSH SAINTS	*Supra*, p. 190 n.
H. B. Workman	*History of Christian Thought to the Reformation* (1911).

INDEX

This index is in the main restricted to names. For subjects, see "Argument" of each chapter. Authors quoted, whether ancient or modern, are not quoted unless some criticism or account is given of them.

Abailard, 247, 267
Abraham, Abba, 155
Accidie, 326 f
Acepsimas, 45
Acts of Thomas, 80
Adamnan, 214
Adolius, 48
Aërius, 19
Agapetae, 62
Aidan, 204
Aksemetae, 49
Aldhelm, 174
Alexandra of Alexandria, 50
Alien Priories, 238
Ambrose, 91
Ammianus Marcellinus, 8, 9
Ammon, 19
Anselm of Aosta, 35, 232, 247
Aṅskar, 176
Anthony, 14, 22, 34, 64, 72, 92–101, 116, 123 n, 346, App. § I, 353
ἀπάθεια, 37
Aphraates, 58 n, 61, 113
Arians, 21
Arsenius, 47, 49
Art, St. Francis and, 307 f
Asella, 116 n
Athanasius, 20, 21, 22, 30 n, 94, 116, 354
Athos, Mount, 128, 153
Augustine of Canterbury, 173
Augustine of Hippo, 22, 39 n, 52, 59, 254, 259 n

Augustine's Oak, 195
Aust, 195 n
Austin Canons, 258 f

Bacon, Roger, 313
Bangor, 197
Basil, 9, 113–5, 127–8, 155, 157
Beasts, Tales of, 36 n, 306
Baths, Monasticism and, 64, 214
Bec, 221–2
Benedict IX, 232
Benedict of Aniane, 225 f
Benedict of Nursia, 19, 135, c. iii, 219, 321
Bernard of Clairvaux, St., 239 f, 244, 307, 349
Bernard of Menthon, 262
Bêth 'Âbhê, 45, 49 n
Birds, St. Francis and, 306
Bishops and Celtic Church, 194 f
Blaesilla, 16, 117
Bobbio, 208
Boniface VII, 231
Boniface of Germany, 175
Bonosus, 32
Boskoi, 45
Brendan, 196
Brethren of the Common Life, 261
Brictio, 103
Bridget, 193 n
Brittany, Celtic invasion of, 197 n; Romans and, 198
Bruno, 251

Caesarius of Arles, 123, 134, 147
Camaldulians, 249
Canon, meaning of, 253, 254 n
Canons, 253 f
Canterbury, 173
Carthusians, 251 f
Cassian, 121 f, 123 n, 131, 147, 359
Cassino, Monte, 142
Cassiodorus, 159 f
Cathari, 40, 275
Cathedrals, English, 258 n
Celestine, pope, 189
Celibacy, 56 f
Celibacy and the Eucharist, 85
Celtic Asceticism, 214
Celtic Church, c. iv
Celtic Wanderings, 196 f
Ceretic, 188
Chaise Dieu, 220
Chapel, meaning of, 110
Chastity, 55 f
Children's Crusade, 288 n
Chrodegang of Metz, 255 f
Cistercians, 238 f
Clara, 285
Clarisses, 285 n
Clonmacnoise, 199
Cluny, 227 f, 235–7, 241–2
Coldingham, 179
Columba, 199, 202 f
Columban, 35, 199, 207 f
Columbus, 196 n
Concordia Regularum, 226
Constantine and the Church, 6
Constantinople, monks in, 113 n
'Conversion,' 4 n
Custodies, 295
Cuthbert, 206
Cyprian, 23

Damasus, pope, 8, 9
Damiani, 233
Danes, 211
Decretals, False, 167
Dedications in Celtic Church, 185 n, 193 n
Deer, 203
defensor, 18
Demons, 97–8
Dichuill, 209
Dicuil, 200 n
Dicul, 205

Disen, 209
Dominic, 292 f, 311
Dominicans, 272 f, 302, 307, 311, 315
Dorotheus, 48, 151
Double Monasteries, 176 f, 262
Drythelm, 214
Dunstan, 175
Durand of Huesca, 293
Dyserth, 186

Eadwine, 204
Ealdhelm, 174
Eastern Monasticism, 53, 114, 152 f, 219
Ebba, 179
Education, Monastics and, 247; friars and, 310 f
Elvira, Council of, 6 n, 82
Ely, 178
Encratites, 81 n
England, Conversion of, 173
'Ephesian liturgy,' 184 n
Episcopate and Monasticism, 163 f
Eroticism, 52 n, 62 f, 72 n
Essenes, 91
Eucheria, 129 n
Euchites, 80 n
Eusebius of Vercellae, 117, 253
Eustathius of Sebaste, 19, 113, 114, 127
Eustochium, 117
Evagrius, 19, 321
Evesham, 174

Farfa, 233
Finnian, 199
Floretum, 287 n
Formosus, 230
Fountains (Abbey), 240 f
Francis of Assisi, 268, c. vi, 347 f; sources of life, 279 n
Franciscans, 68, c. vi
Fridolin, 201
Fulda, 176
Fursa, 205

Gall (St.), 208, 210
Gangra, Council of, 56, 128
Germanus, 186 f

Gilbert of Sempringham, 179, 262 f
Gnosticism, 38 f
Godfrey of Lorraine, 156
Godric, 35
Grandmontines, 250
Gregory VII: *see* Hildebrand
Gregory IX: *see* Ugolini
Gregory the Great, 162; *Regesta* of, 120 n
Groot, Gerard, 261
Grosseteste, Robert, 311
Gualbert, 250
Guthlac, 35
Gyrovagi, 120, 134, 147

'Hallelujah Victory,' 187
Heavenfeld, 204
'Hemerobaptists,' 91
Herlwin, 221-2
Hermas, *Shepherd* of, 79
Hi, 202 n
Hilarion of Gaza, 111 f, 321
Hilary of Poictiers, 105, 106
Hilda, 178
Hildebrand, 28 n, 56, 228 f, 235, 268, 296
Honoratus, 121
Hugh of Avalon, 35
Hugh of Lincoln, 253
Humiliati, 294
Hus, 20, 72 n

Illtud, 191 n, 197
'Inclusi,' 49, 50, 51 n, 84
Injuriosus of Auvergne, 80
Innocent III, 276, 285
Iona, 202 n
Isis, 84
Ivo of Chartres, 258 f, 332

Jacobins, 297 n
Jacopone da Todi, 305, 349
Jacques de Vitry, 273
James the deacon, 204
Jerome, 7, 16, 18, 31, 57, 58, 95, 97, 117-19, 321
Jesuits, 74, 268
John of Jerusalem, Order of, 266
John of Lycopolis, 20, 72 n
John Scotus, 201
John the Short, 72

John XII, pope, 230
Jovinian, 16
Julian of Randan, 53 n
Justinian, *Code* of, 142

κάτοχοι, 84
Kempis, Thomas à, 32, 33 n, 69, 261-2
Kilian, 209

Labour and Monasticism, 154 f, 220-3
Leo the Great, 54
Lérins, 121, 189 n
Liberius, 8
'llans,' 185 f
Lull, Raymund, 302
Lupicinus, 16, 53 n
Lupus of Troyes, 187
Luther, quoted, 338
Luxeuil, 207
Lyons, Poor Men of, 293

Macarius of Alexandria, 36 n, 45 n, 46, 51, 153, 347
Macarius of Egypt, 18, 45 n, 347
Macarius the jeweller, 52
Macrina, 177
Maes Garmon, 187 n
Maildulf, 205
Malmesbury, 205
Mar Awgîn, 113
Marcella, 116
Marcellina, 116
Marcionites, 80
Marina, 71
Martin, 18, 59, 66, 101-10, 120, 121, 142, 346; chronology of, 105 n, 106
Maximus, emperor, 107
Melania, 36 n, 50, 60, 65, 118
Methodism, 243 n, 295 n, 340, 345
'Militia Christi,' 65
Miracles, medieval, 107 n
Missions and Monasticism, 162 f; c. iii, § 4; and friars, 277, 285, 289, 300 f
Mithraism, 83
μονάχός, 124
Montanism, 14, 81

Mucius, 73
Mysticism and Monasticism, 344

Nationalism and Monasticism, 163 f
Neoplatonism, 28, 98
Nitria, 14, 130 f
Norbert, 265
Numbers in Monasteries, 163 f

Obedience and Monasticism, 68 f
Origen, 20, 29 n
Orthodoxy and Monasticism, 20–22, 121
Oswiu, 205, 206

Pachomius, 21, 36 n, 47, 48 n, 63, 87 f, 111, 117, 125, 155, 357
Palaemon, 88, 325
Palladius, 128, 355
Pambo, 150
Paphnutius, 33, 44
Paradise, 347
Parish, origin of, 164
Patrick, 188 f
Paul (abba), 61
Paul (the hermit), 36 n, 96
Paul the Simple, 48
Paul, *Vita* of, 96, 97
Paula, 58, 60, 64, 117, 118
Paulinus, 203
Pelagius, 186 n
Penda, 204
Penitentials, c. iv, § 4
Pershore, 174
Peter the Venerable, 237, 251
Peterborough, 174
Philo, 90
Pillar-saints, 41 n
Pinuphius, 70
Pior, 59
Pontius, 237
Postumian, 9, 19 n, 33, 36 n, 72 n, 129, 132
Poverty and Monasticism, 66 f, 302 f
Premonstratensians, 265 f
Priscillianists, 69, 107
Private Monasteries, 180
Privileges, Monasticism and, 171
Ptolemaeus, 48 n

Radegund, 177
Rahere, 260
Rathbreasail, Synod of, 195 n
Reccared, 122
'Religion,' 4 n
Resurrection of the body, 81
Robert of Molesme, 238
Romances, 62, 63
Romuald, 249
Rosary, 130 n
Rule for 'Inclusi,' 51 n
 of Anthony, 123 n 5, 354
 of Benedict of Aniane, 226 f
 of Benedict of Nursia, 142, 169, c. iii, § 2
 of Carthusians, 252
 of Chrodegang, 256 f
 of Cistercians, 241
 of Clarisses, 285
 of Columban, 207
 of Dominic, 276
 of Francis, 282
 of Gilbert of Sempringham, 264
 of Pachomius, 358
 of St. Augustine, 259 n
Rupert, 209

Sabatier, criticism on, 279 n
'Saints,' 190 f
'Saints' and women, 193
Sampsaeans, 91
Sarabaites, 120, 134, 147
Sarapion Sindonius, 49, 50, 51 n, 350
Saturday and Sunday, 130
Schenoudi, 111, 125, 126
Schoolmen, Friars and, 310 f
Schools, Monasticism and, 161
'Secular,' 4
Senoch of Tours, 53 n
Serapis, 83, 84, 87, 89
Severin, 122
Severus of Treves, 187
Silvia of Bordeaux, 129 n
Sisoes, 48
Spiritual Franciscans, 68
Stephen Harding, 239, 243 n
Stephen of Thiers, 250
'Stigmata,' 291
Studium, the, 49
Sturmi, 176

Stylites, Symeon, 41 f
Sulpicius Severus, 17, 52, 101 n

Telemachus, 52
Templars, 266
Tertiaries, 297 f
Tertullian, 26
Teutonic Knights, 267
Thais, 49, 51 n
Thalelaeus, 43
Theodore of Tarsus, 179, 212
Theodore of the Studium, 115 n
Theonas, 61
Theophilus and Mary, 71
Therapeutae, 90
Thomas, Acts of, 80
Trappists, 246 n
Tribal system in Celtic Church, 190 f

Ugolini, 280 n, 285 n, 290, 304, 314
Universities, Friars and, 311

Vallombrosians, 250
Victor, St. (School of), 261
Vigilantius, 16
Vincent of Lérins, 121
Vita Antonii, 92
Vita Martini, c. ii, § 4
Vita Pauli, 96, 97
Viviers, 159

Walpot, 267
Walpurgis, 176
Waltham, 256 n
Weedon Bec, 222
Wells, 256 n
Wesley, John, 253 n
Whitby, Synod of, 206
Wimborne, 179
Winfrith, 175
Wool-growing, 245 f
Wulflaich of Treves, 53 n

'Zealots' and 'Moderates,' 304 f

www.ingramcontent.com/pod-product-compliance
Lightning Source LLC
Chambersburg PA
CBHW052339230426
43664CB00041B/2205